Offbeat

x

BRITISH CINEMA'S CURIOSITIES, OBSCURITIES AND FORGOTTEN GEMS

EDITED BY JULIAN UPTON

CONTENTS

FOREWORD

When audiences sit in the dark to see our films, they are giving us thirty or ninety or 120 minutes of their life. It's a generous commitment — there should be no place for the shoddy. I wish!

A handful of the films that follow reveal a certain conceit among writers and directors of limited talent who believed they could compete with major filmmakers. There is also a sprinkling of titles to remind us — not that we need reminding — that crap sells. Throwing money at a film has never guaranteed success. Studios keep forgetting this, but audiences know it.

But for the most part, the films here reveal that committed independent and low budget filmmakers, all too aware what a slog it is to get their work up there on the screen, can succeed with meagre resources and limited access to the goodies in the filmmaking toy cupboard. Indeed, with the vital help of creative hands in all departments, they can often produce a gem.

Happily, there are many gems in OFFBEAT.

John Krish
London, September 2011

{ John Krish's long career in British cinema touches on many of the trends and genres featured in OFFBEAT. Starting out in documentaries for such venerable national institutions as the General Post Office and the British Transport Commission, he first came to notice with *The Elephant Will Never Forget* (53). In the 1960s he branched out, initially into B-films (UNEARTHLY STRANGER [63]), then into bigger budget, US-backed fare (*Decline and Fall… of a Birdwatcher* [68]). As for many British filmmakers, work was tighter for Krish in the 1970s and 1980s, but he kept busy with Children's Film Foundation matinees, public information films and shorts, such as the notorious *The Finishing Line* (77). In the 2000s, he was finally 'discovered' by the British Film Institute; in 2011, aged eighty-seven, he was honoured with an Evening Standard Award for Best Documentary for the BFI-released compilation, *A Day in the Life: Four Stories of Post-War Britain*.

INTRODUCTION

AS SEEN ON TV - THE CINEMA OF LOW EXPECTATIONS

BY JULIAN UPTON

I n *Have You Seen?*, his coffee-table-straining 'personal introduction to 1,000 films,' the critic David Thomson, lamenting the dearth of opportunities to experience classic films as they were meant to be shown, says that today "otherwise sensible people write PhD theses on particular movies without ever seeing them on a large screen." [1]

It's a valid point. For *8½, L'Avventura, Ugetsu Monogatari* and *The Searchers* — the kind of 'respectable' films Thomson is talking about — the loss of the theatrical experience is one to be lamented. Certainly, a research student knocking out 50,000 words on Italian westerns is missing a trick if he is only studying Sergio Leone's films on TV in his busy living room, even if he is the proud owner of a 37-inch HD screen.

But sometimes the opposite is true. Many films that were intended only as fillers, as passers of time, or as cheap exploiters of the latest fad or the latest relaxation in censorship, or those simply taking a gamble on a small budget, presenting a skewered approach to a subject or a genre, can sometimes come alive on the small screen in a way that they rarely did — or rarely had chance to — in the theatre.

This was especially the case in the pre-video, pre-satellite, pre-digital era of television, when the film-hungry TV audience lapped up anything they could get. Indeed, for provincial types like me, born thirty years after Thomson, television was the *only* conduit through which to access the delights of cinema, good and bad. The town I was brought up in and many of the towns around it had lost their cinemas before I was born; when I was growing up, a family trip out to the pictures was an *event*. Accordingly, the film had to be worth making the effort for; it had to be a *Star Wars* or a *Superman*, an *ET* or an *Indiana Jones*. Anything less felt like a profound anticlimax.

By the seventies, television had taken over what had once been the cinema's role. The cinema, as Matthew Sweet has pointed out, was "no longer part of the diurnal rhythm of our national life, when the act of spending a few hours in the cheap seats at the Regal required as little forethought as the act of writing home or eating fish on Friday." [2] With television providing this viewing 'mentality,' it replicated the experience "when going to the pictures wasn't a treat."

But films on TV were still very much 'rationed,' and so tended to stand out, regardless of their quality or sense of spectacle. For some of us, *they* were the treats in the decidedly everyday business of watching the box. Television showings of British films that might have left me fairly nonplussed at the

cinema became ingrained in my mind as searing highpoints of my early viewing: *Carry On Screaming!*, TARZAN'S GREATEST ADVENTURE, *The Family Way*, *Run Wild, Run Free*, FLIGHT OF THE DOVES, THE SQUEEZE. Films watched on rainy Sunday afternoons — often so gently twee and lukewarm that expending any kind of physical effort to see them would have seemed ridiculous — are also bathed in a lasting glow: *Trouble in Store*, *Twice Round the Daffodils*, *Crooks in Cloisters*, CASH ON DEMAND. And films caught late at night, films that exuded a very faint aura of 'the forbidden,' have also cast a disproportionately long shadow in my memory: AND SOON THE DARKNESS, GIRL STROKE BOY, REVENGE, *The Vampire Lovers*, *Curse of the Werewolf*, *Theatre of Blood*, DEADLY STRANGERS.

To the schedulers, however, films like these — cheaply purchased as part of a package, not the sort of films geared to drawing huge audiences — were just more television ephemera. Most of the 100-plus titles featured in OFFBEAT had one, maybe two, TV screenings and then disappeared from view. Some have since made their way, quietly, briefly, onto video and DVD, but a great many have not; all that remains of them are distant memories, some long unseen prints and a negative decaying in a vault.

But, revisiting these titles twenty or thirty years after their last TV screenings (via the magic of the internet, low quality bootlegs and the occasional legit release), many seem far from ephemeral. They hold up surprisingly well, and have as much right to be celebrated as those British films whose reputations have been forged and enhanced by frequent television broadcasts and regular, respectful DVD releases — *Peeping Tom*, *Witchfinder General*, *The Italian Job*, *Performance*, *Get Carter*, *Don't Look Now*, *The Wicker Man*, *The Long Good Friday*. Celebration of these 'cult movies' has become de rigeur. So isn't it time some others shared the limelight? (I must add at this point that not all the reviews in OFFBEAT are based on TV screenings or dusty VHS copies. Some of our [slightly] older contributors were able to experience the theatrical showings; a few even harbour vague memories of the short supporting features in circulation at the same time [see the chapter: Wings Of Death].)

OFFBEAT's selection is an unapologetically pick'n'mix one and avoids an auteurist reading of British film history. Nevertheless, certain directors tend to crop up frequently. Val Guest is arguably over represented here, but his output between just 1954 and 64 — when he made *The Quatermass Xperiment*, *Quatermass II*, THE ABOMINABLE SNOWMAN, *Yesterday's Enemy*, *Expresso Bongo*, *Hell is a City*, THE DAY THE EARTH CAUGHT FIRE, JIGSAW and *The Beauty Jungle* — must rank somewhere alongside the entire careers of some of his more celebrated contemporaries. There's also Sidney Hayers. Had

Hayers quit after his first three movies as director — *Circus of Horrors* (60), PAYROLL (61) and NIGHT OF THE EAGLE (62) — he would probably be the subject of a handful of 'serious' studies by now. Like Guest, however, Hayers' crime against re-evaluation seems to be that he was adept enough to stay in constant employment, and pragmatic enough not to believe in the pursuit of an oeuvre.

We're not looking for, or expecting to find, any consistency of vision in the work of Guest or Hayers (or Freddie Francis, Michael Winner, Cliff Owen, Don Sharp or David Greene, for that matter). Most of their films deliver their surprises and charms independently of one another. These are men who, for the most part, just 'got on with it' — men like Roy Ward Baker, who made many a good and one or two great films, but who once expressed dismay at the kind of director who wears a viewfinder around his neck. How pretentious! That's the cameraman's job!

By revisiting these obscurities, curiosities and forgotten gems (spanning the beginnings of the boom in British popular cinema in the mid fifties to its dying days in the early eighties), we hope instead to instil some balance to a British film heritage that still largely ignores the highly productive B-movie activity of the early sixties, that neglects much of the US-financed product that sustained the indigenous industry from the mid sixties to the mid seventies, and that dismisses the seemingly unsinkable exploitation fare that, for twenty-five years, outlasted every other British cinema trend and genre. And we hope to restore some common sense to a populist mood that has become in thrall to a jukebox auteurism and the select band of cult movies mentioned earlier. After all, as OFFBEAT points out, crime movies such as SITTING TARGET and THE SQUEEZE are at least as good as, if not better than, *Get Carter* and *The Long Good Friday*. B-movies such as THE IMPERSONATOR and CASH ON DEMAND far outshine the main features they once supported. And the Children's Film Foundation could occasionally deliver as much charm in one mercilessly cheap hour as Pixar and Disney do on $100 million budgets.

Yes, we look at some of the dross too — that has its place in the story of British cinema we want to tell. But one man's dross is another's 'cult classic' (and vice versa).

So, if you've had a cursory glance at the titles and your expectations are low, so much the better — because there are some treats in store.

1   David Thomson, *Have You Seen?* (London: Allen Lane, 2008), p.xii.
2   Matthew Sweet, 'All the fun of the fleapit,' *The Guardian*, 14 March 2008.

BOOM
BRITISH CINEMA INTO THE SIXTIES

BY JULIAN UPTON

5

F or film exhibitors who'd been operating during the halcyon days of cinema-going in the 1940s (when, at their peak, UK cinema admissions had reached a high of 1,635 million [1]), the dawn of the fifties — particularly from the moment when Queen Elizabeth II's coronation alerted almost everyone in Britain to the possibilities of television — instigated a long period of decline that no trend in film production could really counter.

It wasn't just television that was leading to plummeting cinema admissions (from 1,395 million in 1950 to 581 million in 1959 [2]). The government-set quota demanding that thirty per cent of all exhibited first features and twenty-five per cent of all second features (B-movies) must be British was also helping to drive the punters away. British films, the exhibitors argued, were dross. They were shabby and amateurish; they couldn't compete with their slick Hollywood counterparts.

The immediate postwar Labour government tried to address the film industry's shortcomings with schemes initiated by the new Board of Trade President, Harold Wilson. In 1948 he instigated the National Film Finance Company (NFFCo) to offer state subsidy to ailing film companies. Soon after, this became the National Film Finance Corporation (NFFC), which had a five-year pot of £5 million with which to stimulate British film production.[3] Wilson also proposed the establishment of a levy, named after Treasury official Sir Wilfred Eady. The Eady Levy was to be a tax on all UK cinema tickets sold; the tax would be divided up into a rebate for exhibitors and a fund for producers of British films, to be paid out relative to a British film's earnings at the box office.

Labour lost power in 1951, and the incoming Conservative government was more inclined to distance itself from the British film industry.[4] But under the Tories' watch, the NFFC did become more commercial, and a more tolerant attitude towards American interest in British films developed. Indeed, the NFFC actually started co-financing films with American distributors. As a result, the proportion of British-made films distributed by American companies doubled between 1954 and 1956.[5] This took off further when, in 1957, the Eady Levy was finally established on a statutory basis. With British-made films qualifying for ever more handouts and rebates, the Americans quickly resolved to make more films in Britain.

Although it had been an ongoing source of controversy, US influence over and participation in British films — both main features and B-movies — breathed much-needed life into the British film industry from the mid fifties onwards.

Milking the new 'X' certificate. *Horrors of the Black Museum.*

And enterprising companies such as Hammer were not slow to court their rich American cousins. They gratefully acquiesced to US distributors' demands, such as the casting of US 'stars' in lead roles (for example, the American leading man Brian Donlevy as Professor Quatermass) to maximise the film's market potential back home. And even when the cast and crews remained solidly British (and the narratives decidedly Mittel European), Hammer embraced a punchier, livelier, drive-in style of filmmaking. This paid off in droves with *The Curse of Frankenstein* (57) and *Dracula* (58), which became major box office draws on both sides of the Atlantic and set the studio on the horror path that was soon to define it.

Hammer also understood the power of the new 'X' certificate, which was introduced by the British Board of Film Censors in 1951 to replace 'H' (for Horror) and restrict certain films to the over-sixteens only. Where 'X' had an uncertain beginning, by the mid fifties film marketers were beginning to wear it like a badge of honour. It had actually been introduced to accommodate the increasing amount of non-horror films that were unsuitable for children — films that approached adult themes, not least sex, and social problems more head-on. But, ironically, the enterprising producers of horror films were the first to milk the 'X.' Hammer mischievously re-titled its first adaptation of the BBC *Quatermass* series as *The Quatermass Xperiment* (55), and the company pushed the boundaries of the new certificate with the unprecedented colour blood-letting of *Frankenstein* and *Dracula*.

US schlock, British style. *The Man Without A Body.*

Before long, British Gothic horror had become a mini-boom in itself and American producers were falling over themselves to get a piece of the action. Samuel Z. Arkoff hooked up with Britain's Anglo-Amalgamated for a trio of perverse, colour horror-fests that tried to steal Hammer's thunder: HORRORS OF THE BLACK MUSEUM (59), *Peeping Tom* (59) and *Circus of Horrors* (60). Even Roger Corman got in on the act with *The Masque of the Red Death* (64) and *The Tomb of Ligeia* (64).

At this time, the production of B-movies — still trundling along thanks to a government-set quota and the cinema-going public's refusal to accept less than at least three and half hour's worth of entertainment on one bill — was also enlivened by American interests. The cutback in US B-movie production was leaving provincial American theatres short of programme fillers, so US producers of low budget fare looked to Britain to fill the gap. The result was a spate of British-made but transatlantic-in-tone B-movies, usually starring waning or second-order American stars and tackling heady sci-fi and horror subjects: *Fire Maidens from Outer Space* (56), *The Man Without a Body* (57), *The Headless Ghost* (59).[6] As cheap and cheerful as these were, they were often slicker-looking than previous British B-films (as budgets could rise as high as a dizzying £40,000, from the usual moth-eaten low of £15,000–£20,000[7]) and often a lot more fun.

Homegrown second features also benefited substantially when they were awarded double Eady fund payouts from 1959.[8] The next few years saw a

glut of modest but inventive British Bs, many better than the features they were supporting. The B-movie didn't survive the sixties (double bills came to rely on two 'A' features, or else were abandoned in favour of a main feature and supporting shorts), but the early part of the decade certainly produced some of its best examples: *The Tell-Tale Heart* (60), THE IMPERSONATOR (61), OFFBEAT (61), CASH ON DEMAND (61), UNEARTHLY STRANGER (63).

The real US-led renaissance of British cinema, however, didn't take place until the mid 1960s, when a blossoming youth scene, a new Labour government (this time headed by Harold Wilson) and growing amounts of disposable income saw Britain basking in an apparent mood of optimism. The second-wave 'American invasion' was kickstarted by just a handful of films, all produced in Britain by a Hollywood major (United Artists). First, the James Bond outing, *Dr No* (62), British-made and showcasing a new British star in Sean Connery, became a big, sexy hit. But the Bond formula really took off with *From Russia With Love* (63), and by *Goldfinger* (64) had become an international sensation. This much, of course, had been hoped for, if not expected, by the Bond films producers. But the critical and commercial success of *Tom Jones* (63) — which established Albert Finney as a worldwide star, won a brace of international awards, including the Best Picture Oscar, and made more than $17 million at the US box office (on a budget of $1 million) — took even United Artists (UA) by surprise. A short time later, the Beatles' *A Hard Day's Night* (64), intended as an ephemeral cash-in on what was perceived (by UA at least) as the group's fleeting success, became a worldwide phenomenon and was lauded as an artistic triumph to boot. Suddenly, British films (importantly, films with a British identity) were not just doing major business internationally, but they seemed cooler and fresher and more vibrant than anything that was coming out of Hollywood's dying studio system.

Hollywood reacted by dispatching executives to London by the plane-load. Nineteen sixty-five became a key year for American film companies setting up operations in Britain. Joining those with established British arms like UA and MGM were Columbia, Universal, Filmways and Embassy.[9] As Alexander Walker points out, by 1966 "American finance accounted for seventy-five per cent of 'British' first features or co-features given a circuit release." This figure was to rise to a staggering ninety per cent in 1967 and 1968.[10] The new 'British Hollywood' films like *Catch Us If You Can* (65), *The Knack* (65), *Darling* (65), *The Ipcress File* (65), *Life at the Top* (65), *Georgy Girl* (66), *Blowup* (66), *Modesty Blaise* (66), *Kaleidoscope* (66) and *Alfie* (66) all grabbed the coat-tails of *A Hard Day's Night* and embodied the mood of 'swinging London' (in stark contrast to the 'kitchen sink' films of five years earlier, none were set outside the capital) and almost all were sizeable international hits.

But the hike in London-set films also gave rise to what Robert Murphy would later call 'the anti-swinging London film,'[11] several examples of which we focus on in the pages that follow. These constituted the less attractive flipside to the idea that London life was one long, groovy happening. And as downbeat or even unpalatable as some of them were — PRIVILEGE, CHARLIE BUBBLES, THE STRANGE AFFAIR, OUR MOTHER'S HOUSE, BRONCO BULLFROG, DEEP END — they now serve somewhat more effectively as a 'truer' record of the times.

The rude health of mainstream British cinema in the mid sixties had a knock-on effect on lower budget and less artistically ambitious enterprises, and all manner of filmmaking outfits started riding the wave. Hammer's horror films were of a lower quality than ten years earlier, but it didn't stop the company churning them out profitably enough to win a Queen's Award to Industry in 1968. Cut-price film producer Tony Tenser's Tigon Productions was able to strike up alliances with better-resourced US outfits such as American International Pictures (AIP) and Avco Embassy and embark on a slew of exploitation films, one being Michael Reeves' *Witchfinder General* (68). And the further breakdown of censorship barriers initiated by hip, youth-oriented smashes such as *Blowup* led to a wave of successful British 'sex' films, from 'daring' comedies like *Here We Go Round the Mulberry Bush* (68) and PERCY (71) to the more salacious *School for Sex* (68) and *The Wife Swappers* (70).

So from the dour confines of mid fifties British cinema burst a blast of colour, sex and pop music. And it was paralleled with graphic violence, stark realism and a new preparedness to confront themes that were formerly taboo. By 1967, cinema attendances were still falling (down to 265 million[12]) but the buoyant mood, fervent activity and rising ticket prices more than made up for the decline.

If only it could have lasted.

1   The Cinema Exhibitors' Association Ltd., http://www.cinemauk.org.uk/ukcinemasector/admissions/annualukcinemaadmissions1935-2009/ [Last accessed 6 June 2010].

2   Ibid.

3   Sue Harper and Vincent Porter, *British Cinema of the 1950s — The Decline of Deference* (Oxford: Oxford University Press, 2003), p.8.

4   Ibid., p.24.

5   Ibid., p.30.

6   Steve Chibnall and Brian McFarlance, *The British 'B' Film* (London: BFI, 2010), pp.56–57.

7   Ibid.

8   Ibid., p.58.

9   Alexander Walker, *Hollywood, England* (London: Orion, 2005 edition), p.288.

10   Ibid. p.339.

11   Robert Murphy, *Sixties British Cinema* (London: BFI, 1992), pp.139–60.

12   Cinema Exhibitors' Association Ltd., op.cit.

ANIMAL FARM (1954)

Louis de Rochemont/Halas and Batchelor | 75 mins | colour

Directors/Producers John Halas, Joy Batchelor, from the novel by George Orwell.
Voices Maurice Denham; **Narration** Gordon Neath.

After a rousing speech by their elderly pig patriarch, Old Major, the animals of Manor Farm turn on their cruel, drunken master and take over the running of the farm themselves. Under the benign supervision of Old Major's advocate, Snowball, productivity begins to thrive. But when Snowball is overthrown by rival Napoleon, the pigs assert their power more forcefully, and soon the rest of the animals are worse off than before.

Like many successful animators (and until the 1970s, theirs was the UK's premier animation outfit), John Halas and Joy Batchelor often had to work to outside briefs. They served their apprenticeship making advertising films in the early forties, and during WWII were commandeered by the Ministry of Information to churn out lively propaganda shorts. As late as the 1970s, they were producing factory-line animated fare for television: *The Jackson 5ive*, *The Osmonds*, *The Addams Family*.

Along the way, of course, Halas and Batchelor delivered a good number of shorts that defined their individual style — *The Figurehead* (52), *The History of Cinema* (57), *Automania 2000* (63). But the feature they remain most celebrated for was the one that seemed to allow them the least artistic flexibility: *Animal Farm*.

Production on the film version of George Orwell's potent allegory on the Russian revolution began in 1951, a good few years before American financial and artistic involvement in British films really took off. But despite its very British background, the curious thing about *Animal Farm* is that it wouldn't have been made at all without covert assistance from the US government.

As a 'presentation' of US producer Louis de Rochemont, there was a political context to the film's financing from the outset. De Rochemont was the creator of the *March of Time* news documentaries that ran from the mid thirties to the fifties and which aided US propaganda efforts, particularly during WWII; he had also been an early American detractor of Adolf Hitler's, producing the cautionary *Inside Nazi Germany* a year before the war in Europe started.

The film of *Animal Farm*, however, was not instigated by de Rochemont, but by the CIA. (After decades of rumours, the past few years have seen various books and research papers unearth the paper trail that links the US organisation with the good offices of Halas and Batchelor.[1]) In 1951, a year after Orwell's death, the screen rights to the book were obtained by the Psychological Warfare Workshop, a division of the CIA's Office of Policy Co-ordination, which was engaged in feeding anti-communist sentiments directly into the cultural zeitgeist. The rights purchase was done under the supervision of one E. Howard Hunt (who, among other activities, was later to organise the 1972 break-in of the Watergate building in Washington, DC). Hunt's colleagues found Orwell's widow Sonia relatively easy to sweet-talk into the deal — one condition of the sale was that she could meet her hero, Clark Gable. After arranging this, Hunt chose Louis de Rochemont to handle the film's production.

12

FILM REVIEWS

It seems curious that Walt Disney wasn't at the top of Hunt's list of producers, especially as Disney was known to be vehemently anti-communist (and had gone so far as to shop some of his own employees to the House Committee on Un-American Activities). But it's unlikely that he would have buckled too readily to artistic interference, even if he had wholeheartedly accepted the political principles behind it. Halas and Batchelor were clearly more malleable than Uncle Walt. They were also respected by de Rochemont and his associates for their propaganda and information films. And they weren't so stupid as to pass on the financing — to the tune of £150,000 — for what was to be the first full-length British animated feature.

But what of their artistic input? The script is reputed to be the work of several US government-connected contributors, although much of the dialogue is lifted directly from Orwell's novel. There are no credited screenwriters, but aside from Joy Batchelor they include Philip Stapp and Lothar Wolf, filmmakers who had worked for the European Recovery Program (i.e., the Marshall Plan); J. Bryan and Finis Barr, leader and member, respectively, of the Psychological Warfare Workshop; and John Martin, a longtime associate of de Rochemont.

One result of this 'interference' is a compromise that takes a serious liberty with the original text: the film has a 'happy ending.' In the finale of Orwell's novel, the egregious pigs have invited their hitherto sworn enemies — human beings — to their farm, not only entertaining them warmly but also emulating them by standing on two legs, wearing clothes and drinking alcohol. The starving animals outside look from human to pig and can no longer tell which is which. The film opts to follow this scene (which omits the human visitors) with another animal uprising, which storms the farmhouse and mows down the nasty pigs — a far more palatable, if brutal, 'Hollywood' conclusion. Nevertheless, there is still a strong Halas and Batchelor imprint on *Animal Farm*. It is, for example, almost mercifully free of 'Disneyfication' (one concession being the inclusion of a little yellow duckling, who zealously tries to do his bit for the workers despite his tiny frame). And there is a brave bleakness to it: the violence isn't 'cartoonish' and the general aura of malevolence is unrelenting. The dark mood evoked by the colouring and sketching is embellished by the anthemic score by Matyas Seiber and shrill voice characterisations by Maurice Denham; at times the film achieves an accurate, and thus rather chilling, parody of an austere, breast-beating communist propaganda musical.

---

1   Karl F. Cohen, 'Animated Propaganda during the Cold War' (extract), and Dan Leab, 'Orwell Subverted: The CIA and the Filming of *Animal Farm*' (extract), in Paul Wells (ed.), *Halas & Batchelor Cartoons: An Animated History* (London: Southbank Publishing, 2006).

As for the imposed upbeat ending, Halas later defended it, saying the film needed a glimmer of hope. He was probably right. Orwell's vision is too harsh for mainstream cinema today, let alone in the 1950s. Certainly, a defeatist ending would have killed the film's chances commercially. But even with its glimmer of hope, *Animal Farm* was not a box office success.

Julian Upton

ALIAS JOHN PRESTON (1955)

Danziger Productions Ltd./British Lion Film Corporation | 66 mins | b&w
Director David MacDonald; **Producer** Sid Stone; **Screenplay** Paul Tabori. **Starring** Christopher Lee (John Preston), Betta St John (Sally Sandford), Alexander Knox (Dr Peter Walton).

John Preston arrives in the small town of Deanbridge to carve out a new life for himself in property development. He is welcomed warmly into the community, finding business and romantic success in his new home. But plagued by a series of disturbing nightmares, he begins to worry that all it not as it seems.

Alias *John Preston* is a scarcely referenced film, yet has much to recommend it, with a screenplay by Paul Tabori, author of lurid tomes such as *Crime and the Occult* and *The Social History of Rape*, and the first lead role for horror maestro Christopher Lee. It's easy to see why the film slipped between the cracks, however. While a perfectly well accomplished film, with strong acting and a tight storyline, it lacks any hint of action or intrigue, and has a conclusion that is obvious about halfway through the short running time of sixty-six minutes.

John Preston (Christopher Lee) arrives in the small town of Deanbridge, apparently on impulse after hearing a friend speak of it during the war, where he quickly sets about buying properties and inserting himself into as many important social circles as possible. From his first appearance on screen, Lee establishes the crotchety, domineering character that he would play to perfection in many of his films: the stern father in *The House that Dripped Blood* (70) and upstanding pillar of the community Colonel Bingham in *Nothing but the Night* (72). He is self assured to the point of grandiose over-confidence, striding into the local bank and demanding to see the manager, later employing the same attitude whilst on a date with local girl Sally (Betta St. John). He loses his temper spectacularly at the hapless waiter, having been asked to change tables, then proceeds to lecture poor Sally on the importance of good manners whilst simultaneously expressing his irrational hatred of France. His outbursts become increasingly interesting throughout the film, as he makes no attempt to hide the sulking, simmering anger he feels towards his fellow Board members on the Deanbridge Hospital Board. The Board's decision to appoint a psychiatrist with a psychoanalytic background disturbs Preston to the point where he seems about to leap across the table and physically attack his colleagues, and he makes no secret of his opinion that psychoanalysis is nothing but 'mumbo jumbo.'

Newly appointed psychiatrist (Alexander Knox) appears suspicious of Preston before even meeting him, and it's not long before the chance to analyse Preston presents itself. The latter half of the film chronicles Preston's struggles with his frequent dreams that he is David Garrity, an army deserter rather too familiar with the black market. "What have I done to deserve such nightmares?" he whines childishly at Walton. "Why does it have to happen to *me*?" Lee's forthright façade begins to crumble, until we eventually discover — you've guessed it — that Preston is in fact David Garrity.

This was one of four Danziger brothers' productions that Lee appeared in during the space of one year, also taking roles in episodes of the TV drama series *The Vise* (*The Final Column*, *The Price of Vanity* and *Strangle Hold*). The Danziger's high speed production accounts for the short running time of *Alias John Preston*, which, according to Lee, had as much to do with budgetary constraints as artistic considerations. 'It would have been physically possible, if the spirit hadn't weakened,' he said, 'to make a hundred and twenty films in a year for Harry Lee and Edward J. Danziger, because any film they made that lasted more than three days began to run over budget.'[1] One estimate puts the Danzigers' output at a staggering 351 TV shorts and around fifty-five cinema features.[2] Geoffrey Helman, who worked as assistant director on some of the Danzigers' later films, recalled that shooting schedules typically ran to 'two and a half days for one TV episode, and maybe a couple of weeks for a feature film,' with any running behind schedule occasionally remedied by ripping a page or two out of the script.[3]

In the context of such whistle-stop production, *Alias John Preston* is an impressive feat, and in no way a bad film per se. Its tightly compacted plot and self-conscious intensity though, tire the viewer before becoming somewhat infuriating in their transparency. At the end of it all, you might well feel like taking the advice of Preston's psychiatrist who has perhaps the most sensible response to Preston's shenanigans: "Come along, Sally, I'll get you a drink."

Jennifer Wallis

1   Christopher Lee, *Lord of Misrule: The Autobiography of Christopher Lee* (London: Orion, 2003), pp.165–66.
2   Dinosaur Films and TV: www.78rpm.co.uk/tvd.htm [Last accessed July 2010].
3   Dinosaur Films and TV: www.78rpm.co.uk/tvdd.htm [Last accessed July 2010].

IT KILLS ... BUT CANNOT BE KILLED!

It rises from 2000 miles beneath the earth
to melt everything in its path ...
machine gun bullets, flame throwers ...
nothing can stop it!

the Unknown

Starring
DEAN JAGGER with
EDWARD CHAPMAN
Story and Screen Play by JIMMY SANGSTER
Produced by ANTHONY HINDS
Directed by LESLIE NORMAN

X THE UNKNOWN (1956)

Hammer Film Productions/Exclusive | 81 mins | b&w

Director Leslie Norman; **Producers** Anthony Hinds and Michael Carreras; **Screenplay** Jimmy Sangster. **Starring** Dean Jagger (Dr Adam Royston), Leo McKern (Inspector McGill), Edward Chapman (John Elliott), William Lucas (Peter Elliott), Anthony Newley (LCpl 'Spider' Webb).

A routine army exercise in Scotland is disrupted when a seemingly bottomless fissure appears in the Earth, containing an unknown dark mass that feeds on energy, especially radiation. It terrorises the surrounding area, and with an atomic research institute in the vicinity, an answer needs to be found quickly as to how to arrest its ever-growing power. Hope lies with maverick scientist Dr Adam Royston's unofficial experiments with neutralising atomic energy.

apitalising (literally) on the success of the previous year's 'X' rated *The Quatermass Xperiment*, *X the Unknown* looked not to outer space for the source of its invasive threat, but to deep within the Earth, from where a primordial being has been awakened by an army troop's radiation detection training. Called in to deal with the mystery is Professor Royston, a scientist at the nearby Lochmouth Atomic Institute — a man who spends more time in his shed on his makeshift meccano, pulleys and wireless experiments in neutralising atomic energy safely (or "disintegrating atomic

structure obviating the resultant explosion" as he puts it, to the consternation of a visiting investigator), than on his work, thereby arousing the ire of the Institute's pompous boss (a nicely fussy Edward Chapman).

After radiation is then sucked from a container of trinium in Royston's locked and barred workshop, he realises that what he is dealing with is beyond the bounds of his experience, although not his reason. "Whoever it was came in here must have been most unusual," he says. And unusual it certainly is, the threat in this case coming from a seething black radioactive gloop that spreads its way across the countryside from its home in a Scottish bog (in reality the Gerrard's Cross sand and gravel pits), from where it has been rudely awakened. Royston surmises that it is a being of pure energy which feeds on energy. Unpersuaded by this reading of the situation, however, the army, with a 'these scientists, you know' approach, decide to give it a good licking from their flamethrowers, topping the fissure off with a skim of concrete for good measure. The predictable of course occurs and the creature is soon on the loose again, heading for the Atomic Energy Institute for 'the biggest meal of its life.' Suddenly, Royston's backyard experiments need to be pressed into urgent use.

The characterisation of Professor Royston is interesting. Although the name 'Quatermass' could not be used — his creator Nigel Kneale, disappointed at Hammer turning his pioneering scientist into, as he put it, "a creature with a completely closed mind" through their use of American actor Brian Donlevy in the title role of the film version of *The Quatermass Xperiment*, refused permission — Professor Royston is a Quatermass figure in all but name. And Dean Jagger, in his beanie hat and overcoat, fills his character's boots convincingly. A previous Oscar winner (Best Supporting Actor in *Twelve O'Clock High*), brought in to give the picture some box office prominence in America, he is a man who actually looks as if he knows one end of a Geiger counter from the other. He is sympathetic, quizzical, courteous, and with a slightly distracted gleam in his eye. He really lends the picture some class. It was a nice touch to give him a walking stick as a prop too; he uses it well, stroking the floor with it when he is being reprimanded by his boss, using it to open the door of the ruined tower, sweeping a dangerous canister out of Old Tom's reach (but crucially, waking him with his hand), using it to wave goodbye. He's endearingly fallible too, responding "I don't know" repeatedly to questions, while still retaining an air of scientific authority. And any man who can say the line "How do you kill mud?" not just with a commendably straight face, but convincingly, is well worth his salary.

As for the monster — and, in passing, it's worth noting that United Artists renamed *The Quatermass Xperiment* as *The Creeping Unknown* in the US — there are only so many times you can get away with wide-eyed dread on people's faces before you actually have to show the thing, which initially bubbles out of its crack in a vaguely reptilian spawn. (Early attempts at visualisation had apparently involved tapioca.) It found favour with the producers not least because of its suitability for budgetary constraints; "Cheaper to dig a hole than construct a rocket ship," said production manager and screenplay writer Jimmy Sangster.[1]

Sangster's screenplay took contemporary concerns about nuclear leakage from power plants as one source for his screenplay but, in spite of lines such as Royston's "as long as this thing feeds, it will live, and the more it lives, the more it will grow," it's straining things to call *X The Unknown* a salutary nuclear parable. When asked why he wrote it this or that way, Sangster's reply was, invariably, "for wages."

It's hard to know what more you could feasibly require of the film. As well as an original monstrous threat, it has a maverick scientist, a sceptical boss and his clean-cut heroic son, even a pipe-smoking major. And Leo McKern in a very early role, which sees him adopt a pretty fair private eye act (*Mr* McGill) in his trilby and overcoat. He is a sturdy and respectful presence, not easily swayed from his task of investigating the curious goings on for the UK Atomic Energy Commission (Internal Security Division). Then there are the specific local details that add so much to the experience of watching the films now — the warning poster for Fowl Pest in the police station for example — and some rather lovely location photography from Gerald Gibbs, which nicely captures the hazy light of frosty, early spring days. It has a score from James Bernard too, whose music seethes and boils, as if, deprived of his usual resource of a named horror to build a musical theme around, he concentrated on the movement of the black mousse. Then there are the film's 'blink-and-you-miss-them, did-I-really-see-that moments?' — a grotesquely ballooning finger, a melting face — which caused Hammer some of their many problems with the British Board of Film Censors.

I do have one quibble though. Not about the cavalier disregard for a radioactive substance which seems to be selective about its victims — that's practically a film convention — but about a line from the vicar as he is trying to shepherd his parishioners into his church. "Come on, it's nice and warm inside," he says. There are many things I can believe, but not that.

Graeme Hobbs

---

1   Jimmy Sangster, *Inside Hammer* (London: Reynolds & Hearn, 2001), p.23.

THE ABOMINABLE SNOWMAN (1957)

Clarion Films/Hammer Film Productions/Warner Bros. | 91 mins | b&w

Director Val Guest; **Producer** Aubrey Baring; **Screenplay** Nigel Kneale, from his teleplay *The Creature*. **Starring** Peter Cushing (John Rollason), Forrest Tucker (Tom Friend), Maureen Connell (Helen Rollason), Richard Wattis (Peter Fox), Robert Brown (Ed Shelley), Michael Brill (McNee).

In the high Himalayas, British scientist John Rollason joins an expedition headed by American explorer Tom Friend, who is searching for the legendary Yeti. The team quickly establish that the creature is no myth. They also realise they have underestimated their target: the Yeti are highly intelligent and do not welcome the intrusion of human beings. But Friend is a stubborn man and does not mean to leave the mountain without a trophy...

The legends have it that the Yeti are a placid breed, content to live a reclusive existence in the upper reaches of the Himalayas. And for many years, most folks were happy to respect their privacy. But during the 1950s — as Westerners became more determined to climb the region's vertiginous peaks — interest in the beasts became more intense. Climbing parties photographed mysterious footprints; Edmund Hillary and Sherpa Tenzing reported seeing a series of impressions in the snow as they ascended Everest. In 1954, the *Daily Mail* — who else? — even dispatched a team of crack investigative mountaineers to uncover evidence of Yeti activity. They returned with a circulation-improving set of photographs purporting to show the creature's tracks.

So the expedition led by Tom Friend — as documented by Nigel Kneale and Val Guest — was walking in some well-trodden snow. For Kneale, *The Abominable Snowman* was actually a return journey; it was an adaption of his 1955 BBC teleplay, *The Creature*. Inspired by the Yeti-mania, Kneale's script was a typically thoughtful speculation on the popular subject and a comment on some wider issues.

John Rollason, the film's scientist hero, joins the expedition for the most noble of intentions — to increase the sum total of human knowledge. At first, he believes Tom Friend shares his ambitions but is horrified to learn of the mission's true purpose. Friend is a showman and wants to capture a Yeti, a move he believes will make his fortune.

This division — between the high-minded and the lowbrow — could be said to mirror the different approaches that Guest and Kneale brought to their

DEMON-PROWLER OF MOUNTAIN SHADOWS...DREADED MAN-BEAST OF TIBET...THE TERROR OF ALL THAT IS HUMAN!!

The Abominable Snowman of the Himalayas

WE DARE YOU TO SEE IT ALONE!
Each chilling moment a shock-test for your scare-endurance!!

STARRING **FORREST TUCKER · PETER CUSHING ·**

AUBREY BARING · VAL GUEST · NIGEL KNEALE · Released by 20th CENTURY FOX · **REGALSCOPE** PICTURE

work on this film. Although Guest was no hack, he saw the film principally as an exciting story and approached it as such, charging it with conviction and atmosphere. Kneale, however, clearly had higher aspirations. His script seems determined to say Something Significant.

Kneale uses one 1950s obsession — the Yeti — as a prism through which to consider other contemporary issues. Friend embodies the crass materialism that had taken hold of western societies since the end of WWII, prizing money above humanity. The Yeti are 'abominable' but it's Friend who is the film's real monster, willing to imperil even his closest ally to get what he wants. We are invited to consider the consequences. Looming over all of this is the great spectre of the age — the nuclear bomb, the natural terminus of mankind's greed and aggression. The Lhama of the monastery where Rollason is based tells the scientist that "man is close to forfeiting his right to lead the world" because of such weapons. As they climb the mountain, Rollason ponders the exact nature of the Yeti. He theorises they are a different branch of our own evolutionary tree, ready to replace mankind, should humanity extinguish itself in a burst of uranium.

The film suggests we would do well to learn from the Buddhist monks (presumably Tibetan, although it is not specified). Anticipating the interest in Eastern philosophies that would burgeon in the west during subsequent decades, Rollason is fascinated by the culture and spirituality of his hosts; unlike his little-Englander assistant Foxy (Richard Wattis), he even enjoys drinking their tea — a very different brew from the British cuppa.

As has been traditional since the days of *Lost Horizon*, the Tibetans are
blessed with semi-mystical powers: the Lhama has second sight. He knows, for
instance, that Rollason will join Friend. But he warns the scientist that the Yeti
do not exist. It is a conclusion that Rollason learns to accept after coming face
to face with the creatures. He finally understands the Lhama's warnings: they
must be spared mankind's meddling. Of course, Kneale was too good a writer
to churn out sermons. His script crackles with incident and conflict. However,
in the commentary to the region one DVD, Guest notes how much of Kneale's
philosophising had to be pruned. Guest was surely sympathetic to the writer's
arguments — he would later produce his own anti-nuclear film THE DAY THE
EARTH CAUGHT FIRE (61) — but preferred to make them less overtly.

In the five decades since the film was completed, the threat of the bomb has
abated, the Yeti have not had occasion to leave their caves and Rollason's
hand-wringing seems shrill in consequence. And yet the film remains fresh,
thanks to the remarkable atmosphere that Guest created. Rather than go
for cheap shocks, he builds a gradual mood of unease that increases as the
expedition realises just how powerful the Yeti are.

Obeying the old axiom that what you don't see is more impressive than what
you do, the Yeti are kept largely off screen; the expressions of the actors as
they gaze on the creatures are far more persuasive than anything Hammer's
resource-starved effects department could have cooked up. Peter Cushing was
one of the great screen actors, and this was one of his best roles. While Forrest
Tucker was not in the same class, he plays Friend with bullying aplomb.

Despite a small budget bump that allowed some exterior filming in the
Pyrenees, Guest was otherwise obliged to recreate the Himalayas in the
Home Counties, like a bargain basement *Black Narcissus*. It wasn't just the
monastery that production designer Bernard Robinson had to build: the
mountainsides and snowscapes were largely constructed in Pinewood Studios.
It's to his great credit that the film carries such an evocative sense of place,
reaching beyond the confines of the studio to suggest the peaks and valleys
where the story is set.

Time has been kind to *The Abominable Snowman*; whatever the individual
contributions of Kneale and Guest, their collaboration resulted in an
intelligent, atmospheric adventure that looks increasingly like one of
Hammer's finest productions. As for the Yeti, people are still looking. The
evidence, however, remains inconclusive at best. Maybe they should take a tip
from Rollason and accept they don't want to be found.

James Oliver

THE STRANGE WORLD OF PLANET X (1957)

a.k.a. The Cosmic Monster | Artistes Alliance/Eros Films | 71 mins | b&w

Director Gilbert Gunn; **Producer** George Maynard; **Screenplay** Paul Ryder, based on the novel by Rene Ray. **Starring** Forrest Tucker (Gil); Gaby Andre (Michele); Martin Benson (Mr Smith); Alec Mango (Dr Laird), Wyndham Goldie (Brigadier Cartwright).

An MOD funded experiment goes awry and temporarily disrupts the ionosphere. Harmful gamma rays reach the Earth's surface and bring about mutation in the lower life forms. Soldiers battle colossal insects. The doctor loses his mind and jeopardises the world by taking the experiment to the next level. Flying saucers arrive from Planet X to right the wrongs.

The plot of *The Strange World of Planet X* is pretty standard and formulaic for sci-fi films of that era: a mad scientist tinkers too deeply with nature and creates a monster. However, it is a fascinating sci-fi movie that has many references that can be viewed in an entirely different context by a contemporary audience: MOD sponsored black projects; manipulation of the environment; Adamski-inspired space brothers; and a schoolgirl having clandestine meetings with men in the woods!

The film begins with a pre-credit sequence of stock footage showing a speeding steam train, radio antennas and the detonation of experimental bombs. A narrator advises on man's desire to experiment and advance the boundaries of science. "Since the world began, ever-inventive man has constantly pushed forward into the unknown," he announces in a technically erroneous statement perhaps more befitting creationism than science. The narrator also warns of the perils of such unbridled research: "Man goes forward into the unknown. But how does the unknown react? The unknown planet: Planet X."

Such faux documentary-style openings were common in sci-fi films and they generally succeeded in providing a dash of verisimilitude to the 'science' part, and, indeed, the science in *Planet X* is appealing even by today's standards. Dr Laird is studying the effects of powerful magnetic fields on metals and living tissue. His work is being surreptitiously funded by the Ministry of Defence in what would today be described as a black project — "Do you know how much money we've poured down that drain to date? A quarter of a million pounds," protests Brigadier Cartwright to a government minister. What Laird isn't aware of is that the effects of his experiments are spilling beyond the controlled environment of the lab and into the surrounding location. The clock stops and the TV set explodes at the local pub during one test, for instance.

Efficient special effects. *The Strange World of Planet X*.

The villagers grumble about the doctor's experiments much like the villagers in the Universal *Frankenstein* movies: "Just because they have to muck about with the current for the sake of their blimmin' experiments, we have to suffer," whinges the pub landlord. One almost expects the locals to light torches and march on the doctor's lab.

The similarities with *Frankenstein* don't stop there. When the lab apparatus runs at full power it triggers a lightning storm, which causes the local tramp to be bombarded with cosmic rays and become a facially scarred, deranged creature. Karloffian, he

lumbers about the woods attacking solitary women who stray into the area. But the real 'cosmic monsters' are the insects. For the most part they are real insects shot against miniature foliage, à la Bert I. Gordon, and the effect actually works quite well when people aren't matted into the frame. Also put to use are outsized insect puppets and these, too, are pretty efficient. In one particular scene, where the schoolgirl Jane is in the woods looking for insect larvae, we briefly glimpse the upper part of a man-sized stag beetle standing upright beyond the bushes. It's effectively quite eerie. Another notable scene depicts an attack on a soldier. Overpowered by the insects, the man's face is de-fleshed by gnawing mandibles in a surprisingly gruesome sequence, so much so that it was cut by several seconds in order to achieve an 'A' certificate in 1957.

Thematically reminiscent of *The Day the Earth Stood Still* (51), a space traveller intervenes to advise and correct humanity. 'Mr Smith' arrives by flying saucer and warns Laird's assistants of the dangerous path they walk. The concept of the benevolent 'space brother' was popular at the time, made so by the remarkable claims and influential allegations of so-called contactees like George Adamski and George Van Tassel. Indeed, the saucer in *Planet X* is clearly modelled on the Adamski photographs and as Gil states, "Mr Smith is the legendary character from outer space." Smith helps defeat the insects with his ray gun and summons a back-up saucer to destroy Laird and his lab before bidding farewell.

Typical of the time, the dialogue is unfettered by today's PC attitudes. Brigadier Cartwright announces the news that a replacement assistant has been found for Laird. "A woman?" responds Laird, "you must be joking!"

"She's very highly qualified, doctor," Cartwright counters, "Yeah, I know the type; frustrated, angular spinster, very dedicated to her calling, without a sense of humour, bossy and infuriatingly right every time," bemoans Gil.

When the woman arrives and proves to be French, both Gil and the government minister soon make advances on her in an oblique ménage à trois. Also now seen in a different light are Jane's encounters with strange men in the woods. When her mother rebukes her for chatting to a tramp, she innocently responds: "He's nice. I met him in the woods yesterday... he's promised to give me a flea when he can catch one." Despite her mother's warnings not to speak to strange men, she is soon back in the woods where she meets the sinister-looking raincoated 'Mr Smith' and discusses the oddness of his facial hair. Ironically, lone men with little girls in the woods would seem greater monsters in today's paedophile-obsessed times than the deformed man-eating insects creeping amongst the trees!

Some of the acting is clumsily amateurish, most notably Susan Redway as Jane. Her eyes all too often glance towards the camera or director when delivering her lines, time and money seemingly eliminating the prospect of retakes. But this is forgivable and there are enough familiar faces to counter it. Forrest Tucker's role is similar to that which he plays in another Eros production, THE TROLLENBERG TERROR (58):[1] a boisterous yank who helps defeat the threat and get the girl. Oddly, in the scene where he runs out of the school building to rescue his woman a stand-in is used who bears no resemblance to Tucker. This five-yard dash was seemingly too much for the boisterous yank.

Overall this is fine sci-fi hokum, which stands up to repeated viewings.

Interestingly, the plot pre-empted the real-life HAARP (High Frequency Active Auroral Research Program) experiments by more than thirty years. HAARP, established in 1993, did indeed set out to manipulate the ionosphere. Conspiracy theories and concerns abound as to the dangers that HAARP may unleash upon humanity, but as yet the giant insects haven't made an appearance.

David Slater

---

1   *The Strange World of Planet X* and *The Trollenberg Terror* were released as a double bill in America as *Cosmic Monsters* and *The Crawling Eye*.

THE TROLLENBERG TERROR (1958)

a.k.a. The Crawling Eye | Tempean films/Eros Films | 82 mins | b&w

Director Quentin Lawrence; **Producers** Robert S. Baker, Monty Berman; **Screenplay** Jimmy Sangster. **Starring** Forrest Tucker (Alan Brooks), Laurence Payne (Philip Truscott), Janet Munro (Anne Pilgrim), Jennifer Jayne (Sarah Pilgrim), Warren Mitchell (Professor Crevett), Andrew Faulds (Brett).

There's trouble brewing in the Alpine town of Trollenberg. A number of climbers have met grisly ends on the Trollenberg mountain and no one accepts the official verdict of 'accident.' Then there's the mysterious — and highly radioactive — cloud clinging to the mountainside. United Nations investigator Alan Brooks realises there's an alien invasion afoot; what's more, the aliens have telepathic powers and can invade the human mind...

L et's be clear about this from the start: *The Trollenberg Terror* is a rip off. It began life on television, after the nascent ITV decided to imitate the BBC's tremendously popular *Quatermass* serials. Then it was up-scaled for cinema screens after Tempean films decided to imitate Hammer's tremendously popular *Quatermass* film adaptations. This does not, however, preclude it from being thoroughly entertaining.

To script the film version, the producers recruited Jimmy Sangster. Sangster had form producing *Quatermass* rip offs, having previously penned X THE UNKNOWN (56). Perhaps more pertinently, he was also responsible for writing *The Curse of Frankenstein* (57) and *Dracula* (58): those films informed his script far more than the nominal influence. Despite obeisance to the trappings of sci-fi — there's an observatory populated by wise men in white coats; the aliens make a futuristic beeping noise — the emphasis throughout is on bloodcurdling horror.

It certainly starts as it means to go on; we join three students climbing on the Trollenberg mountain. One gets into difficulties and the aforementioned futuristic beeping noise can be heard... His friends try to rescue their stricken comrade but it is too late: he is dead. What's more, something has removed his head. (Quite why the aliens require human heads is never made clear but it's plainly important: we are later treated to the sight of a head in a rucksack, placed there by their human slave.)

Nor are the aliens' uncanny powers limited to the mountain: on the train to Trollenberg, a young woman senses their presence and passes out. This is Anne Pilgrim, who performs a mind reading act with her sister Sarah. Theirs

Vivid title change for the US release of *The Trollenberg Terror.*

The nightmare terror of the slithering eye that unleashed agonizing horror on a screaming world!

A man dissolves... and out of the oozing mist comes the hungry eye, slave to the demon brain!

THE CRAWLING EYE

FORREST TUCKER LAURENCE PAYNE · JENNIFER JAYNE
Directed by ROBERT S. BAKER, MONTY BERMAN   Produced by QUENTIN LAWRENCE

is no charade, however. Anne is a genuine telepath and has an awareness of when the aliens are up to no good. Naturally, she becomes their target.

Aliens 'possessing' humans is a motif drawn (but of course) from *Quatermass* — variations appeared in every incarnation — but it's used here far more casually: telepathy is presented as an authentic scientific phenomenon. While real scientists will roll their eyes at such notions, it's a fiction that allows a useful sense of disquiet to build. There's an impressive sequence where Anne and Sarah are performing their act in a hotel lounge, when Anne detects alien activity and describes an attack on two climbers on the mountainside as it happens.

Although the film seems most proud of its gruesome goings on, it's these more suspenseful sequences that work best, developing an unsettling tone not often found in monster movies. The most convincing scenes are those involving the aliens' cat's-paw, Brett — a climber whose mind has been taken over. Threatened by Anne Pilgrim's telepathic gifts, the aliens dispatch Brett to kill her. And at first, no one knows he is a threat. There's something inexorable — Terminator-esque almost — about the way he pursues his quarry.

Director Quentin Lawrence deserves praise for his handling of these moments.

Gruesome goings-on in *The Trollenberg Terror.*

He was principally a television director (he handled the original ITV incarnation of *The Trollenberg Terror*) but, on the evidence presented here, should have graduated to better things. Obviously limited by a low budget, he nevertheless manages to include some interesting stylistic flourishes, selecting some unusual angles and using longer takes.

Not all the film is so effective. The intelligent, passionate man of science of Nigel Kneale's *Quatermass* scripts (or even Sangster's X THE UNKNOWN) has regressed into a caricature boffin, played by Warren Mitchell, complete with an is-that-supposed-to-be-German? accent. This character — Professor Crevett — is ostensibly exploring 'cosmic rays,' but turns out to be an expert physician and pathologist too. We should, therefore, not be surprised at the speed with which he becomes an authority on alien behaviour.

Reducing the chief scientist to camp stereotype creates a vacancy for a hero. It's filled by visiting guest star Forrest Tucker, the burly American actor who became an improbable icon of British sci-fi for turns in this, THE ABOMINABLE SNOWMAN and THE STRANGE WORLD OF PLANET X. His character, Alan Brooks, has encountered these aliens during a previous invasion attempt; once he realises that they're up to their old tricks, he springs into action.

And so, the film races towards its rousing climax. All earlier ambitions —
towards atmosphere, towards subtlety — are abandoned in the headlong rush
to beat the monsters. The enslaved Brett tries to kill Anne Pilgrim but Brooks
is on hand to shoot him dead, leading to the film's best effect as the flesh melts
from the enslaved man's bones. This provokes the aliens into launching their
attack; Brooks evacuates everyone to Crevett's observatory, setting the stage
for the traditional final reel siege.

This is conventional monster movie stuff, of course, but handled with such
verve that it's hard to be churlish. The eventual appearance of the aliens is
most satisfactory: huge octopoid globules with a single eye. Brooks' method
for combating these devilish creatures is gloriously irresponsible — he hurls
Molotov cocktails at them; those weapons were later banned from British
screens by the BBFC, who took a dim view of such 'imitable behaviour.'

For all the silly pseudo-science and cheesy sensationalism, *The Trollenberg
Terror* makes the grade as an engaging, fast-paced thriller. Its sins are no
worse than most fifties creature features and its merits elevate it above much
of the genre. In America (where distributors renamed it *The Crawling Eye*),
satisfied customers included a youthful John Carpenter (who was inspired by
it to make *The Fog*) and future superstar novelist Stephen King, who included
a 'crawling eye' in his novel *It*.

The Trollenberg Terror was the last of the *Quatermass* rip offs; the Gothic
horror boom had begun and offered richer pickings for low budget film
producers. And so, the cycle that began with Nigel Kneale's thoughtful,
adult speculations ended with Forrest Tucker lobbing petrol bombs at
rubber blobs. Then again, Sangster and Lawrence did not share Kneale's
lofty ambitions: they just wanted to tell a rollicking yarn and, in that, they
succeeded admirably.

James Oliver

TREAD SOFTLY STRANGER (1958)

Alderdale Films/Renown Pictures Corporation | 90 mins | b&w

Director Gordon Parry; **Producer** Denis O'Dell; **Screenplay** George Minter, Denis O'Dell, from the play *Blind Alley* by Jack Popplewell. **Starring** Diana Dors (Calico), George Baker (Johnny Mansell), Terence Morgan (Dave Mansell), Patrick Allen (Paddy Ryan).

Professional gambler Johnny Mansell returns to his northern working class hometown to find that his supposedly clean-cut younger brother, Dave, has embezzled £300 from the company where he works, so he can lavish gifts on his girlfriend Calico. She persuades Dave to steal the firm's payroll money, but when Johnny tries to stop him, the night watchmen is accidentally killed. Tension mounts between the brothers and Calico as they try to ride out the police investigation.

A quick search for internet reviews of *Tread Softly Stranger* suggests it's a gritty drama with lots going for it. Actually, it's a rather silly offering with two prominent features —both belonging to Diana Dors. And, boy, does she show them off to their full advantage, almost spilling out of sexy lingerie or displayed pert and upright beneath a tight sweater. And after every shot of her getting hot and bothered with the male lead, the editor (Anthony Harvey, who would go on to direct the Oscar-winning *The Lion in Winter* [68]) cuts to a shot of a fiery steelworks foundry — just in case we hadn't noticed how smoulderingly hot she really was.

For those of a certain age, Dors will always be the heavily peroxided woman from Adam and the Ants' *Prince Charming* video, looking bloated but still able to shimmy and strut with the band. She had, of course, once been dubbed Britain's answer to Marilyn Monroe; by the time of her death from ovarian cancer in 1984 at the age of fifty-two, she was more like Shelley Winters, an ageing national treasure willing to share the sometimes harsh life lessons she'd learned over the years.

Dors is better remembered now as a personality than as the decent actress she actually was. Few people can name more than a couple of her films, and those that can rarely mention *Tread Softly Stranger*. But although she's let down on numerous occasions by a weak screenplay here, she manages to give her often laughably poor lines far more conviction than they deserve — and certainly far more than her male co-stars manage.

By the time *Tread Softly* was made, Dors' movie career was in decline. Her

one outstanding film, *Yield to the Night*, had been released two years earlier, and she'd failed to capitalise on its success. Nevertheless, there were those still hopeful that her earthy glamour could pull in the punters — co-writer and executive producer George Minter wanted her for the film so much that he delayed filming in the Rotherham area until she was available. The film gets scant recognition in her autobiography, in which she merely mentions that her fee for it enabled her to buy a fifteenth-century farmhouse. She adds: "I had a very interested taxman and an even more angry agent making enquiries about my earnings on *Tread Softly Stranger*, £10,000 of which I had asked for in cash, unknown to anyone."[1] Relating the film only in terms of money now seems oddly fitting, as it's all about people desperate to get their hands on ready cash.

Dors plays Calico, which the character says is a nickname. Calico is, of course, a cheap fabric — and the character is certainly cheap, willing to accept gifts in return for her charms. Whether the writers had this in mind, or if they merely thought it sounded exotic for somebody who stands out like a sore thumb in her surroundings, is anybody's guess, but it is fitting. Johnny Mansell, a ne'er-do-well whose devil-may-care attitude is established in the pre-credit sequence when he abandons a woman he plans to have his wicked way with after receiving a threatening call from somebody he owes money to, sees through her immediately. They're two of a kind — chancers out to take what

they can. But Johnny isn't impressed with her, claiming "some women are merciless." However, after she thrusts those aforementioned scantily-clad breasts at him a few times, he too can't resist her, despite the fact she's been dating his younger, distinctly less worldly brother Dave.

George Baker is Johnny, but he lacks the dramatic weight to successfully carry the role. He wouldn't come into his own as an actor for some time, eventually becoming a household name for his television role as Chief Inspector Wexford in *The Ruth Rendell Mysteries* in the eighties and nineties. Here, he's stilted and stuttering, putting unnecessary (and distracting) pauses into his lines. Terence Morgan (who was ten years older than Baker in real life) fares better as Dave, whose spectacles and smart appearance mark him out as a stereotypically quiet, bookish man. It's Dave who loses his cool when the robbery at the steel foundry goes horribly wrong, resulting in the death of an old man the brothers have known all their lives. Patrick Allen, he of jutting jaw and dulcet tones (later put to good use in endless TV voiceovers) is the son of the dead man who proves far more useful at tracking down the killers than the local police. Unusually it's his famous voice that lets him down — it's not until about halfway through that you realise he's supposed to be Irish, and that's only after the character announces it!

In fact, the mish-mash of dialects is disconcerting throughout. The producers may have been keen on giving the film some local colour by going on location, but forgot to make sure their stars sounded as if they belonged there. Baker and Morgan's South Yorkshire accents are more RP than anything, while Dors has an odd hint of a transatlantic twang. But it's the dialogue that really lets everyone down. In her big speech Dors actually says, "Remember, I come from a slum, from the gutter, where it's quite a step up to the end of the pavement... I found that I was attractive to the opposite sex. I discovered my legs weren't made just to stand on." But God bless her, she puts her heart and soul into it!

With a little more care with the script (tellingly, the writers subsequently concentrated on their producing careers) and better casting of the male leads, this could have been a real winner. It certainly looks great, with some wonderful night-time shots more akin to *The Third Man* than a B-picture, as you might expect from a cinematographer of the calibre of Douglas Slocombe. But as it stands, *Tread Softly Stranger* is merely an interesting footnote in the career of a star who never really fulfilled her potential.

Sarah Morgan

---

1   Diana Dors, *Dors by Diana* (London: Queen Anne Press, 1981), p.192.

HORRORS OF THE BLACK MUSEUM (1959)

Carmel/Merton Park/Anglo-Amalgamated | 78 mins | colour

Director Arthur Crabtree; **Producer** Jack Greenwood; **Screenplay** Herman Cohen, Aben Kandel.
Starring Michael Gough (Bancroft), Geoffrey Keen (Supt. Graham), Graham Curnow (Rick), Beatrice
Varley (Aggie), June Cunningham, Shirley Anne Field.

*London is in the grip of a killing spree. Young women are being murdered with
instruments of torture similar to those kept in Scotland Yard's infamous 'Black
Museum.' Celebrated writer Edmond Bancroft is obsessed by the crimes, not only
haranguing the police with his theories about the killings but appearing to suffer
physically after each one comes to light. What nobody but his assistant knows is
that Bancroft is running his own Black Museum.*

I n his seminal text on the British horror film, *A Heritage of Horror*
(1973), the teenage David Pirie coined the term 'Sadean trilogy' for
three movies released by Anglo-Amalgamated at the end of the fifties
to challenge Hammer's newfound horror crown. Pirie identified the
trilogy as *Peeping Tom, Circus of Horrors* and *Horrors of the Black Museum,*
all of which were awash with bouts of sadism. They also presented kinky and
perverse subtexts, and — in order to truly give Hammer a run for its money —
were released in glorious Eastmancolor.

Hammer's phenomenal horror revival (*The Curse of Frankenstein*
[57], *Dracula* [58], *The Mummy* [59]) quickly settled into a series of
formulaic, risk-averse, studio-bound costume dramas, but they remained
hugely popular for the next decade. The Sadean trilogy, by contrast, had
contemporary settings, pseudo-psychological pretensions and, not least, a
real desire to upset the viewer. For this reason, they are much more fun to
watch today.

Peeping Tom, since it was reclaimed by Martin Scorsese et al for the
cineastes in the late seventies, now enjoys a healthy reputation as a
masterwork of psychological horror. Sidney Hayers' *Circus of Horrors* is,
equally, perversely entertaining and imaginative but for all its colour and
zeal, does not match up to that director's later NIGHT OF THE EAGLE (62). It's
worth taking a look, however, at *Horrors of the Black Museum* (which was
released first), if only for its shameless commitment to out-grossing (in both
senses of the word) anything that Hammer was doing, and for its streak of
thorough nastiness that clearly influenced the two later Anglo films.

IT ACTUALLY PUTS **YOU** IN THE PICTURE
CAN YOU STAND IT?

HYPNOVISTA

'HORRORS OF THE BLACK MUSEUM

SEE THE VAT OF DEATH!

FEEL THE ICY HANDS!

SEE THE FANTASTIC BINOCULAR MURDER!

FEEL THE TIGHTENING NOOSE!

IN CinemaScope AND COLOR

starring MICHAEL GOUGH · JUNE CUNNINGHAM · GRAHAM CURNOW · SHIRLEY FIELD · Produced by HERMAN COHEN
Written by ABEN KANDEL and HERMAN COHEN · Directed by ARTHUR CRABTREE · a JAMES H. NICHOLSON and SAMUEL Z. ARKOFF Production An AMERICAN INTERNATIONAL Picture

Black Museum certainly doesn't waste any time kicking off. A young woman receives an unexpected parcel in the post and, egged on by her flatmate, quickly opens it to reveal a pair of binoculars. Baffled but excited by the gift, she rushes over to the window to try the binoculars out, suddenly letting out a piercing scream. The glasses drop to the floor and the young woman covers her eyes; blood seeps through her fingers. She collapse next to the binoculars, which we now see have bloody, spring-loaded spikes protruding from the eyepieces. From the end of the opening credits to this moment takes less than two minutes.

When they come, the rest of the murders are equally as abrupt and gory: a shopkeeper is pincered to death with a pair of iron ice tongs, a girl is guillotined as she lays down to sleep in bed, another gets a dagger in the chest upon emerging from a fairground tunnel of love ride. These grisly episodes can raise an eyebrow or draw a tiny gasp today; in 1959 they seemed positively repellent. (All three Sadean movies were met with critical revulsion at the time of their release; Michael Powell's career looks certainly to have been damaged by *Peeping Tom*, although arguments as to whether the film actually destroyed his reputation are ongoing). But they are the highlights that you remember long after you've forgotten the plot.

Gory highlights are not all that *Horrors of the Black Museum* has going for it, however. It also has the deliriously berserk Michael Gough. A contemporary *Monthly Film Bulletin* review criticised *Black Museum* for "Michael Gough's conventional portrait of menace,"[1] but looking at the performance now, this seems a crushing understatement. The film makes no attempt to understand the central character's obsession with murder and torture (as opposed to *Peeping Tom*, which was all about contextualising its protagonist's perversion). But it does give Gough free reign to let loose one of the most ferociously insane performances of pantomime evil in the history of horror movies.

Barking at his vacuous assistant, Gough scales heights of shaking fury that are as alarming as the murders themselves: it looks like his head could explode at any moment. He taps into shuddering, apoplectic rages that seem way out of proportion with the campy lines he has to deliver. But he counters this madness with the public persona of his celebrated crime writer: smooth but arrogant, aggravating the baffled police with his know-it-all theorising and dishing out snide comments to his fans with the scathing dryness of George Sanders in *All About Eve*. Where, say, *Peeping Tom* at least appears to take itself very seriously, Gough makes *Black Museum* impossible to take seriously at all: from his two-tone hair-do to his 'baddie' limp, from his vile unctuousness to his blood-boiling incandescence, he is having the kind of ball

here that only an exploitation film actor can have.

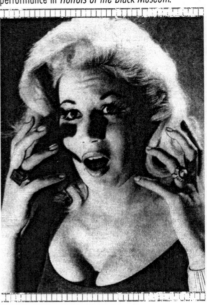

A BBFC examiner reacts to Michael Gough's performance in *Horrors of the Black Museum*.

Director Arthur Crabtree was an ex-cinematographer who, after notably starting his directorial career with a handful of hit melodramas in the forties, was relegated to more serviceable fare in the fifties. Save for a sci-fi horror in the *Quatermass* style (*Fiend Without a Face* [58]) there's nothing on his CV to really prepare one for the unpleasantness that runs through *Black Museum* (Shirley Anne Field's character, for example, is brutally finished off after we've got to know and like her — wooden performance notwithstanding).

It's more likely that this vein of nastiness was implanted (in all three Sadean films) by Anglo-Amalgamated, and compounded, in the case of *Black Museum* and *Circus of Horrors*, by the involvement of US producers like Herman Cohen (who co-wrote the script)[2] and Samuel Z. Arkoff (of Stateside distributors American-International). But we'll never know if Crabtree's dark, distasteful side would have developed further, since *Black Museum* was his last film. A question for further research is whether its damage to his reputation meant he never directed again.

'Thanks' to Cohen and Arkoff, *Black Museum* was released in the USA with a 'Hypnovista' sequence, a fourteen-minute, straight-to-camera scene tagged onto the front of the movie, in which a 'real-life psychiatrist' purported to hypnotise the audience. As an unintentionally hilarious gimmick, it wasn't too out of place with the histrionics that followed. But it served to kill that great shock opening stone dead.

Julian Upton

1   *Monthly Film Bulletin*, 6:300/311 (1959), p.59.
2   Cohen must have been particularly pleased with Michael Gough's handling of this material. Three years later he shipped him to the US to make *Black Zoo*, in which Gough plays a Los Angeles zoo owner who trains his animals to kill his enemies. *Halliwell's Film Guide* describes the film as 'stultifyingly inept.'

PLEASE TURN OVER (1959)

Beaconsfield Productions/Anglo-Amalgamated | 85m | b&w

Director Gerald Thomas; **Producer** Peter Rogers; **Screenplay** Norman Hudis, based on the play *Book of the Month* by Basil Thomas. **Starring** Ted Ray (Edward Halliday), Julia Lockwood (Jo Halliday), Leslie Phillips (Dr Henry Manners), Jean Kent (Janet Halliday), June Jago (Gladys Worth).

Stiff-collared accountant Edward Halliday is concerned his teenage daughter Jo lacks direction or purpose. What he doesn't know is that Jo is spending her nights penning a steamy potboiler, 'Naked Revolt,' featuring fictionalised, sexed-up characters based on her family and the local townsfolk. When the book is published it becomes a sensation, but the town is scandalised and Halliday mortified.

> *"I want to kiss each one of your ribs."*
> *"I say, that is naughty."*

Before they became exclusively pre-occupied with the increasingly lucrative, if decreasingly discerning, *Carry On* series, the producer-director team of Peter Rogers and Gerald Thomas tried their hands at a number of other projects: twee comedies with 'grown-up' asides (*Raising the Wind* [61], *Twice Round the Daffodils* [62], *Nurse on Wheels* [63]), plucky youth pictures (*Circus Friends* [56], *The Duke Wore Jeans* [58]) and, perhaps most successfully, crime thrillers paced with tense economy (*Time Lock* [57], *The Vicious Circle* [57]).

Please Turn Over belongs very much to the first group of films, sharing their genteel milieux, rosy-cheeked approach to sex and dash of middlebrow pretension. But where it begins as a typical 1950s, buttoned-up family comedy, with a cast of interchangeable plummy voiced women exchanging jaunty platitudes with a well meaning if exasperated patriarch, it soon reveals a slightly edgier underside that suggests Rogers and Thomas may have harboured more Boulting-like ambitions before they got caught up on the *Carry On* treadmill. Indeed, the film is actually rather revealing in contrasting what the quaint, provincial English comedies of the 1950s were and what they probably wanted to be. As the story opens, we're at the orderly breakfast table of fussy, middle-aged accountant Edward Halliday (a suitably starchy Ted Ray). It's a typical, quaint, never-had-it-so-good domestic scene: Halliday is calling for quiet so he can read his paper, berating his daughter Jo (Julia Lockwood) for not being efficient and purposeful like his secretary, and sparring with his dutiful wife (Jean Kent) over the general business

of parenting. Only the Hallidays' spinsterish lodger Gladys (June Jago), a puritanical believer in discipline and healthy living, seems beyond reproach.

But when the film slips into the narrative of *Naked Revolt* — the novel the teenage Jo has been penning upstairs using characters based on her family — it becomes something of a playfully subversive romp in which stiff upper-lipped characters mouth sexy dialogue, prim ladies unleash fiery libidos and respectable white-collar workers go to seed over whiskey and women. Halliday's *Naked Revolt* alter ego is an embezzler and an adulterer, stealing money from his firm to keep his toxic, high-maintenance secretary — with whom he is having an affair — in fur and diamonds. His wife is engaged in a passionate, flamboyant affair with family friend Lionel Jeffries. Meanwhile, Gladys is a frustrated, gin-soaked romantic with a desperate lust for her employer, the town's Romeo doctor (Leslie Phillips). Even the Halliday's earthy housekeeper, a scene-stealing Joan Sims, is transformed into a sexy French au pair with an amusing line in Franglais: "*C'eci est une proper turn-up pour le books*," she says, anticipating *Carry On* lines to come.

Of course, 'order' is eventually restored — more's the pity — but there's a sense that the characters, and the film, have all benefited from letting their hair down. It's a long way from *Carry On Abroad*, but that's to *Please Turn Over*'s credit, and shows that Rogers and Thomas might have done well to stay just this side of the vulgar comedy breach. (Here, actors who became forever linked to *Carry On* — Sims, Charles Hawtrey, Dilys Laye — sit perfectly well with more estimable performers such as Jeffries and Joan Hickson.)

The film's strongest point is its acrobatic script by Norman Hudis, which takes the best of its source material (Basil Thomas's play, *Book of the Month*), adds some early *Carry On* vim (Hudis would write the first six entries in that series) and neatly balances a gentle satire of repressed English mores with a precise parody of lurid American potboilers. There are unmistakeable parallels in the story with the brouhaha that accompanied the publication of the US bestseller *Peyton Place*, which, like Jo's book, detailed the sex secrets of a small, outwardly respectable town and was written, scandalously, by a young, unknown female writer.

There's also a moment of surprising comic prescience, albeit unwitting. When the strait-laced townsfolk deluge the bookshop for Jo's steamy novel, the scene prefigures that oft-repeated news footage, taken just a few months later, of bourgeois types standing in line — half ashamed, half unapologetic — for the newly available, unexpurgated edition of *Lady Chatterley's Lover*.

Julian Upton

FILM REVIEWS

TARZAN'S GREATEST ADVENTURE (1959)

Solar Film Productions/Paramount | 88 mins | colour

Director John Guillermin; **Producer** Sy Weintraub; **Screenplay** Berne Giler and John Guillermin from a story by Les Crutchfield, based upon the character created by Edgar Rice Burroughs.
Starring Gordon Scott (Tarzan), Anthony Quayle (Slade), Sara Shane (Angie), Sean Connery (O'Bannion), Niall MacGinnis (Kruger), Scilla Gabel (Toni).

A group of mercenaries, disguised to look like natives, carry out a brutal attack on an African village, stealing supplies and explosives for use in a diamond mine raid. When Tarzan finds out the gang's ringleader is his old enemy, Slade, he sets off in relentless pursuit, resolving to fight them to the death.

T arzan's *Greatest Adventure* wasn't the first of the MGM-RKO-Paramount Tarzan series (which began in 1932 and was sold from studio to studio) to be made with a largely British cast and crew, nor was it the first to be shot in colour and 'scope and filmed partly on location in Africa. It was the first, however, to be produced by Sy Weintraub, who bought the rights from producer Sol Lesser in 1958 and proceeded to breathe some much-needed life into the character's exploits.

Under Lesser, the franchise had grown stale and formulaic; the exotic (and initially erotic) spark that had been ignited by MGM's *Tarzan the Ape Man* (32) and *Tarzan and His Mate* (34) had long been extinguished, giving way to year after year of cheap programmers in which Tarzan swung lazily around an unconvincing studio set, spoke in two-word sentences, enjoyed domestic bliss in a well-kept tree house with Jane and wrestled with a rubber crocodile every time he had to swim across a lake. Aimed squarely at the least demanding nine-year-old boy in the audience, the series would not have lasted much longer had Lesser stayed in the driving seat.

Weintraub changed all that. In *Greatest Adventure*, he elbows Jane out of the picture, has the goofy chimp Cheetah reined in, and, more significantly, sees Tarzan (Gordon Scott) transformed into an earnest, articulate but steel-eyed tracker with a fatalistic streak of vengeance, hunting his criminal quarry with the doggedness of a jungle cat. (Ironically, given that a young Sean Connery puts in an appearance here, this Tarzan is not unlike a loin-clothed James Bond, but without the puns.)

Weintraub was also smart in hiring Brits John Guillermin, Anthony Quayle, Connery and Niall MacGinnis for *Greatest Adventure*, the latter three playing a motley crew of would-be diamond raiders that Tarzan pursues up river. For

Gordon Scott, all man. *Tarzan's Greatest Adventure.*

director Guillermin, it was an early chance to flex the muscles he'd later use to good effect in *The Blue Max* and *The Towering Inferno*. He delivers the epitome of a *Boy's Own* adventure story. We're knee-deep in the action before the credits even come up, as the villains (blacked up to look like natives, oh yes) pull off an audacious midnight raid on a village to relieve it of supplies and explosives, a scene executed with far more panache (and brutality) than Tarzan fans had come to expect. Things turn ugly when the raiders shoot a couple of villagers at point blank, setting the tone for the ramped-up violence to come (characters are later dispatched in quicksand, in man traps, by bow and arrow and with a metal noose, among other modes of death). The film hardly slows down from this high point; it's actually better than a lot of Guillermin's later, higher profile work.

The usually very English Quayle is something of a revelation as the American villain, Slade: he's a cold bastard who thinks nothing of sacrificing his henchmen or his girlfriend as he closes in on his bounty. But he's got a bit of 'previous' with Tarzan and knows the jungle man's strength and resolve; behind Slade's stoic, scarred face there's a trace of fear and respect for his bare-chested pursuer. MacGinnis delivers a typically solid and finely tuned turn as ex-Nazi gang member, Kruger, who is, ironically, perhaps the most sympathetic of this whole egregious bunch. And Connery stands out as the leery, drunken Irish heavy, O'Bannion. He sounds just as Scottish as ever, but already he has a great presence onscreen; looking far more feral than Tarzan, it's no surprise Weintraub was keen to sign him up to play the jungle man after Scott's contact came to an end (Connery had to decline because by then he was being moulded as James Bond). Only the women, exotic as they are, seem redundant: American model Sara Shane has an ineffective Jane-type role as a pilot (no less) who joins forces with Tarzan after crashing her light aircraft, and Italian beauty Scilla Gabel remains firmly in the background as Quayle's girlfriend.

Over fifty years on, with its adult style and decent production values, *Tarzan's Greatest Adventure* still stands up pretty favourably to modern, bigger budget hokum. But compared with most of the other twenty-seven films in the 1932–67 *Tarzan* series, it's an action adventure masterpiece.

Julian Upton

NEVER TAKE SWEETS FROM A STRANGER (1960)

Hammer | 81 minutes | b&w

Director Cyril Frankel; **Producer** Anthony Hinds; **Screenplay** John Hunter, from the play *The Pony Cart* by Roger Garis. **Starring** Gwen Watford (Sally Carter), Patrick Allen (Peter Carter), Felix Aylmer (Clarence Olderberry Sr.), Janina Faye (Jean Carter), Niall MacGinnis (defence counsel).

British teacher Peter Carter takes up the post of high school principal in a small Canadian town. His family's 'outsider' status is heightened when his little daughter Jean claims that she and a playmate have danced naked in front of a reclusive local bigwig, in exchange for 'candy.' The Carters must combat the legal system, the town's founders, and the community as a whole in support of their child's allegations.

A Hammer production in which a group of strangers enter a small insular province, where everyone appears in thrall to a mysterious and powerful dignitary, and where the most vulnerable member of the party is subjected to an ordeal that devastates the lives of all around them. Sounds familiar, no? Add in a final reel during which a hulking brute lurches through gloomy woodland in pursuit of two frightened potential victims, and this might be standard fare from the House of Horror, mixing the whispered secrets of a Transylvanian vampire saga with the monstrous spectacle of yet another of Baron Frankenstein's creations breaking free to wreak havoc. But *Never Take Sweets from a Stranger* sees Hammer in 'social comment' mode, tackling the controversial subjects of paedophilia and the effects of power and corruption on a developing neighbourhood. Ten-year-old Jean (Janina Faye) is the focus of the tale, and her casual revelation to her parents that she and a young friend have visited the mansion of retired business magnate Mr Olderberry, frolicking nude before him, pitches the characters into a world of chaos from an early stage.

John Hunter's script, based on Roger Garis' play *The Pony Cart*, does however allude to the production company's regular supernatural concerns throughout. Jean experiences the delicious thrill of hearing spooky stories told by her babysitting grandmother ("What was tonight's tale of horror?" "A little thing about a witch with three heads and one eye"), but any fireside cosiness is soon replaced by genuine fear, since following her traumatic experiences at the Olderberry place, she imagines something with "white hands" lurking in her bedroom closet, and finds herself persona non grata when attempting to

A different Hammer monster. *Never Take Sweets from a Stranger.*

visit her school chums — whose mothers and fathers cannot step out of line for fear of surrendering their own jobs and lifestyles. They are controlled by the Olderberry clan every bit as much as Dracula exerts his influence over villagers in the Balkan foothills.

Elisabeth Lutyens' score adds to the effect — note the ominous sting when Jean announces the details of her playful romp to her astonished parents, the frequent James Bernard-like passages featuring massed strings, and the grim accompaniment to the shots of Aylmer stumbling through the trees with the girls in his sights towards the climax. The dialogue, too, occasionally suggests connections between the very contemporary shudders of the central kiddy fiddling theme and more primitive myths and anxieties — while defending the Olderberry family to Mr Carter, the police captain lets something slip about keeping away from "a house like that," and suddenly we're right back in the realms of the haunted and shadowy once more.

A pivotal courtroom scene establishes orthodoxy, with Michael Gwynn's brash young prosecutor locking horns with Niall MacGinnis' ruthless defence lawyer. A trumped-up ailment prevents Gwynn from calling Lucille, the other girl involved in the incident, as a witness, leaving Jean's testimony as the sole challenge to Olderberry's reputation. Janina Faye looks so helpless and lost as she takes her place on the stand, her head poking out from the witness box ("If she sits down we won't be able to see her at all," comments the judge), and her use of words such as "think" and "guess" are pounced upon by the wily MacGinnis to dismiss her version of events. He even manages to hint at impropriety within the Carter household ("So, your daddy likes to see you dance naked?"), and after the child breaks down under intense pressure, the family withdraw all charges in order that her stressful situation is not prolonged.

The most challenging film of the decade . . .

NEVER TAKE SWEETS FROM A STRANGER

A HAMMER FILM PRODUCTION
Distributed by COLUMBIA

Carter resigns from his post, canny enough to recognise that the Olderberrys' hold over the townsfolk is simply too strong an iron grip to fracture, and referring to the populace's collective lack of defiance as "an infection" — again, a description perhaps more akin to one of the studio's monster pictures. Inevitably, it all leads to Aylmer's stalking of the two little girls through the forbidding woodland, full of leering close-ups, stray shots of spinning bicycle wheels, and the wide-eyed, open-mouthed expressions of the terrified youngsters. The broken boards of the derelict disused boathouse seem to symbolise something equally cracked in the mind and personality of its owner, and the moment where he grabs the towrope and begins to haul the escaping girls' rowboat back to shore — from an apparent point of safety — is as chilling as anything in the entire Hammer canon.

The movie's lurid poster contains the tagline "A Nightmare Manhunt For Maniac Prowler!" set above a stark image of police and tracker dogs, and the combined human/canine detective work reveals a ghastly outcome for more than one local family, but relief for another. One wonders, however, quite how this shattered society will recover from the shockwaves — the closing shot of the townspeople aimlessly wandering into the darkness offers few clues and scarce redemption.

Darrell Buxton

BABY LOVE
UNDERAGE SEX AND MURDER IN BRITISH CINEMA

BY DAVID KEREKES

Naughty schoolgirls (and George Cole). *The Belles of St Trinian's.*

ne thing that strikes the viewer today about many films covered in this book is the frankness of them. Another thing is the cavalier depiction of subject matter that would now be considered risqué or even taboo, notably that of children in any kind of proximity to sex and sexual danger. These dangers had been spelled out as early as Cyril Frankel's NEVER TAKE SWEETS FROM A STRANGER (60), a Hammer production of a popular stage play that dealt earnestly with the idea of child sexual abuse. Few themes have remained as volatile, but filmmakers of the era were otherwise preoccupied with the censors and how to avoid them, and content to exploit areas of shifting public opinion in their storylines. Consequently the films of the fifties, sixties and seventies take some refreshing twists and turns, if at times they seem to slip off the road altogether.

A love affair with the schoolgirl was ignited in 1954 with *The Belles of St Trinian's.* Directed by Frank Launder and produced by Sidney Gilliat, this gentle comedy is set within the fictitious St Trinian's boarding school for girls, whose unruly pupils get up to misadventure and strike terror into most adults (the local police hit the bottle rather than face the schoolgirl menace). The film was an adaptation of the St Trinian drawings of cartoonist Ronald Searle, while marking similar ground to Launder and Gilliat's own *The Happiest Days of Your Life* (51).[1] But where this earlier film had thrown together girls and boys in a wartime billet resulting in much hilarity, *The Belles of St Trinian's* disperses with the boys and delineates the girls into two distinct groups: the

The lower forms. *The Pure Hell of St Trinian's.*

bedraggled anarchic tomboys of the fourth form and the glamorous, sexually aware young women of the sixth form.[2] In manner and appearance these two groups are a mile apart, but are complicit in fighting both crooks and authority figures.

A number of immediate sequels followed, the sixth form taking an increasingly passive role until, by Launder and Gillait's *The Great St Trinian's Train Robbery* (66), they had become the fishnet and stocking top furniture now associated with the series.[3] But the St Trinian's sixth formers aren't really schoolgirls at all; they're much older than that by their own admission, and should have left school ages ago. The joke in Ronald Searle's original cartoon creation of the 1940s was that ladies sometimes behave badly, too, more specifically little girls being horrid little monsters. In Searle, the older girls were leggier, if little else. But on the big screen the rift is greater, the older girls becoming older and changing in shape and attire, thus avoiding any sexual confusion with children of the lower form, who remain unkempt and squat.

Before the decade was out, a number of films would be made that dashed forever such propriety, unashamedly depicting the schoolgirl not only as sex object but at times a sexual predator. Among these are Richard Donner's Italian/UK co-production *Twinky* (70), a lacklustre farce centred upon the relationship between a schoolgirl and a middle-aged author of lewd novels. Susan George plays the schoolgirl, while an uncomfortably miscast Charles Bronson plays Scott, the author who succumbs to her teen charms, referred to by his peers as a "nymph fetishist." The title song delights in sixteen-year-old girls, who are represented in a montage of bicycles and pedalling white knee socks. Altogether different in tone was Alastair Reed's *Baby Love* (68). *Baby Love* marked the feature film debut of fifteen-year-old Linda Hayden, playing Luci, in a story that parallels Pasolini's *Teorema* that same year. Luci is on a quest to destroy her adoptive family by inflaming its sexual interests and seducing each member in turn. A sequence where she sits painting her face with makeup, to symbolise the innocent as whore, would find a curious place in the family film MELODY, where it is replicated by the eleven-year-old Tracy Hyde. If Luci was a pupil attending St Trinian's (she's actually much too working class for that), she would not be among the childish brats of the fourth form or the sexy adults of the sixth. As the poster art for the film concedes, she is halfway between the two, wearing a school uniform and looking at her naked self in a mirror. *Films and Filming* described Luci as 'prepubescent and provocative'[4] — a remark almost as unthinkable today as the very idea of the film itself.

The schoolgirl as provocateur also found her way into MUMSY, NANNY, SONNY AND GIRLY (70). Directed by Freddie Francis, closely associated with the Hammer and Amicus

Baby Love made *Lolita* look like wholesome entertainment.

Would **you** give a home to a girl like Luci?

ask the man of the house...

or the son...

...or even the wife!

Baby Love

London and General Release
SUNDAY APRIL 20th

horror stables, it is not surprising the games in this instance are imbued with a dark, psychological bent and result in murder. Girly (Vanessa Howard) and Sonny (Howard Trevor) dress and behave like schoolchildren, luring men back to their home with an unspoken promise, toying with them until bored and then killing them.

Popular culture invariably depicts the sexual female to be an untrustworthy entity, and the girls noted in the films above are no exception: the sixth formers of St Trinian's use their wily charms to get their way in the outside world; in *Twinky* the crime is sexual infidelity; in *Baby Love* the family is destroyed; until, in MUMSY, NANNY, SONNY AND GIRLY, we have gone the whole hog with madness and murder. Although the latter performed poorly at the box office it nonetheless heralded a new, if shortlived, direction for horror and psychological drama. British filmmakers who sought to sexualise the schoolgirl had few places they could legitimately travel after *Baby Love*; they certainly couldn't compete with the influx of raunchier material from the continent, notably Ernst Hofbauer's long running *Schulmädchen-Report* ('schoolgirl report') cycle of sexploitation films. Consequently, this misogynistic notion was channelled into some altogether more fantastical

films, where, in lieu of the sinful schoolgirl, children themselves are to be mistrusted and feared (by men). Such sinister connotations can be found in UNMAN, WITTERING AND ZIGO (71), *Nothing but the Night* (72) and *The Wicker Man* (73).

UNMAN, WITTERING AND ZIGO features a school with an unsettling, possibly homicidal group of schoolboys that behaves more like a multifarious organism than it does a group of individuals. In the end they jump quietly off the edge of a cliff like lemmings. A similar ending befalls the children of *Nothing but the Night*. Here, Christopher Lee plays a policeman who is lured to an isolated Scottish isle on the trail of a group of children he believes are in danger. But it's a ruse. The children have actually plotted to use him as a sacrifice (in order to remain children), and he almost pays with his life on a funeral pyre. Beaten, one little girl spits at Lee, "You destroyed my dreams! I curse your cruel God!" And the rest of the children jump quietly off the cliff. All told it's a dry run for the later and better known film, *The Wicker Man*, which also stars Lee.

There are some cautionary tales, too. Retaining a fantastical backdrop, Robert Young's gothic Hammer film, *Vampire Circus* (72), has children being abducted in order to avenge, and to resurrect, a vampire staked by their fathers years ago. The opening sequence, of a little girl lured away to the castle, makes for uncomfortable viewing. As does Sidney Lumet's THE OFFENCE (72) the following year. This is a child sex killer story grounded in a gritty, everyday urban reality that no one much cared for at the box office. The

"Do you take this impetuous, mixed-up loveable teenager to be your lawful wedded wife?"

Twinky

..."I DO"

THE RANK ORGANISATION PRESENTS
CHARLES BRONSON
IN THE JOHN HEYMAN PRODUCTION
"TWINKY" TECHNICOLOR®
AND INTRODUCING
SUSAN GEORGE AS "Twinky"

*Oh no Twinky.
not before
breakfast!"*

ambiguity between hero and villain may not have helped it: Sean Connery as the hardnosed police detective turns out to harbour dark desires similar to that of the suspect, another twitchy role for Ian Bannen. Indeed, he might even be the killer. It's certainly a far cry from Sidney Hayers' clear-cut REVENGE (71), where a suspected molester of children is captured by the family of one victim, beaten senseless and locked in a cellar for the duration. The message is clear, and what's more, the suspect turns out to be guilty after all, reverting to form in the end.

Upstaged by their own raincoats: Cushing and Lee in *Nothing but the Night*.

The notion of child sexual abuse came to the fore of public thinking in the early seventies. There is no one reason for this: the newly established children's charity NSPCC was publishing its findings on the inadequate family, and this in turn became aligned with the growing tide of modern feminism and its focus on male violence and aggression. It certainly couldn't help that adult magazines, in discussing the 'Lolita Syndrome,' would occasionally decry 'that female "children" are not as innocent as is generally supposed'; stating that adolescent girls playing ball in the schoolyard are conscious of the sexual interest they draw and always respond to it.[5] *London Unexpurgated*, a guidebook with 'swing and zing' published by the New English Library in 1969 and openly available, even goes so far as to point out how best to observe the bloom of youth in the capital. 'Where do you find your Lolitas?' asks the section on nymphs and nymphettes. 'We would not like to be accused of encouraging statutory rape,' begins the answer, 'we are only giving you the facts.' There follows a list of dance halls and discothèques, and a selection of the many hundreds of pop star fan clubs ('even a half-way convincing pretence of interest will get you in contact with the enthusiasts'). As to schools, the author, 'Petronius,' concedes: 'Here you are on your own. And watch out — or you may end up doing a stretch.'[6]

Through the early seventies there was the suggestion of a change in the age of consent in Britain, which remains sixteen. The Criminal Law Revision Committee was asked to look into it in 1976, while a little later a number of prosecutions for sex with a minor were widely reported as having met with more lenient sentencing than usual. Pete Walker illustrated the murky travails of such cases with a case study of his own. HOME BEFORE MIDNIGHT (79) is a remarkably sympathetic plight from the point of view of the offending male, in this instance a rock star, who doesn't discover until much too late that his girlfriend is still at school. Unlike *Twinky*, the end of the relationship

isn't a matter of a broken heart and wounded pride, but police questioning, a trial, a criminal record, and the slow dissipation of friends and acquaintances.

Contrary, no clear message is to be weaned from Alan Birkinshaw's KILLER'S MOON (78). Believing they are in a dream, and conditioned to pursue their dreams by contemporary psychiatry, four escaped lunatics unwittingly terrorise, rape and murder a group of schoolgirls stranded at a lonely hotel. Indeed, the whole film plays out like a dream itself, one manufactured in an earlier, more liberal climate that pays no heed to the political and media fracas of around the same time. In 1977, the first of many regular public meetings of PIE (Paedophile Information Exchange) took place in London, which met with violent clashes, and for a time PIE, children, and perverts were rarely out of the press. The concept of a public forum for paedophiles is so far removed from our modern sensibilities it seems almost a joke. But the law of the day didn't consider it illegal to take photographs of naked children, nor to sell them. That particular avenue remained open until the following July, when the Protection of Children Act 1978 was introduced and made it an offence to take, distribute or show indecent photographs of children under sixteen.

By no stretch did KILLER'S MOON violate this law (the schoolgirls in it are clearly older), and it wasn't taken to task because of it. But under the Protection of Children Act 1978 a film such as *Baby Love* certainly could not have been made, given its scenes of a naked fifteen-year-old Linda Hayden. We are thus fortunate that Robin Hardy did not get his way on *The Wicker Man*, when he wanted children dancing around a fire naked, otherwise this once neglected film might have remained neglected, and slipped away into the same cinema landfill that is today inhabited by *Baby Love*.

---

1   Information on the St Trinian's cartoons and films can be found here: Ju Gosling, 'The Parodies of Girls' School Stories: The St Trinian's Film Comedies,' Virtual World of Girls, http://www.ju90.co.uk/indexsho.htm [Last accessed 7 January 2011].

2   The fourth and sixth forms would appear to be the only forms to exist at St Trinian's. There is scant reference to any other.

3   St Trinian's was resurrected in 1980 (*The Wildcats of St Trinian's*), with Frank Launder returning to the director's chair. Despite the proliferation of stocking tops and suspenders, it proved a flop. Had its thunder been stolen by the controversial hardcore porn loops of John Lindsay in the mid to late seventies, devoted to models in school uniform and boarding school themes?

4   Alexander Stuart, 'Assurance: Linda Hayden on sexuality and stardom,' *Films and Filming*, June 1973, p.29.

5   Author not credited, 'Thank heaven for little girls,' *Scorpio* 6 (circa 1971), pp.25–29.

6   'Petronius,' *London Unexpurgate*d (London: New English Library, 1969), pp.96–99. The identity of 'Petronius' was pulp novelist and sex researcher Bernhardt J. Hurwood, according to *The Paperback Fanatic* 22 (April 2012), p.39.

7   Alwyn W. Turner, *Crisis? What Crisis? Britain in the 1970s* (London: Aurum Press, 2009), p.253.

8   Ibid, p.254.

9   Allan Brown, *Inside The Wicker Man: The Morbid Ingenuities* (London: Sidgwick & Jackson, 2000), p.53.

FILM REVIEWS

THE SHAKEDOWN (1960)

Ethiro Productions/Alliance Film Distributors | 92 mins | b&w

Director John Lemont; **Producer** Norman Williams; **Screenplay** John Lemont, Leigh Vance.
Starring Terence Morgan (Augie Cortona), Hazel Court (Mildred Eyde), Donald Pleasence (Jessel), Bill Owen (Spettigue), Robert Beatty (Jarvis), Harry H. Corbett (Gollar), Gene Anderson (Zena).

Fresh out of jail, one time pimp Augie Cortona has a new racket: a respectable photography studio established with naïve photographer Jessel. His rivals and the police are incredulous: is Augie really going straight? Of course not — it's a front. His real scheme involves porn and blackmail. But Augie's overreaching: a lot of people want to take him down.

The *Shakedown* is an easy film to miss. It hasn't, at the time of writing, made it to DVD and it never appeared on VHS. It offers little to tempt film historians into checking it out: it was crafted by journeymen and features no major stars. Since its original outing in 1960, its only escape from the vaults has been infrequent TV screenings — none of which, it seems, were caught by a taste-maker who might revive its fortunes.

It deserves better. Let's not overstate its merits: enthusiasts who inflate a good film to 'great' are burdening their darlings with unfair expectations. But we don't need to add too many caveats since *The Shakedown* is possessed of a gumption worthy of the best American B-pictures. It's a welcome alternative to those prim and stodgy British films that are mistakenly called classics. Indeed, to modern eyes, this scruffy little upstart looks a damn sight more worthwhile than many of the sanctified relics of British cinema.

Our 'hero' is Augie Cortona. We first meet just before he gets out of prison; before his disloyal lieutenant grassed him up and took over the racket, our Augie was Soho's leading pimp.

Censorship conventions of the time meant the filmmakers had to tread lightly but they still succeed in building a dank, squalid atmosphere: upon release, Augie searches for an old flame. When he finally finds her, she's frightened. But he assures her, "My intentions are strictly honourable" — and flashes a bank note. Yup, she's a pro, formally his number one girl. Ever the gentleman, Augie pays the going rate; after he's had his money's worth, he wallops her for setting up shop with his hated rival, Gollar. (She tells Augie she had no choice — otherwise "he'd have marked me." Yuck.)

Augie's in no position to take on Gollar so a new angle is needed. Augie finds it when he meets Jessel (Pleasence), a photographer in recovery from the alcoholism that cost him his business. Augie proposes a new venture: a photographic studio (where the innocent Jessel will produce high class fashion photography)/ model school (to groom the catwalk queens of tomorrow). Of course, they need seed money. That's inadvertently stumped up by Gollar: Augie ambushes him and steals his loot.

The first half of the film shows an interest in the realities of the contemporary vice trade: the slang, the settings, even the ethnicities (Corbett's Gollar — his skin darkened, his accent clipped — is presumably meant to remind viewers of the diverse nature of the underworld at the time; it's an effect that today's more racially aware viewers will find jarring). The second half is more fanciful.

Augie uses his new venture as a cover for seedier activities, inviting respectable gents to photograph nudes after hours. Once they've paid for the privilege, he'll make the amateur pornographers pay again (and again) by blackmailing them: the shakedown of the title. But the police are on his tail (they've planted an undercover cop to find out what he's up to), Gollar's on the war path and Augie's victims have to deal with the cost.

Donald Pleasence isn't given much to do as Jessel but, as was his wont, almost walks off with the film. The timid man (who, it is suggested sotto voce, is gay) is delighted by Augie's kindnesses but when he finally learns what's really going on, he's devastated. Augie's method of pacifying him is a masterpiece of black comedy: he pours a stiff drink and pushes Jessel comprehensively off the wagon. Charming.

Dear old Augustus Cortona. A couple of years later and he might have found his way to the fringes of the Profumo scandal; as it is, his scheme is doomed to failure. He falls for Mildred (Court), one of the pupils at the modelling school; there's something tragic about how the boy from the gutters lusts after the high class dame and their relationship ultimately costs him dear.

As ever, the filmmakers didn't have enough money (the history of writing about British film is largely the history of finding new and inventive ways of saying the filmmakers didn't have enough money). But, just this once, that's to the production's advantage. It plays out in poky apartments and downmarket drinking dens. Everything's just a bit too small and shabby — the perfect ecosystem for these lowlife characters. It feels far more authentically grubby than the kitchen sink dramas that were all the rage when it was made.

Best of all, the low budget meant the producers couldn't afford a bigger name than Terence Morgan. A bit more money and we might have had to endure Laurence Harvey. Morgan was more usually a supporting player but rises to the occasion. Indeed, it's not going too far to say he makes Augie the most charismatic anti-hero in British cinema, investing him with a charm that sets him above the likes of Pinky (*Brighton Rock*) or Jack Carter (*Get Carter*).

The director, John Lemont, was a Canadian who started making army training films before moving into television. His most widely available work is *The Frightened City*, which gives a large role to a pre-Bond Sean Connery. It's a lesser film but enough to confirm him as a useful director with an interest in verisimilitude and an eye for violent sensation. A shame he didn't make more. Parts of *The Shakedown* reveal genuine talent: a scene where one of Augie's unfortunate victims comes close to shooting himself has an intensity seldom found in British film.

And that's the real merit of *The Shakedown*: it shows British film to be tougher and more arresting than is usually allowed. Is this really a singular occurrence or is it a fair representation of low budget film of the period? That a decent film like this can be forgotten shows just how partial and misleading our official cinematic history is. How many more like it are trapped in the archives?

James Oliver

THE SINGER NOT THE SONG (1960)

The Rank Organisation | 132 mins | colour

Director Roy Baker; **Producer** Roy Baker; **Screenplay** Nigel Balchin from the novel by Audrey Erskine Lindop. **Starring** Dirk Bogarde (Anacleto), John Mills (Father Keogh), Mylene Demongeot (Locha de Cortinez), Laurence Naismith (Old Uncle), Roger Delgado (Pedro de Cortinez), Laurence Payne (Pablo).

Catholic priest Father Michael Keogh arrives in his new parish — a remote Mexican town — to find the church shut and his terrified predecessor cowering in his house. The town is under the control of a vicious outlaw, Anacleto, who despises religion. But Keogh is made of sterner stuff. He resolves not simply to defy Anacleto but to save his immortal soul.

I f *The Singer Not The Song* is remembered at all, it is with a snigger. Even the most charitable viewer must concede that Dirk Bogarde was a very imaginative choice to play a brutal Mexican bandit. That he chose to do so wearing tight black leather trousers has earned the film an entirely deserved reputation for high camp.

One of the incidental pleasures of the picture is wondering how such a bizarre concoction ever got made. The short answer is 'desperation.' The Rank Organisation, who had hitherto dominated British film, had been hit hard by the arrival of television. Most of its talent had left for greener pastures, leaving it with only one bona fide star: Dirk Bogarde. And he was making noises about jumping ship once his contract expired. Desperate to retain their only thoroughbred, Rank snapped up the rights to Audrey Erskine Lindop's novel *The Singer Not The Song*. A runaway success with suburban housewives (the bedrock of Bogarde's fan base), Rank reasoned it was just the thing to persuade their star to stay put. After all, he was perfect casting for the priest who tries to redeem the wicked outlaw...

Such a prestige project needed a safe pair of hands so Rank pressured Roy Baker — director of two of their biggest hits (*A Night to Remember* [58] and *The One that Got Away* [58]) — to direct. At first, he declined: he felt no affinity to the story. But the studio was adamant and,

The Singer Not The Song, J. Arthur Rank's only gay western.

Upstaged by his own trousers: Dirk Bogarde in *The Singer Not The Song*.

in time, he crumbled. By the time the reluctant Baker took charge, however, Bogarde was no longer interested in playing the priest. Instead, he'd decided to play the bandit Anacleto. Whatever his misgivings, Baker was in no position to argue.

Neither Bogarde's star power nor even his leather trousers could lure audiences into cinemas for the finished film. The unfortunate Roy Baker carried the can and was exiled to television and, eventually, tacky horror films unworthy of his talents. As he'd intended all along, Bogarde declined to renew his contract with the ailing Rank Organisation. Although he later claimed his final film for the studio as one of his favourites, few shared his high opinion.

And yet, Bogarde was on to something. Like many infamous flops, it is more worthwhile than its reputation would suggest. In direct imitation of Graham Greene (specifically his novel *The Power and the Glory*, set in revolutionary Mexico), the film wrestles with issues of theology but also ventures into areas that *The Power and the Glory* was too tasteful to explore: attentive readers of Greene's masterpiece will find it light on love stories, drunken shoot-outs and, indeed, leather trousers. *The Singer Not The Song* does its best to remedy these omissions.

Like all good melodramas, the film is fundamentally a romance. It's only to be expected that Father Keogh's rugged masculinity captivates local beauty Locha (Demongeot) — 'unobtainable' priests are staple figures in romantic fiction, after all — but she is not the only one with designs on him. Anacleto is fascinated by, and quite plainly attracted to, Keogh. Whereas he terrorised other priests, he engages this one in debate.

The atheist Anacleto struggles to understand religion's appeal. Father Keogh insists it is the message itself — the Song — that attracts people; Anacleto maintains believers are drawn by the charisma of the messengers — the Singer. As the title suggests, Keogh cannot change Anacleto's mind. But the bandit cannot shake his interest in the priest, even killing one of his own gang to protect Keogh.

This might have been one of the screen's great forbidden romances but for an unfortunate piece of miscasting. As written, Father Keogh is a man devoted to his ministry but who exudes a most unclerical sexuality. Both James Mason (who would have been excellent) and Richard Burton (perfect) said 'no,' whereupon John Mills stepped into the breach. Now, Mills was a fine actor but hardly famed for his virility. He plays Father Keogh as a man utterly untroubled by his vow of celibacy.

Bogarde more than makes up for him, though. Contemporary viewers — and the director — maintained that the star upset the tone with his suggestive performance. To modern eyes, however, Bogarde looks to be the only person who understood the film. To be blunt, the film's principal failing is not that it is too camp, it is that it is not camp enough. We should not be too critical of Baker. He certainly exhibits terrific craft: the film is adroitly paced. It's also extremely beautiful, benefiting from Otto Heller's tremendous photography. But Baker's style is altogether too polite for what is, truthfully, lunatic pulp.

From the (inevitably doomed) attempt to stage a Graham Greene style theological meditation within the framework of a bodice-ripping melodrama to the pioneering bisexual love triangle, this is a film that curls its lip at plausibility. Observe the mad way Anacleto maintains his reign of terror, arranging accidents to bump off townsfolk in alphabetical order like something out of Agatha Christie.

Such a heady brew called for a director of wilder temperament: Nicholas Ray, perhaps, or Vincent Minnelli, someone alive to extremities of colour and behaviour. There was a director in Britain perfectly suited to such material. But Michael Powell was in bad odour with Rank's bosses; he had just delivered his own career-ending masterpiece, *Peeping Tom*.

And so it was left to Bogarde to bring the fervid undercurrents of the script to the surface. His performance is amongst his most perfectly pitched, utterly aware of how lurid the film needed to be. Indeed, it should not be seen as the end of his tenure as a matinee idol but the proper start of his career as an acute, cerebral actor.

The Singer Not The Song should be seen not as an oddball disaster but as one of the great baroque westerns, alongside *Duel in the Sun* or *Johnny Guitar*. Like them, it's a film demented by lust and repression, one blissfully unrestrained by the straitjacket of conventional good taste.

James Oliver

CASH ON DEMAND (1961)

Hammer/Woodpecker/Columbia | 66 mins/84 mins/88 mins¹ | b&w

Director Quentin Lawrence; **Producers** Michael Carreras, Anthony Nelson-Keys; **Screenplay** David T. Chantler, Lewis Greifer, from the television play *The Gold Inside* by Jacques Gillies.
Starring Peter Cushing (Fordyce), André Morell (Gore-Hepburn), Richard Vernon (Pearson).

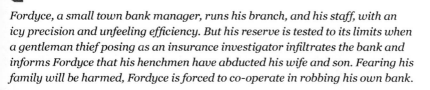

Fordyce, a small town bank manager, runs his branch, and his staff, with an icy precision and unfeeling efficiency. But his reserve is tested to its limits when a gentleman thief posing as an insurance investigator infiltrates the bank and informs Fordyce that his henchmen have abducted his wife and son. Fearing his family will be harmed, Fordyce is forced to co-operate in robbing his own bank.

C ash On Demand is not just vastly superior to the majority of its British B-movie peers, it is also a cut above most of Hammer's output, both horror and 'non-horror.' (If you miss the credits, only the presence of Peter Cushing hints that this could be a Hammer production; it's one of the studio's rare sixties ventures into low-key crime cinema.) Adapted from a television play, *The Gold Inside* (broadcast as part of ITV's Theatre 70 series in 1960), it displays some of the same ingenious economy and sharp characterisation as those staples of US television drama's Golden Age — *12 Angry Men*, *Requiem for a Heavyweight* — that were being brought to the big screen so successfully around the same time.

Cash on Demand, a rather civil bank robbery.

Fordyce, the film's odious bank manager, is probably Peter Cushing's best ever screen role. Priggish, angular, uptight, humourless — he fits the character like a glove. Fordyce is, essentially, Ebenezer Scrooge in modern dress (it's no coincidence the film is set at Christmas time). Reprimanding his honest, decent staff with petty and unfair accusations, turning his nose up at the idea of the staff party, confronting with steely eyes anyone who has the gumption to talk back to him, he is the apotheosis of the gaunt, unsmiling characters Cushing played so well.

But even at his best, Cushing is in danger of being acted off the screen by André Morell, whose louche, urbane bank robber lights up the film like a Christmas tree. Morell had played the criminal, Gore-Hepburn, in the original television play, and he brings an easy, menacing confidence to the role second time around. It's great, guilty fun watching him goad Cushing into submission (although for some it might have carried a spooky echo of Morell's O'Brien torturing Cushing's Winston Smith in the BBC's live broadcast of Orwell's *1984*.) And as his needling begins to reveal the cracks in the bank manager's icy façade, so it intensifies Cushing's performance. It could be that Morell brought out a better actor in Cushing than Christopher Lee ever did.

Cash on Demand is essentially a three-hander, and Richard Vernon, as the bank's second-in-command, Pearson, also gives one of his best performances. His unassuming but unflustered stillness is convincing; you really believe he and Cushing have worked quietly and efficiently at the same bank for over ten years, detesting every minute of each other's company. (It's a shame Vernon ended up almost exclusively doing harrumphing Colonel types in TV guest spots.)

As Fordyce is co-opted by Gore-Hepburn into robbing his own bank, his emotions finally come to the fore, and he is forced to ask for Pearson's charity. By the end of the ordeal, he is a changed man — just like Scrooge after the ghosts are done with him. Now he's even planning to come to the staff party, when the police have finished questioning him. As the original play's title attested to, there was 'gold inside' Fordyce all along, just as there is in the bank; it just took an extreme set of circumstances to get to it.

Like André Morell, director Quentin Lawrence had been involved with the original TV play, and his confidence and familiarity with the material help to give the film version its edge. Keeping things drumskin-tight, while making time to flesh out the characters convincingly, Lawrence delivers as fluid an example of pacing as the B-movie genre has ever seen. It was a loss to British cinema when, after his misfiring next film, the Stanley Baker-starring *The Man Who Finally Died* (62), Lawrence sank back into routine TV assignments for the rest of his career.

Cash on Demand is something like Sidney Lumet's *Dog Day Afternoon* without guns, swearing or loosened clothing. But where *Dog Day* is set in a bustling Brooklyn on the hottest day of the year, *Cash* unfolds in a small, English town on a snowy Christmas Eve. Where *Dog Day*'s bank robbers are highly strung, foulmouthed and incompetent, the men in *Cash* are assured, professional and articulate. *Dog Day* strays into the street and spans into the city, all spotlights, loudspeakers and police sirens; *Cash* stays firmly indoors and is concerned only with talk. In the movies-on-television age, *Dog Day Afternoon* should probably be seen late at night, maybe with an alcoholic beverage. *Cash on Demand* is a film to watch on a rainy weekday afternoon, with a cup of tea and a digestive biscuit.

But the little B-movie is no less tense, gripping and enjoyable than its Hollywood counterpart. It's just that the English prefer their bank heists to have rather less shouting and carrying on.

Julian Upton

---

1   Various sources list *Cash on Demand*'s running time as being, curiously, sixty-six minutes in the UK version and eighty-four or eighty-eight minutes for the USA release. The off air-recorded version I saw came in at around eighty minutes. Also, the film's production and release dates are oddly inconsistent. It appeared in the US in 1962, but seems to have sat on the shelf in the UK for two years, only being released as a supporting feature in 1963. (See Appendix to Steve Chibnall and Brian MacFarlane's *The British 'B' Film* [London: BFI, 2010]).

THE DAY THE EARTH CAUGHT FIRE (1961)

Pax Films/British Lion | 96 mins | b&w

Director Val Guest; **Producers** Frank Sherwin Green, Val Guest; **Screenplay** Val Guest, Wolf Mankowitz. **Starring** Edward Judd (Peter Stenning), Leo McKern (Bill Maguire), Janet Munro (Jeannie Craig), Michael Goodliffe (Night Editor), Bernard Braden (News Editor).

Simultaneous Russian and American nuclear tests at the poles knock the world off its axis, sending its weather haywire. At the Daily Express, *a science correspondent and his disillusioned colleague, with the help of a switchboard operator at the Met Office, try to bring the full story to public attention. As temperatures continue to rise, corrective bombs are called for to set the Earth back on its proper orbit.*

Summer floods at Ascot, Exeter marooned, roads under five feet of water in Devon, dense heat mists, wildfires, water rationing, and a heat wave so severe that the Thames dries up: the only certainty about the world's weather is its unpredictability and unexpected severity — all of which sounds close to our own meteorologically uncertain times. However, this is 1961, and the cause of the trouble in *The Day the Earth Caught Fire* is rooted in the Cold War.

FILM REVIEWS

If its setup is far-fetched — simultaneous American and Russian nuclear explosions at the polar caps have caused a displacement in the direction of the polar axis ('World Tips Over' in headline speak), skewing the Earth off its orbit and sending it towards the sun ('riveting story but bloody balls' said the *Express*' then-science correspondent Chapman Pincher of the screenplay) — then the veracity with which it is treated is riveting. Val Guest, himself an ex-reporter, knew well how to capture the snap of the newsroom, its urgent clamour and chaos fed by the constant buzz and ring of telephones and the clatter of typewriters; he said that he tried to make these scenes as 'documentary' as possible. (This is also the reason why — barring Monty Norman's 'beatnik music' for the doomsday revellers, indulging at the end in their watery orgy of wanton destruction — there is so little music in the film, so as not to clash with its tone of reportage.) The Shepperton set was copied faithfully from the *Daily Express*' newsroom: 'IMPACT! Get it in your first sentence..! Get it in your headlines..! And in pictures — most of all!' implores the banner above the hacks' desks, while the '*Daily Express* for BIG news' poster, with BIG in an explosive burst, lends a heavily ironic touch.

The film also benefits from its use of authentic locations such as Fleet Street (including the *Express*' own offices), Trafalgar Square and Battersea Park, while library footage of an eclipse, drought, and even the Aldermaston peace rally reinforces a tone of urgent uncertainty. It's 'not so much science-fiction as it is a dramatic and imaginative extension of the news,' said Hollis Alpert, writing about the film in *Saturday Review*.

It begins however with Big Ben bathed in a brick red tint, the cracked mud of a dried-up Thames, and evacuated London streets, into which Edward Judd wanders, dazed with heat, trying to summon the energy for one final article. Judd takes the nominal lead as the demoted columnist Peter Stenning ('one-time ace reporter, striving to make a comeback in love and life'), who has turned to the bottle after his divorce and is trying to hold on to the shreds of a relationship with his increasingly estranged son, but his performance is screwed a couple of twists too high; instead it's Leo McKern's hard-bitten hack with a heart Bill Maguire ('the science editor who unearths the deadly facts') who really shoos the film along. And Janet Munro ('the girl on the government switchboard') brings a candid, unaffected and thoroughly seductive naturalism to her role. In fact, Munro, weary of having her breasts bound down in Disney productions, and by way of a recent risqué Harrison Marks photoshoot to help rid herself of her cutesy image, said 'please help me grow up in this' to Val Guest before filming. A scene of Edward Judd admiring her bottom-hugging skirt as she leans over to reach a paper certainly signals this intention early on, and there's a sense that bedsheets were being lowered

to an 'acceptable' limit — and then tugged down just a little more to try it on a bit with the censors. As the mercury rises, so the clothes drop too, with a few frames of a topless towel drape meriting the film an 'X' certificate, though the uncommon and highly suggestive sight of Edward Judd relaxing on Jeannie's bed and casting an appraising eye over her underwear while she is drying her hair in the bathroom helps to steer it firmly in that direction as well.

The film also features newly retired *Daily Express* editor Arthur Christiansen as himself, and though the many cut-arounds in his scenes are testament to his lack of acting ability, Guest knew he was on to something by using him. His presence shows its worth through his use of customary gestures — the picking up of a phone, the issuing of orders, the curt commands and dismissals, all of which would have been lost in some slick portrayal of the part.

Val Guest and Wolf Mankowitz's script, which won a Best British Screenplay BAFTA in 1961, features a healthy cynicism regarding official pronouncements. "I felt it necessary to speak to you all, if only to stop the many wild and irresponsible rumours precipitated by a general lack of facts," says the Prime Minister in measured tones, telling listeners that he has "the utmost confidence that the world's scientists can produce solutions for any of the climatic problems we are likely to meet." No wonder that some of Maguire and Stenning's lines carry the tang of genuine frustrated disgust: "Now they want to read about the filthy, self-destructive force humanity carries around, rotting in its belly," says Judd, adding, "the human race has been poisoning itself for years with a great big smile on its fat face."

'Is this the end — or another beginning?' ran the film's tagline, and although the sky might be tinted a few tones lighter as the bells of St Paul's ring at the end in a celebratory nod towards a successful conclusion (mercifully without the heavenly choir of angels that Guest was prevailed upon to include), the telling shot is the one we have seen a few moments beforehand, with the clocks set at a few minutes to twelve and the two alternative front pages for the next day's newspaper clipped to the printing machinery — World Saved: H-Bomb blasts succeed/World Doomed: H-Bomb blasts fail. That's the real ending.

Oh, and being the *Daily Express* that was the newspaper of choice for the scoop, it also inspired a Giles cartoon from 28 November, 1961: "Give 'em all fire extinguishers" says Father, unhelpfully, from the depths of his armchair, as the rain falls outside the window and Mother puts together her Christmas present list.

Graeme Hobbs

THE IMPERSONATOR (1961)

British Lion/Bryanston/Herald/Eyeline Films | 64 mins | b&w

Director Alfred Shaughnessy; **Producer** Anthony Perry; **Screenplay** Alfred Shaughnessy, Kenneth Cavander. **Starring** John Crawford (Sgt Bradford), Jane Griffiths (Ann), John Salew (Harry Walker/ Mother Goose), Patricia Burke (Mrs Lloyd), John Dare (Tommy Lloyd).

In a small northern town adjoined by a US Air Force base, a prowler is terrorising women. The hostile locals suspect the culprit is an American serviceman. Tasked with improving public relations, USAF Sgt. Bradford makes contact with a primary school teacher in the town to arrange a trip to the local pantomime for the children. But when a local woman is murdered, Bradford finds himself under suspicion.

lfred Shaughnessy works such wonders on *The Impersonator*'s £23,000 budget that you wonder why he wasn't forced at gunpoint to make more movies. A jobbing scriptwriter, this was his fourth and last film as director; despite getting good notices, he decided he didn't have the temperament to carry on directing. Perhaps he was right: the cosy little world that was the British B-picture didn't have much longer to run; before long, he would have found himself managing vaster budgets, under much more pressure, and having to please American paymasters.

As if anticipating that, the theme of frosty Anglo-American relations is one that Shaughnessy explores in *The Impersonator*. Unusually for a British B-picture, the intelligent, balanced view of the 'cold war' that exists between the people of a small northern town and the servicemen from the American base on its outskirts lends it a keen sociological perspective. And this commentary is vital to the plot. Terrorised by a local prowler, the prejudiced townsfolk automatically suspect someone from the US air base. When a woman is murdered, they bay for US blood. Many in the 1960 audience would still strongly identify with this hostility to American soldiers serving in Britain; Shaughnessy uses the sentiment ingeniously as a hook on which to hang his 'wrong man' plot.

There is little slack here — *The Impersonator* hits most of its targets on the nose. The creepy shots in which the women are stalked by an unseen presence on the fringes of the town add up to a minor triumph of night shooting and brisk editing. But the film's real high point is in its theatre sequence, wherein the town's Christmas pantomime is being staged. When the excited young Tommy (who, fortunately, doesn't know that his own mother has become one

Convivial malevolence. John Salew (right) gives us his pantomime dame in *The Impersonator*.

of the prowler's victims) gets a chance to go on stage during a performance of *Mother Goose* and has his first close-up look at one of the actors (whose face he's seen somewhere before), it's a shock moment of cinema worthy of Alfred Hitchcock — a minor piece of bravura that confirms Shaughnessy's growing confidence behind the camera.

There's also a real feel for the pantomime performance, which is staged with a genuinely lively zeal. Shaughnessy draws out the slightly sinister nature of pantomime itself: men dressed as women, women dressed as men, one sex impersonating another, actors impersonating animals. Indeed, the starting point for his original story was the convivial malevolence of the pantomime dame. Like the white-faced clown, with his disquieting painted smile and permanently raised eyebrows, the dame's disguise can hide a multitude of sins. (John Salew, as the actor playing 'Mother Goose,' stands out as one of the most offbeat villains in British film. Shaughnessy gives him a couple of great scenes — a fitting end for a long-standing character actor who died not long after the film came out.)

The regulation B-list cast delivers better than average performances. For once, the American lead is justified — John Crawford (no, not Joan) makes an amiable and charming hero, even if he does look more like a used car dealer than a USAF Sgt. Jane Griffiths' primary schoolteacher Ann has more gravitas than most B-movie heroines — her prim, hard-to-get allure is well played against Crawford's cocky, flirtatious chat-up shtick. Their burgeoning relationship is well handled, and if Griffiths falls for Crawford's charms a bit too suddenly, remember they only have sixty-four minutes to play with.

But the liveliest turn comes from young John Dare as little Tommy. Dare must be one of the campest child performers ever to grace the screen; he strings out his lines so amusingly (if unintentionally) they lift some of the lesser scenes out of the routine. When a police detective asks him "Did you enjoy the panto, Tommy?" he fires back with both barrels, "Ooooohhh yesssssssssss!" as if Frankie Howerd had suddenly gained control of his body. Dare looks inexperienced in front of the camera, but Shaughnessy gets him through some dialogue-heavy stuff without letting him slip into the cringeworthy, which could so often happen with B-movie child actors. It's a shame Dare disappeared; he might have made an endearing adult performer, in *Carry On* films at least.

The Impersonator is a British B-movie par excellence: tightly plotted, sharply realised, atmospheric and economical. But it's a shame that Shaughnessy had to make a key compromise at the scripting stage, making his villain a prowler when he'd originally envisioned a child killer (he'd been inspired by Fritz Lang's *M*). Had he followed this line, the film might now be regarded as a genuinely creepy classic. But British tastes of 1960 dictated that this was a step too far; even if Shaughnessy had got the idea past the releasing company, Bryanston, it would doubtless have been blocked by the censor.

After voluntarily ending his directorial career, Shaughnessy returned exclusively to writing. In the seventies he had major success on TV as head writer on *Upstairs, Downstairs*. And he continued to write occasionally for the big screen, notably for exploitation director Peter Walker. But when you see *The Flesh and Blood Show* (72) and *Tiffany Jones* (73), you really wish he'd carried on directing his own work.

Julian Upton

THE MARK (1961)

Twentieth Century Fox | 127 mins | b&w

Director Guy Green; **Producer** Raymond Stross; **Screenplay** Sidney Buchman, Stanley Mann, from the novel by Charles Israel. **Starring** Stuart Whitman (Fuller), Rod Steiger (Dr McNally), Maria Schell (Ruth), Donald Houston (Austin).

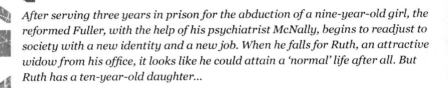

After serving three years in prison for the abduction of a nine-year-old girl, the reformed Fuller, with the help of his psychiatrist McNally, begins to readjust to society with a new identity and a new job. When he falls for Ruth, an attractive widow from his office, it looks like he could attain a 'normal' life after all. But Ruth has a ten-year-old daughter...

Released amidst mainstream cinema's concurrent fascination with all manner of sexual 'deviation' — *Victim* (homosexuality), *Peeping Tom* (voyeurism), *The Children's Hour* (lesbianism), *Suddenly, Last Summer* (take your pick) — and the newly popular belief in the transcendent power of psychotherapy — *The Three Faces of Eve*, *Psycho*, *Freud* — *The Mark*, while combining both heated genres, is perhaps the only film in that company to have failed to have left any kind of, well, mark. And yet the film, dealing as it does with a man who would today be branded a paedophile, is one of the few whose subject matter remains unnerving fifty years on.

For the first hour, the protagonist, Fuller (Stuart Whitman), soaks up our sympathies as he goes about his business nobly trying to adapt to a new life outside prison. He seems a decent, white-collar type, quietly but persistently troubled by his former wrongdoing. Whatever it is he has been in prison for, we conclude, must either have been a miscarriage of justice or a crime seriously misunderstood.

All is eventually revealed, in flashback, when the sexually inadequate Fuller lures a young girl into his car and drives her to a remote spot in the country with the intention of assaulting her. But when the moment comes he is repulsed by the idea, and runs off into the woods to vomit. Taking the girl back home he is met by an angry mob, but instead of trying to defend himself, he begs to be locked up. It is only later, during group therapy sessions in prison with the radical psychiatrist Dr McNally (Steiger), that Fuller begins to realise that he has 'an illness.'

The debate that surrounded *The Mark* at the time of its release balanced the heinousness of Fuller's criminal intention with the worthiness of his inability to carry it out. Some critics were disappointed that the filmmakers didn't have the guts to present a man who actually performed what he'd threatened. In a contemporary review, Pauline Kael weighed in with "what the movie turns out to be about is a man who has expiated a crime he hasn't committed: in other words, he's morally one up on all of us..."[1]

But watching the film in the twenty-first century intensifies its liberal premise (albeit unintentionally) while occasionally rendering it a much more disturbing experience. If Fuller existed today, his internet cache would probably have all

"A FINE PICTURE ...I SALUTE IT!"

"HIGHLY GRATIFYING AND MEMORABLE!"

"A MEMORABLE EXPERIENCE!"

"SOLID ENTERTAINMENT!"

A MOST MATURE MOTION PICTURE!

manner of horrors in it. And yet, because the story takes place when things were much more 'black and white,' he comes across more sympathetically. When he is asked by his girlfriend (that is, his first ever woman friend) to take her ten-year-old daughter to the fair while she cooks dinner, we are uncomfortable, but not because of what he might do to her. Rather, we worry that they will be seen together by the wrong person, and that the wrong conclusions will be jumped to — which, of course, is what happens. The film, nevertheless, has underlined by this point that Fuller means the girl no harm; he would no longer even entertain such a notion.

Helping us, the audience, through this sordid minefield is the seemingly omniscient McNally, who Fuller visits as a condition of his parole and who has such belief in Fuller's rehabilitation that he would doubtless put him in charge of a primary school. The film urges us to look to psychiatry as a pillar of wisdom yet to be scaled by anyone guilty of societal prejudice. Fuller's damaged personality, we are shown, is in fact the result of an overbearing mother and a weak, impotent father. He is also scarred by being the only boy in a litter of strident girls. His 'cure' comes after consummating his love affair with the woman from the office. Freudian psychoanalysis in black and white

An accent too far: Maria Schell, *The Mark.*

indeed! But *The Mark* deserves respect for approaching this rocky territory in the first place. When US movie *The Woodsman* covered similar ground forty years later, it too was obliged to make the child molester at its centre a gentle, misunderstood soul; the subject seems just far too contentious for mainstream cinema to approach any other way.

Whitman is effective in what is, in all fairness, a tricky role; he looks suitably pained and tortured throughout. (Pauline Kael again: "He has no life as a character; he is a walking anxiety." Even so, he bagged an Oscar nomination.) Steiger, much more able to let his hair down, stands out as the psychiatrist. But one wonders what a film *The Mark* could have been if the first-choice cast — Richard Burton, Trevor Howard and Jean Simmons — had been available.

The Austrian Maria Schell (Maximilian's sister) replaced Simmons at the last minute, and her addition is probably an accent too far — the mix already contains the American Whitman doing Canadian and the American Steiger doing Irish blarney. Add to that the fact that, despite being set in an unnamed northern English city, *The Mark* was filmed in Ireland, and you've got a British film whose Britishness is barely noticeable.

The striking monochrome photography (by Douglas Slocombe) manages to capture the agoraphobia of Fuller's world in otherwise unsuitable CinemaScope (a prerequisite of Twentieth Century Fox financing at the time) and director Guy Green handles it all as decently as you'd expect from a sturdy English craftsman: sensibly, soberly and with a fine sense of fair play.

Julian Upton

---

1   Anthologised in Pauline Kael, *I Lost It At the Movies* (NY: Little, Brown, 1965).

OFFBEAT (1961)

Northam Films/ British Lion | 71 mins | b&w

Director Cliff Owen; **Producer** E.M. Smedley-Aston; **Screenplay** Peter Barnes.
Starring William Sylvester (Layton/Steve Ross), Mai Zetterling (Ruth), John Meillon (Johnny), Anthony Dawson (Dawson).

MI5 agent Layton is recruited by the police to infiltrate a well-organised criminal gang. Gaining the gang's acceptance, Layton helps them plan a jewellery heist. But he finds himself forging friendships with the thieves, and falls in love with Ruth, one of their number. He is left to decide whether to betray the criminals or his senior officers at Scotland Yard.

O*ffbeat* takes a decidedly ambivalent view of good and bad, of right and wrong. Other British crime films had displayed touches of sympathy for those on the wrong side of the law, even if they were guilty, but *Offbeat* was quite unique in portraying its workaday villains as 'decent' human beings, doing a 'job' as a means to an end, looking out for each other, engaging in cheery banter and showing their sensitive sides. To underline the point, the film even features a gently postmodern scene that sees the crooks watching a hokey crime drama on TV. Henchman Johnnie complains, "Crime, that's all you get these days. I wouldn't mind if they showed the underworld as it really was"; to which the moll replies: "But then they would have to show criminals as ordinary people trying to make a living."

This is what *Offbeat* valiantly attempts to do. Indeed, the shadiest looking characters here are the police, particularly the poker-faced hero, MI5 agent turned undercover cop Layton (William Sylvester). But when Layton infiltrates the elusive criminal gang and gains their trust, he sees the human face of crime for the first time. And he falls in love — with the blonde moll, Ruth (Mai Zetterling). The 'old-fashioned' view of criminals, the film suggests, may be a bit too clear cut. Real people, whether they are cops or robbers, occupy a greyer zone.

This attempt at moral complexity owes a lot to screenwriter Peter Barnes; a cut above the usual crime genre hack, he went on to prove himself as one of the country's foremost playwrights with *The Ruling Class*. But for all his ambitious ideas, *Offbeat* still betrays its B-movie mentality. The villains are still two-dimensional: in this case they are too nice. The middle-aged gang leader, Dawson, is about as intimidating as a senior civil servant; drainpipe-thin, he wears a dapper suit, looks weary and regal and has ideas on equal

opportunities that are about fifteen years ahead of the rest of the country. Mai Zetterling's Ruth is not given an opportunity to show anything beyond a hapless, butter-wouldn't-melt quality — what she's doing ensconced in a gang of crooks is something of a mystery. She should probably be running a nursery or caring for the elderly. Only John Meillon's Johnnie has a spark of the mischievous about him, but even this seems harmless and endearing. (He was a lot more menacing when he tried to shoot Jenny Agutter at the beginning of *Walkabout* ten years later.)

But seventy-one minutes doesn't give much time for emotional depth, and director Cliff Owen is more concerned with moving things along at a fair peal. He keeps the scenes short and tight, and shows a skill with the noir style dialogue (this is a US thriller in all but accent — American 'star' notwithstanding). One of the characters says Layton "has style and a cool nerve"; he could be describing the movie itself.

William Sylvester's general inexpressiveness actually lends itself well to the moral ambiguity of *Offbeat*'s premise (as it would to Kubrick's clinical *2001: A Space Odyssey* some years later). But we feel for him when he has to shop his new friends at the end. We want him to go through with switching sides, to take the loot and the girl and head for South America. But, of course, crime does not pay, and no B-movie of the time could say otherwise. So we're left with a 'happy' ending that leaves the hero deflated and the audience a little pensive. *Offbeat* indeed.

Julian Upton

PAYROLL (1961)

Lynx Films/Anglo Amalgamated | 102 mins | b&w

Director Sidney Hayers; **Producer** Norman Priggen; **Screenplay** George Baxt, from the novel by Derek Bickerton. **Starring** Michael Craig (Johnny Mellors), Francoise Prevost (Katie Pearson), Billie Whitelaw (Jackie Parker), William Lucas (Dennis Pearson), Kenneth Griffith (Monty), Tom Bell (Blackie).

In the course of a carefully planned raid on a security van carrying a local factory's payroll, two people are killed: the van driver and one of the robbers. The raiders make off with the money, but guilt and recrimination start to break down their post-robbery plans. What's more, the van driver's widow is bent on avenging her husband.

When superstar Steve McQueen saw the low-key British heist movie *Robbery* (67), directed by the relative newcomer Peter Yates, he was so taken by the opening four-cylinder car chase that he invited Yates to Hollywood to direct *Bullitt* (68), just so the Englishman could stage a bigger and better pile-up on the streets of San Francisco. Famously, Yates rose to the occasion, but you get the feeling that had McQueen seen *Payroll* first, the now almost forgotten Sidney Hayers might have been the one to get that Hollywood invitation.

Payroll is not just a better film than the otherwise soporific *Robbery*, but its staging of an audacious raid on a security van after it crosses the Tyne Bridge is just as tense and exhilarating as *Robbery*'s celebrated opening chase. Expertly shot in real urban locations and choreographed with admirable intensity, it's a low budget action sequence that ranks with the second unit work of much more expensive movies.

Hayers was a former editor (he'd worked on notable pictures such as Rank's *A Night to Remember* [58]) and his skill for pacing and building tension is much in evidence in the raid sequence and the dry runs that lead up to it. No British film, not even *Hell Drivers*, had thus far captured a road chase as kinetically as Hayers and his cinematographer Ernest Steward do here. Smartly keeping the use of back projection to a minimum, they shoot the point-of-view action on real roads; the effect must have been quite startling for 1961 theatre audiences expecting another static crime movie.

After the raid scene, *Payroll* looks in danger of becoming the standard thieves-fall-out-after-heist fare. The gang stand around in their hideout shouting and blaming each other for things that went wrong, while the wives of the victims

Sexy noir in 1960s Tyneside. *Payroll.*

suffer obediently in their tidy living rooms. But it's not long before the film's real quirks come to the fore and the supporting actors in the decidedly eclectic cast start to shine through. Kenneth Griffith is excellent as a weary, ageing ex-con who just wants to distance himself from the rest of his gang and get drunk; Tom Bell is reliably petulant as the young buck robber whose cockiness masks his apprehension; and William Lucas, as the thieves' inside man, a henpecked accountant driven to crime by the demands of his dissatisfied wife (Francoise Prevost), cracks spectacularly when the guilt sets in.

But it is Billie Whitelaw as the wife of the killed van driver who really steals *Payroll.* In an instant she turns from loving and dutiful wife to merciless avenger, rejecting the efforts of the police and attempting to hunt down the gang leaders herself (although never once dirtying her prim raincoat in the process). Her quest for vengeance turns the proceedings into something akin to the first feminist crime movie. It's a role that could have become unintentionally comic but, as ever, the complex Whitelaw pulls it off — once she gets that look in her eye, you know she's not to be messed with.

If anything lets *Payroll* down, it is the two leads, although Michael Craig — adventurously cast as a hard-nosed, saturnine villain — is not quite as wooden as usual. With a bit of strict coaching he may have got closer to being dangerous and sexy, something of a proto Clive Owen. But he doesn't quite make it, preferring to glare wildly but ineffectively when he's supposed to be menacing, and never quite shaking his clean-cut, general purpose blandness.

Francoise Prevost looks good but phones in her femme fatale performance and sticks out like a sore thumb as a smouldering Frenchwoman in the middle of suburban Tyneside. It's the type of 'exotic' casting that seems silly now but was pretty prevalent at the time (the celebrated *Room at the Top* [58] must take some of the blame: some may have wondered what French siren Simone Signoret was doing holed up in Bradford, but the Americans gave her an Oscar for it). When Craig and Prevost are together, the whole thing gets sluggish; you keep wishing Hayers would (literally) cut to the chase. He's clearly better with nail-biting pacing than he is with heated sexual tensions of noir.

From a narrative point of view, *Payroll*'s Newcastle setting is entirely incidental — no one attempts a Geordie accent, and the film isn't 'regional' in the way that the New Wave aspired to be. But as a backdrop to the alfresco auto-raid it looks great, even if it was only chosen for the grimy beauty of the Tyne Bridge and the sloping streets adjacent to it. Steward's location photography is first rate, his night shooting stylish and luminescent. Like Hayers, he was a journeyman who occasionally delivered excellent work, and was never less than solid and professional. But he had to go where the jobs took him. By the seventies, he was lighting the last few *Carry On* films.

Hayers himself went on to make a handful of lively British thrillers over the next decade, including one minor classic — NIGHT OF THE EAGLE (62). But by the time he finally did get that Hollywood invitation, he'd been obliged, like so many of his contemporaries, to decamp to television. He spent most of his last twenty years in the USA, churning out episodes of everything from *Magnum P.I.* to *Baywatch*.

Julian Upton

Michael Craig shows his nasty side. *Payroll.*

SEVEN KEYS (1961)

Independent Artists/Anglo-Amalgamated Film Distributors | 57 mins | b&w

Director Pat Jackson; **Producers** Leslie Parkyn, Julian Wintle; **Screenplay** Henry Blyth, Jack Davies
Starring Alan Dobie (Russell), Jeannie Carson (Shirley Steele), Delphi Lawrence (Natalie Worth).

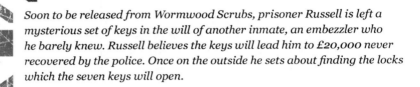

*Soon to be released from Wormwood Scrubs, prisoner Russell is left a
mysterious set of keys in the will of another inmate, an embezzler who
he barely knew. Russell believes the keys will lead him to £20,000 never
recovered by the police. Once on the outside he sets about finding the locks
which the seven keys will open.*

Clocking in at a lean fifty-seven minutes, Pat Jackson's low budget
crime movie *Seven Keys* harks back to the no-frills days of the
1930s quota quickie boom. Jackson would have remembered the
time when British cinema's reputation was tarnished by what the
critical establishment saw as cut-price comedies and crime capers aimed
at the least discerning of audiences. It's doubtful, though, that he would
ever have imagined himself making one. His own career trajectory was
through the documentary movement, widely seen as the Great White Hope
for a distinctive national cinema; he was assistant on the GPO Film Unit's
celebrated *Night Mail* (36) and made his directorial debut with the unit in
1938 before garnering critical plaudits with *Western Approaches* (44), a
gritty wartime tribute to the Merchant Navy. Strikingly shot in colour and
with a cast largely made up of non-professionals, it was a key transitional
film in forging the sort of documentary inflected feature that renounced
the dramaturgy of Hollywood or the West End stage in search of a sort of
redemptive realism.

Postwar realities, though, were of a different kind, and Jackson found himself
working on commercial features, from the worthy hospital drama *White
Corridors* (51) to the horror spoof *What a Carve Up!* (61). *Seven Keys* was
made for Julian Wintle, who'd gained a reputation as an able Rank producer
before moving to Beaconsfield Studios as an independent, where, with Leslie
Parkyn, he helmed an impressive number of low budget films between 1958
and 1963, including the two Sidney Hayers classics, *Circus of Horrors* (60)
and NIGHT OF THE EAGLE (62).

Seven Keys opens with a chap in a sporty motor kissing his girl goodbye and
speeding off into the night. Rather shockingly, he's killed within moments,
smashing into a lorry as the screen goes black. Cut to a police station, where

a weary looking sergeant looks up from his desk and utters the question:
"Dead?"
"Very," replies the PC, setting the film's pleasingly laconic, almost minimal
tone before the credits even roll.

The very dead man, we learn, was Group Captain Jimmy Jefferson, DFC, a
one-time Battle of Britain ace who'd clearly taken to throwing his motor
around like a Spitfire in a dogfight. There's already more than a hint of
something sleazy in the air, of establishment figures compromised by dark
desires, and the next surprise is that Jefferson's respectable accountant father
is banged up in Wormwood Scrubs for embezzlement; or was — he expires
mysteriously at the same moment as his son (an odd synchronicity the film
doesn't follow up).

Equally strange, fellow con Russell finds that Jefferson has left him seven
keys in his will, even though he hardly knew him. Three months later, Russell
is a free man. If he can find the seven locks the keys open, he'll be a rich one
too: £20,000 of Jefferson's ill-gotten gains remains unaccounted for.

In many ways, *Seven Keys* could be seen as a late British noir, with its
existential loner fresh out of prison and the shadow of war hanging over a
gloomy country in search of desperate pleasures. But, appropriately for a film
in which most people have something to hide, it eschews the chiaroscuro of
classic noir in favour of a world that's composed, both visually and morally, of
shades of grey. Jackson's documentary background peeps through at times
in the downbeat location work and the attention paid to casting minor roles
(more like Eisensteinian types than supporting actors); such care, though, is
frequently sabotaged by a gratingly cheery score and an overzealous use of
bongos to signal criminal activity.

Ultimately, despite its high concept set-up of seven keys in search of a lock,
the film seems more interested in its enigmatic central character — not
quite a man with no name, but apparently one with a only a single moniker:
Russell. Understandable enough in the scrubs, but even when he's done
his time Russell never gets a Christian name and remains a cipher — an
inscrutable, impassive one-man operation. Alan Dobie's performance is
particularly memorable — blank-faced and expressionless, his tight mouth
getting no nearer to a smile than a razor thin, faintly amused smirk. Dobie
mostly worked on stage and in television, which is perhaps a shame for British
cinema — on the strength of this performance he could have developed a nice
line in ambiguous anti-heroes.

Of course, if a loner like Russell is ever going to crack then a woman will be his downfall, and the film throws a typical, noirishly opposed pair of them at him. Shirley Steele is old man Jefferson's one-time secretary, and becomes Russell's reluctant partner in unravelling the mystery. She's a respectable working girl who wants to clear her old employer's name; Steele by name and by nature, there's no way she's going to play either secretary or squeeze to Russell, as she makes clear from the outset.

On the other hand, the trail of the keys leads — by a circuitous route that takes in suburbia, new housing estates and an unlikely encounter with veteran Aldwych Farceur Robertson Hare — to a female of another kind: glamour model Natalie Worth. In stark contrast to Shirley, good-time girl Natalie, as her name suggests, is all about the money. Russell soon tumbles to the fact that she's really called Nora Wiggins — another variation on the film's theme of superficial glamour covering up dirty little secrets — and was blackmailing Jefferson senior: Jimmy, it turns out, had been "a very naughty boy," killing a street sweeper in a drunken hit-and-run that dad wanted kept out of the papers.

Despite its probing of a murky modern world which seems to have lost its moral compass, *Seven Keys* settles for a rather reassuring and pedestrian ending; but this short, sharp film must have provided the ideal training in how to tell a ripping yarn with brevity and economy, a skill that Jackson ended up putting to good use directing episodes of *Danger Man*, *The Saint* and *The Prisoner*.

David Sutton

FILM REVIEWS

CAPTAIN CLEGG (1962)

a.k.a. Night Creatures | Hammer Films/Major Productions/Rank Organisation | 82 mins | colour

Director Peter Graham Scott; **Producer** John Temple-Smith; **Screenplay** John Elder (Anthony Hinds), with additional dialogue by Barbara S Harper, from the novel *Dr Syn* by Russell Thorndike (uncredited). **Starring** Peter Cushing (Dr Blyss/Captain Clegg), Yvonne Romain (Imogene), Patrick Allen (Captain Collier), Oliver Reed (Harry).

By day Dr Blyss is a mild-mannered country vicar; by night he's the leader of a gang of brandy smugglers. When Captain Collier and the King's excise men arrive in his parish of Dymchurch near Romney Marsh, Blyss's secret early life as the notorious pirate Captain Clegg seems certain to be exposed.

This was not the first version of Russell Thorndike's novel, nor was it the last. In 1937, Gaumont-British produced a decent adaptation. Then, as *Captain Clegg* was in pre-production, Disney announced its own take, *Dr Syn, Alias the Scarecrow*, starring Patrick McGoohan. Hammer might have been forced to drop their project, but as director Peter Graham Scott later described, the two studios came to an amicable arrangement:

> All of a sudden Disney announced they had bought the rights to the novel *Dr Syn* and we realised we'd only bought the rights to the Gaumont-British script of *Doctor Syn*. But we had acquired it in good faith, so Disney said, "Call it something else." [1]

Hammer's swashbuckler films were somewhat hit-and-miss. *Captain Clegg* is somewhere near their buccaneering best, but it's by no means a masterpiece. In his book *English Gothic*, Jonathan Rigby waxes lyrical about the film's importance, even suggesting that Blyss' duplicity inspired the dubious morality of clergymen in later productions as diverse as *To the Devil... A Daughter* and *Carry On Dick*. [2] In reality, *Clegg* is nothing more than a decent potboiler with two underlying messages: people do have the power to change, and everyone deserves a second chance.

The film begins in dramatic style, with a bombastic score from Don Banks providing the backdrop for a trial aboard a pirate ship that results in a character known as The Mulatto having his ears slashed, his tongue cut out and being left to die alone on a desert island. We later discover he caused the premature birth of Captain Clegg's daughter, and the death of his wife in childbirth. Clegg would have been better off killing The Mulatto outright

when he had the chance, for years later, once Clegg is settled into his new identity, he turns up as the slave of a group of excise men...

He may have appeared in more than his fair share of stinkers over the years, but if there was ever an actor who could be relied on to give a role his all it was Peter Cushing. We first see Cushing as Dr Blyss, who leads his congregation in a heartily sung hymn; he seems your typical bumbling country vicar, the kind we might have seen alongside Derek Nimmo in a seventies sitcom. However, Cushing soon conveys the steely menace beneath Blyss's affable exterior, simply by taking his glasses off and delivering a few clipped lines to his fellow smugglers. Later, he sends shivers down the spine by tricking the excise men and then delivering a chillingly silent laugh as he turns towards the camera.

He also gets to show his agility in several action scenes, including the close-ups in an impressive fight with Milton Reid as Clegg's nemesis, The Mulatto — it's just a shame that it's clearly a stuntman in the longer shots. Reid, a professional wrestler of Scottish and Indian parentage, is perfectly cast here and manages to inspire a complex mix of fear and sympathy; clearly Hammer's casting directors recalled his previous memorable roles for the company in *Terror of the Tongs* and *Camp on Blood Island* before calling on his services again.

Cushing clearly loves every minute of it, probably because it gives him a rare opportunity to appear in something family oriented. In fact, *Captain Clegg* turned into something of a pet project; he worked on tightening up the screenplay with director Peter Graham Scott, [3] and even wrote an unproduced sequel ten years later. [4]

Although it's Cushing who dominates, there are other performances of note, including Oliver Reed, who cuts a dash as Harry, the Squire's son. He's in love with Imogene, Clegg's daughter who was raised by the local innkeeper. (Why Clegg, a seemingly intelligent man, chose to hand his child over to a man who appears to be a spiteful thug is an unexplained mystery.) Hammer stalwart Michael Ripper has a larger role than usual as undertaker Mipps, Clegg's former shipmate; he's bizarrely daubed in burgundy eye makeup and a ludicrous wig, but still manages to make his character likeable. When Clegg is eventually killed by The Mulatto, Ripper provides a surprisingly moving moment, carrying his friend's body to the cemetery and placing him in his grave; the spot has been marked by a stone for years, but has lain empty after the pirate escaped being hung. Sadly, Patrick Allen is as dull as ditchwater as Captain Collier, the leader of the excise men, while David Lodge has little to do as his right-hand man.

THEIR OATH WAS.. *TERROR!* THEIR CRY.. *BLOOD!*

CAPTAIN CLEGG

PRINT BY TECHNICOLOR

PETER CUSHING · YVONNE ROMAIN · PATRICK ALLEN · OLIVER REED

Easily the best moments involve the Marsh Phantoms, or rather Clegg's men dressed as spooks, who roam Romney Marsh, literally scaring the life out of people. Their ghostly appearance was created by painting black costumes with skeletal designs in reflective paint, the same stuff used on road signs. These costumes, coupled with atmospheric marsh scenery and Les Bowie's brilliant matte paintings, give the whole film a supernatural air that wouldn't have looked out of place in one of Hammer's more familiar horror offerings. Released in the US with the title *Night Creatures*, it could be said that, if nothing else, *Captain Clegg* offers the perfect transition from Hammer's most celebrated genre to its now almost forgotten swashbuckling output.

Sarah Morgan

---

1 Brian MacFarlane (ed.), *An Autobiography of British Cinema* (London: Methuen, 1997), quoted in Jonathan Rigby, *English Gothic* (London: Reynolds & Hearn, 2000), p.93.

2 Rigby, *English Gothic*, p.94.

3 Wayne Kinsey, *Hammer Films: The Bray Studio Years* (London: Reynolds & Hearn, 2002), p.228. 4: Rigby, p.94.

SWORDPLAY
THE BRITISH SWASHBUCKLER FILM

BY JAMES OLIVER

T he plot goes something like this: a group of well-provisioned invaders ride in, subjugate the locals and plunder their treasures. But wait! Such behaviour will not go unchallenged! A small band of lively underdogs rise up to take what is rightfully theirs. Facing overwhelming odds and hampered by severe limitations, they still manage to score a number of direct hits.

This is the story of the British swashbuckler, where plucky British filmmakers took on the moustache-twirling Hollywood studios who had hitherto dominated the genre. True, the British producers were actually motivated less by patriotism than a more traditional motive (which is to say, profit). And it cannot be denied that the results sometimes — hell, usually — lacked the polish and pizzazz of the deep-pocketed Americans. Perhaps that's why they sometimes get overlooked.

Aficionados, however, know better: for those with a taste for flashing blades, determined heroes, swooning maidens and last minute escapes, these films are a delight, matching — and sometimes exceeding — Hollywood for energy

THE GIANT SPECTACLE
OF THE ROGUE OF ROGUES AND
HIS MIGHTY OUTLAW BAND!

SEE!
The Siege of Sherwood Forest!
The Rescue of Maid Marion!
The Gallows of Courtney Fair!
The Terror Torture by Fire!
The Villainy of the Norman Traitor!

A Challenge for Robin Hood

STARRING
BARRIE **INGHAM** · JAMES **HAYTER** · LEON **GREENE** · PETER **BLYTHE** · GAY **HAMILTON**
PRODUCED BY CLIFFORD PARKES · DIRECTED BY C. M. PENNINGTON-RICHARDS · SCREENPLAY BY PETER BRYAN · COLOR by DE LUXE · A SEVEN ARTS–HAMMER PRODUCTION
RELEASED BY 20th CENTURY-FOX

81

and enthusiasm. But they were a long time coming. Despite the fact the stories that are the genre's cornerstones — from legends like Robin Hood to novels like *Treasure Island* — were British, indigenous producers had traditionally steered clear of the genre.

There were a few exceptions: Leslie Howard's famous take on *The Scarlet*

Pimpernel (34) or Powell and Pressburger's unfairly maligned stab at the same story, *The Elusive Pimpernel* (50), being perhaps the most notable. A few of the incredibly popular Gainsborough melodramas included sword fighting but the emphasis was, as ever, on romance rather than adventure. But whatever occasioned the British film industry's reluctance to exploit its heritage, it dissipated with the arrival of television, specifically the arrival of commercial television, to Britain's living rooms.

Looking for popular formats to capture their viewer's attention, TV bosses noted that the swashbuckler was enjoying something of a cinematic resurgence with big budget films like *The Master of Ballantrae* (53) and *The Black Knight* (54). Moreover, since most of these films were shot in the UK, there was a ready made stock of costumes, props and settings to plunder. So it was that Richard Greene rode on the screen as Robin Hood, that Roger Moore raised his standard as Ivanhoe and Christian Marquand sallied forth as the Gay Cavalier (no...).

There are multiple ironies here: the big budget films that inspired these small-screen imitations were commissioned by Hollywood to counter the threat of television, to show how the stunted dimensions of the idiot box could never match the grandeur of the cinema. But it was the popularity of televisual rip-offs that finally inspired Britain's filmmakers to break out their rapiers and get into the swashbuckling business.

One company was to dominate this brief cycle: Hammer Films. Always a much more diverse operation than their popular reputation as the house of horror might suggest, Hammer would happily turn their hand to anything they thought might yield financial advantage, be it comedy, crime or sci-fi. If their public showed an appetite for swashbuckling, Hammer were happy to satisfy it.

The history is not quite as straightforward as the above timeline suggests, for Hammer's first Robin Hood adventure was made in 1953, before commercial television had even begun broadcasting. Like most of the studio's productions before the runaway success of *The Quatermass Xperiment* (55) changed their fortunes, *Men of Sherwood Forest* is a cheap, perfunctory affair.

It was Hammer's first film in colour but has little else to commend it. Directed by the normally reliable Val Guest, the plot struggles to retain momentum even over its 1 hr 15 mins running time. Moreover, the film's Robin Hood (American import Don Taylor) sports unwise facial hair that results in an unsettling resemblance to Jimmy Hill.

TV's Robin Hood hits the big screen: Richard Greene in *Sword of Sherwood Forest.*

Altogether better was *Sword of Sherwood Forest* (60). Making a direct pitch
for couch potatoes, Hammer cast Richard Greene, star of the incredibly
popular *The Adventures of Robin Hood*, which had recently concluded its
run on ITV. It's an engaging not-quite conspiracy film, in which Robin foils
an ambitious land-grab orchestrated by the Sheriff of Nottingham. Greene
aside, little else is carried over from television. Robin has an all new band
of Merry Men (including Nigel Green as Little John and Niall McGinnis as
Friar Tuck) and faces a brand new Sheriff (Peter Cushing, arguably definitive).
It's a handsome picture, filmed in the lush Irish countryside (rather than
Hammer's Home Counties base camp at Bray) and shot in colour and 'Scope,
to further distance it from the TV show.

Hammer's final Robin Hood film — *A Challenge for Robin Hood* (67) —
starred Barrie Ingham as a very modish outlaw. It's the only one of the
Hammer Robin Hoods to offer an origin story: Robin is a Norman nobleman
who flees to the forest after being falsely accused of murder and then takes up
the fight against injustice. A lesser film than *Sword of Sherwood Forest*, it's
nonetheless brisk and lively enough to survive the comparison.

Although Hammer dominated the British swashbuckler boom, they weren't
the only game in town. In 1958, the Associated British Picture Corporation

(ABPC) produced *The Moonraker*, a film the word 'romp' might have been invented to describe. It transposes the story of the Scarlet Pimpernel to the English Civil War: Lord Anthony Dawlish (a.k.a. the Moonraker) is a thorn in the flesh of the Roundheads and the film follows him on his most dangerous mission yet — to spirit the future Charles II out of Britain.

The film's origins as a stage play become painfully apparent in the second half, set entirely in a coaching inn. And yet it's a very likeable film: a very young George Baker is a splendid hero and Marius Goring makes for a hissable villain. Director David MacDonald finds exactly the right tone, never taking things too seriously but playing it with enough conviction to keep things involving. He'd clearly been studying Michael Curtiz, the director who worked such wonders with Errol Flynn; there's even a visual nod to the master in the final battle, in which shadows of the duellists — a Curtiz hallmark — are thrown onto the wall.

Perhaps bowing to the inevitable, ABPC teamed up with the mighty Hammer to produce another Civil War adventure, *The Scarlet Blade* (63). Again, it's a story of royalist resistance to Cromwell's forces. (As ever in swashbucklers, the politics are thoroughly conservative; just as Robin Hood will always eventually bend at the knee before King Richard, so the republican roundheads are always the bad guys. The heroes fight not for change but to restate the traditional order.)

'The Scarlet Blade' is another Pimpernel figure, this time determined to rescue Charles I from the clutches of the Parliamentarians. The film was written and directed by John Gilling and displays a number of his preoccupations. Although essentially a writer-director of low budget exploitation films, Gilling returned again and again to the theme of

John Gilling's swashbuckling masterpiece.

RANSACKING A LOST TROPIC ISLAND... FOR A FABULOUS IDOL OF GOLD!

The Pirates of Blood River

COLOR

KERWIN MATHEWS · GLENN CORBETT · CHRISTOPHER LEE · MARLA LANDI

intergenerational conflict, the clash of parent and child. In *The Scarlet Blade*, the battle is between loving-but-repressive Colonel Judd (Lionel Jeffries, excellent) and his daughter Clare (June Thorburn), who turns against him after falling in love with the titular hero.

If any director could be said to be synonymous with the British swashbuckler, it is Gilling. His first outing in the genre was *Fury at Smuggler's Bay* (1961), a tale of smugglers, wreckers and highwaymen along the Cornish coast. The intergenerational conflict here is a father-son battle, with Peter Cushing as a strict Squire, subsequently revealed to be less of a martinet than he appears.

Gilling's masterpiece is *Pirates of Blood River* (62), one of two pirate films produced by Hammer. Given that filming at sea can be an expensive business, it was surprising that the notoriously frugal Hammer even considered a film about characters who plied their trade on water. Their money saving solution was simple: rather than shoot on an ocean, they simply relocated their pirates fifty miles inland. Easy.

Set on a Caribbean island (and filmed in tropical Surrey), it's another father-son conflict. The well-meaning son brings the pirates to the Huguenot settlement governed by his tyrannical dad. But the pirates — led by Christopher Lee, sporting both an eye patch and a thick French accent — have come in search of treasure, not justice.

The settlement is a theocracy and the film takes careful aim at the dogma and hypocrisy of the bigots. It's symbolised beautifully. The community's place of worship — and government — is dominated by a vast statue, embodying the authority that it venerates.

But it is this statue that is the treasure: a layer of paint hides the gold below. They worship gold, in other words: an obvious echo of the biblical golden calf. The pirates haul it towards their ship. But its fate is to fall in the river (filled with the piranhas which provide the film its title); the stern patriarch cannot bear to part with it and clings to it as he goes to his watery grave. It's the sort of demented climax Werner Herzog would be proud of.

Hammer's other pirate film is a more conventional but no less worthwhile affair. *The Devil Ship Pirates* (64), directed by Don Sharp, is again largely set on terra firma. These pirates are refugees from the Spanish Armada, beached in Britain while they repair their vessel. When they are discovered by locals, they pretend the invasion was a roaring success and act as an occupying force, which the British are, naturally, obliged to resist.

The story is redolent of Cavalcanti's wartime thriller *Went the Day Well?* (in which an English village is invaded by a Nazi fifth column). While it never scales the heights of that film, it builds up a useful head of steam and steers towards an explosive climax.

Hammer's finest swashbuckler — the locus classicus of such things — is CAPTAIN CLEGG (62). Freely adapted from Russell Thorndike's *Dr Syn* stories of smuggling in the Kent marshes, it stars Peter Cushing as an ex-pirate (Captain Clegg himself) now trading as a man of the cloth called Dr Blyss by day, while keeping his hand in with a spot of smuggling by night.

Although Clegg is not a real clergymen, he is no hypocrite. He shows his Christian charity by using his ill-gotten gains to fund food and clothing for his less fortunate parishioners. The real villains of the piece are the other figures of authority: Patrick Allen's bullying excise man and the authoritarian Squire. And the government troops just don't have the style of the smugglers.

The director, Peter Graham Scott, was not one of Hammer's regular employees but he does a sterling job here. It's atmospheric enough to be sometimes numbered amongst Hammer's horror films (the smugglers scare away the unwary by disguising themselves as phantoms) and sufficiently well paced for its entertainment value to be undiminished after almost fifty years.

Indeed, it's worth stressing how well these films stand up. Whereas Hammer's more celebrated Gothics are often tawdry and overwrought, their adventure films have endured considerably better and survive as — arguably — the studio's most consistent achievement.

The British swashbuckler boom was a shortlived thing; the cycle had run its course by the mid 1960s. And they are surely a product of their age. These are — in the best possible sense — unsophisticated films. Compare and contrast them to the swashbucklers made by Richard Lester barely a decade later, *The Three Musketeers* (73) and *The Four Musketeers* (74). It isn't just that these films are (much) more expensive; they have a worldliness and irony the Hammer films lack. The comparison is all the more piquant since Lester cast Oliver Reed and Christopher Lee, both Hammer alumni.

And yet the innocence of those early films makes them tremendously attractive to modern viewers. They offer uncomplicated entertainment, a world of simple choices and a promise that everything will be alright. And watched on a wet Sunday afternoon, they can seem nearly perfect.

DILEMMA (1962)

A.C.T. Films/Bryanston | 65 mins | b&w

Director Peter Maxwell; **Producer** Ted Lloyd; **Screenplay** Peter Maxwell, based on an original story by Pip and Jane Baker. **Starring** Peter Halliday (Harry Barnes), Ingrid Hafner (Jean Barnes), Patricia Burke (Edna Jones), Joan Heath (Mrs Barnes).

Schoolteacher Harry Barnes returns home to discover the body of a stranger in his bathroom and his wife missing. Without further ado, he sets about burying the corpse under the floorboards of his dining room.

I like this film a lot. It's a half-cocked misfire that was deemed unfit for general theatrical release (outside of Yorkshire), but now stands as a glorious curio removed from anything else of the period.

It opens with a scream in suburbia and a woman running down the street. Harry Barnes, schoolteacher, returns home from work to discover the front door open, his wife Jean absent (he whistles for her when he walks in), his tea burning in the oven and a strange man stabbed to death on the floor of the bathroom. It is the eve of Harry and Jean's wedding anniversary, which they plan to celebrate with a holiday abroad, or so Harry informs a neighbour. He dotes on his beautiful wife, but no one else it seems likes the woman very much. "Where is she this time?" trills Harry's mother on hearing that Jean is out again. He makes some noises in her defence, unaware that Jean is actually in the midst of packing up and getting out for good, and that her rich, scrap merchant father from Walsall is just a smokescreen for something altogether more sinister.

On discovering the body in the bathroom, Harry launches into its disposal, burying it beneath the dining room. He draws the curtains, turns up the stereo, and rips up the loose floorboards to dig a hole. The operation is constantly on the verge of being undone by a succession of visitors arriving at the house, with at least one of them gaining entrance by the backdoor he has neglected to lock. The unlikely procession of people to this otherwise docile corner of the world includes nuns collecting funds for the abbey, a piano tuner, a piano student, Harry's mother and a nosy neighbour itching to pass opinion on anyone who will care to listen. This aspect of the story parallels that of the murder and robbery of the pawnbroker by Raskolnikov in Dostoevsky's *Crime and Punishment*; here too an unlocked door leads to unwelcome visitors that threaten to usurp the whole sordid enterprise. Raskolnikov, like Harry, is lucky to escape detection.[1] (There is an entire sequence devoted to the piano

tuner, a blind man, hovering unwittingly at the periphery of the hole in Barnes' floor while commenting on the odd acoustics of the room. Other times a face attempts to peer in through the window, drawn by the noise.)

I don't know whether *Crime and Punishment* was in mind when Pip and Jane Baker wrote *Dilemma*, but one thing is certain, the husband and wife writing team (later to pen episodes of *Z Cars*, *Space: 1999*, *Doctor Who* and others) were unhappy with the translation of their work to the screen and requested their names be removed from it. They weren't obliged; the producers didn't want to incur the extra expense of having to re-do the titles.

Dilemma aspires to be a crime thriller with a social conscience, similar in manner to that of *Violent Playground* (58) (bored teenagers) and *Sapphire* (59) (race hate). However, the concept of drug running in suburbia that lies deep at its heart — "a respectable front" being a phrase used more than once — is overshadowed by the narrow gauge of Harry's task. Harry's task is to bury the body and social comment is lost to it.

Harry (an adequate performance by TV mainstay Peter Halliday) appears oblivious to any connection the dead stranger may have to his house, his wife or indeed his bathroom. He simply drags the body downstairs and buries it without question. Not much of a dilemma at all. At the end of the film we discover this hasn't been quite the rash decision it first appeared, that the dying man's death rattle was in actual fact the utterance of a single word: "Snow." It transpires that Jean has been running drugs, and her whole domestic life is a front. Harry clues us in that "almost anybody who has ever read a paperback knows that drugs, cocaine, are called snow." It's

a contrivance lifted from *Citizen Kane* (Rosebud... snow...), but like everything else in *Dilemma*, one that has been fudged and the conundrum reduced to a meaningless act.

One of the few other primary

Dilemma, opening title.

Short, sharp entertainment. Dilemma.

characters in the film is Mrs Jones, a nosy neighbour. She is presented as a humorous counterpoint to the serious matter at hand (and better suits the upbeat musical score by William Davies). But the idea of suburbia twitching behind its curtains has a rather sly connotation, and is perhaps redundant altogether, when one's neighbours really are up to no good. Mrs Jones is expecting high drama and jokingly remarks at one point that maybe Harry has done away with his wife, unaware there really is a body next door and Harry's burying it. "What does it mean? What's he doing in there?" she ponders, watching Harry schlep a large tub into the kitchen that he will use to mix cement to pour under the floorboards.

Bryanston was a small but successful distributor and sometime producer of low budget quickies through the sixties; not so successful in the seventies. *Dilemma* was probably one of their quickest, if not shortest at sixty-five minutes. It concludes with a savvy police inspector to whom Harry spills the beans, but this concession to law and order is irrelevant when one considers the real point seems already to have been made: none of it would have happened if Harry had simply listened to his mother in the first place. Mother was right not to want to trust a beautiful woman who is always out.

When Harry confronts his wife in the final moments, she turns to him and says, "The only thing you can accuse me of is burning that pie."

David Kerekes

---

1   The makeup of *Dilemma* struck me at once as being 'classical' and somehow timeless. Thanks to Thomas Campbell for pointing out the similarity to *Crime and Punishment*.

JIGSAW (1962)

Britannia Films/Figaro/British Lion | 107 mins | b&w

Director, Producer, Screenwriter Val Guest, from the novel *Sleep Long, My Love* by Hilary Waugh.
Starring Jack Warner (Detective Inspector Fred Fellows), Ronald Lewis (Wilks), Michael Goodliffe (Clyde Burchard), Yolande Donlan (Jean Sherman), Moira Redmond (Joan Simpson).

A break-in at an estate agent's premises leads Brighton police to a rented beach house where the dismembered body of a woman is discovered. As Detective Fred Fellows and his men attempt to find the house's missing tenant, John Campbell, they are led through a maze of false trails and blind alleys before the pieces of the puzzle finally fit together.

Leslie Halliwell, in his incomparably pithy *Film Guide*, called *Jigsaw* 'excellent unassuming entertainment.' This pretty much nails it on the head. The film is as unpretentious and dependable as Jack Warner himself, on leave from playing an avuncular, uniformed TV bobby, *Dixon of Dock Green*, to give us the avuncular, plain-clothes Detective Inspector Fellows — sixty-five if he's day and arthritic to boot, yet still tirelessly, and cheerfully, pounding the streets in the name of law and order.

But *Jigsaw*'s absence of artistic indulgence, of profound dialogue, bravura visuals and even incidental music make it easy to forget that you're watching a film constructed with considerable style and flair. For all Warner's (welcome) warmness, this is a punchy, realistic little thriller, surely one of the unsung high points of that evergreen genre, the police procedural.

The film's central murder investigation — which follows the discovery of a woman's dismembered body in a trunk in a rented beach house — is covered in all its fascinating, frustrating detail: dead end leads, painstaking questioning, chance discoveries and spirit-breaking desk work. Rarely has the pertinacity of behind-the-scenes policing been shown quite so enthrallingly. The dialogue consists almost exclusively of quick-fire question and answer sessions as Fellows and his deputy, Wilks (Ronald Lewis), wade through a mire of evidence, witnesses and suspects to find their killer. False trails are followed and leads go cold, but writer-director Val Guest takes care to avoid holes in the plot: every detour is explored with the thoroughness of a four-part TV serial. Only here, things move along at almost double speed. Warner seems to have twice as many lines as the average leading man, and has to get through them in just under two hours. This is still a long running time for an 'unassuming' British crime movie, but *Jigsaw* could never be accused of being sluggish or

FILM REVIEWS

padded. It's as lean as a slice of turkey breast.

The depiction of the detectives' door-to-door canvassing has since become a staple of the TV policier, but in 1962 this kind of location filming was beyond the resources of television drama. Guest superbly captures the Brighton seafront setting, and there's a touch of ingenuity to presenting what was then a sleepy and provincial British holiday town as the scene of a grisly murder (the novel on which it is based is set in Canada). This Brighton isn't one of candy floss, superannuated holidaymakers and walks along the prom; it's more like a barren, windy outpost for exiled misfits and sly opportunists, a hiding place for those up to no good in nearby London.

The unmasking of the killer is likely to catch even an ardent whodunnit fan off-guard, but Guest doesn't bombard us with a shoal of red herrings or colour our view with artistic licence. It's a testament to his manipulation of the semi-documentary approach that we don't leave the film feeling even a little cheated; the stylised opening sequence aside, we see everything as the police do, we see the same jigsaw puzzle, we could be observing a real case unfolding. And it's one that looks unsolvable until the final piece fits into place.

The diligent, versatile Guest went on to make a two more 'gritty' films of note — *80,000 Suspects* (63), a smallpox outbreak drama with soap opera asides, and *The Beauty Jungle* (64), a sharp exposé of the world of beauty contests — before the bigger pay cheques and lavisher budgets of international projects with James Bond aspirations (*Where the Spies Are* [65], *Casino Royale* [67], *Assignment K* [68]) effectively derailed what had been steadily developing as a fascinating directorial career. By the early seventies he was flitting between hack TV work and lowbrow sex comedies like *Au Pair Girls*. At least he left us an abundance of rich pickings from what now looks like his great decade as a filmmaker, 1954–64. Among these, *Jigsaw* is perhaps his most assured and satisfying work.

Julian Upton

NIGHT OF THE EAGLE (1962)

Independent Artists/Anglo-Amalgamated/AIP | 90 mins | b&w

Director Sidney Hayers; **Producers** Albert Fennell, Samuel Z Arkoff; **Screenplay** Charles
Beaumont, Richard Matheson, George Baxt from the novel *Conjure Wife* by Fritz Leiber Jr.
Starring Peter Wyngarde (Professor Norman Taylor), Janet Blair (Tansy Taylor), Margaret Johnson
(Flora Carr), Colin Gordon (Lindsay Carr), Kathleen Byron (Evelyn Sawtelle).

*Professor Norman Taylor takes a dismissive view of the supernatural, so he is
appalled to discover that his own wife is a practitioner of the occult arts. She
is not the only witch in town, however, and when Taylor forces her to burn the
charms that she claims are protecting him, he becomes the target of malicious
sorcery. Bedevilled by strange occurrences, Taylor's trenchant disbelief is soon
placed under severe strain.*

I t's inevitable, given the similarity of both theme and title, that *Night of
the Eagle* should find itself compared to — and too often overshadowed
by — *Night of the Demon* (57). Like Jacques Tourneur's masterful
adaptation of M.R. James' story *Casting the Runes*, Sidney Hayers' film
concerns itself with a sceptical rationalist discovering that the supernatural is
much more threatening than he supposed. *Night of the Eagle* is no imitation
or remake, however. Beyond the broad similarities, it quickly manifests its
own identity and atmosphere.

As the establishing shots make plain, the film takes place on the campus of
Hempnell Medical College, an unprepossessing establishment somewhere
in the English countryside. In one of the seminar rooms, Professor Norman
Taylor is lecturing his students on the psychology of superstition. It is clear
he has strong opinions on the matter. For Taylor, such nonsense is "a morbid
desire to escape from reality." Just in case his students miss the point, he
chalks a bold reminder on the blackboard: I DO NOT BELIEVE.

You don't have to possess Professor Taylor's tremendous intellect to realise
that this statement will soon be challenged. As in most films that pit
rationalism against the occult, it is the man of science who is obliged to justify
his beliefs, ultimately unsuccessfully. As played by Peter Wyngarde, Taylor
contrasts strongly to the other members of the faculty: young, vigorous
and popular with the student body. (Wyngarde's high fashion wardrobe is,
incidentally, quite something to behold. But such élan caused difficulties for
the production team: in certain scenes Wyngarde could only be filmed from
the waist up as he was wearing immodestly tight trousers.)

FILM REVIEWS

Neither Taylor nor his wife Tansy (Janet Blair) find Hempnell to their taste — Tansy spends much of her time at her seaside cottage — but they do their best to fit in, socialising with Taylor's colleagues and hosting tedious evenings of bridge. Taylor is tipped for promotion, something that sets teeth grinding amongst the more experienced members of the college: no matter how accomplished he might be, he is still a newcomer. More even than the men, it is the women who take the greatest umbrage at the perceived slight to their husbands.

The race for promotion clearly brings out the worst in such people; we are soon to discover that Taylor's bracing scepticism is not as widely shared as he might like to suppose. One of the aggrieved parties is determined to place a hex on him, to scupper his chances by means of magic.

The film never really develops this angle, on the petty jealousies that swirl around the cloistered world of academia, which is a pity. It would have made for a wonderful satire — a sort of *Lucky Jim*, with added juju — to see people resorting to such extreme measures to resolve what outsiders would see as trivial tensions. Instead, the film concentrates on thawing Taylor's disbelief. His first shock comes when he learns that his own wife is a devotee of magic; she has filled their home with charms and trinkets. Outraged, this proto-Dawkins insists she burns them all, refusing to listen when she tells him they are for his protection. Once they are consigned to the flames, however, he is no longer under their defence and falls prey to the rival sorcerer.

The first assault comes when he is almost run over by a lorry. He survives but there is worse to come when a student accuses him of rape. There's no (obvious) occult dimension to any of this — such things could happen to any university lecturer and these portions of the film are more effective

for eschewing the supernatural phantasmagoria that usually accompanies curses in cinema.

Night of the Eagle aspires to the ambiguity of the great Val Lewton chillers of the 1940s, where the horrors might just as easily have been the product of a broken mind as black magic. Even after the film tips its hand and Taylor is pursued by a gigantic eagle, the film endeavours to maintain at least some uncertainty — once the attack is called off, there is no trace of the damage that the bird caused. Perhaps he just imagined it...

But while viewers of more rationalist inclinations might prefer to believe that it was all a hypnotic hallucination (and that's certainly possible), Taylor himself has been convinced otherwise. He shelters from the eagle's attack in the classroom where he previously delivered his stirring critique of mumbo-jumbo. In his panic, he brushes up against the blackboard, erasing the word 'not' from his once unequivocal declaration: I DO NOT BELIEVE.

The film was adapted from Fritz Leiber's 1943 novel *Conjure Wife* (previously filmed under the wonderfully prosaic title *Weird Woman* [44]), relocating the action from New England to old. All three of the screenwriters were American: perhaps that's why *Night of the Eagle* moves at a faster clip than most British films, charging through the plot and racing to a crescendo. Which is not to say it stints on mood: it's suffused with an unsettling atmosphere that builds as the pressure of Taylor rises.

True, budgetary constraints are occasionally obvious (perhaps the visible tether attached to the eagle during the nail-biting climax represents the psychic supervision exerted by its controller). But it's hard not to be impressed by the precision with which Sidney Hayers orchestrates it, carefully balancing pace and ambience to create a compelling, creepy film.

Night of the Eagle will forever be twinned with *Night of the Demon* but is too effective to be eclipsed by it. If Hayers never quite matches Jacques Tourneur's achievements then it should be remembered that Tourneur is generally regarded as one of the finest directors in his division, while Hayers — if he is regarded at all — is supposed to be no more than a purveyor of very ordinary formula pictures. That he manages to get within spitting distance of the master, with much reduced resources, suggests a new accounting is necessary.

James Oliver

A PRIZE OF ARMS (1962)

Bryanston/Interstate/ British Lion | 105 mins | b&w

Director Cliff Owen; **Producer** George Maynard; **Screenplay** Paul Ryder, from a story by Nicolas Roeg and Kevin Kavanagh. **Starring** Stanley Baker (Turpin), Helmut Schmid (Swavek), Tom Bell (Fenner), Patrick Magee (Hicks).

Intent on stealing its payroll, three crooks infiltrate an army barracks, disguised as soldiers. With some ingenuity, they blend into the day-to-day activity of the base. Eventually they get to their payload by dressing as military police, starting a fire, and staging an evacuation of the offices. Joining a convoy of outgoing trucks, they successfully leave with £100,000. But just how far will they get?

I f you're the kind of crime movie fan who gets irritated by those obligatory heterosexual asides — you know, the femme fatale getting the hero hot under the collar, the good woman bringing him back to the straight and narrow — then this film is for you. There's not a woman in sight here, just a bunch of villains carrying out a raid on an army barracks, and a base full of shiny booted types who almost let them get away with it.

A Prize of Arms has no time for fannying around — it gets down to business as pragmatically and unemotionally as the crooked protagonists execute their robbery. It's the filmmaking equivalent of a plate of bread and dripping and a mug of hot tea on a cold night on guard duty: it's satisfying, diverting and not un-tasty, but you won't need any fancy French words to describe it. It's a film for plain thinking men — men who like the creases ironed into their trousers.

Only Stanley Baker could be the star of a picture like this. As Turpin, the lead villain, he's edgy and always on his guard, but he also has a core of inner, almost paternal strength; when things get dicey, he can think on his feet. He'd be the sort you'd want on your side, if he wasn't as bent as a nine-bob note. He's been driven to crime by a dishonourable discharge from the army at the end of the war. He's lost his identity; now, all he has are "just three holes on each shoulder where the pips used to be." There isn't much time spent in *A Prize of Arms* on emotional agendas or back stories, but it does allow Baker's character this motivation for breaking into an army base and stealing its payroll. It also makes his fraught interactions with the 'real' military men all the more exciting: will Turpin's jaded authority give him away? He had been an officer before his downfall; now he's mixing in with privates, and he has an axe to grind.

That said, Turpin coordinates the subterfuge necessary to stage the army base robbery with a professionalism bordering on military genius. The Achilles heel of the operation is his young accomplice, the inexperienced Fenner. (Tom Bell gives the classic Tom Bell performance as Fenner: petulant, pouty and presumptuous.) It's his immature slip-ups and general insolence that threaten to bring the whole caper down.

Director Cliff Owen builds here on the taut economy he gave OFFBEAT. The longer running time allows him to spend more attention on the minutiae of the raid, the detail of its execution and the planning that precedes it (down to the cold-air breath of the hideout). He also exhibits a skill — like those brawny American directors Robert Aldrich and Samuel Fuller — for delivering micro-pockets of relationship drama that show the hierarchical resentments of men and how they seep into their stone-faced adherence to protocol, whether they are villains or soldiers.

A Prize of Arms thrives on pacing and tension — there are regular moments of suspense as the army imposters come close to being found out — but there is also a striking visual flourish at the end, as the thieves turn flamethrowers onto their pursuers. Suddenly their anonymous truck becomes a monster in the night, a mechanical fire-breathing dragon. It's an image that could be at home in *Night of the Demon*.

Owen moved out of straight drama after *A Prize of Arms* and spent most of the rest of his career directing comedy, but the flabby scripts he was given began to drag him down with them. He was at the helm of two of Morecambe and Wise's ill-conceived movie capers (*That Riviera Touch* [66] and *The Magnificent Two* [67]); steered the big screen *Steptoe and Son* (72) to domestic box office success at the expense of the series' usually well-crafted dialogue; and was tasked with the unenviable job of delivering a saucy musical version of *Tom Jones* in 1976, the height of the disco/punk era. Sadly, *The Bawdy Adventures of Tom Jones* (76) was a nowhere-near-bawdy enough misadventure, and it effectively finished Owen's career.

Like most journeymen directors, Owen was at the mercy of his material; with a decent script and good actors, he could bring a film to life with real zest. *A Prize of Arms* is taut and gripping until the end. Even then there's no time for reflection. Within a second of the crooks meeting their sudden fate, the film is over, credits and all. Job done.

Julian Upton

THE DAMNED (1963)

a.k.a. These are The Damned | Hammer/Columbia Pictures | 96 mins | b&w

Director Joseph Losey; **Producer** Anthony Hinds; **Screenplay** Evan Jones.
Starring Macdonald Carey (Simon Wells), Shirley Anne Field (Joan), Oliver Reed (King), Alexander Knox (Bernard), Viveca Lindfors (Freya), Kenneth Cope (Sid), James Villiers (Captain Gregory), Walter Gotell (Major Holland).

Attacked by a vicious biker gang, American tourist Simon Wells flees town, with his tormentors in hot pursuit. He takes refuge in a top secret army establishment, where he discovers nine peculiar children, whose skin is cold to the touch. They are the product of a demented experiment to ensure that the human race will continue even after nuclear war, an experiment that will not be stopped because of Wells' interference.

on't let the credits fool you. Although produced by the venerable Hammer Films, *The Damned* has little in common with the other flicks the company churned out. This mad, atomic-powered nightmare operates far outside the studio's comfort zone. Even its admirers must concede that it is a flawed — perhaps profoundly flawed — film, with ambitions that exceed its reach. It has an unfortunate taste for pop psychology and it sports a distracting performance from Shirley Anne Field. The plotting is uneasy and there's a cod rock and roll theme tune ("black

leather, black leather, rock, rock, rock") that's unlikely to find its way onto many iPods. And yet it is a masterpiece, a downbeat — even nihilistic — vision of a society gone insane. Although rooted in the nuclear age, it addresses anxieties that are still regrettably current.

We begin in *Brighton Rock* territory. Simon Wells (Carey), a visiting American yachtsman, has berthed in Weymouth, that jewel in the English Riviera. He catches the eye of a young lady — Joan (Field) — and, in a bravura sequence of crane-and-tracking shots, she lures him on. It is, however, a trap. Joan is the sister of King (a youthful Reed, glowering as only he could), the leader of a local biker gang. Wells is duly beaten and robbed.

King's gang is a parody of British tradition. Their fearless leader drills them like soldiers, even borrowing the vocabulary of a retired colonel ("Forward into battle, dear chaps"). While his troops dress in leathers, he accessorises his outfit with a tweed sports jacket and umbrella, just like a proper toff (if not quite a king). They are, in other words, a product of their environment, both of imperial history and the post-imperial present: when Wells expresses his surprise that such behaviour happens in jolly old England, he is told "The age of senseless violence has caught up with us too." The speaker is Bernard (Knox), a passing stranger who, we learn, runs a top secret military establishment nearby.

As the film progresses, it returns again and again to the question of "senseless violence," drawing explicit links between the violence perpetrated by King and the violence controlled by the state, specifically nuclear weapons. What chance does anything have against naked aggression?

This point is made most forcefully in a scene where King confronts Bernard's lover, Freya (Lindfors). She is a sculptress: he smashes her work — art is powerless before barbarous rage. Freya's work was created by Elizabeth Frink, an artist much preoccupied by nuclear war. Her bronzes recall the crisp bodies of Hiroshima and manifest a terror of the bomb that adds another unsettling layer to the film.

King's visit to Freya comes as he is on the trail of his sister: she has tired of his incestuous designs and has fled with Wells. Knowing that King is hot on their heels, they stray inside the perimeter of Bernard's top secret military base. A fissure in the rock face leads the trespassers into an underground bunker, whereupon the film takes a sharp left into sci-fi fairytale.

Inside are nine children; their skin is cold to the touch. In time, we learn this is because they have been engineered by Bernard to be radioactive; if the grown-ups start an apocalyptic war, then these children will inherit the Earth. Until then, they must be sequestered from the rest of the world; their only contact comes via the telescreens by which Bernard communicates with them.

Bernard means well — he wants to keep his children safe and protect them from the world outside — but he is a remote patriarch. So the children are thrilled to have company. Poignantly, the children want these adults to be their parents, to give them the love they have hitherto been denied. It's a grim portrait of the family in the modern age, isolated and starved of affection — a blackly ironic comment on the 'nuclear family'; these children are literally 'atomised.'

For all Bernard's noble intentions, he can only achieve his ambitions with force. When Wells and Joan orchestrate an escape from the bunker, Bernard rounds up his charges, imprisons them again and kills everyone who knows about them, including his own lover. Wells and Joan make it to his yacht but they will die soon enough. They have been contaminated by the children. The film ends with their boat going around in circles.

Although he later dismissed it, *The Damned* is a triumph for its director (and uncredited co-writer), Joseph Losey and arguably superior to his more celebrated collaborations with Harold Pinter. An American, Losey brought an outsider's eye to England, revealing a very different country to the one depicted by indigenous directors. The English seaside has never looked as cinematic as Weymouth — ordinary, unglamorous Weymouth — does here and he is alert to the violence embedded in British society.

A few years later, another American ex-pat made a film about dandified street gangs; Stanley Kubrick's *A Clockwork Orange* (71) even features a woman being menaced with a sculpture (a rather less respectable piece, admittedly, than the Frinks exhibited by Losey.) Like Losey's film, *A Clockwork Orange* is interested in the society that produced these young hooligans but Kubrick's method is detached and satirical. *The Damned*, by contrast, takes a much less comfortable approach. It's a bleak film that denies hope. We're doomed. The best we can hope for is that Bernard's mad plan succeeds.

Predictably, Hammer were utterly horrified when they saw Losey's first cut; they were a fundamentally conservative institution, with a very British suspicion of intellectualism. Moreover, the overt nuclear politics made them uneasy. So they shelved it for two years, trimmed it down and only finally released it in 1963 as the lower half of a double bill. But it is the most intriguing picture that they ever produced; for all its faults, it has a force and intelligence unique in British cinema.

James Oliver

FRENCH DRESSING (1963)

ABPC/Kenneth Harper Productions/Warner-Pathe | 86 mins | b&w

Director Ken Russell; **Producer** Kenneth Harper; **Screenplay** Peter Brett, Ronald Cass and Peter Myers (original screenplay), Johnny Speight (additional dialogue). **Starring** James Booth (Jim Stephens), Roy Kinnear (Henry Liggot), Marisa Mell (Francoise Fayol), Alita Naughton (Judy), Bryan Pringle (the Mayor).

Deckchair attendant Jim and entertainments manager Henry decide to introduce some changes to the old-fashioned seaside resort of Gormleigh by importing a French sex bomb to launch the town's film festival — a decision that causes chaos in Gormleigh and threatens Jim's relationship with the tomboyish Judy.

One might expect a country surrounded by ocean and dotted with holiday resorts the length and breadth of its coast to have produced more films about that most British of settings, 'the seaside.' But this rich seam — with its eminently photographable landscapes and vivid social tapestry of eccentric landladies and vacationing workers —has been relatively little touched upon over the decades. The Gracie Fields vehicle *Sing As We Go* (34) provides a comic-picaresque view of Blackpool in its heyday; Carol Reed's *Bank Holiday* (38) uses Brighton for its melodramatic backdrop; Ken Annakin's *Holiday Camp* (47) offers a vision of a brave new postwar world of regimented, egalitarian pleasure at Butlins in Filey.

Perversely, perhaps, it's the image of the British holiday resort in decline, caught on a cusp of cultural change, growing consumerism and widening horizons, that has provided our abiding cinematic images of the seaside. Even before package deals and mass foreign tourism dealt home-grown holidays their deathblow there was something melancholic, tawdry even, in cinematic representations: Olivier's faded variety artiste Archie Rice hanging on in an equally faded Morecombe in *The Entertainer* (60); Tony Hancock and John Le Mesurier filling their empty days in Bognor Regis in *The Punch and Judy Man* (63); Sid James' Councillor Fiddler organising a beauty contest in *Carry On Girls* (73), a film which opens with a shot of a dog pissing against a poster welcoming us to the rain-sodden and aptly-named resort of Fircombe.

Ken Russell's long forgotten cinematic debut mines a similar vein at times — there are plenty of gags about the British weather — but it's also a film that embraces change, a proto-swinging sixties movie that looks not just to the youthful future but also across the English Channel for both inspiration and subject. Producer Kenneth Harper had already brought something of a new vision to British cinema with the two Cliff Richard musicals, *The Young Ones* (61) and *Summer Holiday* (63), and *French Dressing* picks up on and continues their central conflict between heady youth and hidebound establishment, albeit without the colour, pop music or star power of the earlier films.

The story concerns deckchair attendant Jim (James Booth), his entertainment manager pal Henry (Roy Kinnear) and his local reporter girlfriend Judy (Alita Naughton), all wasting away in the stultifying confines of the seaside resort of Gormleigh as it gears up for what promises to be another miserable summer season.

Gormleigh, of course, is a microcosm of Little Britain, an Edwardian timewarp boasting a limply flapping Union Jack on its promenade and a troupe of aged, bowler-hatted town councillors to remind us of the declining fortunes and continuing delusions of a post-Suez nation. Early on in the film, the camera tracks along the prom, taking in a distant bandstand with its wheezing brass band before coming to rest on modern ingénue Judy and her transistor radio, blasting out some insistently twangy pop which drowns the dirge-like efforts of the aged musicians. With her sailor top and sunglasses she's a cut-price Anna Karina — just one of Russell's many references to the Nouvelle Vague — reading airline timetables as she dreams of escape.

If escape is impossible, then bringing some Gallic excitement to Gormleigh is the next best thing, and Jim's idea of launching a Continental-style film festival in the town, complete with visiting starlet, drives the plot as he and Henry set out for Le Touquet and return with the modestly talented but well-endowed French sex kitten Francoise Fayol (Marisa Mell) in tow.

The ensuing comedy is predictable, perhaps, with British provincialism coming into conflict with Cannes-style internationalism (witness the

splendidly awful welcoming carnival procession) and Continental sexual liberation finding its response in barely repressed British lust. One suspects that Russell is critiquing British cinema as much as British society here, introducing 'foreign' elements into the stylistic mix — echoes of Tati's seaside sight gags in *Les Vacances de M. Hulot*, an amusingly pastiched Nouvelle Vague film within a film, a Georges Delerue score — and prefiguring the cartoonish visuals of Richard Lester with speeded up sequences, jump cuts and surreal whimsy ever so slightly ahead of its time.

It might all seem a far cry from Russell's later brand of pop romanticism — and none the worse for it — but there are moments where we can see the mature (if that's the word) Russell breaking through, with memorable images of sexual obsession channelled through visual devices: the lecherous mayor cranking the handle of his 'What the Butler Saw' machine in a masturbatory frenzy, a riot in the cinema with brawling audience members disappearing though Mlle Fayol's giant pouting lips on the torn screen.

In the end, though, it's a surprisingly sunny film, with Russell's keen eye making the most of his Herne Bay locations; no snakes and funerals, but piers and promenades work just as well in the film's striking widescreen compositions. If there's a more overcast note, it's in the film's sexual politics: James Booth's leering, know-it-all Jim and his rejection of the tomboyish Judy in favour of the overt sexuality of Francoise leave a bad taste, and there's something genuinely cruel in the scenes of Judy's final humiliation. All's well in the end, but Russell veers briefly into some dark territory here.

The director's own memories of making the film are entirely negative ones; the actors disliked him (the would-be auteur treated them, Hitch-like, as cattle); Russell heartily disliked them, and the film's producers — whom he believed sold the finished product short — even more. And, unsurprisingly, he felt nothing but contempt for the blowsy parochialism of a seaside resort like Herne Bay, even as he created an invaluable visual time capsule of its once celebrated and now forever vanished pier.

Oddly enough, Jim's vision of transforming the British seaside through art has proved prophetic. Travel round the Kent coast today and you'll find that, to the west of Herne Bay, the sleepy old fishing town of Whitstable has reinvented itself with art galleries and a Biennale, while Margate, to the east, may yet be saved from terminal decline by Tracy Emin and the Turner Contemporary.

David Sutton

GIRL IN THE HEADLINES (1963)

British Lion/Viewfinder Films/Bryanston | 94 mins | b&w

Director Michael Truman; **Producer** John Davis; **Screenplay** Patrick Campbell, Vivienne Knight, from the novel *The Nose on My Face* by Laurence Payne. **Starring** Ian Hendry (Chief Inspector Birkett), Ronald Fraser (Sgt Saunders), Jeremy Brett (Jordan Barker), Peter Arne (Hammond Barker), Jane Asher (Lindy Birkett), James Villiers (David Dane).

Police Inspector Birkett and Sgt. Saunders uncover a drug smuggling ring while investigating the murders of Ursula Gray, a drug-addicted model, and David Dane, a TV star who has been blackmailing her.

Police procedural dramas were once a staple of British cinema, but these days they seem to be largely forgotten. And after watching *Girl in the Headlines*, you may be glad that's the case. It's not that it's a bad film — in fact, for the first eighty minutes or so it's a little gem; sadly, it all falls away as the denouement takes place.

Based on a novel by actor/writer Laurence Payne (best known for his starring role in a series of Sexton Blake TV adaptations broadcast in the late sixties), the screenplay was written by journalist and TV personality Patrick Campbell and his wife, publicist/writer Vivienne Knight, whose professional acquaintances, along with those of Payne, no doubt helped inform certain aspects of the plot. Released around the same time as Christine Keeler was making the news for her role in the Profumo affair, the film underwent a name change from *The Nose on My Face*, possibly in a cack-handed attempt to make it sound topical. There seems to be no other reason for the title *Girl in the Headlines* — the dead girl, Ursula Gray, only hits the headlines once she's been murdered; she is not well known beforehand. Admittedly, *The Nose on My Face* is hardly a fitting title either!

The story opens as Chief Inspector Birkett (Ian Hendry) and sidekick Sgt. Saunders (Ronald Fraser) visit the scene of Ursula's murder, a swanky London apartment. She's been shot and the place has been ransacked. Camp TV actor David Dane (the aristocratic James Villiers, giving what can only be described as his best 'screaming queen' impersonation; there's no subtlety here) lives upstairs and wastes no time bad-mouthing his neighbour, a good-time girl never seen with the same guy twice. She clearly had low morals and liked the company of men — a trait Birkett senses Dane shares. He even later tells his wife, "I think he'd rather be married to me." There's no hint of attraction for Birkett from Dane, but his homosexuality is ratified when he's stabbed to

Girl in the Headlines: a great eighty-minute film. Unfortunately it runs to ninety-four.

death in an underground gay club. "David Dane came here often enough with some very tough boys," says the barman, confirming Birkett's suspicions. Such scenes would have been rare in mainstream fare at the time — homosexuality would remain illegal in Britain until 1967— and it's unclear whether Birkett will treat the witnesses to the crime sympathetically; all we know is they're all taken in for questioning. Still, it's interesting to see the subject featured on screen, if only for historical reasons; the film shies away from making any real comment on it.

Birkett himself is quickly established as a cerebral, cultured chap. He plays the piano, he knows about opera, he likes oysters — he's like a family oriented, chirpier precursor to Inspector Morse. He certainly has a similarly simpler-minded sidekick —Saunders is Birkett's answer to *Morse*'s Lewis, a working class chap with a demanding, never-seen wife. But Saunders also has a wisecrack for every occasion; he describes a fellow copper as "walking out with my daughter. Nice lad, very good with clocks." But saves his best line for a discussion about members of the opposite sex: "You can never tell with women. My wife likes custard — on bread." Such descriptions seem oddly placed in a gritty crime drama. Birkett's wife, meanwhile, is revealed to be an almost saintly figure: a stoic, stay-at-home, dutiful housekeeper who makes sure his meals are always on the table on time, and is chiefly responsible for raising their lively teenage daughter Lindy (an annoyingly sickly Jane Asher) during his long, work-related absences from home. But Mrs Birkett does find a crucial early clue — a code hidden in a pen found outside Ursula's flat. "You clever old darling!" exclaims her husband, in a slightly patronising tone.

Casual sexism isn't the only matter that dates the film. The dialogue is, at times, laughable (a murder suspect is described as "that Ted," while an undercover policeman actually states "He tried to scarper but I nailed him." Birkett himself tries to persuade a suspect to surrender with the line, "You've got one round left and then you're a dead duck." It's hard to imagine that anybody ever spoke like that!). And almost everyone has a Home Counties accent; there isn't even the merest hint of the 'kitchen sink' approach so popular at the time.

But the main problem comes in the final scenes. Now, a twist in the tale is all well and good, but even the most casual film viewer knows it has to make some kind of sense. The twist in *Girl in the Headlines* is just plain ridiculous. Birkett and Saunders discover that Ursula was a drug addict and was caught up in a smuggling ring, although its members weren't directly responsible for her death. So, the police hunt for the individual named 'P' in her diary, who seems to have been the last person to see her alive. After overhearing her estranged mother being addressed as 'Phil' by her lover, they deduce that she must have done the deed. You're left exclaiming "Eh?!" at the screen. Mrs Gray is called Edith, and this nickname (or any other, come to think of it) is never previously mentioned — neither is it then explained. After that abrupt episode, we immediately cut to Lindy's birthday party, where Birkett and Saunders surprise her by leading a celebration around the piano. Cheesy? Absolutely — and it grates horribly with the dark nature of the rest of the film. Such juxtaposition would be hilariously funny if it wasn't so damn weird.

It would also have been nice to see more of Jeremy Brett and Peter Arne, who only have limited screen time here. Brett is almost unbearably handsome and soulful as Jordan Barker, who was in love with Ursula; why he didn't become a star until his definitive take on Sherlock Holmes twenty years later is a mystery. As for Arne, as Jordan's brother Hammond, well, nobody did smarmy menace quite like he did. Arne was murdered twenty years later, purportedly by an Italian schoolteacher in a tale far more intriguing than anything seen here.

Sarah Morgan

MANIAC (1963)

a.k.a. The Maniac | Columbia/Hammer Films | 86 mins | b&w

Director Michael Carreras; **Producer** Jimmy Sangster; **Screenplay** Jimmy Sangster.
Starring Liliane Brousse (Annette Beynat), Nadia Gray (Eve Beynat), Donald Houston (Georges Beynat), Kerwin Mathews (Geoff Farrell).

Aspiring artist Geoff Farrell finds himself stranded in a small French village, where he forms a relationship with Eve Beynat, who runs the local hotel with her daughter Annette. Eve's estranged husband is in a local asylum. The lovelorn Geoff is hoodwinked into a plan to spring him, discovering too late that he has unwittingly unleashed a homicidal maniac into the countryside.

The Camargue region of France, one of the world's largest river deltas, enjoys a glittering reputation as a UNESCO world heritage site host to pink flamingos, wild boar and majestic white horses. Tourists are encouraged to sample its specially-bred beef, Fleur de Sel, and red rice before attending the Fête des Gardians which celebrates the skills of the Camargue 'cowboys' who rear the area's bulls for meat or export for Spanish bullfighting. Its picturesque setting, tourist guides are keen to point out, has been used in a number of films including Perret's *Le Gardian de Camargue* (10) and *Roi de Camargue* (34). [1]

They are not however, at pains to note its use for filming Hammer's 1963 film, *Maniac*. Perhaps one famous madman was enough: Vincent Van Gogh lived in the area when he took the decision to present part of his ear to a prostitute at a local brothel before being dispatched to the Saint-Paul de Mausolée Asylum. The painter in *Maniac* is not unhinged, but a man who shamelessly pursues both a stepmother and daughter just hours after being abandoned by his girlfriend is perhaps not without some issues.

The film opens with the scenario leading up to the murder that caused Eve Beynat's husband, Georges, to be imprisoned in the nearby asylum. Fifteen-year-old Annette is walking home from school down a quiet country lane when she is offered a lift by the salivating Janiello (Arnold Diamond). The following sequence is short but arresting: jumping from the car to avoid Janiello's advances, Annette is pursued into the undergrowth. The empty road and lack of action that follow clearly suggests that she is being raped, whilst a wildly inappropriate Bond-esque score plays, tricking the audience into expecting her to return, unscathed, at any moment for an action-packed chase scene. Instead, the scene cuts to a few minutes later, as Annette runs dishevelled into the road to be found by her father who unhesitatingly takes

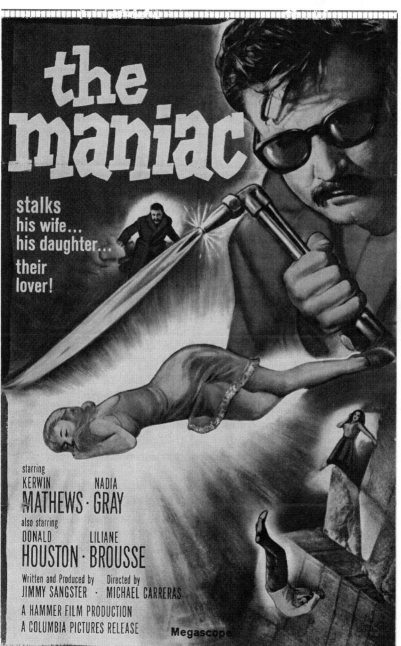

revenge on Janiello. We never actually see Janiello's murder, but it involves something nasty with a blowtorch.

As with NEVER TAKE SWEETS FROM A STRANGER (60), *Maniac* demonstrates a brief Hammer penchant for seedy, uncomfortable elements of sexuality, with perverts ruthlessly pursuing underage girls. Unlike NEVER TAKE SWEETS FROM A STRANGER, however, a 'message' film with an educating purpose, *Maniac* was seemingly without any message and simply sensation for sensation's sake.

Director Michael Carreras was no stranger to sensation, of course, his films often dismissed as cheap supporting feature fodder. Criticisms of *Maniac* — slow pace, lack of action, unbelievable and confusing storyline — are misleading, though, and unwittingly assess the film in comparison to traditional Hammer horror fare. It's true there's not a great deal of horror action, but *Maniac*'s charm lies elsewhere. There is a definite noir quality to it, with Farrell the accidental visitor drawn into a complicated web of crime and madness, and Eve a classic scheming femme fatale. Strong focus on the threat of the roaming psychotic killer, and the suggestion of grisly, inventive murders, also imbue *Maniac* with something of a subdued giallo character.

The filmmakers couldn't resist taking advantage of the French setting to direct a few comedy digs at our neighbours across the Channel. The local policeman is an undisguised picture of French excess, telling Farrell (cue *'Allo 'Allo!* accent): "When on duty, I allow myself three drinks only."

It's interesting to consider the relationship Britain's filmmakers of this era had with France. They saw France at once as a place of exoticism and culture, while at the same time, of foreigners and foolishness. In *The Rebel* (61), the Tony Hancock vehicle, an artist whose work is perceived in Britain as infantile becomes suddenly innovative when he relocates to France. It takes another Englishman, George Sanders, to see through the ruse. In British films, French women are invariably refined and beautiful (Cliff Richard goes to look at them for his *Summer Holiday* [63]), and the men in turn either pompous (Jim Smith, the famous surreal artist in *The Rebel*, has half a moustache) or homicidal (in AND SOON THE DARKNESS [70], the finger of suspicion falls on anything that wears French trousers).

Maniac combines elements of all the above.

Jennifer Wallis

---

1   See, for example, Languedoc website, http://www.languedoc-france.info/07020201_camargue.htm [Last accessed January 2010].

Wilfrid Brambell and Anthony Newley in *The Small World of Sammy Lee*.

THE SMALL WORLD OF SAMMY LEE (1963)

Bryanston/Seven Arts/British Lion | 107 mins | b&w

Director Ken Hughes; **Producer** Frank Godwin; **Screenplay** Ken Hughes, based on his TV play. **Starring** Anthony Newley (Sammy 'Lee' Leeman), Julia Foster (Patsy), Robert Stevens (Sullivan), Wilfrid Brambell (Harry), Kenneth J. Warren (Fred).

Sammy Lee, a compère at a seedy Soho strip club, has racked up one gambling debt too many and needs to call in favours. He is temporarily distracted by the arrival of Patsy, who has travelled to London to declare her love for him after a previous one-night stand. But the desperate man she finds now seems a world away from the classy showbiz entrepreneur she thought he was.

T he Small World of Sammy Lee makes few real attempts to open out its source material (it made its debut as a TV play, written by director Ken Hughes, in 1958), but it does begin with an effective series of tracking shots that trundle wearily through a West End that's just coming to life at the crack of another unremarkable dawn. As the street cleaners hose down the roads outside the Italian and Indian restaurants, and the dustbin men clear the rubbish from the porches of the peepshow houses and adult cinemas, something briefly poetic emerges from these otherwise

prosaic images, something of a fluid and wordless paean to London's ongoing cycle of dirtying and cleansing.

Then the camera catches up with Julia Foster, that fresh-faced doyenne of low budget, slightly daring monochrome dramas of the era. As the pixie-like Patsy, she's just stepped off the bus from 'up north' and into the Soho netherworld to come and work for an unsuspecting former one-night stand, Sammy Lee (Anthony Newley), a Jewish wide boy with showbiz connections who obviously made a big impression on her as he sowed his wild oats around the Yorkshire nightclub circuit some months before. Sammy is the compère at a Windmill-type strip joint — although Patsy initially believes him to be the owner — but at this ungodly hour he is nowhere to be seen. Before he actually turns up, the hapless but unmistakably ripe Patsy is persuaded into auditioning topless for the club's real owner, the egregious Sullivan (Robert Stephens), who gives her a job at twenty quid a week before she's even had a chance to unpack.

Meanwhile, we get acquainted with Newley's Sammy Lee as he crashes out in the embers of an all-night poker game. Dejected, he wanders back to his bedsit before heading off to work, manfully rejecting a sub from his showgirl neighbour. Sammy is small-time, a loser, but he's also endearing and artfully eloquent. From the outset, there's a weary resignation to him, a quiet fatalism, that Newley captures without becoming cloying (he could have so easily gone the other way). It's a remarkable performance. As Sammy resorts increasingly to desperate measures to pay off a threatening bookie to whom he now owes 300 quid, while trying to hold down his job delivering hackneyed gags and asides to an unappreciative audience of hostile middle-aged men keenly awaiting the next on-stage stripper, Newley delivers one of his true tours-de-force. He shows what a good straight actor he could have been if he hadn't always been trying to 'stop the world.'

Sammy's frantic calls to his various contacts as he tries to raise the necessary funds are masterclasses of monologue; he runs the gamut from spiky and amusing to petulant and despairing. *Sammy Lee* may very much be an 'adult' film for its time — evoking its seedy Soho milieu with morsels of partial nudity and bursts of thumping violence — but it is nevertheless at its most powerful when Newley is barking plaintively down a phone, sweat gathering on his brow, a mask of hopelessness etched on his face.

There's a great supporting cast of London lowlifes, spivs and dodgy contacts for Newley to bounce off: Stephens, of course, Wilfrid Brambell, as his aged gofer, Roy Kinnear and Warren Mitchell as Sammy's more level headed if exasperated brother. And Julia Foster holds her own as Patsy — it is through her naïve and provincial eyes that we really see the ugliness of Sammy's life. Ultimately, though, she and the rest of the cast simply operate as a narrative device to guide us into this urban underbelly and to flesh out Sammy's character a little more; in its original TV version, *Sammy Lee* was just a monologue for Newley, and the monologue still outclasses the rest of the material.

Newley gets jiggy with Julia Foster. *The Small World of Sammy Lee.*

The Small World of Sammy Lee was the last of Ken Hughes' minor but intense British noirs (*Confession* [55], *Wicked As They Come* [56], *The Long Haul* [57]); from here he went onto a handful of much more lucrative but far less personal international films: *Of Human Bondage* (US, 64) *Casino Royale* (the silly version, 67), *Chitty Chitty Bang Bang* (68). His career stumbled after the ambitious but staid *Cromwell* (70) and by the mid seventies he was behind the wheel of *Alfie Darling*, a pathetic sequel of sorts to the hit of a decade earlier, with former Animal Alan Price standing in for Michael Caine. Hughes' final offering was the eminently forgettable and unrepresentative US slasher flick, *Night School* (81).

In films, Anthony Newley never found his form, but then the kind of 'all-round entertainer' vehicles he sought to make went rapidly out of favour. His eye-wateringly indulgent autobiographical musical fantasia, *Can Heironymus Merkin Ever Forget Mercy Humppe and Find True Happiness?* (69), which he wrote, directed, produced, scored, starred in and made the sandwiches for, was one of several productions that contributed to the near-sinking of Twentieth Century Fox at the end of the sixties. After that, Newley generally stayed away (or was kept away) from the big screen, juggling jobbing actor work on television with his myriad other showbiz activities, from writing pop singles to performing in revues. Not long before his death, he took a role in the TV soap *EastEnders*, playing an aged and crooked car dealer. It wasn't a million miles from where Sammy Lee could have ended up.

Julian Upton

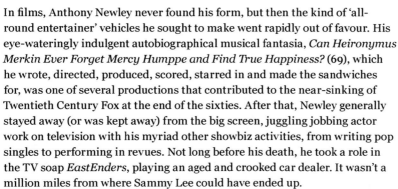

UNEARTHLY STRANGER (1963)

Independent Artists/Anglo-Amalgamated | 78 mins | b&w

Director John Krish; **Producer** Albert Fennell; **Screenplay** Rex Carlton, from an idea by Jeffrey Stone. **Starring** John Neville (Dr Mark Davidson), Philip Stone (Professor John Lancaster), Gabriella Licudi (Julie Davidson), Patrick Newell (Major Clark), Jean Marsh, Warren Mitchell.

A leading astro-scientist gets his brains fried by an unseen and unknown force. His replacement has recently married a woman who doesn't blink and has no pulse. She turns out to be an alien agent with orders to kill. She herself is killed when she falls in love with her human husband, leading him to discover a sinister conspiracy of extraterrestrial interlopers

U nearthly Stranger is a very odd but rewarding experience. It's shot on tuppence ha'penny in a rather staid television style (two-shots and talking head close-ups abound) on the smallest studio sets available. For example, a space research institute is made up of two offices and a corridor and is staffed by about five people. But, for some reason, it has its own morgue. You can tell it's a space research institute because it has a big poster of the moon on the wall and four (yes, four) clipboards. You can have fun when you notice they only had the one poster when you see it in two locations positioned at different angles.

Of course, this is nit picking. John Krish knows how to do 'Dutch' angles for when Davidson (John Neville) is running through the streets of London, and he knows the best way to shoot a spiral staircase, looking down from on high to get that concentric effect. He also has a field day getting the lighting to turn the good looking Neville into a pointy-faced freak.

The central story is insane. The scientists are trying to travel the galaxy using the power of concentration. They maintain you can get to any planet you want to by thinking very hard indeed. Plus, in that wonderfully bonkers and stiff-upper-lipped British sci-fi fashion, there's even a formula to do so. This involves the equally mad notion of a "dormant region at the back of every brain known as TP91." Well, cheers for that, Doc. I'm off to alert the staff at Broadmoor to order some extra rolls of rubber wallpaper.

All this of course is annoying the invading aliens (well, not so much invading as waiting around for something to happen), who are all unblinking women (except when they do blink), prepared to off anyone who's worked out 'the formula.'

FILM REVIEWS

Something to do with the dormant part of the brain known as TP91... *Unearthly Stranger.*

OK, it sounds a bit naff. But there are some gems contained within the running time. There's a scene about a third of the way through when we've finally escaped the pokey studio and ventured out on location. We join happy-go-lucky alien Julie (Gabriella Licudi) as she goes shopping for a bit of pasta. Outside a shop she spies a baby in a pram and goes in for the time-honoured 'coochie-coo' manoeuvre. We cut to a close-up of the baby becoming agitated and then visibly distressed. The camera cuts back to the puzzled Ms Licudi. She carries on her trek around the unnamed town (which looks like Ealing actually) until she comes across a primary school at playtime. She stops at the chain link fence to watch the children, a big soppy smile on her face. But we see that, one by one, the children are stopping their games and japes and becoming still and silent as they become aware of Julie's presence. As one they slowly start to back away, step by deliberate step, until, unable to control their panic, they flee to the safety of the school buildings. All the while we keep cutting back to Julie's face as her emotions go from joy to puzzlement to horror and finally tears.

It's a brilliant piece of cinema. Most film and TV directors know there's something inherently creepy about gangs of kids doing stuff en masse and unchildlike (see *Village of the Damned* [60] or the BBC serial *Torchwood: Children of Earth*). Mr Krish does it splendidly. Plus there's a nice coda when we see that crying has burnt grooves into Julie's face. Creepy.

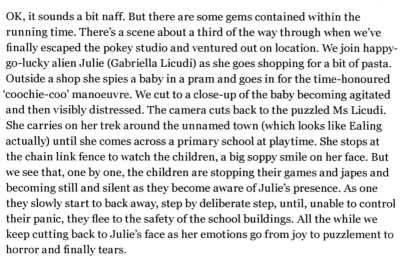

So we come to what, I think, is the central appeal of the film. Patrick Newell's performance as Major Clark is nothing short of outrageous. It's so fruity you could make jam out of it. With his Bunterish appearance, mad bow ties and tweedy tomfoolery, he dominates every scene he's in. He's the finest exponent in what must have been the masterclass for all the thesps on display in this flick:

1. Even when you don't have a line, fiddle with props all the time. Be it an unopened bottle of Johnnie Walker, a bag of sweeties, even a humble sofa, you must wrestle with it like wanno until we're forced to stare at you and you alone.

2. Deliver lines about horrible death with the same jocularity as you would relaying your recent trip to see a maiden aunt. (Of course, Newell could have received direction that his character, a security chief, is simply playing avuncular to wrongfoot someone until they say "Soviet Union" in a suspicious manner, and then drag them off screaming to the torture room. But he obviously hasn't.)

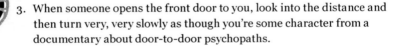

3. When someone opens the front door to you, look into the distance and then turn very, very slowly as though you're some character from a documentary about door-to-door psychopaths.

All this campery means that when the alien death force does fry Major Clark, we're rather sad to see him leave the film (even if he gives the impression he's about to throw in an aside announcing "Still available for panto!" before he disappears).

The denouement arrives with the humble secretary (Jean Marsh) revealing herself as the alien 'sleeper' at the institute, which leads to a bizarre chase around a desk with a chloroformed hanky and an ungainly fall out of a window. Ms Marsh then evaporates, leaving an empty dress and a gang of unblinking ladies in headscarves (mostly looking like Meddlesome Ratbag from *Viz*) gathering around to stare at the lens.

Unearthly Stranger is an interesting curate's egg of a production. Caught on the cusp between the fifties sci-fi paranoia of *Quatermass* (note the 'BLAAAAH!' style of music) and the Op-Art wackiness of *Doctor Who*[1] and Emma Peel-era *The Avengers*, it's a nice little segue into the rest of the sixties.

Phil Tonge

---

1   *Doctor Who* actually debuted on 23 November of the same year as *Unearthly Stranger*. Its opening episode was called *An Unearthly Child*. Coincidence? I'm afraid so.

THE YELLOW TEDDY BEARS (1963)

a.k.a. Gutter Girls a.k.a. Thrill Seekers | Compton-Tekli/Animated Motion Pictures | 88 mins | b&w

Director Robert Hartford-Davis; **Producers** Tony Tenser, Michael Klinger; **Screenplay** Derek Ford and Donald Ford. **Starring** Annette Whiteley (Linda), Jacqueline Ellis (Anne Mason), Iain Gregory, Georgina Patterson, John Bonney.

A select group of schoolgirls wear teddy bear brooches to indicate (to those in the know) that they have lost their virginity. When their teacher finds out, she makes an impassioned plea for them to treat sex as a private and highly personal matter, and to value its importance to a loving relationship. But this comes too late for the group's ringleader Linda, whose unreliable boyfriend has already got her pregnant.

Next to what Derek Ford went on to become 'famous' for — that is, a seemingly insatiable force behind some of the more risible examples of the seventies British sex film: *The Wife Swappers* (70), *Suburban Wives* (71), *Keep It Up, Jack* (73), *The Sexplorer* (75), *Diversions* (75), *What's Up Nurse!* (77) — his screenplay for *The Yellow Teddy Bears* looks like a high watermark of social progressiveness.

Coming straight from the tabloid headlines, the film's premise — which sees a gang of schoolgirls wear teddy bear brooches to let each other know that they've lost their virginity — marked *Teddy Bears* as an exploitation film from the outset (it was released in the US as *Gutter Girls*). But the narrative is actually threaded with what appears to be a strongly liberal message about the perils of teenage sex and unwanted pregnancy. The epilogue — in which socially conscious biology teacher Miss Mason (Jacqueline Ellis) defends her decision to talk to the schoolgirls openly about her own sexual experiences — is so dry, lengthy and moralistic, it would probably have sat better in a serious-minded TV discussion show than as the denouement to a salacious programmer.

The boldness of the language will be lost on modern audiences (a tea-time TV soap would deal casually with these issues now), but given that the film was released in 1963 — not long after the point where, as poet Philip Larkin later famously suggested, "sexual intercourse began" — *Teddy Bears* tackles its subject with some surprising frankness. Initially, the script pussyfoots around any explicit mention of what it is actually about, but when it finally takes the plunge, it seems to take great pleasure in teasing us with words like 'sex,' 'prostitute,' 'slag' and 'bastard,' using them rather like a horror

movie would provide tantalising glimpses of its rubber-suited monster. When pregnant schoolgirl Linda's father finally cries "abortion," it looks like it's going to bring the house down.

And well it might have done. This was a time when society looked down on sex outside marriage when a woman was over twenty-one, let alone sixteen. Pregnancy outside marriage was a definite no-no. Abortion was still illegal and although progressive, critically acclaimed films like *Saturday Night and Sunday Morning* had already started to touch upon the topic, none went so far as to have a character articulate the actual word. Even today, *Teddy Bears* retains a reputation as a sleazy exploration into 'forbidden territory.' Its late nineties VHS video release, courtesy of Salvation Films' ironic Jezebel label, featured on the cover an overgrown schoolgirl provocatively biting the tip of her finger (an effect albeit somewhat diluted by the accompanying 'PG' certificate).

For all this, *Teddy Bears* is very much a pre-sexual revolution film. As such, it is an interesting record of how girls and young women were held back by the values of austerity Britain, how taking the wrong path after 'getting into trouble' could very well lead to a whole life misspent. When the pregnant Linda (Annette Whiteley) heads off to London with an openly lecherous lorry driver, we know for sure she isn't going to find happiness in the capital; she'll be on the game before she gets to Watford Junction. Similarly, her teacher looks likely to be blacklisted even for talking (very discreetly) to the grown-up girls in her class about her own sexual history.

The Yellow Teddy Bears is either brave or lazy in leaving these issues unresolved; there is no pat happy ending (Linda losing the baby would have been a 'happy' ending of sorts). And with none of the sex or nudity hinted at by the marketing campaign, thrill-seekers leaving a 1963 screening were likely to be nursing a keen sense of disappointment, if not betrayal. But they would at least have had some issues to chew over as they left the cinema foyer.

Director Robert Hartford-Davis filmed a couple more Donald and Derek Ford scripts but, wisely, didn't follow Derek further into soft porn territory. Hartford-Davies' patchy career focused largely on horror before he decamped to the US in the mid seventies to direct series television (he died shortly afterwards, aged fifty-three). There isn't much on his CV to celebrate, but he was also responsible for the Lulu-starring rock and roll sci-fi flick *Gonks Go Beat* (65), a film too far out even for this book.

Julian Upton

CLASH BY NIGHT (1963)

a.k.a. Escape By Night | Eternal Films/Grand National Pictures/Allied Artists | 72 mins | b&w

Director Montgomery Tully; **Producer** Maurice Wilson; **Screenplay** Montgomery Tully, Maurice Wilson, from the novel *Clash by Night* by Rupert Croft-Cooke. **Starring** Harry Fowler (Doug Roberts), Terence Longdon (Martin Lord), Peter Sallis (Victor Lush), Alan Wheatley (Ronald Grey-Simmons), Tom Bowman (Bart Rennison).

A plot to secure the release of hardened criminal Bart Rennison results in a prison bus being held up on a deserted country lane. In order to allow Rennison to make good his escape, the van is locked — with screws and remaining prisoners — in a paraffin-soaked hay barn. The men are warned that the barn will be torched should they try to escape, while the Bonfire Night festivities might just ignite the place anyway. Some men plan to make a break for it, others turn on one another.

D irector Montgomery Tully certainly couldn't be accused of being a one trick pony. His career, spanning over twenty years, encompassed B-movie crime, period romances and sci-fi, as well as forays into serials with an episode of the *Edgar Wallace Mystery Theatre* in 1960. Tully's filmography is a little like browsing the pulp paperback shelf of a second-hand book store, with gold-toothed, gun-toting criminals and blonde, heaving-bosomed beauties jumping out from the covers. His films were certainly eclectic: *The Glass Cage* (55) was set in a travelling freak show, while *Girdle of Gold* (52) followed the exploits of a cheating wife whose husband stashes his ill-gotten monetary gains inside her corset. Even as film critics decried the poor production values of Tully's films, there is the impression that, actually, they really rather enjoyed them. Bosley Crowther, reviewing Tully's take on the romance between George IV and Roman Catholic Maria Fitzherbert in *Mrs Fitzherbert* (47), wrote: '[Tully] has compelled [his actors] to rear back and utter such violet-festooned lines as: "But, you see, I am only Mrs Fitzherbert and you are..." (significant pause).'[1]

Clash by Night then, is rather an oddity: it's very well-acted and is more intelligent drama than supporting feature fare. Not to be confused with Fritz Lang's 1952 film of the same name (and released in the US as *Escape by Night* for this reason), it is positively sedate in comparison to some of Tully's earlier offerings. Much of the film appears better suited to a stage play: once the prisoners have been secured inside the barn, all focus is on their personal circumstances and the relationships between them, and a curious bunch they are too. The chief problem with *Clash by Night* is the frankly unbelievable

collection of characters bound for the cells on the same day: a simple-minded murderer, an upright ex-army officer found guilty of fraud, a husband who shot his wife's attacker, a missionary who "carried brotherly love a bit too far," and the obligatory cheeky Cockney thief.

Central to the plot are thief Doug Roberts (Harry Fowler) and accidental murderer Martin Lord (Terence Longdon), who become firm friends on the prison bus. Roberts is a loveable rogue, chirping at the prison officer like a naughty schoolboy: "Can we smoke, Sir?" He is also one of the more seasoned criminals, along with his polar opposite, aspiring Mafioso Bart Rennison (Tom Bowman) who is responsible for the escape plot. "The type of characters they get in prisons these days," laments Roberts. "I wonder why I keep going back there."

Relationships form between the unlikely characters as a means for each to tell their story: Major Grey-Simmons (Alan Wheatley) befriends prison officer Watts (Richard Carpenter), ever respectful of authority and desperate to make a favourable impression. His army background leads him to ridiculous degrees of obedience, reprimanding Watts for removing the men's handcuffs: "I will remind you, Officer, that you are responsible for keeping these men under restraint."

The most interesting pairing develops between murderer Victor Lush (Peter Sallis) and preacher of the faith Sydney Selwyn (Mark Dignam). Lush isn't quite all there — "I don't know why they send us these nutcases" — and has been charged with the murder of a young girl. "Everyone's afraid of me," he tells Selwyn, as he recounts how the girl refused to take a bunch of primroses from him. "I told her to stop crying but she wouldn't. It was a funny sort of crying... She made these little noises. That's why I had to stop her — you do see that, don't you?" It's a shame that we see very little of Lush until the end of the film, when his paranoia and homicidal tendencies get the better of him: convinced that everyone hates him and "tells lies" about him, he gleefully torches the barn with everyone in it. It is by far one of Sallis' most engaging performances, though conspicuous by its absence in his autobiography: instead he concentrates on his appearance, around the same time, as Dr Watson in a musical version of Sherlock Holmes on Broadway (the mind boggles).[2]

Lush may be a homicidal maniac, and Grey-Simmons a high-level fraudster, but all the criminals are frightfully proper and English. Even the apparently dangerous Rennison is the picture of polite restraint: "That was a silly thing to do" he tells his driver after shooting prison officer Mawsley (Robert Brown).

What you might expect of a paraffin-soaked barn on Bonfire Night. *Clash by Night*, the finale.

Unlike most sixties crime films, *Clash by Night* has the old-fashioned air of an Ealing production about it ("What do you want to know the time for?" quips Mawsley to Roberts. "You need a calendar, not a clock."). The film's opening scene, in the bar of a dog track, has a distinct noir quality, but this quickly gives way to a more relaxed atmosphere; the focus is never really Rennison's escape attempt, but the characters of the other prisoners, with very little crime action taking place at all. *Clash by Night*'s appeal then is probably limited, but if nothing else it is a striking picture of 'old England' produced by an industry that would just six years later offer up the cult image of hip modern criminals that was *The Italian Job*.

Jennifer Wallis

1   Bosley Crowther, 'Review: *Mrs Fitzherbert*,' *New York Times*, 11 May 1950.
2   Peter Sallis, *Fading into the Limelight: The Autobiography* (London: Orion, 2006), p.239.

DEVIL DOLL (1964)

Galaworldfilm Productions/Gordon Films | 81 mins | b&w

Director Lindsay Shonteff; **Producers** Richard Gordon, Lindsay Shonteff; **Screenplay** Ronald Kinnoch (credited as George Barclay) and Charles F. Vetter (credited as Lance Z. Hargreaves), based on the short story, *The Devil Doll*, by Frederick E. Smith. **Starring** Bryant Haliday (The Great Vorelli), William Sylvester (Mark English), Yvonne Romain (Marianne Horn), Sandra Dorne (Magda Gardinas), Karel Stepanek (Dr Heller), Francis de Wolff (Dr Keisling), Sadie Corre (Hugo, uncredited).

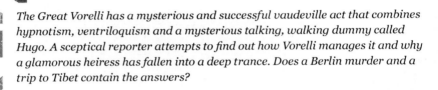

The Great Vorelli has a mysterious and successful vaudeville act that combines hypnotism, ventriloquism and a mysterious talking, walking dummy called Hugo. A sceptical reporter attempts to find out how Vorelli manages it and why a glamorous heiress has fallen into a deep trance. Does a Berlin murder and a trip to Tibet contain the answers?

Devil Doll could have been a very different film from the one that finally hit the screens in 1964. The project was originally in the hands of Sidney J. Furie, who decided that the chance to direct *The Ipcress File* was too good to ignore, so recommended Canadian compatriot Lindsay Shonteff for the job. Furie stayed around to give bits of advice, but as his feature film debut, *Devil Doll* is sterling Shonteff.

Although based on a pulp short story, *Devil Doll* has its roots firmly planted in two classic films that preceded it: the Ealing portmanteau chiller *Dead of Night* (45), where ventriloquist Michael Redgrave is haunted by his dummy, also called Hugo, and *The Great Gabbo* (29), where insane Erich von Stroheim has to struggle with little Otto. There has always been something sinister about inanimate objects coming to life, none more so when it's a little wooden human with a fixed, slightly unhinged grin.

So, it is from this staple horror tenet that *Devil Doll* draws its inspiration and suspense. The Great Vorelli (Haliday) is suave and stern. We first see him taking his exit from the stage and returning to his dressing room, where he tells Hugo: "You'll never win, you'll always lose," before locking him in a cage and covering him with a black sheet. There is obviously a relationship between man and dummy that is not quite normal.

It seems that Vorelli's act is causing a stir and newspaper reporter Mark English (Sylvester) is sent along to the next show to see what all the fuss is about. He is accompanied by his girlfriend, the delicious, rich heiress Marianne Horn (Romain), who is persuaded on stage and hypnotised into an uncharacteristic bit of dirty dancing. We also see more of the dark side

Devil Doll: early career high point for Lindsay Shonteff.

of Vorelli, who brings a member of the audience to his knees and hypnotises him into thinking he is about to be executed. With cold menace Vorelli tells him repeatedly: "Wait for the sound of the gun, and the pain of the bullet smashing into your head..." Nothing like a bit of light entertainment.

Of course, English is the archetypal sceptic, dismissing hypnotism and everything connected to it as phooey, but he is still intrigued as to how Hugo can walk around by itself and how Vorelli controls his subjects. Is it something mechanical? At all times the tension between the dummy and Vorelli is palpable. At a charity night organised by Marianne that Vorelli attends to entertain the guests, English takes the chance to try and discover more about Hugo. He examines the dummy and finds nothing, but, during the night, it comes to his room and asks for help, and drops a cryptic clue about Berlin, 1948. Has English imagined it all?

Vorelli has decided that the evening is his chance to seduce Marianne mentally, gain control of her mind and eventually her money. After the charity gig, she is left in a trance by Vorelli, who has hatched a plot to make her his wife. When she wakes she tells English that she is now in love with Vorelli and intends to marry him. With the motiveless and odd murder of Magda (Dorne), Vorelli's lover and stage assistant, English is now convinced that Vorelli is up to something sinister.

English decides to travel to Germany (as instructed by Hugo) to investigate Vorelli's past. In Berlin, he finds that Vorelli trained as a doctor before being struck off, then spent years travelling in Egypt and India before training with Lama mystics in Tibet. He has seemingly perfected the art of separating a man from his soul. Here we find out that Hugo was once part of Vorelli's

stage act and was murdered, with his soul transferred to the ventriloquist's dummy. It is now clear that Vorelli is planning to groom Marianne to be killed, and have her spirit transferred into a newly-prepared female doll, while Vorelli inherits her estate.

WHAT iS THE STRANGE, TERRIFYING EVIL SECRET OF THE DUMMY... AND WHY iS iT LOCKED iN A CAGE EVERY NIGHT?

Richard Gordon presents

Can a beautiful woman be enslaved against her will?

DEVIL DOLL

CAN YOU KEEP THE SECRET OF THE MOST DIABOLICAL ENDING EVER FILMED? NO ONE ADMITTED DURING THE LAST 10 MINUTES!

WILLIAM SYLVESTER · BRYANT HALIDAY · YVONNE ROMAIN ASSOCIATED FILM DIST. CORP.

After an atmospheric build up, the final scenes are, sadly, a bit clumsy. Vorelli gets ready to head off to Spain, where he will spend the next few years planning the soul transfer and death of Marianne. Hugo decides to launch an attack on Vorelli and they get into a dressing room fight where somehow the souls and voices of Hugo

and Vorelli are swapped over. Vorelli is now trapped inside the body of Hugo and vice versa. The tables are turned. Unfortunately, after a well-paced little shocker, this denouement and final twist are abrupt, weak and unsophisticated.

Arguably, there is nothing original in the murderous, possessive ventriloquist's dummy or evil hypnotist, but for the most part Shonteff delivers it with panache. There is a definite hostile edge to the Hugo/Vorelli relationship, and throughout there is a distinct air of unpleasantness to the film. Haliday in particular plays the perfect cruel villain — he really does have an aura of menace surrounding him. The uncut 'X' rated version has a few touches of nudity and a stage scene where Vorelli convinces a starchy classical musician to do a striptease, but these were chopped out for the US release. Perhaps this taste of exploitation (a sign of where Shonteff would eventually end up) has been the reason the film has not enjoyed the copious TV outings of the likes of *Night of the Demon*, *The Devil Rides Out*, *The Wicker Man* et al. It's a minor tragedy that *Devil Doll* has missed out on generations of viewers' eye-time, as the film deserves to rub shoulders with all of the above, and should rightly be regarded as a classic example of prime cut, low budget Brit horror.

Gary Ramsay

WITCHCRAFT (1964)

Lippert Films/Twentieth Century Fox | 79 mins | b&w

Director Don Sharp; **Producers** Robert L. Lippert, Jack Parsons; **Screenplay** Harry Spalding.
Starring Lon Chaney Jr, billed as Lon Chaney (Morgan Whitlock), Jack Hedley (Bill Lanier), Jill Dixon
(Tracy Lanier), David Weston (Todd Lanier), Diane Clare (Amy Whitlock), Yvette Rees (Vanessa
Whitlock), Barry Linehan (Myles Forrester), Marie Ney (Malvina Lanier).

*When an ancient cemetery is bulldozed to make way for a modern housing
development, a long-dead seventeenth century witch rises from the grave to
exact a terrible revenge on the family of a town planner whose ancestors were
responsible for her death.*

Witchcraft was one of the many films churned out by latter-day
quickie producer Robert Lippert for Fox's operation in Britain.
Directed by Don Sharp — who'd already made a mark in the genre
with *Kiss of the Vampire* (63) for Hammer and went on to direct
the unforgettable bikers-from-hell classic *Psychomania* (72) — it remains the
least known of a small but significant group of black and white, non-Hammer
horrors from the era that includes Sidney Hayers' NIGHT OF THE EAGLE and
City of the Dead.

The film opens with a shot of a suburban main road with traffic passing
noisily by; a gas tower looms in the distance through the grey murk. It looks
as though we're in kitchen sink territory. Then, the camera pans round to
reveal a Victorian cemetery, brooding quietly just yards away from the tumult
of the modern world. The sounds of traffic fade away, replaced by ominously
beating drums and a crescendo of snarling brass and woodwind. In wibbly-
wobbly white letters the word 'Witchcraft' grows to fill the screen.

The persistence of the Gothic — whether in the legacies of revivalist
architecture or the national literary sensibility — has been clearly signalled.
But this isn't the luridly coloured never-never land of Hammer's recent string of
successes. This is modern Britain in the not-quite swinging sixties, dizzy with
the notion of progress, especially in terms of its most visible expression, 'the
built environment'; an age when cast iron fireplaces and ornate ceiling roses
were ripped out of Victorian houses across the land and utopian visions in
concrete reached their tentacles farther into the countryside than ever before.

No surprise, then, when we cut straight from the title screen to a bulldozer
ploughing through the cemetery, upturning gravestones and scooping them
into heaps like piles of bodies. The premise of the film's opening shot — that

the Gothic co-exists alongside the modern — is upturned too: in fact, the old ways are under serious threat from the new — there's a war going on.

From his first entrance — clad in a black cape and waving a heavy cane — it's obvious that Lon Chaney's Morgan Whitlock is not on the side of progress: "Stop that! This is blasphemy! Go back, I say!" he bellows, sounding like a demon (drink)-possessed Daffy Duck.

He has good reason to be up in arms; in the drawing room of a rambling old pile — blind to the architectural hypocrisies involved —

Double trouble: *Witchcraft* shares the bill with another cut-price Lippert flick.

successful town planner Bill Lanier and his new Canadian wife Tracy fiddle with a model of the New Town that's about to go up on the old graveyard and wonder where the children's playground should go.

These days, we all know that you should never, ever plonk a housing development on an ancient burial ground, but Whitlock turns up to spell it out to these dim-witted modernisers: "The Whitlocks have used that cemetery for 800 years. What right does an upstart like you have to run sewers through their coffins, put buildings over their graves?"

What right, indeed? Bill blames his thrusting partner Myles Forrester for the outrage, before paying a moonlit visit to the cemetery where he finds a bit of broken masonry bearing a mysterious occult symbol that matches one carved into the Lanier fireplace. But why?

Grandma Lanier knows the truth: it's a witches circle, sign of a pact with the

Devil. Back in the early 1600s the Laniers accused the Whitlocks of witchcraft and Vanessa Whitlock paid the price. "She wasn't burned," says old Malvina with a look of horror, "but taken out and buried alive!"

A crash of thunder and a cut to Vanessa's now empty tomb confirms our suspicions: the camera tracks across to a pair of feet, up the length of a shroud-like dress and stops on the well preserved but completely bonkers looking face of the risen Vanessa, who turns and walks with glazed eyes into an extremely localised fall of studio rain.

Younger brother Todd fills in the rest of the story, revealing that the house once belonged to the Whitlocks before the Laniers drove them off their land. Progress, it seems, has always been a problematic business in Britain. The family feud has continued down the centuries — although Todd and Whitlock's young niece Amy are enjoying a Romeo and Juliet style romance — and now spooky Vanessa (a splendid, wordless turn from Yvette Rees, giving Barbara Steele a run for her money) starts bumping off the family and its allies one by one. First for the chop is the ghastly Forrester, whose rampant coiff — a great, wobbling Brylcreem mass that looks like a dead animal perched atop his head — steals every scene it appears in; even as he is drowned in his own bath by invisible hands his hair seems to have a life of its own.

Unusually, the rational/supernatural debate that usually kicks in at this point is given short shrift in *Witchcraft*: in an effective use of the traditional association between femininity and the supernatural, it's obvious that the Lanier womenfolk simply know that dark forces are at work — and, in that sense, are linked to the vengeful Vanessa — while the Lanier men are merely in cheerful denial about the murky origins of their comfortable lifestyle. At least, that is, until Vanessa starts ticking the Lanier females off her To Kill list and Tracy discovers a cowl-wearing coven of Devil-worshipping witches in the old Lanier family crypt (a nice touch in this class-conscious yarn that the cemetery-destroying Laniers retain a fine and private resting place for their own privileged dead).

As in so many horror movies before and since, *Witchcraft* ends with a cleansing conflagration as the mansion goes up in smoke, taking with it Vanessa and Amy, past and future, locked in a deadly final embrace. It's a more ambiguous bonfire of the vanities than many, though: Malvina's final words — "Born in evil — death in flames" — while seemingly spoken in judgement on the undead Vanessa could just as well refer to the Lanier's ancient, purloined property.

David Sutton

THE EARTH DIES SCREAMING (1965)

Lippert Films/Twentieth Century Fox | 62 mins | b&w

Director Terence Fisher; **Producers** Robert L. Lippert and Jack Parsons; **Screenplay** Harry Spalding (as Henry Cross). **Starring** Willard Parker (Jeff Nolan), Virginia Field (Peggy), Dennis Price (Quinn Taggart), Thorley Walters (Edgar Otis), Vanda Godsell (Violet Courtland).

A sudden alien gas attack has apparently wiped out the population of Britain. A few survivors, led by American test pilot Jeff Nolan, take refuge in a village hotel. With indestructible alien robots in the streets and people returning to life as blank-eyed zombies, they must discover how to neutralise the alien influence. Jeff is given a clue by the hum that emanates from the robots.

"Er... hello? Is there anybody out there? Hello... help!" (A strangulated gurgling follows and then the sound of a head thumping on a desk.) Such was the continuity announcer's introduction to Channel 4's graveyard screening of *The Earth Dies Screaming* back in the day, which led us straight into a train ploughing through a level crossing, a car crash-banging into a brick wall and a plane dropping from the sky, followed by the inevitable plume of black smoke rising from behind trees. After the camera takes in bodies sprawled on pavements and on grass, it tilts upwards, above a parkland cedar, until we are left looking at the sky as the title comes looming in aslant. Yes, the Earth in general, and Surrey in particular, is dying, and — despite the overly dramatic promise of the title — it is doing it silently, with (as we learn later) the smell of mushrooms.

In fact these first few minutes are the most eerie and engaging of the film as — accompanied only by Elisabeth Lutyens' soundtrack of dissonant strings and foreboding woodwind, occasionally underpinned by martial drums — Willard Parker's test pilot, Jeff Nolan, drives his Land Rover into a village (Shere, near Guildford), lifts a radio from the shop (needs must), and with rifle in hand, installs himself in a hotel, where he tries the TV and the radio, only to receive nothing but a curious oscillating hum. Eight minutes into the film, the spell is finally broken by the first words, from Dennis Price's decidedly untrustworthy Quinn Taggart, who has walked in unnoticed: "Turn it off."

If Jeff Nolan is a man to have around in a crisis — a solid, dependable American, unfazed by aliens and zombies (in fact, just the sort of man that you can imagine selling real estate, which is exactly what Parker retired to do after making the film) — then Quinn Taggart is his opposite. He is accompanied by Peggy, a woman he has told to pose as his wife (and played

WHO...OR WHAT WERE THEY...
Who Tried To Wipe All Living Creatures Off The Face Of This Earth?

Be There When THE EARTH DIES SCREAMING

STARRING
WILLARD PARKER · VIRGINIA FIELD · DENNIS PRICE
PRODUCED BY ROBERT L. LIPPERT and JACK PARSONS
DIRECTED BY TERENCE FISHER   WRITTEN BY HENRY CROSS
A LIPPERT FILMS LTD PRODUCTION   RELEASED BY 20TH CENTURY-FOX

by Willard Parker's wife, Virginia Field). They are later joined by Otis and (wink, wink) Vi, both a little worse for wear after the company's twenty-fifth anniversary bash, and, rolling into the village in a stolen Vauxhall, young punk Mel, with stripy tie and crotch-hugging white trousers, and his girlfriend, heavy with child. "That's all we need, a cheeky kid and a pregnant girl," says Quinn. "They're probably the most important people on Earth right now," replies Nolan. They are survivors all — cocooned from the mysterious event by a test plane, an oxygen tent, a lab, and an air raid shelter.

The theme is familiar: with the rest of the country apparently lifeless, an unlikely group assembles and does its best to survive, battling whatever it is that is threatening to take over — which in this case, are rudimentary remote control zombie robots, nut-and-bolted together from the contents of various back rooms at Shepperton. Whatever is controlling these proto-cybermen has its designs on the humans too, wanting to turn them into 'sightless, mindless slaves,' as Nolan has it. The group alternate between hotel and village drill hall as they stand guard and attempt to repel the slow-moving robots that,

along with the now blob-eyed villagers, reawakened into zombie life, threaten their existence.

Now here's a curious scene. Lorna, the pregnant girl, rises in the middle of the night to get herself a glass of milk. Nolan watches her protectively from the shadows. A clarinet and strings play a pleasant interlude — until a cyber-zombie approaches from down an alleyway and turns to watch the oblivious girl through the window. Nolan watches it watching Lorna, the music builds to a crescendo — and then the girl turns the light off and walks out of the room, and the zombie-robot turns and teeters past Nolan, who wonders if he should clunk it over the head with his rifle, but doesn't, and lets it walk off. No fuss, no mess. I rather admire a film that only just breaks the hour mark but which is so relaxed about how it spends its time. (Maybe they could only afford to destroy the one costume, which happens when Nolan smashes into a robot in his Land Rover, leaving a smoking heap of circuitry and tin foil in the road.)

Enthusiasts of 'curious goings on down English country lanes' films will realise that *The Earth Dies Screaming* shares a few points of comparison with Wolf Rilla's 1960 film *Village of the Damned* (adapted from John Wyndham's *The Midwich Cuckoos*), in which another undefined event of extraterrestrial origin occurs in a Home Counties setting and leaves a lasting effect. It also shares with this earlier film a minimum budget/maximum effectiveness aesthetic. In this regard, *Village*'s supreme moment comes with Peter Vaughan's village bobby walking his bicycle into the infected area and simply falling over, out cold, to show its potency; *The Earth Dies Screaming* uses this technique early on as a bowler hatted city chap drops his briefcase and umbrella (though not his newspaper) and falls backwards onto a luggage cart on a suburban railway platform.

Lutyens' music certainly lends distinction to the material, and Fisher's direction is admirably spare and unfussy. And if that means that you know the closer a character gets to the camera, the more likely it is they will soon be receiving a nasty surprise, and that when a character says "It's as quiet as a tomb here," they are sorely tempting fate, well that can be filed under 'rewarded expectation.'

At the end, the survivors take off in a plane, hoping that their flight will attract other survivors throughout the land. As I began this review with the words of continuity man Trevor Nichols, it seems only fair to give him the last words too: "Nice to see the traffic moving steadily down that arterial road in the final shot," he said before closedown. Cheeky pup.

Graeme Hobbs

FOUR IN THE MORNING (1965)

West One Films | 94 mins | b&w

Director Anthony Simmons; **Producer** John Morris; **Screenplay** Anthony Simmons.
Starring Judi Dench, Norman Rodway, Ann Lynn, Brian Phelan, Joe Melia.

*London, a summer morning, four a.m. A girl's body is dragged from the
Thames. Further up the river, a nightclub dancer meets her boyfriend, but
resists his attempts to have sex. In another riverside location, an exhausted
young mother is pushed to the edge by her drunken husband. As the day
begins, the mother leaves, but has nowhere to go, the dancer is abandoned by
her boyfriend, and the dead girl remains unidentified.*

According to Charlotte Brundson's study *London in Cinema*,[1] *Four
in the Morning* was conceived originally as a short, wordless film
about an anonymous girl's suicide on the Thames. Had I been
reviewing that, I think I would only have had good things to say
about it, and it's fortunate that enigmatic premise survives and is weaved
through the narrative here. But *Four in the Morning*'s attempts to expand its
reach further along the Thames and link the suicide episode meaningfully
to two, considerably wordier relationship dramas leave it somewhat adrift
in the current, rather like a pooh-stick in choppier waters. Even so, the
three interlinked but unrelated stories do give writer-director Simmons an
opportunity to try his hand at three different filmmaking styles. And although
the episodes don't hang together very successfully, this creative audacity lends
the film a uniqueness that makes it worth seeking out.

The story of the dancer (Ann Lynn) and her reckless boyfriend (Brian Phelan)
is pure European art cinema. As they frolic along the banks of the river, in
turn indulging in heavy petting and sub-existential quarrelling, they could
be Jean-Paul Belmondo and Jean Seberg in *À bout de souffle*, or Monica Vitti
and Alain Delon in *L'Eclisse*. They're on their way to Hammersmith, but they
could be in Paris, Rome or Madrid. Ann Lynn actually looks Italian; Phelan
could pass for French. The story becomes increasingly self-conscious and
pretentious, as the couple articulate cryptic, fractured thoughts and exchange
loaded glances. But it's probably for these scenes that the film won its hatful
of European film festival awards (details of which are served up in a pre-
credit sequence). Where the lovers' story does resonate with the real, ordinary
lives of a young audience is when their true desires come to the fore: he just
wants casual sex; she wants love, a marriage. She may be a nightclub dancer,
a swinger, but she doesn't want sex without love. He feels he's backed a loser,
and storms off unsatisfied.

A young Judi Dench. *Four in the Morning.*

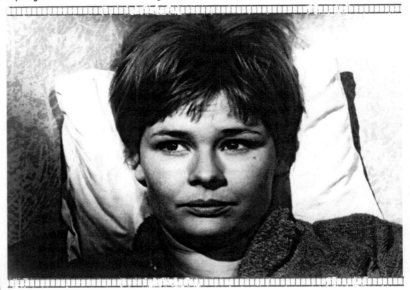

The domestic drama with Judi Dench as a young, stressed-out mother is strident 'kitchen sink' stuff. Dench is excellent (she won a Best Newcomer BAFTA); the early scenes where she struggles to get her baby to sleep (feeding him crushed aspirin in one desperate attempt) pack a real punch — you feel that she may actually become violent to him. But when her drunken Irish husband (Norman Rodway) crashes in with his joke-a-minute friend (Joe Melia), things soon descend into *EastEnders*-level histrionics, which gets tiresome and goes nowhere until the young mother decides to abandon her family. But the highly naturalistic dialogue is convincing and well-played, particularly by Dench and Melia; it's just that Simmons can't really sustain half a film with it, let alone a whole one.

The framing story, as Charlotte Brundson calls it, concerns the young dead girl being dragged from the river. These scenes have Simmons' own stamp on them: starkly vérité in style, yet lyrical and beautiful at the same time. It makes you wish he'd stuck with that original short. The film opens to a haunting image of the river police pulling the rigor-mortis-stiffened girl out of the water, but it's effectively devoid of cheap sensation. The police, certainly, have no time to get alarmed about it. It's just another suicide. Instead they haul the girl around like an item of only modest value; she's treated with

1   Charlotte Brundson, *London in Cinema: The Cinematic City Since 1945* (London: BFI, 2007), pp.200–202.

workaday care rather than respect. And there's a harsh, almost indecent realism to the scene at the mortuary, where her clothes are cut off and she is washed down (a few years ahead of a similar scene in Dusan Makavejev's controversial *The Switchboard Operator* [67]). The camera never flinches, but it's not tasteless. Instead, we see this stiff, anonymous figure as a human being for the first time, as a young girl who's experienced some untold suffering. In itself, it is a fascinating illumination of the Thames' dark and decidedly unromantic side.

There's more to *Four in the Morning* than initially meets the eye. Simmons has done his thinking, and we are left to draw our own conclusions. The Thames flows through the film like blood through a vein. As a linking device, it's quite ingenious; it carries us from one story to another and back again. And it forces us to compare the lives of the three women. All are or have been trapped in some way: Dench by her baby and her loveless marriage, Lynn by her own apparent sexual availability, and the dead girl by some unidentified but equally terrible condition that led to her taking her own life.

I wondered for a while whether the director had been playing around with the chronology of events; maybe it was Dench's or Lynn's character being pulled out of the water at the start of the film. But if it's not one of them this time, there's a possibility it might be one day. The murky Thames is far from a stream of life and regeneration; instead, it's a place for dampened passions and washed-away lives.

Julian Upton

CHARLIE BUBBLES (1967)

Universal/Memorial Enterprises | 89 mins | colour

Director Albert Finney; **Producer** Michael Medwin; **Screenplay** Shelagh Delaney.
Starring Albert Finney (Charlie Bubbles), Billie Whitelaw (Lottie Bubbles), Liza Minnelli (Eliza), Colin Blakely (Smokey), Timothy Garland (Jack Bubbles).

Bored with the trappings of wealth and success in London, novelist Charlie Bubbles, a working class-boy-made-good, travels back to his Manchester roots. But the trip leaves him feeling empty, and he fails to connect with his son and ex-wife when he drops in at their Derbyshire farmhouse. So when he spots an unusual chance to escape, he takes it.

Charlie Bubbles is about a lot of things — class displacement, 'success' and alienation, the English north-south divide — but one of its most revealing preoccupations is with food. Food fills the film, rather like it does Hitchcock's Covent Garden-set *Frenzy* (72). If the characters aren't eating, they're preparing food or talking about it. Charlie's formidable housekeeper castigates him for planning a trip away and not telling her, thus leaving the Sunday roast to go to waste. She further complains about having to make a cheese sandwich for his drinking buddy Smokey in the middle of the night. Back at his old farmhouse in Derbyshire, Charlie's ex-wife talks about food almost constantly, from her mountain of home-made jam to the quality of the eggs she gets from her free range hens. And like a mother hen herself, she fusses around their nine-year-old son's eating habits as if it were her sole purpose in life.

But Charlie (Albert Finney) can't eat. He tries a couple of bites of his wife's home-made bread but can't manage it. ("Aren't you supposed to put yeast in it?") At an expensive restaurant with his lawyers and advisers he runs into Smokey and they run up a huge bill, but not by eating the à la carte food — by dumping it over each other's heads.

Charlie has lost his hunger. The irony is, as a bestselling young author, he can afford all the delicacies he could ever want.

The parallels with Finney's own life are indelible: this is as autobiographical a self-directed film as any star has made. Charlie is a success, he's the northern-working class-boy-made-good, living a life of London glamour. But he is displaced. He is passive and unemotional, nothing stimulates him anymore. He returns to the north in his Rolls-Royce, but he can't fit in. He has no present and he can't go back to his past. His ex-wife is antagonistic

Charlie Bubbles: a preoccupation with food.

and his son indifferent. One day he sees an air balloon tethered in a field. He climbs into it and throws out the sandbags. And that's the last we see of him.

Charlie Bubbles is a fascinating film, and its unevenness adds to its appeal. Finney's sole directorial effort for the big screen, it's a uniquely postmodern addendum to the gritty New Wave dramas that helped make his name. But in rejecting the wholesale realism of that genre in favour of an episodic, semi-surreal narrative and 'progressive' visuals that evoke the work of European masters from Antonioni to Tati, it tells Finney's (and writer Shelagh Delaney's) story with much more poignancy than any straight drama could do.

The pubs and factories and waste ground patches of the north that defined Finney in *Saturday Night and Sunday Morning* — even if he was reacting violently against them — seem alien to him here. Once the rebel, he's now the outsider, a stranger in a strange land. Not even the beauty of Derbyshire (dazzlingly captured by cinematographer Peter Suschtizky) can stimulate him; he remains numb to its rural charms. Within just a handful of years, thanks to his 'London success,' Finney, like Charlie, is unable to exist in the landscape that was his old, hell-raising stomping ground.

If, as critic and chronicler Alexander Walker has said, British cinema moved from the grimy north to the swinging south when it followed Julie Christie from Bradford at the end of *Billy Liar* (63) to her next stop as London's *Darling* in 1965, then *Charlie Bubbles* captures the end of that 'London dream' and speculates on what that new wave of stars might do next. If they couldn't go home again, where could they go? Hollywood, maybe. But what about those who'd already become disillusioned?

When Charlie flies away in the balloon, leaving his life behind, the image might have served as wish fulfilment for Finney, whose identity crisis was brought on, among other things, by the international success of *Tom Jones* (63). But if the actor hadn't the courage in real life to turn his back on what he'd achieved, British stars such as Terence Stamp and James Fox were to do just that. Stamp

disappeared to India for the best part of a decade as the sixties came to a close; Fox gave up acting after *Performance* (70) to sell Bibles, only returning to the screen in 1983. Each had different reasons for moving out of the limelight, but both must have felt some kinship with *Charlie Bubbles*.

Less thoughtful British films carried on swinging for several more years, but *Charlie Bubbles* could already see, in 1967, the slow hangover that the seventies was going to be. There may be something of the hippy mentality in Charlie's final, defiant rejection of materialism, but it goes beyond the modish 'drop-out' philosophy extolled by Timothy Leary et al. Charlie is also rejecting family, roots, friends, stimulants and society; he is pursuing a solitude and an escape that no alignment to a 'cause' could give him.

Perhaps unsurprisingly, this disillusionment with and rejection of 'success' failed to find an audience in Britain and the USA. Finney was appalled by UK distributor Rank's decision not to give the film a circuit release, but within a year or two, the actor was talking about *Charlie Bubbles* with the kind of defeatism all too evident in Charlie's own behaviour. As it made its faltering way around the country in a 'staggered release' of special screenings, he told one audience, "I think my performance spoils the picture." At the same screening he admitted that he'd received a recent statement showing the film's takings in Australia for the previous month: "Thirteen dollars," he said. "Four people on a very rainy night in Brisbane stayed out for the late night show." [1]

But Finney was being hard on himself; he is great in *Charlie Bubbles*, it's just that his character is tired and detached. And as a directorial debut by an actor, it's not outrageous to rank *Charlie Bubbles* alongside Charles Laughton's *Night of the Hunter*. Both films have a beguiling innocence about them — even when dealing with subjects that are dark or cynical — and both display the ambitious audacity of the talented amateur. Finney and Laughton were shaken by seeing their films fail: neither directed for the cinema again. But it would have been great to see what these experimenters would have turned their attention to next.

At least Finney stayed in the film production business. Memorial Enterprises, the company he set up with fellow actor Michael Medwin to make *Charlie Bubbles*, went on to produce some of the most interesting British films of the next few years: PRIVILEGE (67), Mike Leigh's big screen debut *Bleak Moments* (71), the Finney-starring *Gumshoe* (71), and the first two films in Lindsay Anderson's loose 'Mick Travis trilogy,' *If....* (68) and *O Lucky Man!* (73).

Julian Upton

1   Quoted in Alexander Walker, *Hollywood, England* (London: Orion, 2005 edition), pp.332, 351–54.

HEROSTRATUS (1967)

BFI Experimental Film Fund/BBC | 137 mins | colour

Director Don Levy; **Producers** Don Levy and James Quinn; **Screenplay** Don Levy, from an original idea by Don Levy and Alan Daiches. **Starring** Michael Gothard (Max), Gabriella Licudi (Clio), Peter Stephens (Farson), Antony Paul (Pointer), Helen Mirren.

As a protest against modern society, disillusioned young poet Max offers his suicide to Farson's ad agency so they can market his death. Intrigued, Farson plays along with his wishes. Duped into thinking it is the day of his jump, Max goes to the chosen rooftop, where a photographer who tries to prevent him jumping falls to his death in the scuffle. A desperate Max runs through the London streets.

Conceived in 1962, shot between August 1964 and June 1965, assembled into a final edit in 1967, given its premiere in May 1968 when it was the first film shown at London's ICA cinema, and unavailable on any home-viewing format until its release on DVD and Blu-ray forty-one years later in 2009, *Herostratus* now looks like a key film of the 1960s — though you would be well advised to leave any Aquarian age preconceptions about the era at the door. If the film has a totem it is Francis Bacon's 1954 painting *Figure with Meat*, while its signature sound is a raw and desperate scream that is only sometimes silent.

The film (which takes its title from the fame-seeking man who sought to immortalise his name through the destruction of one of the seven wonders of the ancient world — the Temple of Artemis at Ephesus) is ostensibly about

Helen Mirren. *Herostratus.*

Youthful liberation undermined by vanity. *Herostratus*.

a young poet, Max, who offers his suicide to a marketing agency as an act of protest against modern society. However, this is only half the story. In his only recorded interview about the film with Clare Spark in 1973, Levy said that the film — he calls it a documentary in fact — was edited together to form "a network of resonances," with its narrative set like "jewels in a necklace." Indeed, as much as its story, the film is composed around the rhythm and punctuation of sounds and silence, emotional ripples, colour, the flashes and repetition of scenes from elsewhere in its narrative cycle, and even the gestures and movements of its characters.

It begins with the exhausted Max, seen in snatches of running through streets and across waste ground, fetching up in his cheerless room in a dilapidated house next to a main road. The room, scrawled with layers of broken slogans, pasted flyers and cut-up thoughts, is an extension of himself. It is irredeemably stained and even appears to be rusting — with this colour echoed by a low winter sun catching and reddening Max's blond hair. Throughout, traffic drones and buzzes by. The few of Max's thoughts that do surface through this noise are pounded into submission by the sporadic sound of a trench rammer, working on a site somewhere in the distance. As Max looks at himself in the mirror, flash frames slash through his own self-pitying sighs and the film's linearity, showing us glimpses of his fate.

He then embarks on an exhilarating, axe-wielding bout of cathartic destruction in his room, which he leaves with axe and tape player in hand to seek out ad-man Farson, or 'Fars' as he calls him, to sell him his death. "I am going to commit suicide," he says to him. "My congratulations," replies the icy-eyed Farson, calling his bluff. "Why do you want to commit suicide?" he asks

Max. "I've got a headache," he replies.

Soon, Farson and his hatchet man Pointer are outlining their plans for Max's jump from a building. They need to give him a 'good selling image for the general public.' "What do you think I am, a box of detergent or something?" says Max. "As far as we're concerned, you are," replies Farson, who adds that they feel, on consideration, that the best time for a jump is on a Monday at a quarter to two... to help people get over their 'black Monday' feeling. "They're dying for something to happen," says Pointer, without irony.

HEROSTRATUS

Sensuality is never far from the grotesque in *Herostratus*. A striptease is juxtaposed with scenes from an abattoir, while Max, now in Farson's studio bed, spends his time cutting and collaging magazine pictures. Breasts are served on a silver salver, a woman eats hair, and in a *Family Circle* treatment of the Francis Bacon theme, a housewife's head with large upside-down lips emerges from a roast joint of lamb. The comparisons with Bacon are here made more explicit as disturbing time-lapse collages of Max's distorted face are created and held in moments of brief and terrible silence. All of these scenes, together with the archive footage of the century's obscenities, make the bodies of Max and Clio on the bed (Clio, Farson's secretary, offers Max a sympathetic ear and they make love) all the warmer and more precious, and the blue-white morning fog that Max steps out into all the colder.

But Clio is bought and Max is betrayed — or perhaps just gets what he deserves by offering his life to a "Human Crapology Machine, selling it to the native" (as he describes Farson). What Max is blinded to by youthful egotism is that 'human crapology machine' applies as much to self-pitying poets placing themselves voluntarily on 'the scrapheap of humanity' as it does to cynical ad men looking for new material to exploit. For all Max's youthful posturing, it's seen-it-all ad-man Farson who runs the game: "You've been

Herostratus: powered by the peculiar energy of the age.

doodling on water... go through with it... achieve something," he says. His predatory circling of Max on the bed as he reduces him to a fame-seeking failure is bracingly cruel.

There are only two credits in the film; at the beginning, the title, and then at the end, that very word. It seems appropriate for a film that, as Levy said, "scoured the truth of ourselves" during its making. Neither Levy nor his cinematographer Keith Allams made another feature. Gabriella Licudi, whom Levy describes as being 'busted' after the film, gave up acting in 1974, Don Levy took his own life in 1987, Michael Gothard took his in 1992.

Herostratus is important today because it helps to explain some of the peculiar energy of the age. It provides the psychological mortar behind such films as Antonioni's *Blowup* (66) — filmed after *Herostratus*, released before it — with Michael Gothard a close cousin to David Hemmings' photographer (even down to the blond hair and white jeans). It shows how revolutionary energy and liberating, youthful destruction is underpinned, and eventually undermined, by vain, attention-seeking egocentricity. It's a brilliant, if depressingly clear-sighted premise that, especially in the light of Max's involvement with advertising, resonates in our own fame-hungry, image-greedy age.

Graeme Hobbs

THE JOKERS (1967)

Gildor-Scimitar/Adastra/Universal | 94 mins | colour

Director Michael Winner; **Producers** Ben Arbeid, Maurice Foster; **Screenplay** Dick Clement and Ian La Frenais, from a story by Michael Winner. **Starring** Michael Crawford (Michael Tremayne), Oliver Reed (David Tremayne), Harry Andrews (Inspector Marryatt), Brian Wilde (Sgt. Catchpole).

When upper-class rebel Michael Tremayne is thrown out of Sandhurst military school for failing to follow orders, he teams up with his seemingly high achieving but equally mischievous architect brother David to rock the establishment with a series of audacious pranks, culminating in the 'borrowing' of the Crown Jewels. But when the police track them down, one brother betrays the other.

Returning to Britain after his lengthy Hollywood sojourn in the seventies, Michael Winner soon came to be regarded as a bit of a joke. His uncouth 1983 version of *The Wicked Lady* garnered some of the worst reviews of his career — no small achievement — and the press sniped with haughty dismay as he embarked on yet another *Death Wish* movie (his third). His private life was also up for criticism, with the tabloids tut-tutting at the affair he began with the twenty-plus-years-younger actress, Jenny Seagrove.

Over the next decade and a half, he blithely carried on making the movies he wanted to make. By the time he made *Bullseye!* (90), *Dirty Weekend* (93) and *Parting Shots* (98) he seemed hopelessly out of touch as a filmmaker.

But what did Winner care? He had thirty million in the bank, and he could still earn good money as a TV personality and all-round bon viveur. Criticism seemed irrelevant. So it was very easy to forget that he had once been a prolific and versatile director of some actually rather good films.

In the late fifties, barely out of his teens, the precocious Winner talked himself into a job with Harold Baim, a producer of travelogues and shorts. Learning his craft quickly, by his mid twenties he was directing features. After an obligatory nudie-cutie (*Some Like It Cool* [62]) and an oddball Gilbert and Sullivan adaptation starring Frankie Howerd (*The Cool Mikado* [63]), he found his stride with a series of progressively ambitious comedies and dramas, all of which could sit comfortably within these pages: *West 11* (63), *The System* (64), *You Must Be Joking* (65), *I'll Never Forget What's'isname* (67) and *Hannibal Brooks* (68). But perhaps the most effective and successful of this impressive run was *The Jokers*.

MICHAEL CRAWFORD
OLIVER REED
HARRY ANDREWS

THE JOKERS

TECHNICOLOR

"JAMES DONALD

DANIEL MASSEY MICHAEL HORDERN GABRIELLA LICUDI LOTTE TARP

An Outrageous film!

OPENS THURSDAY 15th JUNE Leicester Sq. Theatre

Fuelled by the optimism of a carefree, affluent sixties London, *The Jokers* shamelessly embraces all that was 'swinging.' It's a film that could only have been made by a director in touch enough with the times to recognise that lack of depth was itself a raison d'etre. But for all its rampant superficiality, *The Jokers* is infectious.

Just the presence of Michael Crawford and Oliver Reed as upper class, rebellious brothers waging mischievous war on the establishment, captures the era perfectly: Crawford was fresh from *The Knack* (65), perhaps the epitome of the swinging London comedy; Reed was steeped in the sexy, urbane dangerousness of a new breed of star. Articulate, moneyed, well dressed, the brothers represent the groovy young sticking it to the dusty old; there's something of a Bonnie and Clyde sensibility to their criminal pranks — the anti-heroes as heroes. But these rebels are well connected and debonair, not seedy or desperate; they've turned to crime for kicks, not from desperation. They're a bit like Leopold and Loeb, but without the dash of perversity.

This is post-Great-Train-Robbery era villainy. There's a measure of respect for the would-be thieves. Crime might not pay, but it sure looks like a lot of fun, glamorous even, and it's better than working. Even though we're just a few years down the line, *The Jokers* seems a generation away from the austere, monochrome thrillers of Stanley Baker (although Crawford initially wanted Baker to play his brother), and the crime comedies of Ealing and Peter Sellers. The sun's come up on the caper movie, and everyone's out for the party.

FILM REVIEWS

'A one-man film industry' said *CinemaTV Today* magazine of Winner in December 1972.

Winner's night out

Michael Winner (left) is seen here with **Stanley** and **Mrs Baker** at the premiere of his latest film, "The Mechanic." Winner has recently been described as "a one-man film industry"—"The Mechanic" took more than £10,000 in its first four days. (See CHB-W's Box Office.)

Of course, it's all very silly, but Winner moves things along fast enough to stop you really noticing. Crawford and Reed look nothing like brothers (Reed stocky and saturnine, Crawford like he's just pecked his way out of an egg), but they do have chemistry and sharp, lively dialogue, courtesy of Dick Clement and Ian La Frenais, to keep them afloat.

Winner, for his part, employs all the trendy visual tricks in the book (none of them his own) — jazzy, *Ipcress File* camera angles, frenetic editing, Dick Lester-style undercranking — and it serves the comedy well (*The Jokers* is his funniest film). But there's still a trace of ugliness here: when Reed, always convincingly nasty, is roughing up a couple of guards, it's a touch more brutal than it needs to be, and momentarily scratches the feelgood veneer of the film. This proved ominous: it soon transpired that Winner wasn't really about comedy at all, he was about violence. Not long after *The Jokers*, he decamped to the US, where he traded laughs for blows in an effective series of thrillers and actioners — *Lawman* (70), *Chato's Land* (72), *The Stone Killer* (73), *Scorpio* (73) — that culminated in the first (and best) of the ugly and cold hearted but commercially triumphant *Death Wish* series.

But before that, the director had a very offbeat British stew of violence (and sex) to inflict on us: THE NIGHTCOMERS.

Julian Upton

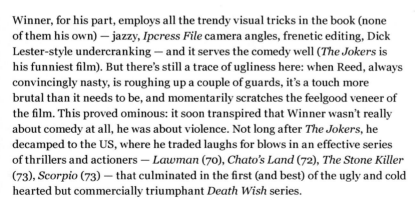

OUR MOTHER'S HOUSE (1967)

Filmways Pictures/Heron Film Productions/MGM | 101 mins | colour

Director Jack Clayton; **Producer** Jack Clayton; **Screenplay** Jeremy Brooks and Haya Harareet, from the novel *Our Mother's House* by Julian Gloag. **Starring** Dirk Bogarde (Charlie Hook), Margaret Brooks (Elsa Hook), Pamela Franklin (Diana Hook), Mark Lester (Jiminee).

Seven children, fearful of life in an orphanage, bury their recently deceased mother in the garden where her grave becomes a macabre place of worship. Tensions grow between the children as keeping their tragic situation a secret becomes increasingly difficult. Matters take an unexpected twist when Charlie Hook, purported father of the brood, arrives to get his hands on the inheritance.

ur Mother's House is a grim little film. Set in suburban sixties Croydon, everything is distinctly drab in tone, from the large Victorian house to the schoolyard of grey-uniformed children. Gothic melodrama pervades the atmosphere from the outset, as we witness the death of frail Violet Hook (Annette Carell) in her sickbed, eyes upturned in her cadaverous face, a hand dangling limply from the edge of the bed. Her children, just preparing themselves for 'Mother time,' react with varying degrees of panic, sorrow and bewilderment, but eventually agree that burying Mother in the garden is the best course of action.

Mother's bedroom furniture is hastily transferred to the garden shed, which becomes 'the tabernacle' where 'Mother time' continues, now by candlelight and with Diana (Pamela Franklin) acting as medium. "Speak to us, oh Mother, for we love you," she intones, swaying unnervingly in Mother's rocking chair. We are never sure whether Diana genuinely contacts her Mother's spirit, but the salient point is the act of mediumship itself, fraudulent or otherwise. A pious Christian woman, Mother has instilled in the children a fervent religiosity: their key reference point is the Bible and young Dunstan (John Gugolka) certainly has the makings of a preacher as he repeatedly explodes at his siblings. "God will rip your insides out and leave you to rot if you play in the garden anymore!" he rages at younger sister Gerty (Phoebe Nicholls). The children see no conflict between their staunch Christian upbringing and these nightly séances. Their improvised religion seems to have the makings of a central theme, but it quickly disappears with the arrival of estranged father Charlie, his appearance marking a sudden and rather abrupt reorientation of focus.

With Charlie ensconced in Mother's house, Victorian drama begins to co-exist uneasily with hints of swinging London. A gambler and womaniser partial to a beer or two, Cockney Charlie is a mysterious character: not wholly

Distinctly drab: Dirk Bogarde and clan in *Our Mother's House*.

reprehensible, but not completely likeable either. His interaction with the children smacks of the absent father given a second chance, but his activities suggest to the viewer he is not all that he seems; he is visibly impressed at little Jiminee's (Mark Lester) talent for forging his mum's signature on the monthly annuity cheque. As he begins to make himself at home, bringing home women and throwing parties, daughter Elsa becomes visibly distraught. "Doreen!" she scoffs, listening to Charlie greeting a young woman at the door. "What a common name. They're whores if you ask me."

Despite the trappings of a quaint family tale, the sexual undercurrent of sixties exploitation is still beneath the surface. Chasing the children around the garden, Charlie knocks himself and Diana to the ground. Laid on the grass, she looks back at him with coy approval, a faint smile playing on her lips, and Charlie hurriedly extricates himself from the situation to join the other children. Any illusions of incestuous romance she might have about her newly found father are quashed when she later discovers the wayward Doreen lounging in Charlie's bed, provoking a swift and tearful exit.

Pamela Franklin's performance as Diana is just one of a host of stunning turns by the children, with even the youngest cast members performing competently throughout — many of whom had never appeared on screen before. "I'm old stale Quayle,"[1] pronounces Jiminee, prancing around the kitchen in a calculatedly cute opening scene. "And I'm going to give you a

proper dusting." It's unfortunate we don't see very much of home help Mrs Quayle (Yootha Joyce), as her unsympathetic demeanour and dowdy glamour add a welcome bit of humour to the early sections of the film. The big name is of course Dirk Bogarde but, as Roger Ebert notes, 'it really isn't his picture... It belongs to the kids.'[2] Bogarde's character, though initially intriguing, is a stock one and not particularly difficult to analyse, whereas the children manage to maintain the viewer's attention throughout.

Our Mother's House defies simple classification. Parallels with Clayton's earlier *The Innocents* (61) are clear: the same sense of unease, the implied threats of a gloomy Gothic mansion, but the film is more psychological suspense than straight horror: there's no hint of sensationalism and watching the children crowd around their mother's body is more touching than shocking. The most disturbing aspect of the film is the move to a primitive 'us and them' mentality, as the children demarcate themselves into those loyal to dear Mother and those who resist the spiritual interventions of Diana. "Do you think you know better than Mother?" cries Dunstan, as elder brother Hubert voices his objections. "Do you think you know better than God?" Upon the film's release in 1967, Roger Ebert mused: 'It is, I suppose, a horror film. It is set in a bleak old Gothic mansion, and it has dead bodies and communication with the spirit world and all that. But it is a ghost story without ghosts.'[3] Looming over the whole thing however, are the ghosts of the past. Mother remains something of an enigma to the children, yet her presence remains in her stuffy bedroom empire to exercise an imaginary control. "Mother wouldn't like it" is Elsa's unrelenting refrain, whilst Charlie openly battles the memory of Mother, removing her furniture from the tabernacle and introducing copious amounts of alcohol into the religious household.

The dichotomy between Gothic tragedy and trendy sixties London is interesting, but too jarring at times to work together effectively, with the presence of *Playboy* and flashy open-topped cars just a tad too obvious. It is 'almost perversely unfashionable' says Robert Murphy, and Alexander Walker seems to agree, noting that 'Its Dickensian terrors [fit] awkwardly into Welfare State England.'[4] That said, *Our Mother's House* is a well-executed drama with Clayton's trademark air of disquiet just discernible enough to remain compelling.

Jennifer Wallis

1   Neil Sinyard, *Jack Clayton* (Manchester: Manchester University Press, 2000), p.134.
2   Roger Ebert, 'Review: *Our Mother's House*,' Chicago Sun-Times, 13 November 1967. http://rogerebert. suntimes.com [Last accessed August 2009].
3   Ibid.
4   Robert Murphy, *Sixties British Cinema* (London: BFI, 1992), p.81. Alexander Walker, *Hollywood, England: The British Film Industry in the Sixties* (London: Orion, 2005), p.363

PRIVILEGE (1967)

World Film Services Ltd./Memorial Enterprises Ltd./Universal | 103 mins | colour

Director Peter Watkins; **Producers** John Heyman and Timothy Burrill; **Screenplay** Norman Bogner, from an original story by Johnny Speight, with additional scenes and dialogue by Peter Watkins. **Starring** Paul Jones (Steven Shorter), Jean Shrimpton (Vanessa Ritchie), Mark London (Alvin Kirsch), William Job (Andrew Butler), Jeremy Child (Martin Crossley).

Steven Shorter is a pop music phenomenon, whose carefully managed stage act is used by Steven Shorter Enterprises Ltd. and the British coalition government, first as a means of deflecting public attention away from political involvement, and then as a way of converting people to faith and flag. Steven meanwhile, experiencing a little human warmth with a woman hired to paint his portrait, is beginning to question his role.

'A film so bizarre, so controversial, it shall crucify your mind to the tree of conscience.' Nope, I don't know what it means either, but these words – written to the right of the disjointed puppet figure of Paul Jones, wearing Jean Shrimpton's face for his breastplate on the US release of *Privilege*'s soundtrack album – alert you to a number of things about the film: it eludes easy reduction, it's seriously absurd, it may well be vaguely offensive to those of a religious bent, and lastly, even though its intent is entirely serious (showing how the entertainment industry can serve as an officially sanctioned outlet for energies that might otherwise be directed into political disruption) you watch it too seriously at your own peril; i.e., it's OK to laugh. After all, this is a film that starts with the acne-pocked pop singer Steven Shorter, 'the most desperately loved entertainer in the world,' complete with 'SS'-initialled lapels, raising his hand in a half-hearted Nazi salute as he is paraded in an open top vehicle through the ticker-taped streets of Birmingham.

Watkins partially based his film on *Lonely Boy*, the 1962 film from the National Film Board of Canada about Paul Anka and the new phenomenon of 'the astonishing transformation of an entertainer into an idol, worshipped by millions of fans around the world.' "Paul, you no longer belong to yourself, you belong to the world," says Anka's manager at one point. This view is taken to extremes in *Privilege* where Steven Shorter belongs to Steven Shorter Enterprises Ltd. ("He is, in every sense of the word, a gilt-edged investment," says his press officer). Three hundred Steven Shorter discothèques throughout the land, built 'to spread happiness throughout Britain,' are abutted by Steve Dream Palaces — 'designed to keep people happy and buying British.'

Pop will eat itself. *Privilege.*

Privilege is a brave, unsettling oddity of a film. Its lead is, deliberately, a character-free zombie, leached of drive by the parasitic life that feeds on him from all sides. Unsurprisingly, the one woman who tries to get close to him, Jean Shrimpton's artist, commissioned by the Ministry of Culture to paint his portrait, sees 'a strange sort of emptiness' in him. Both Jones and Shrimpton received pitiless reviews for their performances, but their scenes together have a ring of halting authenticity that contrasts with the cynical product and presentation that Shorter represents. As for Manfred Mann singer Paul Jones, his portrayal of Shorter is a thankless one. Anyone going to the film based on seeing him rocking out on some of the promotional posters would have wondered what on Earth they had come to see. His wearied, flat and fluey delivery of lines such as "Quite a phenomenon, aren't I" seems like exactly what was required of the role, but it was never going to win him many plaudits.

Jones was chosen for the role ahead of Eric Burdon and Marc Bolan, both of whom filmed screen tests, but it's hard to imagine either of them hitting the stranded, strained, nervy and desperate look that Jones gets from the very opening shot when he announces how happy he apparently is to be back in Britain after his American tour. Witness too the scene at the promotional party when he turns and stares over his shoulder directly out of the camera and at us, with a 'get me out of here' look, a moment that anticipates the many glances to camera in Watkins' 1974 film, *Edvard Munch.*

After a while, Steven Shorter Enterprises Ltd., backed by the coalition government, which up to that point had 'asked all entertainment agencies to usefully divert the violence of youth' by keeping them happy, off the streets and out of politics, decides that a change of tack is needed 'for the sake of national cohesion and survival.' Thus commences 'Christian Crusade week' — a 'great drive for God,' to promote one faith, one God and one flag. The cathartic violence of Shorter's previous stage show, which provided the public with a necessary release from the state of the world, changes to an opportunity for him, and them, to repent. With the 'He is Coming' posters already printed, his band — now dressed in Franciscan sandals and tonsure toupees — rehearse an excruciating version of Onward Christian Soldiers, at which their assembled Reverend holinesses smile sourly and admit that it might help their cause. Shorter is newly clad in Cardinal's vermillion.

The climactic concert for Christian week is really quite a sight, resembling a mixture of Nazi rally, Ku Klux Klan meeting, Bonfire Night, a cacophonous battle of brass bands, pop concert and cut-price Olympic opening ceremony all in one. After a Hitler-esque Reverend takes the podium to promote the message 'We Will Conform,' and a blackshirted Hitler-saluting band play Jerusalem, Shorter takes the stage, inspires the lame to rise from their wheelchairs, and, as we learn later, persuades 49,000 people in the stadium to pledge themselves to God. (Ironically, given his role as a vessel for wholesale conversion in the film, Paul Jones himself devoted his life to Christ's ministry after Cliff Richard took him and his wife to see evangelist Luis Palau at White City in 1984.)

Meanwhile, Shorter is cracking up. One song of his has the words "Forgive me please, I've been a bad, bad boy." Well, at an industry beano he really is a bad, bad boy. As the guests wait in excruciating silence for his words, he holds the absurd, tawdry bauble with which he has been presented, a platinum statuette of a singer with a rotating microphone that earlier had taken the position of a large erection, glinting in the light, flicks the switch and listens to his own song wind down as the batteries go. "You've made me nothing... I hate you," he says to the assembled guests. Overnight, Steven Shorter becomes 'a bad investment,' having misused his position of privilege 'to disturb the public's peace of mind.' *Privilege* ends with Watkins' foreboding narration: "It's going to be a happy year, in Britain, this year, in the near future."

At the time of going to press, *Privilege* was Watkins' last British film, after which he went into self-imposed exile. It is a measure of his film's originality that it is utterly resistant to being assimilated into anyone else's vision.

Graeme Hobbs

THE ANNIVERSARY (1968)

Hammer/Warner Bros.-Seven Arts| 95 mins | colour

Director Roy Ward Baker; **Producer** Jimmy Sangster; **Screenplay** Jimmy Sangster, from the play by Bill MacIlwraith. **Starring** Bette Davis (Mrs Taggart), Jack Hedley (Terry Taggart), Sheila Hancock (Karen Taggart), James Cossins (Henry Taggart), Christian Roberts (Tom Taggart), Elaine Taylor.

During the course of another of their domineering mother's wedding anniversary celebrations (which she continues to host despite her husband being dead), the Taggart brothers and their partners are once again belittled, ridiculed, manipulated and verbally abused by the old lady. But this time Tom Taggart's new girlfriend decides to stand up to her.

A peculiar film for Hammer to release near the peak of its horror wave, *The Anniversary* is a waspishly funny chamber piece, a comedy of bad manners, which makes almost no attempt to open out its highly theatrical source material. But in Bette Davis's grotesque, one-eyed Mrs Taggart — festooned in a hellish gown of traffic light red, morbidly complemented by an eye patch of the same colour — the studio was actually unleashing a monster to match its ongoing parade of vampires, werewolves and ghouls.

As a play, *The Anniversary* had been a hit during the West End's 1966 season, with Mona Washbourne holding court as the egregious Mrs Taggart. But after Hammer's success importing Bette Davis for the more conventionally thrilling *The Nanny* three years earlier, the studio decided the material was ideally suited to her. Davis's flagging career had been re-energised by the guignol-esque *What Ever Happened to Baby Jane* in 1962, and she had stayed in the horror vein ever since. But, at sixty, she was now nearing the end of her time as a leading lady, even in campy horror films; *The Anniversary* was clearly a platform for her to bow out with a bang.

This she certainly did, both on and off screen. Despite her dimming star, Davis was still more than able to act the diva, issuing haughty demands before the production started (as well as trying to force writer-producer Jimmy Sangster into sexual submission after a meal at her Hollywood home)[1] and throwing her weight around on-set, antagonising the rest of the cast (most of whom had come from the original stage production) and getting the original director, Alvin Rakoff, fired three weeks into filming.

Hammer, rather unused to this kind of horseplay, dealt with Davis's demands

I Spy
with my little eye
Something
beginning with
SEX...
and I mean to put
a stop to it.

BETTE DAVIS
THE ANNIVERSARY

smoothly and diplomatically, and made an intelligent choice in quickly drafting in director Roy Ward Baker, who had known Davis from his sojourn in Hollywood in the early fifties. Not only was Baker a friendly face, he was also solid and efficient and, although he threw out all the previously filmed material, he had the production back on track in good time.

And at this point Baker was still glad of the work. After the critical mauling of his THE SINGER NOT THE SONG (60) and the commercial failure of his 'youth picture' *Two Left Feet* (63), the former Rank golden boy had gone into television exile, churning out episodes of *The Saint*, *The Champions* and *Department 'S.'* So humbled was he by this experience that when Hammer called on him to direct *Quatermass and the Pit* (67) — his first big screen assignment in four years — he agreed to change his screen credit from Roy Baker to Roy Ward Baker to avoid confusion with one of the studio's young dubbing mixers. That he was able to 'discard' his old (and hard-won) identity for the benefit of an otherwise anonymous sound engineer is testament to the 'get on and make do' philosophy that personified the kind of directors that usually worked for Hammer. As David Thomson has said: "Hammer horrors have always seemed the work of decent men who tended the garden on weekends." [2]

So while Baker was 'getting on and making do,' Bette Davis was busy winding up the cast, telling Sheila Hancock, for example, that she would have preferred Jill Bennett in her part, even though Hancock had created the role

Firing on all bitchy cylinders: Bette Davis in *The Anniversary*.

on stage. The result of this, however, probably helped the film more than Baker's sensible handling did. There is a real indignation in the interplay of the cast, particularly between the women: both Sheila Hancock and Elaine Taylor, as the unfortunate daughter-in-law and would-be daughter-in-law respectively, are effective in standing up to Davis; there is a burning frustration in their performances that must have been partly exacerbated by the older star's needling. The men are less successful, but James Cossins stands out as the perverted loner brother, given to stealing pantyhose from washing lines and pegging up ten bob notes in their place.

The Anniversary is of value as a serviceable record of an entertaining, campy play that would otherwise have been long forgotten — it's like a high key, domestic sitcom version of Pinter's *The Homecoming*, with a fearsome harridan replacing the bullying patriarch. But its lasting appeal is as a vehicle for Bette Davis to deliver what is effectively the last magnificent shrew of her screen career. Davis had always excelled at acidic, catty dialogue, and she gets her fair share in *The Anniversary* (to her son Tom's girlfriend, minutes after meeting her: "Shirley, my dear, would you mind sitting somewhere else? Body odour offends me."), spewing out every line with a spectacular, shrill vindictiveness while enjoying every minute of the opulent turmoil she is creating.

Davis was less successful in her subsequent leading roles on the big screen — she came back to the UK for another, far more forgettable stage-to-screen transfer, *Connecting Rooms* (69); was humiliated in hippy clothes in the embarrassingly 'with it' *Bunny O'Hare* (71); and chewed the scenery in the espionage hokum *Madame Sin* (72). By the mid seventies she was doing

1   Jimmy Sangster, *Inside Hammer* (London: Reynolds & Hearn, 2001), p.118.

2   David Thomson, *A Biographical Dictionary of Film*, (London: Andre Deutsch, 1994 edition), p.244.

her best work on television. But she did get a chance, at nearly eighty, for a distinguished swansong, alongside fellow screen legend Lillian Gish, in Lindsay Anderson's gently elegiac *The Whales of August* (87). But she was frail then, and far less dangerous. Thankfully, *The Anniversary* catches her firing on all bitchy cylinders!

Julian Upton

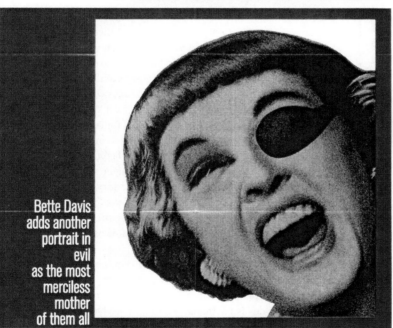

BETTE DAVIS IN THE ANNIVERSARY

Bette Davis adds another portrait in evil as the most merciless mother of them all

...and remember, Mum's the word for depravity!

Also Starring SHEILA HANCOCK · JACK HEDLEY · CHRISTIAN ROBERTS · JAMES COSSINS · ELAINE TAYLOR
Produced by JIMMY SANGSTER · Directed by ROY BAKER · Screenplay by JIMMY SANGSTER · Color by DeLuxe · A Seven Arts-Hammer Production

151

THE BIRTHDAY PARTY (1968)

Amicus/ABC/Palomar Pictures | 119 mins | colour

Director William Friedkin; **Producers** Max J. Rosenberg and Milton Subotsky; **Screenplay** Harold Pinter, from his stage play. **Starring** Robert Shaw (Stanley), Patrick Magee (McCann), Dandy Nichols (Meg), Sydney Tafler (Goldberg), Moultrie Kelsall (Petey), Helen Fraser.

Stanley is the only guest at a rundown, seaside boarding house owned by Meg and Petey. Into their dreary lives come two strangers, Goldberg and McCann, who have apparently been sent by 'the organisation' to retrieve Stanley. A birthday party, held for the reluctant Stanley, alters the course of events.

Harold Pinter's original, controversial stage play, *The Birthday Party*, was first performed in 1958 in Cambridge and then revived by the Royal Shakespeare Company in 1964. Initially, it was panned by the critics, who found its confusing, combative atmosphere over the top. So it's hardly surprising that this film version is 'forgotten,' given that the drab, postwar British landscape it depicts lacks both the saucy comedy of the *Carry On* films and the overt political stance of the British New Wave movement. (The grimy and unpleasant boarding house setting of Pinter's original production is retained, exaggerated even; here, the kitchen sink is all sour milk, gravy tea and blackened fried bread.) But the device of conjuring psychological horrors out of the supposed calm of a holiday boarding house has a fairly established tradition — from Roald Dahl's 1959 short story *The Landlady* through films such as *10 Rillington Place* and television's *The League of Gentlemen* by way of Alan Bennett. And, although it is directed (effectively) by an American, *The Birthday Party* is a British film that is entirely English.

The film is set on the south coast of England (filmed in the Sussex town of Worthing), but the joy generally associated with holidays by the sea is singularly lacking — the opening shot of a row of deckchairs being laid out on a terminally grey day is particularly memorable. The dislocation that runs through the entire film begins with the title sequence, as a plush limousine makes its way through the terraced streets accompanied by the painful, greatly amplified sound of tearing paper. The landscape is briefly viewed through the curved lens of a car wing mirror, one of a number of elliptical shots in the film. But the fragmentary nature of the psychodrama comes mainly from the dialogue. Pinter was the first to include 'realistic' conversation into drama, and the pauses, mis-hearings, non sequiturs and grunts are maintained in this production. The film's text, like the play, is a clever fusion of outbursts, soliloquies, cricketing metaphors and Irish ballads. The mood is intensely claustrophobic even though the action in the film,

Robert Shaw is hysterical. *The Birthday Party.*

unlike the play, occasionally moves out of the sitting/ dining room. Indeed, when the setting moves beyond the threshold, this claustrophobia is intensified. At one point Stanley is seen mooching outside the front door looking bewildered and lost. Friedkin exaggerates the mood of the living room with a fish-eye lens and alienating effects such as shifts from colour to monochrome and solarisation.

Although occasionally hysterical, Robert Shaw makes an effectively troubled Stanley; his lopsided, malicious grin makes him almost impossible to like even when he is being besieged by the two strangers. But his technique is at odds with the understated gloom of the other characters, who seem to have transferred their stage characters better onto film. The two strangers who have "come to do a job" — Goldberg (flashy, Jewish) and McCann (menacing, psychotic) — are built on that fine British cinematic construct of the smart-yet-sleazy hood, later perfected in films such as *Performance* (70) and *Get Carter* (71). And Goldberg delivers to Stanley one of cinema's great understated threats: "When did you last wash up a cup?"

Needless to say, the climactic 'birthday party' is a disaster. Meg and Goldberg both make emotional speeches that have no effect on the visibly crumbling Stanley. The pivotal game of blind man's bluff is truly terrifying. A harmless children's activity becomes a deranged nightmare. McCann stumbles around the room like a demented Frankenstein's monster. When the lights fail during the game, a torch becomes the only source of illumination. The fragmentary glimpse of the sadism being perpetrated in the dark leaves the viewer breathless. With hindsight, it is hard not to view this part of the film as laying the ground for Friedkin's later *The Exorcist* (73).

The haunting beauty of Pinter's writing has often been difficult to render on the big screen. But the grim tragedy of this film is worth celebrating. As famed *New York Times* critic Vincent Canby once noted: '*The Birthday Party* may not be a great movie, but it's a good recording of an extraordinary play.'

Mark Goodall

THE BOFORS GUN (1968)

Copelfilms/Everglades Productions/Rank | 105 mins | colour

Director Jack Gold; **Producers** Robert Goldston and Otto Plaschkes; **Screenplay** John McGrath, from his play *Events While Guarding the Bofors Gun*. **Starring** David Warner (Lance-Bombardier Evans), Nicol Williamson (O'Rourke), Ian Holm (Flynn), John Thaw (Featherstone), Donald Gee (Crawley), Peter Vaughan, Barbara Jefford.

Before his return to England from Germany to begin a second attempt at officer training, Lance Bombardier Terry Evans has to suffer a final stint on guard duty with a bunch of embittered, cynical old squaddies. The night is centred on a battle of wills between Evans and the unruly Gunner Danny O'Rourke, a force of nature determined to ruin everything for everyone. Inevitably, tragedy befalls both men.

Why Jack Gold's feature film debut has slipped through the cracks of British film history is puzzling. Rarely seen on television screens in over forty years, its first DVD release wasn't until 2012. A dour portrayal of the humdrum duties of 1950s National Service it may be, but *The Bofors Gun* is spliced together with a powerful, neurotic interplay between David Warner as Evans, a well-meaning but ineffectual young officer wannabe, and his guard room nemesis Nicol Williamson (O'Rourke), a simmering barrel of resentment, intent to cause chaos at every step.

A film revolving around class and responsibility, or lack of it, the drama is set in the pressure cooker atmosphere of a guard room and barracks in Germany in 1954. Undoubtedly an actor's piece, it is slow and wordy but far from static; the cross-conversations and banter are occasionally prodigious as Warner jousts with Williamson and his band of supporting players that includes a scornful Donald Gee, a fresh-faced Ian Holm and John Thaw (with whom director Gold would remain a close friend and associate for the rest of his life).

The tone is set immediately. Our first view of Evans sees him listening to a genteel string recital before his return to barracks to complete his last night as an NCO; he is set to return to England to give officer training a final try — failure is not an option. This is not a man cut out for the rigours of rank and file army life. But, as Evans sniffs at one point, what is the alternative — to return to Manchester and end up like his father, selling paraffin?

On his return to the barracks, Evans finds that his final night is to be spent as the officer in charge of an awkward, rum bunch of bored troopers, intent

A sinewy portrayal of class war. Nicol Williamson and Ian Holm in *The Bofors Gun*.

on giving him as hard a time as possible. The main event of the evening is the war of wills between Evans and the elemental Irishman O'Rourke. They are poles apart: Warner is fragile and wishy-washy, while Williamson, in his finest big screen role, is jovial, cynical, passive-aggressive, an explosion waiting to happen; he sees it as his personal duty to goad and probe the weaker Evans. After one spat between O'Rourke and Evans, the most memorable scene of the film sees O'Rourke asking whether Evans is "a fox man or a hound man," before O'Rourke calmly walks to a brazier and picks out a burning coal with his bare hand, glaring icily at Evans and dropping it smouldering on his desk.

In between them, acting as a strange counterbalance, is Ian Holm as Flynn. He is sympathetic to Evans and understands his 'duty,' but also holds any kind of authority in disdain. "I despise people taken in by pips and stripes and wigs and chains," he says at one point. But if Evans can't control a guard room overnight, what chance does he have of being raised to an officer and 'getting on'? This 'getting on' is one of the fulcrums on which the film swings. Social mobility was one of the yardsticks by which most challenging cultural material was judged throughout the 1960s. Know your place. Class suspicions. Privilege does not breed popularity. All of this the timid handwringer Evans knows, but he is desperate to escape from it.

O'Rourke's endless needling descends into destruction when he slopes off to get drunk at the NAAFI. In an unintentionally funny scene, he runs full pelt and jumps through an open window, nearly killing himself on the parade ground below. This is controversy that will jeopardise Evans' trip back to England for sure. If his commanding officers get to know about it, his chance of an officer's life is finished. The unravelling of the evening is handled well by Gold: Evans has empathy for O'Rourke and doesn't want to punish him more than he is already punishing himself, but once again, his shortcomings as officer material are only amplified. He is just simply too nice.

The film ends on a stiff, bathetic note. No doubt it worked well on stage, but as a screen moment it becomes overly contrived and melodramatic. After going AWOL and staggering around the compound, O'Rourke bellows: "No more excuses," before meeting his demise at his owns hands on the stroke of midnight, on what would have been his thirtieth birthday. But the final victory, it seems, is O'Rourke's, as one of Evans' commanding officers calmly tells him: "You won't be going home for donkey's years."

The Bofors Gun has weathered well. Jack Gold forges a sinewy portrayal of class war that starkly picks out the frustration, anger and burgeoning social mobility of the mid 1960s, with a frisson of post-WWII nuclear scaremongering thrown in. The film was a critical success on release. Ian Holm picked up a Best Supporting Actor award at the 1969 BAFTAs, although Nicol Williamson was overlooked as Best Actor in favour of a sentimental nod to the late Spencer Tracey for *Guess Who's Coming to Dinner*. Looking back from a distance, Williamson's lack of a more solid and rewarding film career is frustrating, as frustrating as the fact that *The Bofors Gun* continues to be unseen and overlooked.

Gary Ramsay

CORRUPTION (1968)

a.k.a. Laser Killer, a.k.a. Carnage | Oakshire Productions/Titan International/Columbia Pictures

Director Robert Hartford-Davis; **Producer** Peter Newbrook; **Screenplay** Donald and Derek Ford. **Starring** Peter Cushing (Sir John Rowan), Sue Lloyd (Lynn Nolan), Noel Trevarthen (Steve Harris), Kate O'Mara (Val Nolan), David Lodge (Groper).

When he disfigures his fiancée in an accident, the noted surgeon Sir John Rowan comes up with an innovative procedure that restores her beauty. But it's only a temporary fix requiring a regular supply of unwitting female donors, who Sir John begrudgingly murders in the name of love.

Lurking in the less frequented annals of British cinema, the horror film *Corruption* tries at once to offer something new while paying lip service to those that have inspired it, and burns up spectacularly in the process. It dumps on the British Gothic tradition in favour of a more aggressive Continental approach — almost an anti-Hammer film if you will — and places at its centre Peter Cushing in a role that serves him no favours.

Poor Peter Cushing. The gentleman of horror has never looked as crestfallen as he does here, in the role of Sir John Rowan, a surgeon of some repute. Cushing is perfectly comfortable leaning over books at his desk, and on vacation serving drinks in a cravat and jaunty sailor's cap. But engaged in *Corruption*'s less wholesome pursuits the usually indomitable actor crumbles under the strain. An amorous Cushing canoodling at a party is alarming enough a sight, yet it is nothing next to our very own 'Baron Frankenstein' wrestling with a topless prostitute and stabbing her mercilessly on the floor of a Soho knocking shop. Cushing gives his all, of course, throwing himself around as might a younger man,

Peter Cushing, masking his embarrassment. *Corruption.*

but he is desperate, as if by flailing hard enough he will disengage himself from the whole sordid business. By the time the second victim comes around, Cushing can no longer hide his disdain. Sizing up a lone woman on a train, he sweeps his eyes from his bag of murder tools to fix the camera a gaze quite unlike any Cushing we have witnessed before.

The veteran actor said in interview that "*Corruption* was gratuitously vicious, fearsomely sick. But it was a good script, which just goes to show how important the presentation is."[1] According to Stanley Long, with whom the actor would work next on *The Blood Beast Terror* (68), Cushing in truth was "deeply ashamed" of his part in the film.[2]

Written by exploitation stalwarts Donald and Derek Ford, *Corruption* is set against the swinging London of Antonioni's *Blowup* (66). It even gives David Hemmings a low rent refit in the guise of Anthony Booth, here playing a photographer called Mike. Booth was familiar to audiences as the 'randy Scouse git,' the thorn in Alf Garnett's side in the BBC sitcom *Till Death Us Do Part*, and it is no accident he appears early in *Corruption* to put Cushing on a bad footing. When Sir John turns up at a party dressed in a suit, Booth mocks him by suggesting it's a police raid. Soon afterwards, jealous of the attention his fiancée Lynn is receiving, Sir John tussles with Mike and inadvertently knocks over the flood lamp that will disfigure her.

Wracked with guilt, Sir John throws himself into repairing Lynn's good looks. But the treatment, which involves the pituitary gland from a cadaver, offers only a short term fix and Lynn becomes increasingly deranged because of her ugliness, demanding that Sir John murders young women so that he may replicate the process.

The story is a nod to Hammer's intriguing *Stolen Face* (52), about a surgeon who repairs faces (which, too, features a death on a train and equates disfigurement with criminal psychosis), as much as it is Georges Franju's *Eyes Without a Face* (59). Director Robert Hartford-Davis was inspired by advancements in medical science taking place in the sixties, where the laser had become a viable substitute for the scalpel. Of course in the hands of screenwriters Donald and Derek Ford technology here doesn't have much to do but explode and kill everyone at the end of the film.

The laser is an awkward presence, clumsily wedged into the story: Sir John even takes it on holiday to his cottage retreat in Seaford, near Brighton. Yet the laser isn't the only half-baked element of the film. Gearing towards its final act, *Corruption* introduces a new set of characters and yet another

Suitably PC promotional campaign for *Corruption*.

"CORRUPTION" IS NOT A WOMAN'S PICTURE!

where will the bodies turn up next? ...under a car seat? ...in a valise?

...or in a deep-freeze?

THEREFORE: NO WOMAN WILL BE ADMITTED ALONE TO SEE THIS SUPER-SHOCK FILM!!

COLUMBIA PICTURES PRESENTS PETER CUSHING AND SUE LLOYD IN "CORRUPTION"

Screenplay by DONALD and DEREK FORD · Produced and Photographed by PETER NEWBROOK · Directed by ROBERT HARTFORD-DAVIS · A PETER NEWBROOK and ROBERT HARTFORD-DAVIS Production · COLUMBIACOLOR   Suggested For Mature Audiences

modern conundrum for Cushing in the form of young thugs who break into his Seaford retreat, ostensibly to rob it but soon exhibiting a more nefarious intent. The gang is dressed outlandishly and among them a giggling dimwit called Groper (a cross between Cosmo Smallpiece and a *Strawberry Fields* John Lennon), who answers only to the gang leader and is eager to administer some of the ultraviolence. If nothing else, the sequence is an interesting precursor to Kubrick's *A Clockwork Orange* (71).

Similarly pointless, but more confusing, is the coda that posits Cushing back at the party at the start of the film, where he fights with Mike and scars Lynn in the process. The look on Cushing's face at the prospect of having to go through it all again is priceless...

Corruption was a Titan International production, a company formed and owned by Hartford-Davis and producer Peter Newbrook. Despite misfires with *Gonks Go Beat* (65) and *The Sandwich Man* (66), Titan landed a three-picture deal with the American Oakshire Films for distribution through Columbia, but of these films only *Corruption* emerged and it flopped at the box office.

Corruption was made in two versions: one for the domestic market and another, containing nudity and more gore, for export. (This was no secret: *Premiere* magazine referenced the overseas version shortly following the film's release.) Ironically the uncut export print of this altogether scarce movie has proven easier to locate (under the title *Laser Killer* with French subtitles) and forms the basis of this review. The extra materials are scenes involving Cushing that were clearly shot back to back with their more staid domestic counterparts. Most noteworthy are the offal-loaded shots of a severed head in the fridge and the murders, in particular that of the prostitute, who is topless in the export version (and by all accounts a different actress). Having stabbed the woman to death, Sir John dismissively wipes the back of his hands on her bloodied breasts, which may be interpreted as a two-fingered salutation to the British censor on the part of the filmmakers.

As for Cushing, he would face the indignity of the new permissive era once again in Hammer's *Dracula A.D. 1972* (72), a similarly myopic observation of modern times and modern horror.

David Kerekes

---

1   Alan Frank, 'The Life and Times of Peter Cushing,' *The House of Hammer 2:6* (March 1978), p.32.
2   Stanley Long, with Simon Sheridan, *X-Rated: Adventures of an Exploitation Filmmaker* (London: Reynolds & Hearn, 2008), p.132.
     Sources: Production notes at *The Encyclopaedia of Fantastic Film and Television* http://www.eofftv. com/notes/c/corruption_notes.htm [Last accessed October 2010]

NEGATIVES (1970)

Kettledrum/Silvio Nazzarino Productions/Continental Distributing/Walter Reade Organization Inc | 98 mins | colour

Director Peter Medak; **Producer** Judd Bernard; **Screenplay** Peter Everett and Roger Lowry, based on the novel *Negatives* by Peter Everett. **Starring** Peter McEnery (Theo), Diane Cilento (Reingard), Glenda Jackson (Vivien), Billy Russell.

Because modern life is mundane, Theo and his partner Vivien spend their leisure time in the guise of Dr Crippen and Crippen's wife (or mistress). But Theo is tired of the charade. Influenced by a charismatic German woman, he determines he is less like the bespectacled Victorian murderer and more akin to Manfred von Richthofen, a WWI ace fighter pilot. Theo's relationship with Vivien breaks down, as it does with reality, when he 'becomes' von Richthofen.

Peter Medak's work in recent years has been in American television: a run of competent if not entirely distinctive cop shows that offer few clues to his interesting and occasionally classy British films. He was assistant director on Hammer's CAPTAIN CLEGG (62), directed the acclaimed *The Ruling Class* (71) and, later on, the true crime biopics *The Krays* (90) and *Let Him Have It* (91). His directorial debut, *Negatives*, is altogether different and much more idiosyncratic, and its lukewarm reception (negative, actually) no doubt curtailed his inclination to pursue similarly outré trajectories. Filmed in 1968, but unreleased until 1970, *Negatives* was an experiment that failed to endear itself to critics generally sympathetic to cinema's newer waves — or those sympathetic to European directors from the communist bloc, such as the Hungarian-born Medak.

It stars Glenda Jackson (on the cusp of an Oscar for *Women in Love* [69]) and Peter McEnery, as a couple who attempt to alleviate their dreary modern life by sitting around the house in period dress, play acting the characters of murderer-physician Hawley Harvey Crippen and his wife or mistress. Theo, disillusioned with Crippen, later adopts another role, that of German WWI fighter ace Manfred von Richthofen, and the line between make believe and reality breaks down completely — as does conventional filmmaking when the story adopts a sympathetically schizophrenic approach. *Negatives* is about personal identity being eroded by familial pressures and power struggles within relationships. The *Monthly Film Bulletin* tried not to be too disappointed by it, peppering its review with the words 'fussy,' 'fidgety' and 'messy'; the *New York Times* was very disappointed, however, likening the film to *Peanuts* with Theo as the gallant Red Baron.

PETER McENERY · DIANE CILENTO
GLENDA JACKSON

"THIS IS AMONG THE MOST EROTIC OF MOVIES!"

NEGATIVES

with MAURICE DENHAM

COLOUR

162

"I was Crippen all day," moans Theo in his Victorian gentleman's apparel and uncomfortable spectacles, frustrated at Vivien's refusal to be herself. Theo runs an antique shop, so even at work he is surrounded by other peoples' lives. He visits his sick father in hospital, a patient on the Marie Celeste ward. When an enigmatic German woman enters the picture, Theo believes he has something exciting in his life, but actually his brittle sense of self is pushed closer to collapse. "I wonder why people are so interested in Crippen?" asks the German woman, before volunteering that Peter Kürten, the vampire of Düsseldorf, is so much more interesting.

There is no explanation why this fascination with a doctor who poisoned his wife in 1910;[1] any figure from history could have serviced the story. The film even begins with a transcript of Crippen's sentencing at the Old Bailey. Perhaps a clue lies with Madame Tussaud's waxworks, where *Negatives* spends an inordinate amount of time in the middle section: In reality, Crippen's wax effigy was a mainstay of the London exhibition, and a newsworthy item in itself following its rescue from a fire in 1925, having its head split in half by an earthquake in 1931, and being one of only two residents from the Chamber of Horrors to survive the Blitz in 1940.

Modern life is rubbish. Peter McEnery in *Negatives*.

Having lost interest in Crippen, Theo salvages a German biplane from a scrap yard, before lapsing totally into his fantasy of von Richthofen, inspired to do so by his meetings with the German woman. Theo sees himself in full battledress in the cockpit of his plane, engaged in a fearsome dog fight. His partner, Vivien, on the other hand sees none of this, only Theo pottering about the backyard, and she calls down from a window for him to join her once again as Crippen. At this point the po-faced *Negatives* becomes altogether more farcical, akin to something Richard Lester might cook up, with jump cuts between the caterwauling Vivien at the window and the delusional Theo engaged in battle. But Theo has gone quite mad and, bleeding from a direct hit, he might even be dying.

Nineteen sixty-eight was a turbulent year with riots and civil unrest in America and Europe. Some British films adopted themes of youth in revolt and sought to question the status quo. Much as the angry young men films of the early sixties — such as *Saturday Night and Sunday Morning* (60), which spat forth Albert Finney and his kind from the provinces, disillusioned with their lot in the north — the late sixties had its own reactionary young men on film, though in this instance from a different social class. The most famous of these films is probably *If....*, presenting public schoolboys as no less a metaphor for the invasion of Czechoslovakia by Warsaw Pact armies. Made in the same year as *Negatives*, both films share a similarly cataclysmic ending.[2]

David Kerekes

---

1   Calls to grant Crippen a posthumous pardon failed in 2009.

2   Also from the same year is Peter Sykes' much less known *the committee* (anarchistic lowercase). Screened theatrically upon its release in 1968 and rarely since, *the committee* features Paul Jones as a disaffected young everyman (by association an extension of Jones' defeated pop idol in PRIVILEGE [67]). Adapted from a story by sociologist Max Steuer, *the committee* has no obvious plot to speak of: A group of people of all ages, races and classes, gather at a country retreat for a meeting of 'the committee,' which has the suggestion of purpose about it but is simply an excuse for vexed revolutionary psychobabble. Jones, billed as the 'central figure,' arrives at the meeting a disillusioned man and leaves a disillusioned man (despite the unexpected appearance of The Crazy World of Arthur Brown in full pyrotechnic regalia, performing for the assembled guests). "Other people, that's what happens," enunciates Robert Lloyd as the committee director. The clatter of an original Pink Floyd score heralds the more obtuse diatribes.
The committee's most striking sequence has Jones decapitating a motorist who offers him a lift, simply because the man is boring with a boring wife and kid. Then he sews the head back on.

THE STRANGE AFFAIR (1968)

Paramount | 106 mins | colour

Director David Greene; **Producers** Howard Harrison, Rene Dupont; **Screenplay** Stanley Mann, adapted from the novel *The Strange Affair* by Bernard Toms. **Starring** Michael York (Peter Strange), Jeremy Kemp (Detective Sgt. Pierce), Susan George (Fred March), Jack Watson (Quince).

After failing in his university endeavours, Peter Strange joins the police force, keen to root out crime and avoid becoming, like many of his colleagues, a 'bent copper.' Gradually though, the unassuming Strange is dragged into the seedy world of police corruption, and put in ever more difficult situations by his superior, Detective Sgt. Pierce, and underage girlfriend, Fred.

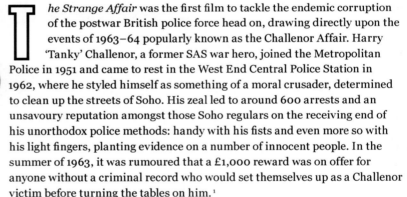

The *Strange Affair* was the first film to tackle the endemic corruption of the postwar British police force head on, drawing directly upon the events of 1963–64 popularly known as the Challenor Affair. Harry 'Tanky' Challenor, a former SAS war hero, joined the Metropolitan Police in 1951 and came to rest in the West End Central Police Station in 1962, where he styled himself as something of a moral crusader, determined to clean up the streets of Soho. His zeal led to around 600 arrests and an unsavoury reputation amongst those Soho regulars on the receiving end of his unorthodox police methods: handy with his fists and even more so with his light fingers, planting evidence on a number of innocent people. In the summer of 1963, it was rumoured that a £1,000 reward was on offer for anyone without a criminal record who would set themselves up as a Challenor victim before turning the tables on him. [1]

Things went sour for Challenor in July 1963, when he planted a half brick on left-wing protestor Donald Rooum who had been marching with a banner outside Claridge's Hotel, voicing his opposition to the visit of former Hitler Youth-ite Queen Frederika of Greece. "There you are, me old darling," Challenor is reported to have said. "Carrying an offensive weapon can get you two years." Rooum, a member of the National Council for Civil Liberties, employed forensic evidence to prove that the brick had never been in his possession. In the ensuing court case, Challenor was diagnosed as a paranoid schizophrenic and deemed unfit to stand trial, whilst three of his colleagues were sentenced to three years each for their involvement in his shenanigans. [2]

In *The Strange Affair*, we see a loose interpretation of the Challenor Affair through the eyes of new police officer Peter Strange, who despite his promising name actually does very little. Rather, he is an axis around which the bulk of the action happens; only late in the film do we realise that upright Detective Sgt. Pierce is the Challenor character, persuading Strange to plant heroin in the pocket of notorious local criminal Quince (Jack Watson). Jeremy Kemp is a menacing presence as Pierce, brooding in the background like Frankenstein's Monster, but crumbling rapidly under the pressure of the eventual trial. Perhaps wisely, Greene chose not to imbue him with the more colourful aspects of Challenor's character

which reportedly included singing "Bongo, bongo, bongo, I don't want to leave the Congo" at a black prisoner.

Indeed, contemporary reviewers had enough trouble with the plausibility of the film without such diversions. *New York Times* reviewer A.H. Weiler wrote that the 'aptly titled' *The Strange Affair* depicted 'bizarre destructive circumstances so contrived as to be hardly acceptable.'[3] Nowhere is this more evident than in the relationship between Strange and his young girlfriend — a product of artistic licence rather than a take on the Challenor Affair. Fifteen-year-old Fred's (Susan George) seduction of the wide-eyed officer leads to a bedroom romp which is secretly filmed by her eccentric Aunt Mary and Uncle Bertrand, pornographers extraordinaire, stills of which find their way into the grubby paws of Pierce, who then uses them to blackmail Strange into abetting his underhand methods.

Strange's desire for young Fred is equally incomprehensible: from her first toothy appearance on the screen, she is an irritating character with not even a Lolita-esque charm about her, being just too darn obvious. A badass equivalent of Hayley Mills, Susan George looks painfully out of place, and appears no more than twelve at times, never mind fifteen.

Despite the obligatory elements of sixties-sploitation — nude frolics on round beds, scar-faced rogues and flower-painted hippy children — *The Strange Affair* has nothing of the glamour of other films set in swinging London. There are no glimpses of tourist spots here; Strange and his partner clamber over piles of bricks and rubbish on their beat, and rag-and-bone men ride past ugly high rises in rickety carts. It is here that the film stands out from its contemporaries, depicting a realistic and decrepit capital, which, for all its crassness, is a visually arresting portrait of a city caught between postwar slum life and modern development. Nothing is dressed up and grimy locations are put to good use; there is a genuinely disturbing scene in a junkyard in which the vicious Quince brothers (David Glaisyer and Richard Vanstone), laughing hysterically, crush associate Charley (Barry Fantoni) beneath a toppling pile of rusty cars, and a grisly meeting with them later in a dank industrial basement sees Strange terrorised with an electric drill.

There is some light relief from supporting actors Madge Ryan and George Benson as the sex-crazed Aunt and Uncle. "Do you know anyone on the Vice Squad?" asks Uncle Bertrand eagerly on meeting Strange for the first time. "Must be fascinating work." Aunt Mary is a fantastic domineering presence, whose passion for erotica is complemented by a playful sadistic streak directed towards her husband. "You disgusting little man," she exclaims, rapping the top of the piano. "I told you to stop that racket!"

The Strange Affair might be an ideal candidate to represent the beginnings of a shift towards the 'anti-swinging London' genre described by Robert Murphy[4] and evidenced by earlier films such as *Life at the Top* (65). It depicts a Britain marred by drugs, pornography and petty crime which even respectable citizens seem powerless to resist, and it is this depressing picture, rather than the corrupting influence of a single officer, that emerges as the film's cause célèbre.

Jennifer Wallis

1   James Morton, *Bent Coppers: A Survey of Police Corruption* (London: Little, Brown, 1993), p.116.
2   For a first-hand account of events, see Harold Challenor, *Tanky Challenor: SAS and the Met* (London: Leo Cooper, 1990).
3   A.H. Weiler, 'The Strange Affair,' *New York Times*, 25 July 1968.
4   See Robert Murphy, *Sixties British Cinema* (London: BFI, 1992), pp.139–60.

THE TOUCHABLES (1968)

Film Designs/Twentieth Century Fox | 97 mins | colour

Director Robert Freeman; **Producer** John Bryan; **Screenplay** Ian La Frenais, based on a script by David and Donald Cammell from an original idea by Robert Freeman. **Starring** Judy Huxtable (Sadie), Ester Anderson (Melanie), Marilyn Rickard (Busbee), Kathy Simmonds (Samson), David Anthony (Christian), Rick Starr (Ricki), Harry Baird (Lillywhite), Joan Bakewell, Michael Chow, William Dexter.

Four punishingly gorgeous, doe-eyed swinging sixties chicks kidnap a pretty boy pop star and keep him as a sex slave inside a gigantic lakeside pleasure bubble. Meanwhile, a wrestler-cum-gangster attempts to track them all down for his own dubious ends — cue perfect lipstick, blissed-out psychobabble and plenty of half nelsons.

The promo poster was clear: 'Are You Ready To Turn On With The Try Anything Generation?' With additional promises of 'Love in the fifth Dimension,' possibly some ultraviolence, guns, drug-fuelled orgies and Lord knows what else, what is there not to look forward to? It certainly put the wind up the censors, who rated *The Touchables* 'X' for supposedly overt kinky sexual action. It is difficult to assess how scurrilous this was on original release, as on reflection it is so sweetly tame really; this is not a film that should be approached by anyone seeking carnal thrills. Instead, you find yourself spending some time with the stylish pop art British cousin of Russ Meyer's *Beyond the Valley of the Dolls*.

In a pre-credit sequence, our gang of girls, led by Sadie (Judy Huxtable), steal a waxwork dummy of Michael Caine from a typically modish sixties party and bundle it into the back of a sporty two-seater before bombing off into the night. This leads into a perfectly formed dreamy title sequence designed by director Robert Freeman. (Freeman was a hot ticket in 1968. He had made a name for himself as one of the Beatles' inner circle, designing and photographing five of their album covers including the iconic *With the Beatles*; he had also worked as the title designer on *A Hard Day's Night* [64] and *Help!* [65], as well as Richard Lester's *The Knack* [65].) We see Sadie, Melanie, Busbee and Samson in a fashion shoot, all billowing beautiful hair and makeup, blowing bubbles and fluttering their eyelashes. This is backed by the song All Of Us, a perfect piece of lush flower pop by the UK psych band Nirvana. It is a delightful start.

Unfortunately, this is something of a high point for *The Touchables*. For the most part Freeman and screenwriter Ian La Frenais serve up an 'action comedy' that is best looked at rather than understood. The mish-mash story

centres on our bored freewheeling girls looking to capture and 'punish' Christian (David Anthony), an aimless identikit pop star of the era, given to mouthing platitudes with vague philosophical undercurrents. At one point he is interviewed by a demure and mildly foxy Joan Bakewell (yes I know...) to discuss "traditional morality being replaced by fashionable morality." There are many similar grating, semi-intellectual postures littered amongst the Spider-man wallpaper, Jimi Hendrix posters and clockwork robots.

Love in the fifth dimension

20th Century-Fox Presents
JOHN BRYAN's production
THE TOUCHABLES
starring JUDY HUXTABLE · ESTHER ANDERSON · MARILYN RICKARD · KATHY SIMMONDS
and DAVID ANTHONY Directed by ROBERT FREEMAN Screenplay by IAN LA FRENAIS

Christian also has a penchant for visiting wrestling clubs. At one particular event, he catches the eye of Lillywhite (Harry Baird), a gay, roughneck masked wrestler and gangster, who 'wants' Christian. You don't need to be a genius to work out what for. The fulcrum between the girls and Lillywhite is Ricki (Rick Starr), the real life ballet dancer turned wrestler, playing a camp millionaire playboy and sugar daddy to the girls. There are quite a few wrestling scenes throughout the movie and they are fun to watch, with some of the fights also including another professional grappler in Steve Veidor a.k.a. The Handsome Hearthrob.

After the trial run with the waxwork of Michael Caine, the girls decide to go for the real thing. At one of Ricki's wrestling nights, Sadie et al dress as nuns and kidnap Christian, tie him to a wheelchair and bundle him off

FILM REVIEWS

The Touchables: forged inside the heart of swinging London.

to the countryside. And this is where the fun truly begins. Here they hide inside an enormous geodesic inflatable bubble, where they strip him to his undies, strap him to a revolving bed and get ready for some "indoor Olympics." What those are we don't see unfortunately, but they seem to spend plenty of time frolicking about playing pinball, bar billiards and table football. We can only guess at what happens in between, but when Christian screams at one point that he has about as much love as he can take, you know what kind he is talking about. And when he says he is feeling 'tender,' you can guess where.

When Christian has had his fill of loving, he tries to escape in a handy speedboat but is shot by über-doll Sadie and returned to the love bubble. While this is all going on, Lillywhite, who wants Christian for his own sexual dalliances, has finally found where they are hiding and sends his goons to bring him back. Fights then ensue inside the sci-fi pleasure dome, where eventually everything is rendered pointless as the dome deflates to signal the end of the film and Sadie and the gang swan off to build another bubble, presumably to embark on other trippy adventures. And that is that — 1968 vintage girl power.

A certain mystique has grown up around *The Touchables*, mainly due to the involvement of Donald Cammell — whose personal excesses were allegedly on a par with the 'indoor Olympics' of the pleasure dome — but Robert Freeman's Beatles connections and the hand of Ian La Frenais will always maintain interest in the film. Capturing the zeitgeist can see a film conquer everything in its path, but it can also lock it inside a time capsule and render it aged and twee, as is evidenced here. From the chiming first chords of Nirvana's All Of Us, you know that this is a film forged inside the heart of swinging London. It is difficult not to feel a tinge of delight watching the girls cavort around their sex dome, playing psychedelic table tennis in their miniskirts, but ultimately, without the sepia coating of nostalgia, *The Touchables* is a period piece that is both delightful and incoherent in equal measures.

Gary Ramsay

TWISTED NERVE (1968)

Charter Films/British Lion | 118 mins | colour

Director Roy Boulting; **Producers** John Boulting, Frank Granat, George W. George; **Screenplay** Roy Boulting, Leo Marks, from a story by Roger Marshall. **Starring** Hywel Bennett (Martin Durnley), Hayley Mills (Susan Harper), Billie Whitelaw (Joan Harper), Barry Foster (Gerry).

Martin Durnley's repeated clashes with his parents lead him to seek refuge with mother and daughter Joan and Susan Harper, where he establishes himself as the challenged baby of the family. All is not as it seems however, and Susan slowly uncovers the shocking truth about his background, fearing she may be the ultimate target of his murderous tendencies.

It's hard not to like *Twisted Nerve*. The blatant political incorrectness, awfully clichéd characters and glib sexual innuendo all combine to make the film a model of late sixties exploitation cinema. The result of a collaboration with screenwriter Leo Marks of *Peeping Tom* fame, *Twisted Nerve* was the Boulting Brothers' attempt to make their mark in the British exploitation market. Rather a bold transition from their previous fare of light comedies such as *Heavens Above!* (63), it immediately came to the attention of disability rights campaigners — before its theatrical release — due to its portrayal of Down's Syndrome, tactfully referred to throughout as 'mongolism.' Coined by nineteenth-century doctor John Langdon Down, the term reflected his belief that Down's Syndrome sufferers represented a reversion to a 'mongoloid race.' In the early 1960s, when understandings of the condition were improved, calls to drop the antiquated term and replace it with Down's Syndrome were voiced in *The Lancet*, and in 1965 the World Health Organisation ended all reference to mongolism. The Boultings apparently missed this development, but did add a hasty disclaimer to the opening credits, reminding viewers that there was of course 'no established scientific connection between Mongolism and psychotic or criminal behaviour.' The VHS to DVD transfer used for this review unfortunately lacked this curiosity due to the delayed reactions of whoever recorded it from ATV's Cinema Showcase (proving that it did, in some distant and more permissive past, merit a television screening).

The film revolves around Martin (Hywel Bennett), whose 'mongoloid' brother resides in an institution whilst his mother and stepfather focus on more important matters, such as dispatching their remaining son to Australia. Bennett's performance is startling as he switches between the rebellious Martin and his second (or cleverly fabricated — we are never quite sure

COMING SOON AT **A B C** AND OTHER LEADING CINEMAS

Enough to make even Hitchcock **jump!**

YOU ARE INSURED FOR £25,000 IN CASE YOU DIE OF FRIGHT WHILE SEEING 'TWISTED NERVE'

THE BOULTING BROTHERS'

HAYLEY MILLS **HYWEL BENNETT**

TWISTED NERVE 'X'

BILLIE WHITELAW **PHYLLIS CALVERT** BARRY FOSTER SALMAAN PEER
Guest star FRANK FINLAY

Produced by GEORGE W GEORGE & FRANK GRANAT   Screenplay by LEO MARKS & ROY BOULTING   EASTMAN COLOUR
A BRITISH LION PRESENTATION

which) personality, six-year-old Georgie. Our first glimpse of Georgie comes as he is hauled into the manager's office at a toy store, having just pocketed a small toy duck. Susan Harper (Hayley Mills), accused of being in cahoots with the young thief, is sympathetic and puts an end to the matter by paying for the toy. Big mistake. The film quickly degenerates into a suspenseful nightmare in which Georgie/Martin stalks Susan, managing to install himself in the boarding house run by her mother Joan (Billie Whitelaw), and involving himself in all manner of unseemly situations until the film reaches its climax in Susan's bedroom, with Georgie's mask slipping to reveal the psychotic Martin.

Twisted Nerve is more psychological thriller than exploitation flick, yet its ad campaign sold the film as a slasher horror. 'Cleaver. Cleaver. Chop. Chop,' ran the tagline. 'First the mom and then the pop. Then we'll get the pretty girl. We'll get her right between the curl.'[1] Such inane nonsense does the film some injustice. Filmgoers hoping for a grubby gore-fest would undoubtedly have been disappointed, but as an exercise in psychological suspense the film works remarkably well. The sinister voyeurism of *Peeping Tom* is recreated in a scene in the boarding house kitchen. About to sneak out to murder his father with Mrs Harper's kitchen scissors, Martin is interrupted by Susan clearing up the evening's cutlery. He hides in a cupboard, where he watches her through a twee heart-shaped stencil in the cupboard door, waiting for his chance to escape but also, we suspect, getting a prurient kick out of Susan pottering around the kitchen in her *Chelsea Girl* attire.

The jaunty score by Bernard Herrmann, recycled for Quentin Tarantino's *Kill Bill* (2003), is a recurring element adding to the general atmosphere of unease. Martin whistles it as he strides menacingly down the street in pursuit of Susan, having lain in wait outside her house to follow her to the local library where she works. Its use alongside a somewhat psychedelic title sequence perhaps suggested to the cinema audience this might not be a run of the mill horror flick, even if Herrmann biographer Steven Smith described the tune as conveying an overarching impression of 'boredom.'[2]

The Boulting brothers, John and Roy.

Unlike other films of its ilk, *Twisted Nerve* has an impressive cast of competent actors who rise to the challenge of their somewhat formulaic characters. We have the nymphomaniac, middle-aged boarding house owner (Whitelaw), who appears to have a rent 'arrangement' with certain members of the household, and is visibly disturbed by her physical attraction to the backward Georgie (though not disturbed enough to turn him out of her bed after a nightmare, later imploring him to "Tell Mummy all about it" whilst caressing his bare chest in the woodshed). Next up is the lecherous male boarder Gerry (Barry Foster) who, when not cracking racist jokes to fellow boarder Shashie (Salmaan Peer), is leering at young Susan. "She'll be begging for it by the time she's forty," he opines after yet another frosty response to his advances. Timothy West is magnificent as Superintendent Dakin — not a million miles away from *Life on Mars'* Gene Hunt — and librarian Mr Groom (Timothy Bateson) is a likeable if marginal presence as petulant dictator of his bookish empire.

Despite being a focal point of the film, Hayley Mills is upstaged by the eminently more capable Whitelaw (who received a BAFTA for Best Supporting Actress) and, although Mills' typecast naïve charity allows most of the action to unfold, her performance seems even more vacuous than usual. Explaining the real identity of Georgie to housemate Shashie, she remains sympathetic towards the murderous delinquent to an extent that is almost comical, and which bears a striking resemblance to Marilyn Monroe's (intentionally) comic overacting in *The Seven Year Itch*.

Another hysterical poster for *Twisted Nerve*.

Not that *Twisted Nerve* is without its comedic moments. Amongst the cringeworthy racial jokes which passed as normal conversation in the late sixties ("Maybe," considers Susan, her father went to Africa "to get something he couldn't get on the National Health." "Yes, black women," quips her mother), there are some truly inspired snippets of dialogue from the supporting actors. Clarkie, the housekeeper (Gretchen Franklin), muses over the breakfast table whether a recent murder might have been committed by "one of these psychoprats," whilst Superintendent Dakin considers young women with skirts "just long enough to cover their parking meters."

A box office failure when it was released, *Twisted Nerve* is still interesting for exactly the same reasons it was condemned in 1968. The ingrained smutty innuendo and casual racism, alongside the notion that chromosomal abnormalities invariably make a psychotic killer, are the epitome of British exploitation bad taste. The disturbing thing is that it's all executed with such finesse.

Jennifer Wallis

1   See Harvey F. Chartrand, '*The Horrors of Hayley Mills*' at Horror-Wood webzine. http://www.horror-wood.com/hayley.htm [Last accessed November 2009].

2   Steven C. Smith, *A Heart at Fire's Center: The Life and Music of Bernard Herrmann* (California: University of California Press, 1991), p.293.

BUST
BRITISH CINEMA 1969-85

BY JULIAN UPTON

By the 1970s, all that was left of the US-backed British cinema boom was debris. As early as mid 1967, the smoke had started to clear; more astute observers could see that London was no longer swinging — if it ever really had done. This took some time to sink into Hollywood heads, who continued to urge filmmakers to keep the party going. But when the hits stopped coming, Hollywood finally sat up and took notice.

For the US executives, there was also a crisis back home to take care of: in 1969, the major film companies were quickly heading for bankruptcy. MGM announced a loss of $35 million, Twentieth Century Fox lost over $36 million and Warners, $52 million.[1] Not only were the studios failing to gauge the mood in Britain, they had desperately misjudged the climate in their own market. Back in the States, Fox, for example, had been pumping millions into inflated, anachronistic musicals like *Star!* and *Hello, Dolly!*, which duly bombed; young Americans were more interested in indie, counterculture fare like *Easy Rider*. So, as quickly as the US executives had arrived in London, they cleared out. Universal and Twentieth Century Fox shut down their UK production bases in 1969. United Artists and Paramount started slashing production the following year. MGM reported it was closing its British studios.

The effects weren't immediately apparent to the cinema-going public. For the first two or three years of the seventies, the British film production line looked as busy as ever. Behind the scenes, however, the pinch was being felt. Even directors with solid sixties successes behind them, like John Schlesinger and Richard Lester, suddenly had trouble raising finance. US money was still available, but, increasingly, it was channeled into low risk, low budget films. And even these were proving unprofitable. By 1975, the cash flow from the States had dried up almost completely.

The US withdrawal dropped the British film industry back on its own two, shaky feet. There was no domestic B-movie production now; the ubiquity of television had brought that to a halt around 1965. And with cinema attendance in 1969 falling to 214 million[2] and the introduction of colour television offering a vastly improved viewing experience at home, British filmmakers had to go to new extremes to get the patrons into the theatres.

Domestically produced British cinema in the seventies, then, consisted largely of low budget genre and exploitation films, sex and soft porn comedies, TV spin-offs and the *Carry On* series.

Fortunately, that still leaves pretty rich pickings for this book. But the end was nigh for this kind of populist cinema too.

Death on the Nile: short-changed by the Eady Levy.

The inequities of the Eady Levy fund — which, to simplify it brutally, taxed foreign (that is, mainly US) films exhibited in Britain and paid extra money to the producers of a British film for every pound it took at the home box office (the payout for shorts was doubled) — were becoming more apparent. Big budget films registered as British but actually Hollywood subsidised (such as the Bond movies and *Superman* [78]) were qualifying for massive Eady payouts, while genuine, low budget British fare was seeing very little of it. The farcical extreme of this saw a British made short documentary about drag racing, *Hot Wheels* (78), which was on general release with the crowd pleaser *Grease*, receive a whopping £250,000 from the Eady fund (more than the British hit feature *Death on the Nile* [78] received). Since the short film had been acquired by an American company for British distribution, this money found its way back to Hollywood. [3]

A Harold Wilson-chaired working party, The Interim Action Committee on the Film Industry, responded by recommending the capping of Eady Levy payments on the highest earning (i.e., mainly Hollywood-backed) films. Later, the cap was set at £500,000, and the practice of awarding double payouts to short films was stopped. But this did nothing to ease the condition of the cash-strapped but commercially focused British filmmaker. By then, the Eady Levy pot was pretty drained anyway, thanks to several years of diminishing investment and descending ticket sales.

Harold Wilson may have personally continued to support British cinema, but his own government's tax laws were not so sympathetic. Returning as Labour Prime Minister in 1974, his party immediately put the highest rate of income tax up to eighty-three per cent, payable on earnings of just £20,000 a year. The result was another mass exodus, this time not just of American executives, but of home-grown British talent like Michael Caine and Sean

But *Come Play with Me* didn't needy Eady money. It had a ready-made audience of gullible soft porn consumers.

Connery, directors such as John Schlesinger and London-based American exile Joseph Losey, and even, for a time, the Great White Hope of British cinema, David Puttnam. The evacuation of personnel of this magnitude may not have struck low budget or genre cinema directly, but it served to further destabilise the climate of commercial filmmaking in Britain, and certainly extinguished the mood of optimism so prevalent in the previous decade. "These years," said critic Alexander Walker of the mid seventies, "were the lowest, most shameful nadir of the British film industry."[4]

The lower budget and lower brow British films that succeeded in the seventies did so largely with indifference to government-assisted financing or incentives. (The UK's other source of film funding, the National Film Finance Corporation [NFFC] was a choosy outfit; it tended to avoid films that were blatantly 'commercial' or not representative of modern British culture and society, rather like Channel 4 was to do in the eighties.) But there were some domestic success stories. The film of the popular TV sitcom *On the Buses*, produced by Hammer for £89,000 in 1971, became the second most profitable film at the UK box office that year,[5] grossing £1 million. In 1974, the Columbia-backed *Confessions of a Window Cleaner* grossed a higher sum per dollar spent (outside the US market) than any other film backed by the studio.[6] As late as 1977, David Sullivan's soft porn comedy *Come Play with Me* made its modest budget back many times over, running for four straight years

Confessions of a Window Cleaner also cleaned up at the British box office.

The dirty window cleaner reveals everything!

COLUMBIA PICTURES Presents

Confessions OF A WINDOW CLEANER

in one London cinema,[7] mainly thanks to a heated marketing campaign in Sullivan's own stable of porn mags.

By 1979, however, both the lucrative TV spin-off and the sex comedy were on their last legs. Not even the *Carry On* series was to see the decade out. Margaret Thatcher's Tory government had come to power, and it definitely did not place British films (or indeed any of the arts) high on its agenda. Soon, the remaining avenues of state finance were closed off completely.

But more wounding was the arrival, around the same time, of a shiny machine called the videocassette recorder. This, more than anything, was about to put the final nail in the coffin of popular British cinema.

1   Alexander Walker, *Hollywood, England* (London: Orion, 2005 edition), p.442.
2   The Cinema Exhibitors' Association Ltd., http://www.cinemauk.org.uk/ukcinemasector/admissions/annualukcinemaadmissions1935-2009/ [Last accessed 6 January 2010].
3   John Walker, *The Once and Future Film* (London: Methuen, 1985), p.24.
4   Alexander Walker, *National Heroes* (London: Orion, 2005 edition), p.136.
5   Adrian Garvey, 'Pre-sold to Millions: The Sitcom Films of the 1970s,' in Paul Newland (ed.), *Don't Look Now: British Cinema in the 1970s* (Bristol: Intellect, 2010), pp.182–83.
6   The Elstree Company, http://www.adjs96.dial.pipex.com/profile.htm [Last accessed 9 June 2010].
7   David McGillivray, *Doing Rude Things: The History of the British Sex Film 1957–1981* (London: Sun Tavern Fields, 1992), p.78.

FILM REVIEWS

I START COUNTING (1969)

United Artists/Triumvirate Productions | 105 mins | colour

Director David Greene; **Producer** David Greene; **Screenplay** Richard Harris, from the novel by Audrey Erskine Lindop. **Starring** Jenny Agutter (Wynne), Bryan Marshall (George), Clare Sutcliffe (Corinne), Simon Ward (Bus Conductor), Madge Ryan (Mother), Billy Russell (Granddad).

Fourteen-year-old schoolgirl Wynne's crush on her much older foster brother George develops, perversely, into an infatuation when she suspects he might be the killer of a number of local women. Desperate to find out more about his nocturnal activities, she sets about spying on him. But even with her suspicions, she is not prepared for what she finds out.

I Start Counting's 'Is my brother/father/son/husband (delete as appropriate) the local sex killer?' plot may be an off-the-peg one, but the film itself is saved by a committed performance from a young Jenny Agutter as Wynne and some interesting, suspenseful flourishes from director David Greene. And despite — with its theme of teenage sexuality burgeoning in an antiseptic new town — sharing some similarities with the Stevenage-set sex romp *Here We Go Round the Mulberry Bush* (68), it is also another prime example of what Robert Murphy called the 'anti-swinging London film.'

Any sense of personal awakening and national optimism that *Mulberry Bush* may have wrung from its concrete suburbia is effectively inverted in *I Start Counting*, however. The ongoing redevelopment of a crumbling town (in this case Bracknell, Berkshire) into an impersonal, featureless landscape of high rise flats and prefabricated precincts serves as an unsettling leitmotif; the demolition of rows of tumbledown terraces to make space for a vast, ugly building site signals Wynne's (and perhaps Britain's) painful loss of innocence, or at least loss of 'quaintness,' as well as providing a derelict environment for a killer to operate freely at night. Further, the abnormally white interiors of Wynne's high rise home — airy, spotless and flooded with skylight — become, ironically, a place for shadowy secrets and dark suspicion. For not only has she begun to harbour a sexual yearning for her much older foster brother, George (Bryan Marshall), but these feelings have intensified with her belief that he may be said local serial killer.

And we believe that too, especially as Greene throws red herrings at us as if he's feeding a pool full of sea lions. Wynne retrieves a jumper that George has secretly dumped in a bin — and it's got blood on it. Wynne finds out that George hasn't been visiting his aunt every Friday to put shelves up — but he

says he has. Wynne ogles George as he's washing in the bathroom — and he's got deep scratches over his back. And so on. But all's fair in love and psycho-sexual thrillers, and this is nothing that Hitchcock wouldn't have teased us with. (One can wonder with some relish how Hitchcock might have handled this material; the story, after all, is no more hackneyed than the one he returned to Britain to film: *Frenzy* [72].) Indeed, Greene does pull off some sub-Hitchcockian moments quite effectively, such as Wynne's stowaway ride in the back of George's van. There's also the poker-faced turn by Marshall as George, whose rigid countenance refuses to give anything away.

While a general 'anti-swinging' sense prevails, the era does occasionally show itself; for example, there's Wynne and her friend's acutely short miniskirts (could this have been standard uniform at a Catholic school in the late sixties?) and the appearance at Wynne's family flat of a 'longhair,' a friend of Wynne's other brother, Jim. (But the hippy is treated as a novelty rather than an ordinary visitor; when he says he's spent the morning talking to the police, old Granddad proffers: "I'm not surprised!"). Also, in a droll scene where a priest is giving the school assembly a decidedly ineffective sex education sermon, one girl pipes up: "What's the Pope got against the pill?"

The preoccupation with adolescent sexuality certainly marks *I Start Counting* out as a product of its time; such endeavours seem somewhat riskier now, especially the sexualisation of a girl as young as Jenny Agutter, who was still on the wrong side of sixteen as far as all this malarkey was concerned. (Agutter tended to have this dangerous effect on her much older, male directors; only a year later Nicolas Roeg was shooting languorous scenes of her swimming naked in *Walkabout*). Nevertheless, there is actually a strong conservatism at work here. We sympathise with Agutter's naïve and misguided crush on her brother, but her outspoken friend Corinne (Clare Sutcliffe) pays the ultimate price for her more 'vulgar' attitude to sex. And the final shot of bulldozers tearing through the earth and razing another dilapidated street to the ground does leave us with some ambiguity: was the 'old world' — with its traditional values, propriety and chastity — better, or is the new?

For all its churning concrete, *I Start Counting* didn't cement Greene's career on the big screen. This is a shame, because it builds on the promise he showed in his first three British features: *The Shuttered Room* (67), *Sebastian* (68) and *The Strange Affair* (68). Aside from a handful of fairly random films in subsequent years (including the movie version of *Godspell* [73], of all things), he returned to directing television drama in the US, working there successfully and prolifically until his retirement in the late 1990s.

Julian Upton

THE RECKONING (1969)

Columbia Pictures | 111 mins | colour

Director Jack Gold; **Producer** Ronald Shedlo; **Screenplay** John McGrath, from the novel *The Harp That Once* by Patrick Hall. **Starring** Nicol Williamson (Michael Marler), Rachel Roberts (Joyce Eglington), Ann Bell (Rosemary Marler), Paul Rogers (Hazlitt), J.G. Devlin (Cocky Burke), Christine Hargreaves (Kath), Gwen Nelson (Marler's mother).

Michael Marler, a successful, aggressive, young London businessman, heads back to his native city of Liverpool after many years away when he hears his father is dying, but does not make it back in time. Paying his respects, Marler notices severe bruises over the old man's body, and later discovers that his father was badly beaten by a local youth. Marler goes back to London, but cannot rest until the score is settled.

nd, lo, over a year before *Get Carter*, there was *The Reckoning*. But *The Reckoning* is much more than just a rough and tumble revenge drama. It astutely juxtaposes the violent honour of the provincial slums with the aggressive backstabbing of the business world.

Its 'hero,' Michael Marler (Nicol Williamson), has exchanged the former for the latter. Marler is from a tough Irish immigrant family in Liverpool, but has long since started a new life of expensive watches, fast Jags, elegant threads and a fragrant, blow-dried wife (Ann Bell) — trappings of his success as a rapidly rising executive at a large London-based company. Back home, he was recognisably a product of his environment, but in the business world he's a whirlwind. Dapper in his pricey suits, he's nonetheless a near-Neanderthal to the squares he works with. He drives to work like a Kamikaze pilot, calls his colleagues 'twats' and takes aspirin without water as he rushes from one testosterone-

fuelled meeting to another. What's more, he makes love roughly to his wife, decks colleagues at fancy soirées and mercilessly bullies his boss, Hazlitt ("You pin-striped get!").

Where *Get Carter*'s protagonist is largely machine-like, *The Reckoning* is much more interesting as a character study. We can believe how Marler has clawed himself up from uncouth northern urchin to pugnacious executive. We can see why his colleagues (and his boss) are scared of him. But there's also a profound gentleness and respect in the way he interacts with his family. The expression on his face when he sees his father has died is heartbreaking, and he is tender and attentive with his mother and sister. But the attack on his family sends him back to brute force after years of conducting his battles only in the boardroom.

Nicol Williamson, giving a powerhouse performance, was not unlike Marler himself: volatile, confrontational, but deeply vulnerable and capable of brilliance. He too was from a provincial, working class background, and had soared to success early in adulthood. In Williamson's case, he was the talk of the West End stage by his mid twenties. He was revered by Laurence Olivier and the theatrical establishment. He was courted by Hollywood. He was invited by President Nixon to perform a one-man show at the White House. But where he graciously tackled some artistic endeavours, others he fought against or violently rejected. He stormed off the stage minutes into a major production of *Hamlet*, saying he couldn't perform that night and offering the audience its money back. He was known for physically attacking other actors, sometimes during a performance. And he could be heart-stoppingly antisocial in polite company.

In *The Reckoning*, there are plenty of glimpses of what made Williamson the enigmatic British actor du jour. (He never went on to become a film star, but you get the impression it's because he never wanted to.) He's powerfully built and imposing, like Caine in *Carter*, but has a feline grace about him (unlike Caine). His voice is commanding and authoritative, but also nasal, sometimes almost camp. His countenance is both rubber-faced and steely-eyed. And although his ginger-blond hair is manfully receding on top, it billows out around his head like thespian sailcloth. He's a walking storm of paradoxes. As Marler he looks like a parody now, but he was exactly the kind of anti-hero the sixties sat up and took notice of.

Reuniting THE BOFORS GUN's triumvirate of Williamson, director Jack Gold and screenwriter John McGrath, *The Reckoning* draws sterling work from all three. Gold precedes *Get Carter*'s director Mike Hodges in striking a balance

Nicol Williamson and Rachel Roberts. *The Reckoning.*

between stylised brutality and almost anthropological social realism (although *The Reckoning*'s smoky working men's club was created in a studio). He's also more prepared to tell the story visually, either through Williamson's face or via nicely judged montages of location shots: we can see Marler's mind turning over as he observes what his life down south has become and what he must do to settle the score up north. Gold also delivers an audacious ending that derails your expectations. It's a complete departure from the staginess of *Bofors Gun*, and makes you wish he'd done more work for the big screen (although he did go on to great success on television). As for McGrath's script, it's a grown-up piece of writing. Marler emerges fully rounded, if a little twisted. You believe totally that he's from where he's from and is where he is. (Can you say that about *Carter*?) And his dialogue, at times, is quite uproariously funny.

And then, for unconventional (and extra-marital) romantic relief, there's Rachel Roberts as Joyce, offering a small but poignant glimpse into the frustrated, love-hungry life of a once attractive, unhappily married woman. As soon as Marler lays eyes on her, she's giving him the kind of look the office cougar gives the handsome postboy, three weeks ahead of the Christmas party. Before long, they're "at it like knives" in the decidedly unromantic setting of a local scrap yard. Fitting enough, as she's on the scrap heap. (Harsh, but she'd be the first to admit it.) When Marler sees her dragging her reluctant child along a particularly ugly stretch of tower block at the end of the film, you know he knows he's had a lucky escape.

The Reckoning is as much about redemption and family honour as it is about violent revenge and its white-collar equivalent. Marler learns something from his experience up north, but he doesn't come back to London a better man. If anything, he's more ruthless, more sly, more prepared to stab people in the back (and front). He gets back with his trophy wife, but he doesn't love her. We know that, as much as he needed to break away, home is where his heart is. The pansies down south are just there to be trampled on.

Julian Upton

PERMISSIVE (1970)

Lindsay Shonteff Film Productions/Tigon | 75 mins | colour

Director Lindsay Shonteff; **Producer** Jack Shulton; **Screenplay** Jeremy Craig Dryden.
Starring Maggie Stride (Suzy), Gay Singleton (Fiona), Gilbert Wynne (Jimi), Robert Daubigny (Pogo),
Forever More (themselves: Alan Gorrie, Stuart Francis, Mick Travis (Mick), Onnie Mair), Madeleine
Collinson, Mary Collinson.

*Milk-faced country girl Suzy comes to London looking for adventure. After
hooking up with her old school friend Fiona, she becomes part of the 'groupie
scene' surrounding rock band Forever More. Suzy soon becomes acclimatised to
the sex, drugs and backbiting that fuels this circle of girls and quickly inherits
the role of queen bitch, with destructive consequences.*

I f interest to musicologists and cineastes alike, *Permissive* is a
compelling, if grubby, portrayal of London life and the underground
music scene, as the 1960s hippy dream dissolved into the troubled
murk of the 1970s. Known at various times as *Suzy Superscrew* and
The Now Child, even the gloss of a recent high definition DVD makeover by
the BFI (under its admirable Flipside programme), can't disguise the coating
of grime covering Lindsay Shonteff's cautionary tale of sexploitation and
pub rock.

As far removed from the amped-up lollipop colours of psychedelic London
as you can get, Suzy (Maggie Stride), clad in a distinctly unhip duffel coat,
arrives in the drab city and is taken under the wing of Fiona (Gay Singleton),
who is living with Lee (Alan Gorrie), the lead singer of rock band Forever
More. Initially out of her depth, Suzy finds herself taking cues from Fiona,
living a low rent life in the land of bedsit shittery, goalpost spliffs, predatory
men and vacuous, bitchy women. Suzy is seemingly baffled by the blatant
drug taking and bedroom merry-go-round of Fiona and her 'friends.'

Shonteff shoots all of this with a convincing verité feel that includes various
flash-forward scenes to future events in the narrative and gives the film a
slightly hallucinatory, disjointed aura. The 'fly on the wall' camera gives it
the feel of a *World in Action* TV documentary, investigating the seedy side of
youth culture, drugs and promiscuous sex.

When Forever More hit the road, Fiona goes with them to do her duty: "a
bit of cooking, bit of washing, a lot of loving," and Suzy is left behind to
look after herself. During one of the many backstage parties, Suzy feels she
has found a soul mate in Pogo (Robert Daubigny), a hip but empty-headed

Maggie Stride descends into groupiedom. *Permissive.*

madman, who takes her on a trek through London, strolling through building sites and grim parks, before finding a church where he embarks on a lunatic, impromptu sermon, railing against God, 'the man' and the 'fat cats.' Then the police turn up and they scarper off to continue their sojourn around the bleak, rainy streets of Camden. Unfortunately, Pogo's charm is shortlived, as he is promptly and almost comically run over by a Ford Capri Mk1.

Suzy is now a changed and hardened woman. The duffel coat is replaced by coloured beads, headscarves and a vicarious carefree attitude. When Forever More eventually roll back into town, Suzy begins to manipulate those around her — including Fiona — and starts to screw her way through the band. This includes stealing the 'hairy' Lee from Fiona. This is all too mind blowing for Fiona, who takes on the mantle of Suzy and spends many handwringing hours strolling around the same dingy London streets Suzy and Pogo had pounded earlier. As Forever More are preparing to take off on another tour with Suzy as the new head girl, Fiona slits her wrists in the bath. The final scenes have Suzy calmly checking her eyeliner before staring at Fiona with a typically baleful expression, then slamming the door and leaving her to bleed out in the bath — an indelible and fittingly desolate final scene.

The music is as important to *Permissive* as the tale of Suzy's descent into groupiedom. Forever More with Alan Gorrie at the helm were a real band with a real career.

Add to this the inclusion to the soundtrack of Titus Groan and cult acid folk heroes Comus, and the film is a rare glimpse into a little-seen part of British underground music of the era. There are several live segments showing Forever More belting out their prog rock in various smoky clubs, and it is here that *Permissive* offers a superb insight into the world of touring in a clapped-out transit van. Anyone that has been in a band will totally relate to the heady atmosphere of boredom, mixed with a dose of micro-fame, plus

You can't tell if they're girls or boys nowadays. Two lovebirds get *Permissive.*

permissive

groupie girls who
really want to
make it big!

COLOR

MAGGIE STRIDE
GAY SINGLETON
GILBERT WYNNE

Music by FOREVER MORE

endless hours driving up and down the motorway in a joss stick fug, playing crap gigs in crap towns. But looking at the film with the benefit of historical hindsight, it is bewildering to see the seemingly artless Alan Gorrie and believe that only a couple of years later he would form The Average White Band, write Pick Up The Pieces, be Number One in the USA and be famously marched into consciousness in Cher's apartment after accidentally overdosing on strychnine-laced heroin.

Permissive would prove to be the last film Lindsay Shonteff would direct of any merit before he descended into progressively inane and amateurish spoof comedy. He delivers an unpleasant undertow to the film; even the sex and nudity — much of which was cut on original release — is coldly unerotic and uninteresting. Shonteff the sexploiter offers no judgement of the pointless use and abuse of the young girls led astray in this would-be morality tale; he presents it all within a framework of youthful indifference. Groupies come and groupies go. People live and people die. Adults beware. Certainly, the London counterculture he shows is gloomy, tarnished and compulsively depressing: the flipside indeed to the flowery sunshine and communal love-ins of San Francisco. Because of that, *Permissive*, with its haphazard blankness, is a very British affair, and all the more memorable for it.

Gary Ramsay

AND SOON THE DARKNESS (1970)

Associated British Picture Corporation/EMI | 98 mins | colour

Director Robert Fuest; **Producers** Albert Fennell and Brian Clemens; **Screenplay** Brian Clemens and Terry Nation, from their original story. **Starring** Pamela Franklin (Jane), Michele Dotrice (Cathy), Sandor Eles (Paul), John Nettleton (Gendarme).

Jane and Cathy, two attractive young English nurses, are on a cycling holiday through France. After an argument, they separate. But when her friend fails to catch up with her, Jane begins to worry as to where Cathy has gone, and reluctantly teams up with a mysterious young man who had been following them earlier in the day.

A thriller stripped down to its basic components, *And Soon the Darkness* remains a chilling experience simply because the location used completely overpowers any attempts by the filmmakers to add story, character or sub-plots of depth. Considering the production crew involved, at times it seems to play out like second-unit filler footage from *The Avengers*. Director Robert Fuest was a graduate from that TV show, as were writers Brian Clemens and Terry Nation, two men set deep in the high-turnover world of serial scriptwriting. The languid, near-silent pace of *And Soon the Darkness* must have seemed like a short holiday to them, and there is little indication from Fuest that he would go on to helm the art-deco sadistic nightmare of *The Abominable Dr Phibes* the following year.

After only a few days, the endless ghost roads of Normandy already seem to be straining the relationship between Jane and Cathy. The former wants to crack on with their itinerary, the latter wants to chase the opposite sex. Function and fun cannot co-exist for long and soon the travelling companions part in the heat of an argument. But who is the handsome man who has been chasing them on his Lambretta, stopping only at an eerie roadside cemetery to visit a dead girl's grave? This is one of many clues that are not actually clues in the film — an empty camera, a scythe hung on a window frame, an abandoned car (a bicycle underneath it), a closed police station — because nothing can distract from the straight route that all the characters take, from beginning to end.

Alone, Jane cycles on, whilst Cathy sunbathes by the roadside, just far enough away from it for her not to be seen. Despite the clear landscape, Jane is constantly looking over her shoulder. Perhaps Pamela Franklin cannot adjust to the vast space that engulfs her? The exact opposite of her roles within the suffocating homes of *The Innocents* (61) and OUR MOTHER'S HOUSE (67). It may be open country, but why does everything seem so

hidden, so empty? Like scarecrows, figures watch her from fields. At a village further on, she waits. Jane seems to spend all her time waiting, suspicious of others she encounters who may or may not want to help. The handsome

A stripped-down thriller. *And Soon the Darkness.*

man introduces himself as Detective Paul Samon — played by Sandor Eles as if gratefully released from the frockcoats of Hammer — and talks of a previous murder on the same road. A reluctant Englishwoman gives Jane a lift. "Loathsome business," she tells the girl. "It was more than murder, if you know what I mean?" A café owner offers a warning (and alternative film title) in her limited English: "Bad road..."

Back at the roadside, Cathy hangs her washed underwear on branches to dry out. It triggers a genuinely unnerving sequence in which traffic, civilisation, help, seems a million miles in the other direction. Whilst she dozes, a shadow passes over Cathy's face. She wakes to silence. A plane flies high overhead, cutting through the blue sky. Slowly realising that such a thing could not have made the shadow that stirred her, Cathy is no longer the flirtatious girl at the start of the film, and the day is no longer there to sunbathe and laze, and dream of a boy in the next town. Earlier, before they had parted, Cathy offered a moment of reflection to Jane:

"That delivery last week, y'know, the difficult one? The baby died, y'know. It was only a day old. I don't suppose they know anything... feel anything, I mean, when they're one day old, do they?"
"Whatever made you think of that?"
"I don't know. A day like this... it seems such a pity. She wasn't even married."

But a day is more than enough time to die in, as Cathy soon discovers. And her actual killer? By the end of the film, the denouement seems immaterial because in *And Soon the Darkness* — to paraphrase Roger Corman — the road is the killer.

Martin Jones

BRONCO BULLFROG (1970)

Maya Films/British Lion | 86 mins | b&w

Director Barney Platts-Mills; **Producer** Andrew St. John; **Screenplay** Barney Platts-Mills. **Starring** Del Walker (Del Quant), Anne Gooding (Irene), Sam Shepherd (Bronco Bullfrog), Roy Haywood (Roy), Freda Shepherd (Irene's mother), Dick Philpott (Del's father).

London's East End, late sixties. Del, an apprentice welder, spends his spare time roaming the fringes of delinquency with his teenage friends. He starts a faltering romance with fifteen-year-old Irene, whose father is in prison. When Del's father and Irene's mother react vehemently to the couple's relationship, they elope and stay with Del's friend, Bronco Bullfrog, a more seasoned criminal with a flat full of stolen goods. Irene's mother responds by alerting the police to her daughter's 'abduction.'

We touch on the flipside to the swinging sixties many times in these pages, but few London films are more antithetical to that artificial orgy of free love and wide-eyed optimism than *Bronco Bullfrog*, shot in black and white for £18,000 on the streets of the East End with an unprofessional cast of teenagers from Joan Littlewood's Playbarn youth theatre project. While Carnaby Street may have been groovin' to the fashions and tunes of the era, the Stratford of *Bronco Bullfrog* is very much the depressing pit it always had been. Despite the odd signifier of the times — such as protagonist Del's Dave Davies haircut and pal Bronco's suedehead threads — this is, sadly, a timeless landscape; it could be the bombed-out London of the early fifties or the jobless underbelly of Thatcher-era Britain.

Bronco Bullfrog: Central London might have been swinging, Stratford wasn't.

Bronco Bullfrog: a rare moment of youthful exuberance.

Del, who looks like David Warner's beleaguered younger brother, is so bored with his environment that he can barely summon the energy to speak. The only stimulation he and his mates have is petty crime — a dash of breaking and entering, the odd bit of thieving — and you can't really blame them. As inexpressive as Del is, his repetition of "There's nothing to do round here" becomes a pointed refrain; the antisocial behaviour (as we would call it now) he gets caught up in is borne only of frustration — there is no real sourness in his heart. But there are no prospects where he lives, no money. The area is heading straight from postwar slumland poverty to a desolate 'No Future' cityscape of tower blocks and urban violence, with nothing in between. Stratford's proximity to the consumerist delights of central London is meaningless. Its high rise flats might as well be stacked cages; once Del and his mates accept their fate, they know there'll be be no chance to escape.

Bronco Bullfrog has its place in a British cinema chronology that spans the Free Cinema documentaries of the fifties to the films of Shane Meadows — by way of Ken Loach, Mike Leigh and Alan Clarke, even The Who's *Quadrophenia* — but in many ways the film is more representative of the 'cinema of social work' than it is of socialist cinema. The Playbarn theatre project was set up as an extension of Joan Littlewood's world famous Theatre Workshop to give kids like Del and Bronco something to do with their time, to steer them away from exactly the kind of fate they end up with in the film. Platts-Mills got involved with Playbarn to make a documentary about it (*Everybody's An Actor, Shakespeare Said* [68]) and was then encouraged by the participants to develop a feature film with them; at twenty-five — not that much older than most of the cast — the director wasn't so much using the young performers to make a sociological point as helping them make their own point, working with them 'on the ground,' letting the film's narrative evolve loosely around their ideas and personalities.

The results are, not surprisingly, unpolished. The non-professionalism of the cast is heavily apparent and their delivery of the improvised dialogue can make things hard to follow, but, as most reviewers who take themselves seriously will tell you, this adds to the 'authenticity' of the piece. It is revealing, however, that the film garnered good reviews when it was released in New York, where it had to play with subtitles. To audiences who think they're watching a foreign language film, *Bullfrog* looks something like an Italian neo-realist masterpiece: a *Rome*, *Open City* or a *Bicycle Thieves*. Platts-Mills was, by his own admission, influenced by the neo-realist movement, and he certainly has an eye for drawing human drama from the impoverished locations.

Dave Davies? No, Del Walker. *Bronco Bullfrog.*

Impressive as it is in its depiction of a teenage wasteland, *Bullfrog* also coasts on a warm stream of laconic humour. The kids are likeable, despite their casual disregard for law and order. No one stones any babies to death. Even Bronco, the 'hardened' borstal boy, has a Neanderthal charm about him. At the end we see him racing off into the middle distance, pursued by 'the Man,' just like Sweet Sweetback in Melvin Van Peebles' iconic *Sweet Sweetback's Baadasssss Song* (71), but here the effect is more mischievous than radical. And at the centre of it all is a love story (of sorts) between Del and Irene, a love story that, for all its inarticulacy and lack of romance, is believable and sometimes quite tender.

Today, *Bronco Bullfrog* dips in and out of view at film festivals and has received a prestigious Blu-ray BFI release. But it's still not well known, and probably never will be. Left on the shelf for a year after it was made, its distribution was uneven to say the least, despite making a small, if belated, impact at Cannes and selected international cities. But we're lucky to be able to see it at all. Platts-Mills has recounted that the film's 35mm negative was saved for the archives only after it was rescued from a rubbish pile at the bankrupt Humphries Laboratories by a sharp-eyed employee (a story all too believable — the British film industry still has a lot of making up to do for past sins regarding the preservation of its legacy). Today, BFI releases notwithstanding, DVD transfers of the film are always available from the director himself at www.platts-mills.com.

Julian Upton

DEEP END (1970)

Maran Films/Bavaria-Atelia/Kettledrum | 91 mins | colour

Director Jerzy Skolimowski; **Producer** Helmut Jedels; **Screenplay** Jerzy Skolimowski, Jerzy Gruza, Boleslaw Sulik. **Starring** John Moulder-Brown (Mike), Jane Asher (Susan), Diana Dors, Karl Michael Vogler.

School-leaver Mike starts a job at a London bathhouse. His beautiful co-worker Susan suggests he swaps his male clients for her female ones, in order for them both to make better tips from 'attending to them.' Mike agrees but is not interested in his ageing female clientele. Instead he develops a crush on Susan, which becomes more obsessive and destructive when he finds she is having an affair with the baths' swimming instructor.

At a May 2011 BFI screening of a digitally restored *Deep End*, I sat in an audience that seemed to find every instance of visual absurdity and awkward dialogue hysterically funny, and yet I still find the film something of an unsettling 'sex comedy,' even as it passes forty years old. [1]

At least I'm in good company in not finding the film riotously funny. Its star, the fragrant Jane Asher, was in the audience for the screening and gamely took questions afterwards. "I don't think a lot of it was actually intended to be funny," she proffered, good naturedly. Alas, no one seemed to believe her, not even her co-star John Moulder-Brown (who, with a preciousness befitting a golden-haired child actor but not really a man of nearly sixty, turned up for the debate but couldn't watch the film because he 'didn't have the courage.' Still, he had some vague memories of shooting it. Very useful for the Q&A).

None of this is to say I don't like *Deep End*. In fact, I like it a lot: not for its clunky, artificial, largely post-synched dialogue, or for its uneasy mix of German and British actors who can barely understand a word the other is saying, but for its bold evocation of a run-down setting, its provocative use of primary colours and, not least, its downright lurid seediness. Few of that era's youth-oriented films caught the grubbiness of an unvarnished, late sixties Britain with such spiky individuality. And although many of *Deep End*'s exterior

Radiating sex: Jane Asher in *Deep End*.

JANE ASHER
JOHN MOULDER-BROWN · DIANA DORS
in
DEEP END(X)
Directed by JERZY SKOLIMOWSKI

scenes were shot in Munich — "Was that to foster a sense of displacement?" asked one beard-stroker in the BFI audience; "Not really; it was down to money," said Asher — the film seems to encapsulate 'permissive-era' England far more convincingly than anything from the cinema of swinging London. In its unique, semi-surreal way, *Deep End* channels the frustrating reality of late adolescence in a grey, ascetic country that was only being teased and tormented with the promise of rampant debauchery.

Even so, without being explicit, *Deep End* pulsates with sexuality. But it's rarely joyful; the sex here is dirty, cheap, unwanted or dishonest. And, ultimately, it's unsatisfying.

From the moment school leaver Mike (Moulder-Brown) starts his new job at the decrepit swimming baths and sets eyes on the beautiful, slightly older attendant Susan (Asher), he is thrust not only into the deep end of adult work and responsibility, but also into the midst of a sexual storm. As his teenage

yearnings overwhelm him, Susan becomes not just an object of lust and desire, but of jealousy and obsession. And all around Mike there are predatory or cynical attitudes to sex: from the overheated, middle-aged female patrons of the bath house (such as Diana Dors, who molests him while screaming orgasmically about footballer George Best in a scene that, perhaps shamefully, is actually funny)

Schizoid flirting: Asher is ogled by John Moulder-Brown. *Deep E...*

and the budding teenage girl swimmers and their touchy-feely male instructor (hey, it was the seventies) to Susan's casual dispensing of 'extra services' to male clients for ten bob each. Later, Mike stalks Susan and her fiancé through seedy Soho streets awash with crummy soft porn cinemas, gaudy hookers ("You can't imagine the things we can do for three quid") and window displays promising naked dancing girls. But it's a landscape of puerile sexuality: there's nothing really liberated about it. To director Skolimowski's outsider's eye, there isn't much evidence of a sexual revolution in swinging London, just a juvenile frustration. Everything remains at arm's length, in a manner of speaking.

Any genuine sexiness in the film radiates from Jane Asher. She and Moulder-Brown are pretty good together; there is chemistry to their schizoid relationship. Sometimes they seem like brother and older sister: one minute trading vindictive exchanges and physically fighting, the next showing camaraderie and affection. There's a playful flirtatiousness between them, before it turns dangerous. Ultimately, though, Asher is too much for the naïve and hormonal Moulder-Brown to handle: she is a truly sexual person while he is still grasping at the idea. But by the end, as she fends off his lumbering advances in the deep end of the empty swimming pool, she's merely naked and vulnerable, as pale and helpless as an uncooked supermarket chicken.

It's not a particularly funny image, but it's one that sticks with you.

Julian Upton

---

1   The over-egged laughter at the screening annoyed me. What is it with 'sophisticated' audiences that find mildly amusing passages in arthouse films so uproariously funny? Do they have to loudly prove they 'get it'? Were they laughing because the refined programme notes 'confirmed' it was a comedy? Would they have laughed so hard if the film had been gloomily described as a dark tale of destructive obsession and sexual harassment? We'd probably get a truer response to *Deep End* from a multiplex full of sullen teenagers. Of course, we'd have to chain them to their seats first...

GIRL STROKE BOY (1971)

Hemdale/Virgin Films/London Screen | 82 mins | colour

Director Bob Kellett; **Producers** Terry Glinwood, Ned Sherrin; **Screenplay** Caryl Brahms, Ned Sherrin, adapted from the David Percival play *Girlfriend*. **Starring** Clive Francis (Laurie Mason), Peter Straker (Jo Delaney), Joan Greenwood (Lettice Mason), Michael Hordern (George Mason).

Laurie arrives at the family home to visit parents George and Lettice, bringing with him new sweetheart Jo, who is not quite what the status-conscious middle-class couple expect. George is easily charmed by the exotic Jo, but Lettice is worried and determined to discover Jo's true identity, even if it is at the cost of her son's happiness.

A s Spike Milligan played for politically incorrect laughs as 'Paki Paddy' in the late sixties LWT sitcom *Curry and Chips* and Mary Whitehouse was railing against the filth peddled by the BBC, a group of London theatregoers were engaged in silent revolution. In 1970 David Percival's play, *Girlfriend*, ran at Shaftesbury Avenue's Apollo Theatre, relating the story of a young man who brings home his new — and rather mysterious — companion to meet his parents. *Girl Stroke Boy* adapts Percival's play into a genuinely interesting film that defies genre conventions of its day, placing a gay black man at the centre of the action.

Guess Who's Coming to Dinner (67) had previously investigated the issue of inter-racial relationships, presenting a well spoken Sidney Poitier who eventually charms the family of his fiancé with his intelligent amiability. *Girl Stroke Boy* goes one step further, challenging existing portrayals of black men by placing the flamboyant Jo (Peter Straker) centre stage: "I hope I'm not too much of a shock," he ponders, spritzing cologne across his satin shirt and tight embroidered dungarees. The contrast with *Guess Who's Coming to Dinner* seems no accident as mother Lettice (Joan Greenwood) thunders "No one's coming to dinner!," and hatches plans to get rid of their expected dinner guests lest they catch a glimpse of Jo.

In the excited moments before the arrival of son Laurie (Clive Francis) and his new partner, Lettice and husband George (Michael Hordern) congratulate themselves on their open-mindedness. Laurie has already divulged the news that Jo is West Indian and 'with it' Lettice is positively gushing over the possibility: "You know that on the colour question, I am a pioneer," she says. Poor George couldn't care less, and Michael Hordern plays the bumbling husband with the same wit as he did most of his clueless scholarly characters.

Guess who's coming to dinner... *Girl Stroke Boy.*

IN COLOUR

His experiences of life outside their rural middle-class abode leave him cold, even the Head Girl at his secondary modern who frequently "expose[s] herself." The unrelenting wry dialogue throughout keeps up the pace, even if it is from the mouths of characters too stereotyped to be taken as anything but comedic. Patricia Routledge of *Keeping Up Appearances* fame even puts in a brief turn as one of the

dinner guests, earning a swift reprisal from Lettice on her choice of dress: "Pamela! You know perfectly well that it won't look good against my chairs."

This humorous element makes it difficult to label *Girl Stroke Boy* in any straightforward manner, with jokes sitting oddly alongside what is essentially a serious drama of social mores. The jokes though, are all on the parents. Jo's appearance may be outlandish against the backdrop of the Masons' magnolia and wicker furnishings, but the most extreme reactions come from Lettice, whose distress at her son's new relationship is painfully palpable. Bemoaning Laurie's fragile mental condition, she becomes the picture of madness herself — jumping up and down on the bed to implore George to 'do something about it.' Lettice's unhinged demeanour is a clever riposte to the popular idea of homosexuality as a genuine mental 'problem.' A survey of British psychiatrists in the early seventies, for example, found that sixty-nine per cent still viewed homosexuality as an 'aberrant behaviour pattern.'[1]

Within such a climate, *Girl Stroke Boy*'s non-judgmental depiction of a gay relationship not surprisingly had its critics. Even before the film's theatrical release, the filmmakers were in trouble with the Advertising Viewing Committee: a poster depicting the soles of a couple's feet in 'an inverted missionary position' were deemed too sexually suggestive and the feet rearranged into a more acceptable side by side arrangement. On its release,

1   P.A. Morris, 'Doctors' attitudes to homosexuality,' *British Journal of Psychiatry 122* (1973), pp.435–36.
2   Richard Afton, *Evening News* [original date not cited]. Cited in Bourne, Stephen, *Black in the British Frame: Black People in British Film and Television 1896–1996* (London: Cassell, 1998), pp.182–83.
3   Matt Cook, 'From Gay Reform to Gaydar, 1967–2006' in Matt Cook (ed.), *A Gay History of Britain: Love and Sex Between Men Since the Middle-ages* (Oxford: Greenwood World Publishing, 2007), p.187. Thanks are also due to Stephe Feldman at Androgyne Online, http://androgyne.ocatch.com/gsb.htm [Last accessed November 2009].

Richard Afton's comment —'Seeing men kissing each other and making love is not my idea of entertainment'[2] — was typical of the generally hostile and homophobic reaction the film received. For its first (rare) TV appearance in 1978 it was billed as a 'Saturday adult movie.' Perhaps it was this showing that led some film historians to label *Girl Stroke Boy* a 'sex film,' alongside the likes of *The Wife Swappers* (70) and *Virgin Witch* (70).

Allusions to sex there are, and a couple of fleeting kisses, but nothing to merit slotting the film into the British sexploitation bracket. Essentially, *Girl Stroke Boy* is a gay pride film, a coming out drama, because as hard as the filmmakers may have tried to maintain an aura of mystery around the androgynous Jo, it's quite clear that 'she' is a he. In the closing credits, Jo is billed simply as 'Straker': the first and only lead role for Peter Straker, an original *Hair* cast member who went on to star in a number of minor TV roles after a brief foray into camp comedy territory when he was cast as 'the Arab' in *Up the Chastity Belt* (71). He is probably best remembered by *Doctor Who* fans as Commander Sharrel from the Destiny Of The Daleks episodes in 1979, but by 2000 had been reduced to small parts in BBC's *Casualty*.

The film, forgotten though it may be, represents a subtle turning point. Appearing the same year as Schlesinger's *Sunday, Bloody Sunday, Girl Stroke Boy*'s depiction of an inter-racial gay couple was food for thought for white, straight society, as well as that element of the gay community that considered the black gay man as a stereotypical hypersexualised 'other.'[3] It presented a challenge to those films of the sixties which celebrated an aggressive, ultra-masculine and often misogynistic strain of British youth culture, by replacing them with a more all-encompassing version of manhood. *Girl Stroke Boy* was one of many small but significant voices in the wider campaign for gay rights that took hold in the 1970s, with its speedy disappearance from British screens perhaps the strongest testament to its importance.

Jennifer Wallis

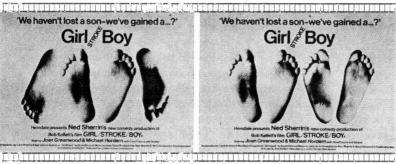

Rejected advertising campaign for *Girl Stroke Boy* (left) and the approved model.

GOODBYE GEMINI (1970)

a.k.a. Twinsanity | Josef Shaftel Productions/Cinerama Releasing | 89 mins | colour

Director Alan Gibson; **Producer** Peter Snell; **Screenplay** Edmund Ward, based on the novel *Ask Agamemnon* by Jenni Hall. **Starring** Marion Diamond (Denise Pryce-Fletcher), Judy Geeson (Jacki), Martin Potter (Julian), Alexis Kanner (Clive Landseer), Michael Redgrave (James Harrington-Smith).

Arriving in London, twins Julian and Jacki quickly come to the attention of some of the city's seedier characters. As Jacki attracts significant male interest, Julian becomes increasingly unhinged, his incestuous interests in his sister taking him down a slippery slope to blackmail, prostitution and murder.

lan Gibson is better known for his Hammer films *The Satanic Rites of Dracula* (73) and *Dracula A.D. 1972*, which may be why there is some argument whether *Goodbye Gemini* is a horror film in the true sense. Gibson devotees are perhaps over-keen to align it with his later Gothic fare. Indeed, the tagline 'In the Age of Aquarius the twins Julian and Jacki share everything — love, men and murder!' hints at sinister New Age goings on, but horror fiends will likely be disappointed by the slow paced drama for little gory reward.

The horror of *Goodbye Gemini* is primarily psychological, charting a struggle for dominance between unfeasibly attractive twins Julian and Jacki as they navigate the underbelly of swinging London. Their arrival in the big city leads almost instantly to the demise of their housekeeper, aided in her fall down the stairs by Agamemnon, the twin's ever-present teddy bear. The twins appear to be in their early twenties but exist in a childlike world where role play is the order of the day and life resembles a perverse parody of an Enid Blyton book: *"Oh Julian, you are super!"* Anyone who encroaches upon their fantasies risks meeting a sticky end. Their unconventional relationship — witness, for example, a distinctly unsettling slow dance sequence — proves irresistible to pimp Clive and his girlfriend Denise who shamelessly pursue Jacki and Julian, heightening tensions between the twins.

Predictably in the tradition of the twin film (marginal as it is), mental states steadily unravel as the film progresses. Helping to convey the psychological breakdown of the duo are mirrors. Throughout, Julian avoids his own reflection except on those occasions when it appears alongside that of Jacki: following an assault by two transvestites in a seedy hotel room, he turns hurriedly away from a large mirror to see himself instead reflected physically in the face of his sister. Only in the closing scene, having strangled Jacki, is he able to face himself in the mirror: shivering, crying and distraught, Julian's fantasy world is finally exposed as a sham. Another scene sees Jacki in a mirror as she runs along the upper deck of a bus, attempting to escape her reflection/Julian. Although Jacki appears to hold the reins in the relationship ("He's a little bastard. Sometimes he needs hitting about every ten minutes."), Julian persistently tries to assert his authority and becomes wildly jealous should another man speak to his sister. Jacki tolerates his incestuous designs to a degree, but more than once is seen pushing him away as his affections become too close for comfort. The liberating experience of London changes Jacki,

as she pulls further away from her brother and out into a glamorous world of new friends and experiences; her increasingly headstrong manner is evident in her speech, most memorably when she rebuffs the odious Clive with the ultimate put-down: "If you touch me... I think I'll be sick."

Alongside the twins, there is a crucial third element to the relationship: Agamemnon, the beribboned teddy bear who is whisked along with the duo to all manner of hip places. Although the authority of glassy-eyed Agamemnon is nothing more than a figment of childish imagination, at times he is an oddly unsettling presence. Invited by Clive to find somewhere 'private' to drink together, Julian engages in a whispered conversation with the bear in order to gain his permission. Later, setting the scene for Clive's murder, Agamemnon is carefully positioned on the bed where, from his vantage point, he looks on as the twins swiftly do away with their friend. (This scene wouldn't be out of place in a Hammer production, as Jacki and Julian appear shrouded

in white sheets, towering over Clive brandishing Samurai swords before brutally slashing his throat.) In Greek mythology, Agamemnon commanded armies in the Trojan War and his family history — like that of many Greek notables — was a catalogue of murder, rape and incest. The idea that cuddly Agamemnon is the silent commander of his own small army may be subtle almost to the point of invisibility, but it is an interesting background touch. When Jacki visits the scene of Clive's murder, her blood-curdling scream from the house is presented as a reaction not to Clive's

Doomed: Judy Geeson and Alexis Kanner. *Goodbye Gemini.*

bloodied body, but to Agamemnon, who has been disembowelled, stuffing spilling from his black fur. His 'death' marks the end of childhood, as Julian hides in the hotel room intended for his prostitution and Jacki wanders the streets barefoot and blood-spattered.

Goodbye Gemini enjoys something of a cult following, and reviewers rightly locate the film within the 'enclosed universe' trend, akin to MUMSY, NANNY, SONNY AND GIRLY (70), as well as a classic example of the swinging London genre that included gems such as *Cool It, Carol* (70).[1] Like other swinging London flicks, the film is positively gasping to cram in as much social 'comment' as possible, meaning that side-plots like the relationship between MP Harrington-Smith and delightfully camp duo David Curry (Freddie Jones) and Nigel Garfield (Terry Scully) are unfortunately presented almost as an afterthought. The film's charms though are clear to see, with possibly the most visually arresting duo ever put together on film a perfect complement to the sheer weirdness of it all.

Jennifer Wallis

1   See Kim Newman, *'Goodbye Gemini'* in Harvey Fenton and David Flint (eds.), *Ten Years of Terror: British Horror Films of the 1970s* (Guildford: Fab Press, 2001), p.28.

LET IT BE (1970)

Apple Corps/United Artists | 81 mins | colour

Director Michael Lindsay-Hogg; **Producers** The Beatles, Neil Aspinall, Mal Evans. **Starring** [not credited] John Lennon, Paul McCartney, George Harrison, Ringo Starr.

A documentary showing the Beatles rehearsing songs for a new album, culminating in what was to be their last live performance as a group: the impromptu concert on the Apple Corps building rooftop in January 1969.

A concert by the Rolling Stones at Altamont speedway track in November 1969 is regarded as the black cloud that washed away the era of peace and love. Presided over by Hell's Angels, whose approach to crowd management led to one count of murder, the ill-fated concert was the subject of a feature length documentary, released theatrically in December 1970 as *Gimme Shelter*. It is a landmark film, despite having repulsed cinemagoers of the day who were expecting something akin to *Woodstock* but starring Mick and Keith.

Gimme Shelter has an antecedent. A few months prior to its release, cinema seats were being vacated for yet another feature length music documentary starring another musical demigod: the Beatles. *Let It Be* is a strange mirror to *Gimme Shelter*. It is not a concert film, but a film about a concert that never really happens. It's a film that captures the slow and painful disintegration of the Beatles as a working unit, the most important cultural bookmark of the 1960s.

In January 1969, only months prior to a messy divorce, John Lennon, Paul McCartney, George Harrison and Ringo Starr, known collectively as the Beatles, convened at Twickenham film studios to prepare material for a proposed live Beatles concert, the first since their self imposed exile in 1967. It was a far cry from the cosy confines of Abbey Road studios, where the Beatles usually worked and recorded: Twickenham was the size of an aircraft hanger and in it the Beatles were very insignificant indeed.

The band was barely working as a unit at this point; it was effectively four solo artists with whom the others sometimes begrudgingly still played. At Twickenham it got much worse. Conflicts within the group were accelerating, due in part to their failing Apple business empire and an inability to agree on a business manager, ending up instead with two. Another conflict was that Lennon would bring to the sessions his new girlfriend, Yoko Ono, insisting she

should have as much say in the group as he. This was when Lennon bothered to turn up at all.[1]

And the icing on the cake? A film crew was present to record every moment for the contractually obliged new Beatles film. The most remarkable aspect of the resultant film is the resolute dreariness of such a once dynamic force.

The Beatles' film career started on a commercial and critical high with Richard Lester's sartorial *A Hard Day's Night* in 1964. The follow-up, *Help!* (65), was another success but the Beatles were already bored with the trite conventions of stardom and their film career hereafter takes a path to avoid it. The script for a possible third feature by hip playwright Joe Orton was completed but ultimately rejected. In its place came *Magical Mystery Tour* (67), an abstract made-for-TV venture conceived and directed by the Beatles themselves. It befuddled the BBC Boxing Day audience that tuned in to watch its premiere. *Yellow Submarine* (68) is an animated feature that utilises Beatle songs and the Beatle personas (dubbed by actors), but the Beatles actually had very little to do with it.

Let It Be came next, an idea borrowed from a 1968 TV special orchestrated by the Rolling Stones entitled *The Rolling Stones Rock and Roll Circus*. It showcased performances by some of the biggest names in rock music, among them John Lennon. Its director, Michael Lindsay-Hogg, a young veteran of TV drama and comedy, was invited next to film the Beatles.

The plan for *Let It Be* was a fly-on-the-wall TV special, removed from the type of theatrics that defined *Rock and Roll Circus*. McCartney wanted bright lights, not moody lighting, for a warts and all study. It's unlikely anyone was expecting quite so ugly a close-up, however. The opening sequence, in which McCartney draws a fragmented melody from a piano while Ringo Starr gazes into middle distance, a half eaten apple between them, is perfectly indicative of the film to follow. The live concert idea was aborted mid project, and the band concentrated on a new back-to-basics album instead, the eponymous *Let It Be*. Lennon later described these sessions as the lowest of the low. The band do little more than sit and chat about last night's telly, occasionally alleviating the tedium with some jaundiced rock and roll covers and a lackadaisical stab at new material. They bicker a lot, with the relationship between McCartney and Harrison being particularly frayed. McCartney at one point accuses Harrison of deliberately misinterpreting everything he says, and later gripes about his band mate to a nonplussed Lennon; Harrison on the other hand introduces a new composition, stating he doesn't care whether McCartney likes it or not.

Paul at the wheel in *Let It Be.*

Filming each day commenced with the arrival at the studio of the first Beatle and concluded when the last one departed. It is a remarkable time capsule, but, in spite of the sheer volume of material committed to tape, it is one that provides very little actual insight into the group or its workings. The fault isn't entirely with Lindsay-Hogg;[2] the Beatles influenced the cut of the film, calling for scenes to be removed. At one point Harrison quit the band only to return days later, but this pivotal moment is missing from the final print. McCartney is an overriding presence in what is left; more than once the documentary is jettisoned so he may play songs to camera in the model of a music video.

Let It Be hasn't surfaced in any official capacity since its home video release in the early eighties. Its last British TV screening was 1982. The insatiable appetite for all things Beatles along with Apple's continued reinvention of the Beatles catalogue makes for a strange, if not unexpected, absence. The film portrays the Beatles in a bad light. Despite one moment of warmth and the impromptu rooftop concert that closes the film with the threat of police arrest, *Let It Be* is a doleful and wasted exercise. It makes the brutal epitaph of *Gimme Shelter* entirely necessary.

David Kerekes

Offbeat

Let It Be rooftop concert. Ringo has his sights on *Son of Dracula.*

1   Much like the film itself, the book that originally came with the *Let It Be* album gives nothing of this
     away. Ethan A. Russell, Jonathan Cott and David Dalton, *The Beatles Get Back* (London: Apple, 1969).
2   In his memoirs, *Luck and Circumstance* (NY: Knopf, 2011) , Lindsay-Hogg confirms the rumour that he
     is Orson Welles' son.
NOTES Following the Beatles split, George Harrison and Ringo Starr would remain active in films.
Harrison formed HandMade Films in the late seventies, the production and distribution company
behind *Monty Python's Life of Brian* (79), *A Private Function* (85) and *Withnail and I* (87). Starr on
the other hand took to acting. He played in the decent THAT'LL BE THE DAY (73) but generally had roles
in rather quirky, unsuccessful movies. In Frank Zappa's *200 Motels* (71) he plays Frank Zappa, and in
Ken Russell's *Listzomania* (75) he plays the Pope. Most quirky of all however is *Son of Dracula* (74).
Produced by Ringo Starr under the Apple banner, this obscure horror musical directed by Freddie
Francis warrants attention here. Starr plays Merlin the magician and cohort to singer/songwriter Harry
Nilsson's vampire, Count Down, who is attempting to beat Baron Frankenstein (Freddie Jones) to the
crown king of the Netherworld. Set in contemporary London, the film has several musical interludes
consisting of Nilsson performing songs to camera with guest musicians Keith Moon, John Bonham and
Peter Frampton. (It sounds better on paper.) The amalgamation of rock music and horror convention
is tragic, and the film feels like it is being scripted as it goes along. But everyone except Starr plays it
straight; even Dennis Price, who is on hand as Van Helsing, plays it straight. Nilsson is incapable of
playing it any other way because his capacity as an actor is nil, and he has no screen presence, while
Starr simply reprises his comedy wizard shtick from *Magical Mystery Tour* (altogether less fun at
feature length). The film gets off to a promising start, invoking a sense of nightmare in its pre-credit
sequence (looking as if it was modelled for 3D), but hereafter loses steam and ideas, like so much rock
and roll inspired cinema. *Son of Dracula* is assuredly a curio, but one less entertaining than Anthony
Balch's *Horror Hospital* (73) or Paul Morrissey's *Blood for Dracula* (74), which it evokes at times.
John Lennon's final album (with Yoko Ono), *Double Fantasy*, poorly received on its release in 1980,
sounds greatly influenced by Nilsson. One can easily imagine Nilsson performing the material on it.

MUMSY, NANNY, SONNY & GIRLY (1970)

a.k.a. Girly | Brigitte/Fitzroy Films/Ronald J. Kahn Productions | 102 mins | colour

Director Freddie Francis; **Producer** Ronald J. Khan; **Screenplay** Brian Comport, based on the play *Happy Family* by Masie Mosco. **Starring** Michael Bryant (New Friend), Ursula Howells (Mumsy), Pat Heywood (Nanny), Howard Trevor (Sonny), Vanessa Howard (Girly).

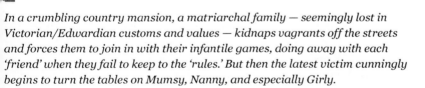

In a crumbling country mansion, a matriarchal family — seemingly lost in Victorian/Edwardian customs and values — kidnaps vagrants off the streets and forces them to join in with their infantile games, doing away with each 'friend' when they fail to keep to the 'rules.' But then the latest victim cunningly begins to turn the tables on Mumsy, Nanny, and especially Girly.

Knitting in the conservatory. Playing cowboys and Indians. Administering bromide and castor oil. Nailing shut bedroom doors. All wholesome family activities. Side-stepping the safety of Hammer/Amicus for one moment, Freddie Francis' *Mumsy, Nanny, Sonny and Girly* exists in a polite English borderland of dust and decay, simultaneously doffing an ill-fitting school cap to the past whilst brutally ridiculing it. The Victorian Gothic structure of Oakley Court, Berkshire, is the setting for this peculiar story. Once a Hammer location for the likes of *Plague of the Zombies* (65) and *The Reptile* (66), here it has fallen into

grand disrepair; a smothering Petri dish, where unsuitable questions are not allowed at the dinner table. Where did these people come from? Why are they acting this way? Where's 'Daddy'? Why are they playing a game? The only answer to that is: "You've *got* to play the game."

Sonny and Girly like to stray from home, seeking out new friends. Tramps, drunks. After running riot round a zoo, tormenting horror heirloom Michael Ripper, they find a man called Soldier (Robert Swann) asleep on a park bench, wake him, tempt him ("Nice drinkie?"), bury him up to his neck in a nearby sandpit and then usher him home. There's a sandpit back there, as well. In the film's opening scenes it sums up the children's temperament nicely: you've got to play with it, otherwise the weeds start to show through. "In a happy family you must always have rules," the prim Mumsy tells Soldier as they gather for afternoon tea. But, over a pink blancmange rabbit, he's not having any of it: "What about my teacake?!" he demands. "Where's my bleeding medicine?!" Outside, in the afternoon sun, the instigation of a nursery rhyme game signals the lecherous Soldier's end, and the chopper comes to chop off his head...

Enter Michael Bryant and hot-but-doomed Imogen Hassall, fresh from a hip party. Sonny and Girly dip into this world in order to obtain a new friend. After some nocturnal playground fun, Hassall makes a flying exit and Bryant, enticed by Girly, becomes New Friend, waking to a terrible morning-after nightmare (curiously, just like Murray Brown in the 1974 Oakley Hall-set degenerate classic *Vampyres*) and suddenly forced into gruesome parlour games and ghoulish pranks, the lovely corpse of his girlfriend never far away.

But New Friend becomes canny to this world, falling in with 'the game.' Accustomed to seduction, he sets to work almost straight away, using Mumsy as a way to get to the devastatingly attractive, dangerously unhinged Girly. His amorous attentions confuse her, and New Friend is for some time unaware that he is playing with fire, blinded perhaps by Girly's schoolgirl get-up and frilly blue knickers. A homicidal Alice, innocent and vain. So what happens if you don't play the game? "We send you to the angels." She also reminds him that there are plenty more dollies in the toy cupboard, but already the damage is done: Mumsy, Girly and Nanny are bedded (if New Friend seduced Sonny as well, it might have pitched the film uneasily into the contemporary urban decadence of 1970's GOODBYE GEMINI), and the seeds of mistrust begin to grow into full-scale downfall.

The family uses the perverse justification of 'rules' and 'structure' as a way of stopping a dip into true insanity... or should that be into 'normality'? Once these rules are broken, deadly acid becomes the medicine of choice, an axe makes a perfect accompaniment to impromptu nursery rhymes, and New Friend finds out what happens when you don't play the game, courtesy of the locked-up Friend in Five (a forever mute Hugh Armstrong from *Death Line*). Because he misses the actual murder itself, the family gladly allows New Friend to watch it on their home projector, again and again and again...

Play the game. *Mumsy, Nanny, Sonny & Girly.*

A sign around his dead girlfriend's neck says it all: 'RULE NO 1: PLAY THE GAME.' Everything is there for a reason; everyone plays their part. But what happens when someone goes off the script? Fittingly, the film's origins are stage-based. It is a play on a dilapidated set, with a disruptive audience of one in the form of New Friend, leering down from the circle. All the actors play their parts admirably straight: Bryant (rock solid supernatural regular), Howells (alluring TV matriarch), Heywood (Zeferrelli cast-off), Trevor (obscurity) and especially Vanessa Howard. After late sixties dolly bird bit parts in the likes of *Here We Go Round the Mulberry Bush* (68), and the gob smacking Peter Cushing nasty CORRUPTION (68), she got the role of a lifetime with Girly: sexy, innocent, wicked and murderous, it's no surprise that her part was pushed to the fore in the limited, re-titled (*Girly*) American release of the film.

"Not mad," she tells New Friend in an unguarded moment. "We're happy. We're a happy family." But where they sprung from, or who created the rules, we shall never know. Mumsy quotes one of Charles Dickens' sentimental statements concerning childhood, but it is in fact a passing reference to Charles Kingsley's *The Water Babies* that best sums up the family: all the strenuous attempts to present an idealised version of purity and virtue to the world in fact merely allows the audience to glimpse, horrified, at unearthed preoccupations of an unnatural, sexual nature...

Such a disturbing take on supposed normality makes *Mumsy, Nanny, Sonny and Girly* a truly deranged classic, and also home to one of the most biting put-downs ever uttered in British cinema: "Just remember," Mumsy tells her subordinate. "You're only the Nanny. I'm the Mumsy."

Martin Jones

MY LOVER, MY SON (1970)

Sagittarius/MGM | 95 mins | colour

Director John Newland; **Producer** Wilbur Stark; **Screenplay** William Marchant and Jenni Hall, based on the novel *Reputation for a Song* by Edward Grierson. **Starring** Romy Schneider (Francesca Anderson), Donald Houston (Robert), Dennis Waterman (James); Patricia Brake (Julie).

Because his wealthy father is often away from home on business, James is free to take his place and lounge about the pool with his mother. This unhealthy relationship is usurped when James finds himself a girlfriend. Later, believing he has been responsible for the death of his father during a domestic fraças, James finally breaks free of mother altogether when he discovers the truth.

T he taboo of homosexuality had been well and truly dusted by Basil Dearden in *Victim* (61) when John Newland took this similarly sensational pop at the law of exogamy and sexual morality. Despite the clue of its title, the image on the film poster and the salacious intent of every scene shared by Romy Schneider and Dennis Waterman, *My Lover, My Son* isn't a meditation on the subject of incest as one might expect [1] or Newland had perhaps hoped. In fact it isn't much of a meditation on any one thing at all, and is a bit of mess.

Newland had already directed many episodes in some enormously popular US TV shows (*Peyton Place, Star Trek, Dr Kildare*) when he came to Britain for *My Lover, My Son*. He returned to familiar territory quickly afterwards when it was over.

Romy Schneider is akin to European cinema royalty. Dennis Waterman is not. So their pairing is somewhat jarring even before we know what's afoot. Waterman plays James Anderson, a rather tiresome young man enraptured by the idea of the new permissiveness and the times that are changing around him, but of which he has absolutely no part. He drives his girlfriend through town in a flash sports car and feeds on the wealth of his father, Robert, a hardworking man of the old school with whom he is often at loggerheads. He drops a bombshell when he tells the old man he won't be going to university, with no contingency for anything else but to swan about the family mansion playing silly games with his mother, Francesca (Schneider).

It's a role that requires plenty of emotion and depth of expression, and, at twenty-one, the miscast Waterman – better suited to his later hard man turns on TV in *The Sweeney* and *Minder* – is too old to be playing it. Another

Romy Schneider and Dennis Waterman: together at last!

more fundamental problem is that the film doesn't have any clear idea about what it wants to be. It opens with James pretending to chat up Francesca, a familiar diversion for this mother and son we are led to believe. She has just had one of several hallucinatory moments, reliving the tragedy that befell her first husband, Macer, who drowned in a swimming pool. She evidently loved him very much and when she looks at her son, it is in fact Macer she sees. (They share a similar taste in swimming trunks.) James is dismayed when his father

returns from a business trip to Kenya, if only because it puts a stop to him bursting in on his mother without first knocking. Throwing a party for friends and associates, Robert cannot help but notice that Francesca and James behave more like a courting couple in a slow dance than mother and son.

This is as close as the film gets to an overt description of the doomed relationship. A desperate ballad on the soundtrack implores "What's on your mind?" with horrible regularity, certainly with every close-up on Romy Schneider's face, but that's about it. The viewer is ill prepared for the film's final stretch, when Robert is killed following a family quarrel and James is put on trial for his murder. He can't remember what actually happened and is acquitted, but later Francesca confesses he was never responsible at all — she was. Even with a flashback it's all very improbable stuff.

Without its incest theme it's no stretch to imagine that *My Lover, My Son* would make for even duller viewing, but incest is almost irrelevant anyway when Francesca is revealed in the end to be quite mad and something of a black widow (having murdered Robert and very likely Macer before him), as well as possessing a weird, unexplained mind control power over James.

James' girlfriend Patricia is the embodiment of the new liberalism he so fondly talks about. She has a high tech job in that male dominated institution, the BBC, while wearing some of the shortest miniskirts on cinema record. It is Patricia who helps the sexually retarded James break the hold his mother has over him, being neither shocked nor surprised to discover the 'truth.'

In court, we learn from the prosecution that James dares sleep in bed without pyjamas. It's an interesting charge. Earlier in the film James' father laments to a mistress that he has little in common with his son, informing her that James only likes "experimental films in foreign languages. And they bore me!"

With this, crusty old dad, the deal-making suit and tie, puts himself in diametric opposition to permissiveness, liberalism and art, and as a consequence his fate is sealed; this appears by far a greater crime in the eyes of the 'now' than any number of mangled taboos, madness or even murder. In the face of it James and Francesca are absolved, leaving space enough for James to run to the miniskirted Patricia and greet the new dawn by her houseboat on the Thames.

David Kerekes

1   In his autobiography, *Reminder*, Dennis Waterman says the film was shot under a different title and that he was unaware of the incest theme until he saw the finished film. This seems unlikely. He says he was shocked by its salacious implication as he was by the film in general. Throughout Europe the title translated simply as *Incest*. See Dennis Waterman, *Reminder* (London: Hutchinson, 2000).

NO BLADE OF GRASS (1970)

Theodora Productions/MGM | 96 mins | colour

Director Cornel Wilde; **Producer** Cornel Wilde; **Screenplay** Sean Forestal and Cornel Wilde, from the novel *The Death of Grass* by John Christopher. **Starring** Nigel Davenport (John Custance), Jean Wallace (Ann Custance), John Hamill (Roger Burnham), Lynne Frederick (Mary Custance), Anthony May (Pirrie), Wendy Richard (Clara).

A virus that leads to the death of all grass-related plants is spreading from the East; worldwide famine is taking hold and desperate emergency measures are being enforced. In Britain, after hearing that cities are going to be closed off, John Custance leads his family away from riot-filled London in the hope of making it to his brother's farm in Yorkshire, encountering checkpoints, renegade military and motorbike gangs along the way.

As the opening credits roll over bleached, cracked earth, an apocalyptic orange sun and sketches of fleeing figures that recall prehistoric rock paintings, to the tune of a doleful guitar, Roger Whittaker sings words that — if you weren't already aware of John Christopher's flintily unsentimental 1957 source novel — give a fair idea that things are going to end badly, for everyone: "No blade of grass grows and birds sing no more / No joy or laughter where waves washed the shore / Gone all the answers, lost all we have won / Gone is the hope that life will go on."

"By the beginning of the seventies," says director Cornel Wilde, also on narrator duty, in words that chime closely with the sharpened concerns of our own age, "man had brought the destruction of his environment close to the point of no return. Of course there was a great deal of rhetoric about saving the Earth, but in reality, very little was done." To press home the point, stock footage of car dumps, belching chimneys, sulphurous skies, exhaust fumes, clogged roads, and brown smog blanketing a city lead us into the film, and then — to press home the point a little harder — there's more footage of smoke-belching chimneys, sewage-spouting pipes, poisonous river spume, opencast mining, oil spills and dead fish. And then a nuclear explosion to cap it all off. "No

Lynne Frederick and John Hamill. *No Blade of Grass.*

blade of grass here and no blue above / No you and me, it's the end of love," sings Roger.

"And then, one day, the polluted Earth could take no more," says Wilde, as the blue planet seen from space is smeared with orange clouds. Welcome to Earth, circa 1970, where London is no longer any place to be, a fact to which architect John Custance is alerted by a middle of the night phone call from his daughter's boyfriend Roger, telling him that, as they have been expecting for some while, the situation has suddenly turned critical and the government is sealing off the cities. As

they grab their suitcases and ready themselves for a hasty exit, the film winds back a year to the news breaking on television of a desperate famine in China and southeast Asia caused by an epidemic of grass disease, derived, according to the 'emergency committee of world ecology,' from cumulative residues of pollutants and pesticides. As joints of ham are carved on a buffet table and diners feed their faces, images of famine appear on the screen. More worrying reports then come through of cannibalism, and, in China, nerve gas bombings of major population areas. Well at least that couldn't happen here. Could it?

With the themes of eco-disaster and over-consumption now well and truly established, the film then — barring a few intermittent fill frames of more dead fish — drops them for a by-the-numbers treatment of the well-worn theme of a band of disparate survivors travelling through a decimated, dangerous country of unofficial checkpoints and intermittent crackly wireless news, mixing action scenes with disconsolate wandering across bare moors as the party head to the safe haven of Blind Gill, a Yorkshire farm owned by John's brother. Nigel Davenport plays the eyepatch-sporting leader of the group, the archetypal decent man forced to adjust his behaviour to the needs of the time, while Jean Wallace (the director's wife) takes the role of Mrs Custance. Their party is boosted by Pirrie, handy with a rifle, and his pouty, petulant wife (a black-haired and well-upholstered Wendy Richard), who has an eye for anything in trousers. Her attempted seduction of Custance leads Pirrie to debate throwing her out of the group. "She's got a survival kit between her legs," he says, but then he shoots her anyway so she doesn't get the chance to use it.

Although Wilde attempts to jazz up proceedings with flash-forwards that signal (in tinted blinking red) the dangers they will face along the way, including a rape and an attack by horned-helmeted bikers, the leaden script, which veers between shock one-liners and flaccid sentimentality ("A year ago I wouldn't have believed it could happen to us"), means the film loses its way on the journey. At one point, Burnell Whibley's music signals, somewhat unexpectedly, that we are in a western, following a group of pioneers on the trail, but by the time we get to watching a biker's nightmare as a motorbike hits a rock and explodes in slow motion, the plot, and any focus on ecological issues, has long taken a back seat to set pieces and not-so-fancy effects. It doesn't help that some time before a coup has been announced on the car radio (by a spokesperson who seems to be none other than Peter Sellers in the guise of Fred Kite): "This is the, er, citizen's emergency committee in London," he says, "we've taken charge of the BBC." Let's just say that the film's ambition outstrips the talent and judgement available for its realisation.

It does capture some of the matter of fact, casual brutality of Christopher's novel in which killing has become a necessary part of survival, and a scene that plays out in negative, in which men seem to kill a squealing dog for food with rocks and a spade, is genuinely unsettling. ("No living creature was killed or mistreated in the making of this film," assures a disclaimer.) In the end though it can't justify its grandiloquent final claim that "this motion picture is not a documentary... but it could be."

As evidenced by Penguin's 2009 Modern Classics edition of the original novel, with an introduction by Robert Macfarlane (who notes that Wilde's film is so "arrestingly bad that Christopher himself has never been able to watch more than a few minutes of it"), the story itself still carries a powerful charge and relevance over half a century after its creation. It still awaits a film adaptation that does it justice.

Graeme Hobbs

TOOMORROW (1970)

Lowndes Productions/Rank | 95 mins | colour

Director Val Guest; **Producers** Harry Saltzman, Don Kirshner; **Screenplay** Val Guest.
Starring Olivia Newton-John (Olivia), Roy Dotrice (John Williams), Benny Thomas (Benny), Karl
Chambers (Karl), Roy Marsden (Alpha).

*The Alphoids, an alien race, are dying out — and only the music of an Earthling
pop group, Toomorrow, can revive their civilisation. An Alphoid agent on
Earth approaches the group, who are busy with their own career and the
groovy London scene, and arranges an intergalactic concert.*

One of the rarest British sci-fi films, *Toomorrow* opened and closed
inside a fortnight and then disappeared. An expensive production,
a personal project for ex-Bond producer Harry Saltzman, it had
a complicated history, with an early draft script from David
Benedictus junked and rewritten from scratch by director Val Guest — who
had a habit of rewriting scripts by everyone from Nigel Kneale to J.G. Ballard
in order to secure screen credit and extra payment. In the event, Guest had
the film injuncted because Saltzman hadn't paid him before opening it;
some suggest he did this in a spasm of embarrassment, but since he had no
problem letting folks see *Confessions of a Window Cleaner* a few years later
that seems unlikely.

The psychedelically bizarre sci-fi content (cue expensive effects work from
John Stears) is no more important to the pop musical hijinx than, say, the
space ambassador business used in the earlier British sci-fi pop musical
Gonks Go Beat (65). *Toomorrow* is really a weirdly middle-aged attempt to
make a 'happening' youth film built around a cobbled-together-for-this-movie
group, and as concerned with student protest sit-ins (remember them?) as
saving the dying Alphoid race.

Alien anthropologist John Williams (Roy Dotrice) has lived on Earth for
centuries, making Ford Prefect-like reports on how uninteresting human
achievements are to his bosses. One day, a *Barbarella*-style lightshow
ship beams John aboard, where he reverts to a grey alien form (now cliché,
then a fairly new-minted look) and is told his species is dying out through
lack of exciting vibrations. Luckily, an Earth pop group called Toomorrow
has invented the electronic instrument ('a tonaliser'), which will keep the
Alphoids going. Naturally, a never-before-unearthed collaboration of the
Beatles, Mozart, Elvis and Spike Jones couldn't live up to the universe-
saving rep bestowed on Toomorrow before we hear them, so their pleasantly

As bad as it looks. Olivia Newton-John in *Toomorrow*.

forgettable, hardly-cutting-edge-even-for-1970 tones can't hope to be convincing.

That said, the vast ambition of the script and its saving-a-species-with-rock-music concept plays better (who knows what aliens dig?) than if the film had suggested Toomorrow might have a number one hit or cheer up a sickly child or sell some albums. Indeed, the most unbelievable scene has the bland combo wowing seemingly unstoned crowds at a 'pop festival.'

Don Kirshner (who co-produced, with Saltzman) had been involved with the Monkees, but the template had changed in the few years since the debut of the original Prefab Four, so a blonde girl and a black dude are required to give *Toomorrow* a bit more diverse appeal. Tunesmiths Ritchie Adams and Mark Barkan don't come up with songs on a par with the Monkees' catalogue and Guest doesn't give the young folks (who use their own first names) much to play with in comic or drama scenes. Olivia Newton-John, who toiled for a few more years before becoming a proper pop and movie star, is the bright-eyed girl singer with a mild antipodean twang (she calls someone a 'drongo'); the rest of the band, who didn't go on to anything like stardom, are Karl Chambers (hat-wearing drummer — described by *Variety* as 'a lively Negro skinbeater'), Benny Thomas (lead guitar, banjo, vocals) and Vic Cooper (sax, keyboards, organ, tonaliser). There are tiresome, footage-eating troubled romances: Benny with a faculty member (Tracey Crisp), Vic with a ballet dancer (Imogen Hassall, held over from Guest's *When Dinosaurs Ruled the Earth*) and Karl with a stunning, terribly thin, slightly nude model (Kubi Chaza) who gets the script's worst line ("I'm all for integration, but not with my cat!") and has the worst dialogue delivery.

The band hustle to get it together to play an eight-minute slot at the Roundhouse introduced by disc jockey Stuart Henry, vaguely take part in a student protest (no mention of a war or anything — the issue that prompts the sit-in is student faculty representation on committees dominated by bureaucrats, which sounds surprisingly credible) and are kidnapped by a spaceship to save the Alphoids, which they manage to do with a couple of tunes before zapping back to Earth where it might all have been a dream but then again probably wasn't. With Margaret Nolan ('Dink' from *Goldfinger*) as an alien innocent who doesn't realise she's been given the body of a sex bomb — she wanders about as if expecting this to turn into a raunchier film, like, say, *The Sexplorer* (75) or *Outer Touch* (79). Composer Hugo Montenegro — known in the UK for his hit cover version of The Good, The Bad And The Ugly and an album of music from *The Man From U.N.C.L.E.* — provides the jolly, tonaliser-heavy incidental music.

Toomorrow is inoffensive and has nothing to say, but remains a fascinating relic from that period when hopeless entertainment industry squares were trying to get hip and hook the affluent but disaffected youth audience. Costumes, hairstyles, aliens, spaceships, disco lights and student décor provide acute visual reminders of those precise two weeks (in September 1970) when the film was in cinemas.

Kim Newman

OVER THE CLIFF
THE BRITISH ROCK AND ROLL FILM

217

BY JAMES OLIVER

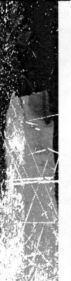

The US had Elvis movies. Britain had Cliff's.

In the grand scheme of things, Britain's contribution to the world of cinema is hardly spectacular. Oh, patriotic film fans might splutter, pointing to the majesty of Powell, Lean or the many worthwhile titles contained within this present volume. But compared to the film heritage of other countries — notably our French neighbours — the UK has long punched below its weight. Shift things onto rock and roll, however, and things look different. America may claim the patent on contemporary musical forms, but Britain has provided the most accomplished practitioners. How many truly great French rock and roll records are there, eh? Take that Johnny Hallyday!

Although it took its cues from the States, British rock evolved in different directions. Few things illustrate this better than the way the two countries treated their rock movies. In America, once the initial popularity of rock and roll music faded, the priority was to extend the career of the artistes. The obvious solution was to get 'em into pictures. Hey, it worked for Bing Crosby, didn't it? Elvis fans complain that their hero was neutered by Hollywood. But that was the whole point: to clean him up and tone him down so he was palatable to ticket buyers otherwise unconvinced by his gyrations.

It didn't play out like that in the UK. After a faltering start, the British rock movie grew into something quite distinct. They were motivated by the same

financial considerations as their American counterparts but the results were a world away artistically. What's more, these films project a very British identity. Indeed, they offer a more truthful picture of Britain over the last fifty years, both culturally and creatively, than the respectful costume dramas, breeze-block realism and ingratiating comedies said to represent 'British film.'

It starts, as these things so often do, with Cliff. Six decades of Eurovision, religious piety and tennis obscure Cliff Richard's status as Britain's first proper rocker: our Elvis. Although Cliff's records suffer by comparison to his idol's, the films he made surpass those of The King. While Elvis' film work is basically only of interest to his devoted fan base, Cliff's movies are breezy enough to stand on their own merits.

Moreover, they established the traditions of the British music film. It's stretching things to say that Cliff established any sort of template but the distinctive character of the British rock movie can, if you're so minded, be traced back to Cliff's films. Certainly, they illustrate the essential differences between the British and American approaches.

Although both Elvis and Cliff were singing superstars, their films were hardly prestige productions and were accordingly handled by uncelebrated directors. For Elvis, this meant old timers like Richard Thorpe or Norman Taurog, grizzled veterans of the studio system for whom the hip-wiggling hillbilly was just another assignment.

By contrast, Cliff's films were assigned to newcomers. *The Young Ones* (61) and *Wonderful Life* (64) were both handled by Sidney J. Furie (who would later make *The Ipcress File*),while Peter Yates (future director of *Bullitt*) took the wheel for *Summer Holiday* (63). The fact that, post-Cliff, British producers saw rock movies as a training ground rather than a retirement home was crucial to establishing the distinctive tone of British rock movies: younger directors were keen to make their mark, more in tune with their times and consequently more adventurous.

Cliff's best movie is his second, *Expresso Bongo* (59). He plays a bongo player propelled to stardom by unscrupulous music promoter Laurence Harvey. A satire on the music business, it's far more cynical than American films on the same subject, like *The Girl Can't Help It* (56). Once again, Cliff blazed a trail British music films would follow: anchoring themselves in a semi-recognisable reality and never skirting the downside of stardom nor the grubby profiteers of the record industry.

Catch Us If You Can: Among other things, John Boorman's directorial debut.

These two strands — younger, more flexible filmmakers and a willingness to de-mythologise the music industry — recur throughout the British rock movie. Take, for example, the Beatles' *A Hard Day's Night* (64), generally reckoned to be the best rock movie (British or otherwise): the director was an unconventional up-and-comer (in this case, the American ex-pat Richard Lester) and his film is a lightly fictionalised version of life in the Beatle bubble, never shying away from the isolation their fame has brought them. It is the quintessential British rock movie.

It was also enormously successful, ensuring a rash of imitators as the Beatles' competitors rushed to get themselves into pictures. The best of these is *Catch Us If You Can* (65), starring the Dave Clarke Five. Many British invasion bands went to Hollywood to make their films, with apparently disastrous consequences (has anyone under the age of fifty seen a film starring Herman's Hermits?)

But The Five not only chose to make their film at home, they also found John Boorman, one of Britain's truly great directors, at the start of his career. True, *Catch Us If You Can* does not number amongst his masterpieces but it deserves respect for its intelligence and downbeat atmosphere: qualities not usually associated with the films of Herman's Hermits.

Whither the Rolling Stones? The Beatles' principal rivals have, over the length of their career, shown more commitment to cinema than any other group. Most of that commitment, however, has taken the form of documentaries (American-produced documentaries, at that — technically beyond the remit of this book.) Their brand of rebellious insouciance did not lend itself to the conventional sort of pop music movie.

The most promising prospect was an adaption of *A Clockwork Orange*, which came to nothing. (Stanley Kubrick's eventual version of Anthony Burgess' shocker deserves at least a parenthetical mention in these pages as one of the great touchstones of British youth culture: bands from Heaven 17 to Moloko took their name from it, while Wendy Carlos' electronic score influenced a generation to take up synthesisers.) It wasn't until *Performance* (70) that the Stones — well, Mick Jagger — made a feature film. It borrowed plentifully from Losey's *The Servant* (63), right down to having James Fox being tormented by mind games. This time, however, Fox was the working class interloper — a wry comment on how the new celebrity aristocracy had supplanted the old order.

Performance captures the moment as the optimism of the 1960s curdled into the cynicism of the seventies with unusual prescience: it was filmed in 1968, in the afterglow of the summer of love but was shelved for two years, allegedly because the on-screen debauchery induced the wife of a Warner Brothers executive to vomit. ("Even the bath water is dirty," complained one suit.) By the time it was ultimately unleashed, the nihilism and depravity were no longer an emetic but an accurate reflection of what was going on outside.

Things were changing. 'Pop' entered puberty and became 'rock,' no longer cheap and disposable but weighted by adolescent bombast and self importance. The films these groups produced were equally grandiloquent. The worst offenders were Led Zepplin (*The Song Remains The Same* [76], which pads out histrionic concert footage with over-ripe fantasy sequences) and The Who (*Tommy* [75], which — as one would expect from Ken Russell — is nothing but over-ripe fantasy sequences).

As if to atone, The Who later produced *Quadrophenia* (79). It might be the best film about what music means to its audiences. [Each to his own. *Ed.*] It represented a return to realism after the grim extravagances of *Tommy*; although specifically about the sixties mod culture, the drugs, shagging and fighting give it a universal recognition, ensuring it has been co-opted by every generation since.

Indeed, films of the 1970s moved away from the let's-put-on-the-show-right-here! pantomimes of the previous decade to consider the wider culture of rock and roll, its institutions and its impact. For instance, in his semi-musical *O Lucky Man!* (73), Lindsay Anderson used ex-Animal Alan Price's songs as a Greek chorus. Elsewhere, Chris Petit's remarkable *Radio On* (79) is one of the great films about music and movement, boasting a killer soundtrack to boot.

The UK in the seventies was a grim place, stumbling around under a post-Imperial hangover, beset by economic stagnation and political paralysis. Such apocalyptic times called for a soundtrack to match: punk.

Punk's DIY aesthetic inspired many low budget filmmakers but no one captured the movement better than Derek Jarman did with JUBILEE (78). Jarman drew on punk's art school ancestry to create something as ragged, bewildering and confrontational as the unholy noises coming out of the clubs. If some movies are like fine wines, this one's like sniffing glue: a brutal deconstruction of traditional British genres like the costume drama (it begins in Elizabethan England) and urban realism (it continues in a war zone that represents modern Britain), a mockery, indeed, of the traditional British music film itself. Of all the artefacts surrounding punk, JUBILEE is just about the only one still capable of putting the wind up the *Daily Mail*. Many people loathe JUBILEE and this viewer suspects that's just the way Jarman would have wanted it.

Punk brought forth the last great flowering of British music movies. The Sex Pistols (or rather their manager, Malcolm McLaren) gave *The Great Rock'n'Roll Swindle* (80) to the world; The Clash produced *Rude Boy* (80), the story of a young Clash fan who ends up as a roadie for his favourite band and discovers life on the road is a lot less romantic than it sounds. *Take It Or Leave It* (81) was a fictionalised version of the rise of Madness, while *Breaking Glass* (80) had Hazel O'Connor as a determined wannabe.

The most interesting movie of this period was *Babylon* (80), a portrait of London's reggae scene. It's a raw film that doesn't shy away from the pressures of the time, notably the police and the then-ascendant National Front.

It couldn't last: MTV saw to that. What band wanted to make a gritty, low budget feature film about how the music industry screws over its artists when they could spend the same dough on a high-gloss promo, complete with models and yachts and the like? Video not only killed the radio star, it gave music films a bloody good kicking too.

The last flowering of the British music movie.

There were sporadic flickers of life, and not simply the dispiriting likes of *Spice World* (97). To mark the release of their epic record Weekender (92), London band Flowered Up commissioned the singularly named 'Wiz' to make a short film inspired by their tune. The plot is minimal — the title character goes out, takes drugs and comes down hard — and since it's only fifteen minutes long, some will argue it has no business in this selection. But it is a more vibrant document of the rave scene than the tiresome *Human Traffic* (99) and says more about youth culture than any film since *Quadrophenia*.

The glory days might have faded but British cinema's affair with popular music has only grown more passionate. Dead rock stars have replaced classic novels as the default subject for the heritage-obsessed UK film industry. Take your pick from early Beatle Stuart Sutcliffe (*Backbeat* [94]); his mate John Lennon (*The Hours and the Times* [91], *Nowhere Boy* [2009]); Brian Jones (*Stoned* [2005]); Sid Vicious (Alex Cox's over-romanticised *Sid and Nancy* [86]); Ian Dury (*Sex & Drugs & Rock & Roll* [2010]). You want a eulogy to Ian Curtis of Joy Division? Choose between *24 Hour Party People* (2002) and *Control* (2007).

There's nothing wrong with this in theory — they're good stories, after all — but it's hard not to feel that the respectability of all these films (honourable exception: the thoroughly irreverent *24 Hour Party People*) is contra to the rebellion that rock and roll is supposed to represent. This is the National Trust version of rock history, placed behind glass for grown ups to gawp at from a safe distance.

At least the back catalogue is healthy. From Cliff to *Babylon* (80), the British music film represents one of the strongest, most reliably inventive strains of our cinema culture. Often overlooked in favour of more clean-living fare, it's time to recognise the importance — and the quality — of these pictures.

FLIGHT OF THE DOVES (1971)

Rainbow Productions/Columbia | 101 mins | colour

Director Ralph Nelson; **Producer** Ralph Nelson; **Screenplay** Ralph Nelson, Frank Gabrielson, from the novel by Walter Macken. **Starring** Ron Moody (Hawk Dove), Jack Wild (Finn Dove), Helen Raye (Derval Dove), Dorothy McGuire (Granny O'Flaherty), Willie Rushton (Tobias Cromwell), Dana (Sheila).

Bullied by their tyrannical stepfather, thirteen-year-old Finn and his seven-year-old sister Derval run away from their Liverpool home to try to find their kindly grandmother's house in Galway, Ireland. Pursued by the police and their evil uncle Hawk, the siblings need their wits about them to get safely to their destination.

To cynics well versed in the history of British family cinema (if such people exist), *Flight of the Doves* might seem little more than a lame cash-in on *Oliver!* (68). It re-teams Fagin and the Artful Dodger (Ron Moody and Jack Wild) and thrusts them into an adventure that is contemporary-set but looks curiously Dickensian. There's an elaborate musical number, in which our brother and sister heroes, Finn and Derval Dove (Wild and Helen Raye), join a St. Patrick's Day parade singing You Don't Have To Be Irish To Be Irish, and later, in a moment of respite, they are comforted by a gentle but no less optimistic ballad by tinker girl Sheila, played with decidedly Nancy-esque gusto by Eurovision Song Contest winner Dana.

As an *Oliver!* cash-in, *Flight of the Doves* <u>is</u> pretty lame. It only has the two musical numbers above and they fall far short of Consider Yourself or Food Glorious Food. The production values are somewhat grubbier, and there's no classic source material to draw from. What's more, Jack Wild is getting way past his cheeky-chirpy stage here. He's eighteen playing thirteen, and although he only looks fifteen, there's something about his raspy voice and unkempt hair that point inexorably to the unkind ravages of puberty. And he's more subdued than he was as the Dodger; looking after his younger sister, he displays a touching parental concern, not the plucky camaraderie he showered on Mark Lester in the earlier film.

But let's not be cynical, because *Flight of the Doves* is really nothing like *Oliver!* It isn't a musical, it's a Saturday morning feature; it's like an epic Children's Film Foundation effort. It's also a showcase for Ron Moody's versatility. As failed performer Hawk Dove, in murderous pursuit of Finn and Derval to relieve them of their inheritance, he is the epitome of the pantomime baddie: a menacing, comic master of disguise. Impersonating

224

FILM REVIEWS

policemen, lawyers, country bumpkins and even a flamboyant female journalist — all feather boas and high-pitched trilling — Moody has a great time here, impressing the audience's adults with his repertoire of regional accents and scaring the children witless with his gurning, handwringing leer. (And he is scary for little children —

that dark grimace is never completely hidden by his disguises.) Probably the only other actor capable of attacking the role with this much gusto was Peter Sellers (who Columbia Pictures had actually wanted for Fagin in *Oliver!*). But Sellers lacked Moody's air of danger, at least on film.

As for Jack Wild, although he's packed into clothes that wouldn't have been out of place on a ten-year-old Victorian chimney sweep, he shows a maturity that suggests he could have gone on to more grown-up roles if he hadn't been hamstrung by his diminutive size and the success he'd had in *Oliver!* He not only takes responsibility for his scenes with the young Helen Raye, but he's also remarkably generous with her. (Raye is cute as a button and gets the funny lines, but she proved to be yet another British child performer who vanished after one movie.) But Wild was reaching the end of his stardom by now. After playing a couple more 'child-man' roles, his career went into sharp decline.

Immediately before taking on this film, US director Ralph Nelson had shaken audiences and upset censors with the notoriously violent western, *Soldier Blue* (70). Turning his attentions to the lurking danger of a picturesque but untamed Celtic community could well have resulted in another *Straw Dogs*. (Like Nelson, *Straw Dogs*' director Sam Peckinpah had recently come from a savage western, *The Wild Bunch*). Certainly, this film contains undercurrents of male violence that evoke the lawlessness of the Wild West. But, fortunately, Nelson didn't want to foist all that brutality on us again. The villains in *Flight of the Doves* just need a good booing from the kids in the audience.

Julian Upton

MELODY (1971)

a.k.a. S.W.A.L.K. | Hemdale Group/Sagittarius Productions/Goodtimes Enterprises
| 107 mins | colour

Director Warris Hussein; **Producer** David Puttnam; **Screenplay** Alan Parker, from his story.
Starring Mark Lester (Daniel), Tracy Hyde (Melody), Jack Wild (Ornshaw), James Cossins
(Headmaster).

*Daniel and Ornshaw go to the same school in south London. Despite their
different backgrounds and personality, they are firm friends but this
relationship is threatened when Daniel meets a girl: Melody. Deciding they will
get married, Daniel and Melody elope to the railway arches for an impromptu
ceremony conducted by Ornshaw. With the unexpected arrival of frantic
family members and the entire school staff, Ornshaw helps the couple escape.*

D avid Puttnam has been a champion of a middling type of British film
over the years. He has also been completely fearless in putting his
name to things like *Melody*, a celebration of adult themes masked
as youth and innocence. *Bugsy Malone* (76), for instance, a gangster
story starring only children shooting splurge guns that fire cream not bullets,
is as bizarre now as it seemed then, while *P'tang, Yang, Kipperbang* (82)
and *Those Glory Glory Days* (86) are similar variations on the rosy idea
that schooldays are the best days. *Melody* was the first film that Puttnam
produced.

Melody made much of its two child stars, Jack Wild and Mark Lester, still
relatively fresh from the hit musical *Oliver!* (68), but already saddled to the
stereotype that would forever haunt them: Lester the cherubic innocent to
Wild's goodhearted rapscallion. They are both capable young actors, but Wild
in particular is a perfect natural and brims with wit and confidence. The
film introduces Tracy Hyde as the lass who steals Lester's heart, making up
the trio around which the film evolves. She acts sweet and strolls down the
road with a contemplative expression, the way of girls twice her age ("Melody,
Melody, remember you're a girl," is a helpful refrain on the soundtrack).
Adults are all silly authoritarian figures waiting to be taken down a peg or two,
portrayed here by familiar character actors, such as Ken Jones (the history
teacher with a convoluted mnemonic for Wellington's Iberian campaign),
James Cossins as the headmaster ("The Jewish children may leave for their
studies — not you, O'Leary and Ornshaw."), Kate Williams (soon to appear
opposite Jack Smethurst in Britain's best-loved sitcom, *Love Thy Neighbour*),
as well as an underused Roy Kinnear and an uncredited Keith Barron.

'How old is old enough?' questioned the film poster, while the press ads disingenuously promised 'the happiest film of all time.'

Daniel is losing interest in his stamp collection and toy rocketship, turning his attention instead to the opposite sex. His mother removes a glamour magazine that a boy gave to him at school, which Daniel is using as a template for some interesting drawings in his bedroom. Later he spies Melody in dance class and is smitten. From this point on, Daniel's relationship with his protective best friend Ornshaw is on rocky ground, or so it would seem. Daniel and Melody go to the seaside and talk about love while building sandcastles. "The sea*side*?" roars the headmaster on hearing the news. The world just doesn't understand.

The film initially met with decent if reserved reviews both in the UK and US, but distributors weren't quite so confident. In the US it played only

as a supporting feature, while British Lion in the UK changed the title to *S.W.A.L.K.* for general release, despite theatrical engagements and reviews as *Melody*.[1] This proved a disaster, but then *Melody* was essentially a kids film desperate to appeal to adults and is neither here nor there. The first part is quite funny, showing the children at their respective homes while taking comfortable swipes at class, family and education. But the sickly rich refraction towards the loveliness of childhood doesn't ever falter and becomes hard to stomach. An audience of ten-year-olds might like the ending, where the kids run circles around the teachers and kick them in the seat of their pants, but the public in general was in no mood for such a flam. Alan Parker, who wrote the original story and screenplay, later to direct many successful films, was certainly under no illusion that *Melody* was anything but "a beginning for all of us."

By contrast, the film was a big hit in Japan — as one might expect of Japan in the face of a schoolgirl screen star. Even the soundtrack album, featuring horrible occidentalists the Bee Gees, went to number one because of it. I did some research on the internet and discovered that the eleven-year-old Tracy Hyde, who plays the love interest Melody, has quite a fan club. She isn't, of course, eleven these days, but few of her fans seem to have noticed. The bikini-clad preteen adorns the homepage of one such site, an image lifted at a guess from a Japanese film magazine of the seventies. The starlet was a regular face in these magazines, as evidenced by the pages that show her relaxing with her young co-stars, and even at home doing the ironing. She visited Japan to receive an award for Best Actress 1977 as voted by the readers of *Screen*. She was now seventeen-years-old, working as a secretary in London and still yet to make another movie. But the fans loved her and their loyalty was rewarded with a limited edition seven-inch of Tracy thanking them for voting for her, as well as all the children who sent her presents, concluding with a fumbling reminiscence about the amusement park at the foot of Mount Fuji.

Unavailable since its video release in the UK in the eighties, the film was finally submitted for classification in 2010 by Optimum Home Entertainment and is now out on DVD. The print under review hails from Japan, where I suspect *Melody* has always been available. Its success there certainly saved David Puttnam's bacon.

David Kerekes

---

1   *The Monthly Film Bulletin* reviewed the film as *Melody* in their issue dated May 1971. In August they noted the title change to *S.W.A.L.K.* (which stands for 'sealed with a loving kiss,' a phrase familiar among the burgeoning loves of Britain's schoolyards). Over the years the titles have become almost interchangeable, with *Melody* the most popular and more common outside the UK.

THE NIGHT DIGGER (1971)

Tacitus Productions/Youngstreet/MGM | 100 mins | colour

Director Alastair Reid; **Producers** Alan Courtney, Norman Powell; **Screenplay** Roald Dahl, based on the novel *Nest in a Falling Tree* by Joy Cowley. **Starring** Patricia Neal (Maura Price), Nicholas Clay (Billy), Pamela Brown (Mother), Graham Crowden (Mr Bolton).

Billy appears at the crumbling house of Maura Price and her ageing mother, winning them over with a combination of rugged good looks and handyman skills. As Maura becomes increasingly conscious of her attraction to the young man, Billy's demons surface to unsettle his newfound stability, leading the two to seek solace in an unlikely and ultimately doomed relationship.

T he Night Digger — a marginal improvement on original title *The Road Builder* — is an interesting artefact from the MGM archive, who shelved it after an initial New York release as a tax write-off. The film is still an oddity: not quite sure whether it wants to be a suspenseful drama, atmospheric horror, or a sleazy foray into *The Graduate* territory.

Based on *Nest in a Falling Tree* by New Zealand author Joy Cowley, *The Night Digger* chronicles the uneasy and intense relationship between Maura, a middle-aged Plain Jane looking after her cantankerous mother, and twenty-year-old Billy Jarvis. Billy's innocent demeanour, embellished with tales of his poor mother dying in a fire, masks a man tormented by memories of his rape at the hands of a hideous group of gypsy women. Flashbacks to Billy's past reveal his repeated sexual failures and embarrassments: unable to prove his virility, his frustration ferments into murderous anger. He sneaks from the house during the night, roaring away on his motorcycle to pursue his female victims: one scene sees him enter a girl's bedroom before stealthily tying her up whilst

Unsavoury atmosphere. Patricia Neal and Nicholas Clay. *The Night Digger.*

she sleeps. She ends up buried beneath the local motorway, where Billy has dumped her body to be covered in cement by road workers the next morning.

His rapes and murders aside, Billy is — confusingly — generally a quite likeable character, unlike the clueless Maura. With more than a little of Bette Davis about her, Maura cuts a slightly sinister figure. Her simmering anger with her situation — caring for a demanding elderly mother and with no romantic memories to speak of — threatens to explode at any moment, her depressing presence in the gloomy house becoming almost claustrophobic to watch. Throughout the film, as Billy goes on his homicidal jaunts, there remains the possibility that perhaps there is as much to fear from Maura, who Patricia Neal plays with an edge of realism that borders on the magnificent.

As wife of screenwriter Roald Dahl, Neal hoped the film would act as a showcase for her recovery from a recent stroke: job offers had dried up following her appearance in 1968's *The Subject Was Roses*, with directors apparently wary of employing a lead with underlying health problems. Her stroke is deftly worked into the script, as she explains to Billy that her slight limp is due to 'bleeding on the brain'; her job also involves working with recovering stroke patients. Dahl was keen that Neal get her deserved credit for the film, to the point of arguing with composer Bernard Herrmann. "This is Pat's film!" Dahl reportedly roared at Herrmann on finding out his script had been altered to fit the score. [1] Neal and Dahl were disappointed with the final film however, primarily concerned by the strong sexual theme running through it. To add insult to injury, Neal, Dahl and director Reid never received any money, having deferred payments to royalties. Says Reid: "The only guy who came out okay was Bernard Herrmann, who insisted on money up front." [2]

Continuing the unsavoury atmosphere, Graham Crowden is hugely entertaining as the village gossip, especially when considering the wave of murders in the area. "He does most of them in their own bedrooms," he whispers to Mrs Price and Mrs McMurtrey (Jean Anderson), undisguised prurient delight in his voice. "Rips off their nighties and..." His unbridled tongue gives rise to a misunderstanding among the locals: after suggesting that Reverend Palafox's wife (Yootha Joyce) has the character of a man rather than a woman, the conclusion is drawn that the couple are about to undergo simultaneous sex changes. "Mrs Palafox will become the Minister!"

The confusion descends into *Carry On*-style innuendo which, though mildly amusing, is completely out of place in the film. Discussing an upcoming operation the Reverend is having to remove a mole, the dialogue is more suited to *Are You Being Served?* than serious drama:

Mrs Palafox: They're just going to snip it off.
Mrs McMurtrey: Snip it off?
Mrs Palafox: Well, you see, it's got a lot bigger lately. And that scares me.

Although typical of the trademark black humour of Dahl, the tension between comedy and suspense does little to help a film whose central premise already tests the limits of believability. The relationship between Billy

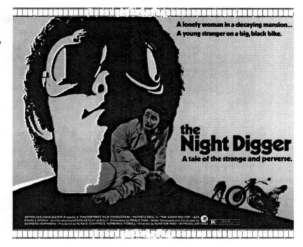

and Maura may be heartfelt, but is more bizarre than touching as the two are so startlingly different in both appearance and character. The *New York Times* noted upon the film's release that Maura did 'not appear to be the type who would fall for a strange, shifty young man who has insinuated himself into the household.'[3] Indeed, her initial apprehension at the prospect of the forlorn Billy staying on as a handyman inexplicably shifts halfway through the film to a passionate and unconditional love. The reasons behind this are a mystery, but Maura enters into her new persona with enthusiasm, gushing over Billy as he lies dispirited on his bed and giving herself a makeover which makes her look even more unsuited to her young Romeo than she did previously.

Matters progress unfeasibly quickly, as Maura empties her savings account to pay for the couple's relocation to a remote cottage on the Scottish coast. We have barely had time to adjust to this sudden change in location when the film's finale comes limping into view. Suspecting that Billy has been sleeping with their neighbour Jenny (Jenny McCracken), Maura wanders the cliffs despairingly. Billy roars up on his motorcycle and their eyes meet before he rides determinedly over the edge of the cliff (a strange, *almost* parallel with the same year's *Harold and Maude*). Whatever was contained in this brief glance was clearly meaningful but is unfortunately lost on the viewer. The cast may be engaging but the material they have to work with is vague at best, and it's not especially surprising that MGM decided it was best forgotten about.

Jennifer Wallis

1   Steven C. Smith, *A Heart at Fire's Center: The Life and Music of Bernard Herrmann* (California: University of California Press, 1991), p.301.

2   Smith, *A Heart at Fire's Center*, p.303: excerpt from an interview with Alastair Reid, 6 June 1984.

3   A.H. Weiler, 'The Night Digger,' *New York Times*, 13 May 1971.

THE NIGHTCOMERS (1971)

Scimitar/Avco Embassy | 96 mins | colour

Director Michael Winner; **Producers** Michael Winner, Elliot Kastner; **Screenplay** Michael Hastings, based on characters from *The Turn of the Screw* by Henry James. **Starring** Marlon Brando (Peter Quint), Stephanie Beacham (Miss Jessel), Thora Hird (Mrs Grose), Christopher Ellis (Miles), Verna Ellis (Flora).

Orphaned siblings Miles and Flora are looked after by their governess, Miss Jessel, and housekeeper, Mrs Grose, in the generous surroundings of their uncle's country mansion. They spend much of their time with the uncouth but entertaining Quint, a groundsman who is kept away from the house. The children discover that Quint and Miss Jessel are locked in a passionate but destructive affair. Naively, they try to intervene — with tragic consequences.

ack Clayton's 1961 film *The Innocents* brought Henry James' haunting and darkly mischievous work, *The Turn of the Screw*, to the big screen in a handsome, respectful version that threw in the odd, unsettling twist of its own. Simplifying the language of the original novella, it still captured the central enigma very faithfully, balancing ghost story elements with a suggestion of madness. Does the governess in charge of two precocious young orphans actually see the spectres of their former nanny, Miss Jessel, and her lover, Quint, around the grounds of their opulent country house? Are the children 'in on it'? Or is she just imagining it?

As the new governess, *The Innocents'* Deborah Kerr tapped elegantly into a reserve of controlled hysteria as she degenerated from the children's loving and protective guardian to their distrustful inquisitor. And her paranoia was compounded by a repression that spilled out in two disquieting scenes where she kisses the young boy in her charge full on the lips. Absent from the original text, this hint of sexual deviation gave a nod to trendy Freudian interpretations of the story, and made an already eerie tale all the more unnerving for modern audiences.

But where Jack Clayton used sexual aberration to show the cracks in the governess's troubled psyche in *The Innocents*, Michael Winner tries to firebomb the story with debauchery in *The Nightcomers*, an imagined 'prequel' that attempts to explore just what Miss Jessel got up to with Mr Quint.

In Winner's film, Miss Jessel (Stephanie Beacham) and Quint (Marlon Brando) aren't just illicit lovers (a fact that was delicately alluded to in the

FILM REVIEWS

original) — they regularly indulge in full-on, sado-masochistic bondage sessions.

To James purists and fans of the earlier film, taking such liberties with the source material is surely tantamount to artistic treason. But *The Nightcomers* isn't as bad as a lot of people would have you believe. Indeed, there's something ingenious in the way it winds back James' story and brings flesh to his ghosts. It's not inconceivable that the *The Innocents* and *The Nightcomers* could be watched in 'chronological order' — though, admittedly, screening Winner's film directly before Clayton's might be like preceding a crystal-cut glass of quality cognac with a plastic tumbler of cooking sherry.

"Gripping, Spine-Tingling and Terrific!"
—REX REED in the N.Y. Daily News

"A horror scenario of dramatic drive and sinister chill...excellently acted!" THOMAS QUINN CURTISS in the New York Times

JOSEPH E. LEVINE presents AN AVCO EMBASSY PICTURE
MARLON BRANDO
In a MICHAEL WINNER Film
"THE NIGHTCOMERS"
Co-starring STEPHANIE BEACHAM · THORA HIRD and HARRY ANDREWS
Music by JERRY FIELDING · Written by MICHAEL HASTINGS
Produced and Directed by MICHAEL WINNER
An ELLIOTT KASTNER-JAY KANTER-ALAN LADD, JR.-SCIMITAR PRODUCTION
COLOR by Technicolor® Prints by Deluxe® **An Avco Embassy Release**
R

Even so, if it wasn't for the bursts of murderous violence and sexual bondage, *The Nightcomers* might have made quite an agreeable family movie. Winner allows Brando's Quint free reign to entertain his two admiring charges with tall tales and boyish charisma. This could so easily have become pretentious, but Brando is quite engaging; the young actors are in awe of him, just as young Miles and Flora are in awe of Quint. He seems to be having real fun larking around with them — but then, as an actor, he had nothing to prove any more. Winner got his money's worth with Brando here: the star's stock was at its lowest, and Universal, with whom he had a contract with one film left to

Brando appeared for a cut-price fee in *The Nightcomers*. Wonder why?

run, was prepared to do anything to get rid of him. Winner struck a deal and Universal paid Brando his remaining $300,000 for doing *The Nightcomers* even though it wasn't their film. What Universal didn't foresee was that the following year Brando was to become white hot again, thanks to *The Godfather* and

Last Tango in Paris. By 1978 he was effectively the highest paid screen actor in the world, netting $14 million for a ten-minute appearance in *Superman*.

The touches of paternal whimsy that run through the scenes of Quint and the children naturally make the film's overheated moments all the more alarming. When the orphan Miles discovers that Quint is embroiled in a sexual relationship with the otherwise buttoned-up Miss Jessel (the scenes of Quint tying her up for another S&M session, albeit brief and heavily cut, can still raise an eyebrow), it is at a cost to his (and his sister's) innocence, not to mention sanity. (It certainly seems enough of a traumatic experience to turn Miles into the slightly warped man-child of the James story proper.)

The Nightcomers was largely reviled on its release — a critical reaction Winner would later get used to (and even start to court). It marked the beginning of his ongoing affair with blatant tastelessness, something that he was able to indulge in more frequently as censorship relaxed further. But the passage of time has served to dilute its excesses and coax out its (admittedly few) charms. For the most part, it now looks quite admirably restrained (no pun intended), in parts even tranquil. It remains an intriguing curiosity on Winner's CV: the only film in which he tackles 'higher brow' material, and in which he aspires to and largely achieves something of an arthouse sensibility.

Julian Upton

PERCY (1971)

Anglo-EMI/Nat Cohen/Wellbeck | 103 mins | colour

Director Ralph Thomas; **Producer** Betty E. Box; **Screenplay** Hugh Leonard, Terence Freely, from the novel by Raymond Hitchcock. **Starring** Hywel Bennett (Edwin), Denholm Elliott (Emmanuel Whitbread), Janet Key (Hazel Anthony), Patrick Mower (James), Cyd Hayman (Moira), Elke Sommer, Britt Ekland.

When shy antiques dealer Edwin Anthony loses his manhood in a freak accident — involving a chandelier he is delivering and a naked philanderer falling from a bedroom window — he becomes the subject of the world's first penis transplant. The operation is a success, but Edwin is restless and vows to find out about the promiscuous donor by visiting all his conquests.

Percy had a lot to answer for in its day. Coming on the heels of the so-called sexual revolution, it stood for what many otherwise sensible couples regarded as a dirty night out in 1971. Its popularity led to a lot more of the same, so it has to be held at least partly responsible for unleashing the glut of desperate soft porn comedies that saturated domestic British cinema for the rest of the decade (for more of which, see ESKIMO NELL).

Percy is concerned with a transplanted penis, but, of course, the organ is never shown and very rarely even referred to as a penis. Rather, in that puerile, schoolboy way that was occasionally endearing in the *Carry On*s but was to become wearisome and threadbare by the *Confessions* era, the grafted-on member is referred to throughout in double entendres of variable quality (Whitbread, the surgeon, addressing the press: "I will make a further statement when the occasion arises.") and visual jokes, such as the ubiquitous presence of London's Post Office Tower.

To more discerning 1971 cinemagoers, all this ribaldry epitomised plummeting standards and the shameless vulgarisation of screen comedy. The most disturbing part was that it was made by the celebrated Betty E. Box and Ralph Thomas, the team behind the successful *Doctor* comedies — those twee, cheerful romps that ran on the big screen for nearly twenty years — and some of the most memorable films of the Rank Organisation's heyday: *Campbell's Kingdom* (57), *A Tale of Two Cities* (57), *Hot Enough for June* (64). But where *Doctor in the House* (54) was brisk, solidly made and charming, *Percy* is sluggish, shoddy and uneven. The first half looks like a paean to British cinema at its worst. The wink-wink references to the transplant, risible enough even back then, look painfully laboured now; the staging is flat and unimaginative; and the cheapo set designs (particularly the hospital)

HYWEL BENNETT in
PERCY x
with guest stars
ELKE SOMMER
BRITT EKLAND
also starring
DENHOLM ELLIOTT
introducing
CYD HAYMAN

are woefully uninspired. Much of it looks as unpolished as an out-and-out grindhouse film. It would have had J. Arthur Rank spinning in his grave, had he been dead by then.

So it's hard to find anything good to say about *Percy*. But Denholm Elliott is on good form as the suave, arrogant transplant surgeon; he seems to have gauged the depth of the project rather more accurately than anyone else. And the film is fortunate to be blessed with an original Ray Davies score, performed by the Kinks. Tracks like God's Children and Animals In The Zoo interpret the proceedings far more wittily than the script and direction do.

Perhaps the best thing in the film, though, is Hywel Bennett, who brings some sensitivity to a role that doesn't really demand it. Desperate for information about the late, philandering donor of his new member, his melancholy demeanour turns the film into a series of downbeat, semi-comic vignettes, not just a string of vulgar sketches. These add to *Percy*'s unevenness, but they are at least a little more grown up than the madcap first half hour. The scenes Bennett shares with Cyd Hayman, as the donor's regularly cuckolded widow Moira, look like they belong in a much more serious and rather better film: there's believability to their slow-burning relationship, despite its ludicrous context. They give the enterprise rather more class than it deserves. (Robin Askwith and Linda Hayden would have probably suited its purpose better.)

Watching Bennett in *Percy* is also rather poignant now. To his credit, he didn't return for the 1974 sequel, *Percy's Progress* (which featured, of all people, Vincent Price). He had already proved himself as one of the most engaging young actors of the era — and one with a penchant for offbeat roles: sexually inadequate in *The Family Way* (66), psychotic in TWISTED NERVE (68) and *Endless Night* (72) — so he didn't need dragging further into the sex movie mire. Instead he headed for television, where he was to have his greatest success as the eponymous dropout in ten series' of the ITV sitcom *Shelley* (79–92), a good vehicle for his sardonic style of delivery. But his career went into steep decline not long after this. Battling booze, he became bloated and ugly, appearing less frequently onscreen, confined to guest spots. *Percy*, then, at least serves as a reminder of the days when a handsome, fresh-faced Bennett could dignify even the ropiest of projects with his presence.

Julian Upton

QUEST FOR LOVE (1971)

Peter Rogers Productions/Rank Organisation | 87 mins | colour

Director Ralph Thomas; **Producer** Peter Eton; **Screenplay** Terence Feely, from the short story 'Random Quest' by John Wyndham. **Starring** Tom Bell (Colin Trafford), Joan Collins (Ottilie Trafford/Tracy Fletcher), Denholm Elliott (Tom Lewis).

Scientist Colin Trafford is involved in an accident whilst demonstrating a new piece of equipment at his laboratory. He finds himself transported to a parallel world in which he is a successful but thoroughly unlikeable playwright, whose wife Ottilie is battling an inoperable heart condition. After Ottilie's death, Colin vows to seek out the Ottilie in 'his' world in a race against time to save the life of his true love.

The brief synopsis on the (pirate) DVD case for *Quest for Love*, incorporating time travel with a good old-fashioned love story sounds, frankly, pretty awful. Upon viewing, it becomes clear the film is a real rarity, deftly mixing together sci-fi, alternative history and tragic romance with an understated flair, all backed up by sterling performances from Joan Collins, Denholm Elliot and a host of other seventies favourites.

The original tale *Quest for Love* is based upon comes from a 1961 short story collection by John Wyndham, *Consider Her Ways and Others*, where it was titled 'Random Quest.' The tale of scientific experiments gone awry, parallel worlds and marital disharmony was picked up by the BBC for an episode of the *Out of the Unknown* series in 1969 which — like many other Brit TV classics — has been wiped completely, with only a brief clip and two short audio extracts of the 'Random Quest' episode known to survive.[1] The BBC attempted to redeem itself in 2007 with a feature length version on BBC4 starring Samuel West and Kate Ashfield — unsurprisingly hardly comparable to the original film version.

The VHS release of the film from Independent United Distributors promised 'Joan Collins... as you'd like to see her!,' capitalising on Collins' role reversal as playwright Colin's long-suffering wife, Ottilie. Rumour was that the part was originally envisioned for Britt Ekland, but fell to Collins; Ekland fans may be rather put out by this, but there's no doubt Collins adds a degree of depth and interest that likely wouldn't have been bestowed by Ekland. REVENGE, also released in 1971, saw Collins play her usual ruthless and wildly unsympathetic stock character, but *Quest for Love* offers a side of her never seen before. She looks even more gorgeous than usual: gone is the harsh overdone makeup, and on occasion she even effects an expression of genuine wide-eyed

Joan Collins and Tom Bell, *Quest For love*: a good old fashioned, time travelling love story.

innocence. Far from being the maligned bitch, we find ourselves feeling sorry for Ottilie as she discovers her philandering husband in the arms of another woman at a party, and genuinely saddened by her death in the arms of 'new' husband, physicist Colin.

Tom Bell is engaging as Colin, with his struggle to comprehend his new situation graphically conveyed as he loses control at his after-show party, drunkenly telling his guests that they are "not on the same plane" as he is before breaking down and ordering everyone to leave. Denholm Elliott is Tom, Colin's best friend in both worlds and, we suspect, harbouring a painful unrequited love for Ottilie; it's unfortunate that the writers chose to distinguish the two Toms by removing an arm from one, and Elliott's performances are somewhat damaged by the suspicious shape of his jacket. There's a turn from Johnny Briggs, later of *Coronation Street* fame, as a teddy boy barman, and a fresh-faced Simon Ward as one of Colin's friends. Laurence Naismith puts in a brilliant, if brief, performance as eccentric scientist Langstein, rushing around his lab with chalk in hand as he explains the mechanics of Colin's crossing into the 'other' world.

And this is a model tale of parallel worlds: Colin's experience proves Langstein's rejected theory that time can be divided, with different events happening to the same person at the same time — like a train track splitting in two, Langstein explains. Assessing the discrepancies between Colin's two

lives, they conclude the split occurred in 1938. In playwright Colin's world, WWII and Vietnam never happened, John F. Kennedy is still alive and Mount Everest has yet to be conquered.

Time travel, however, is more a mechanism to explore the notion of soulmates than the basis of a solid sci-fi plot, and *Quest for Love* is not without its flaws. We are never quite sure why, in the second world, Colin is a thoroughly unlikeable character — "You really are a bastard, aren't you?" whispers bit-on-the side Stella (Geraldine Moffat) at a party — yet in both worlds, Collins' character is the picture of virtue. Scientist Langstein also never divulges

where exactly the 'evil' Colin disappears to whilst his double charms the pants off Ottilie. Viewers expecting to see futuristic sets and silver lame catsuits will be somewhat put out; the most advanced effect we see is some startling hand-held camera work whilst Colin clamps his hands to his head in horror as the 'random particle accelerator' creaks into action.

Also slightly disappointing is the changing atmosphere of the film, from the initial distinct Wyndham atmosphere of unease to more traditional romance. It is, though, genuinely heartwarming to watch Collins' reactions to her husband's changed demeanour, as he sharply rebuffs the advances of actress Geri (Juliet Harmer). "Promise me that you'll find me — the other me — in the other world. I know I'm there," whispers Ottilie before dying in Colin's arms; terribly kitsch, yes, but by this time Collins has charmed us so perfectly that even the most unromantic viewer must feel a slight lump in the throat. Her complete role reversal for *Quest for Love* overshadows the film's sometimes lax approach to scientific details or continuity, making it a genuine and enjoyable piece of seventies pseudo-sci-fi.

Jennifer Wallis

1   See www.zetaminor.com/cult/out_unknown/ootu_clips_guide_s3.htm, for a comprehensive guide to the last remnants of *Out of the Unknown* [Last accessed December 2009].

REVENGE (1971)

George H. Brown Productions/Rank | 89 minutes | colour

Director Sidney Hayers; **Producer** George H. Brown; **Screenplay** John Kruse.
Starring James Booth (Jim Radford), Joan Collins (Carol Radford), Kenneth Griffith (Seely), Ray Barrett (Harry), Tom Marshall (Lee Radford), Sinead Cusack (Rose).

A bereaved publican whose young daughter has been murdered by a paedophile decides to take a stand, kidnapping a nearby loner whom he holds responsible for the girl's death, and locking him in the pub cellar. The presence of this figure disrupts the entire household, and his unwillingness to confess, coupled with contradictory reports from the newspapers, make the landlord and his co-conspirators wonder whether they have abducted the right man after all.

The tradition of making motion pictures 'ripped from today's headlines!' is one that sadly seems to have vanished in recent years. As a consequence, British cinema has been deprived of grubby grindhouse gems centred upon, say, the Brinks Mat robbery, Rochdale's 'satanic abuse' fiasco, the life and times of Jade Goody, and so on. One subject from which modern filmmakers have noticeably steered clear, despite its popularity among hack journos and red-top editors and its prominence on our tabloid front pages, is paedophilia — so, no Gary Glitter exposé, no Huntley and Carr biopic, no direct-to-DVD 'Jonathan King Story.'

It was all very different in the early 1970s, which saw a welter of grim British movies on this most controversial of themes. There was *Assault* (71), directed by Sidney Hayers, with Lesley-Ann Down and her gymslip chums menaced by a woodland lurker on their way home from school; Sidney Lumet's searing THE OFFENCE, with Sean Connery's harangued/haunted detective driven as barmy as the perverted suspect he pursues and interrogates; and I START COUNTING's sexually precocious teenagers Jenny Agutter and Clare Sutcliffe caught up with a local killer prowling the town for underage victims. Even telly got in on the act with *Out of the Unknown*'s notorious *To Lay A Ghost* episode (transmitted April 1971), with Lesley-Ann Down (her again) attacked by another roving predator as an adolescent, the experience scarring her in unexpected and outrage-provoking ways when she encounters a supernatural manifestation in later adult life. And, from *Carry On* producer Peter Rogers, in tandem with Sidney Hayers (him again), came the starkly titled *Revenge*.

Revenge, of all the representatives of this seedy subgenre, is the one perhaps tailored most towards a rabble-rousing, mob mentality — the film's very name makes this most evident, although, weirdly, the actual content spins events

Hate Lust Fear

They took their own

Revenge

THE RANK ORGANISATION PRESENTS · PETER ROGERS PRODUCTION
JOAN COLLINS · JAMES BOOTH
Revenge x
co-starring RAY BARRETT · SINEAD CUSACK
with KENNETH GRIFFITH AS THE VICTIM

FOR SECOND FEATURE
SEE LOCAL PRESS!

ON GENERAL RELEASE SEPT 19 AT PRINCIPAL ODEON AND OTHER IMPORTANT THEATRES

off on some odd tangents which muddy the waters somewhat. Having lost one daughter to a crazed killer, and presumably fearing for the safety of his other child currently studying for her exams, the grief-stricken James Booth rounds up a couple of mates to assist him in stalking and trapping the neighbourhood weirdo (Kenneth Griffith in fashion statement bottle bottom specs and half-mast trousers). In a scene as tawdry as they come at this level of fleapit tat, they bundle their targeted victim into a hatchback under cover of darkness and whisk him away to Booth's boozer, intending to shut him away in the cellar in the hope they can force a confession out of the hapless, bewildered hermit.

Naturally, everything spirals out of control, and Booth's exasperation as his scheme and his whole life begin to unravel gives *Revenge* an oddly cosmic/karmic quality. Truly, there wasn't another domestic dramatic arc like this until perhaps television's *Fawlty Towers* a few years on — Booth and Joan Collins here exist in a relationship apparently built on mutual loathing, highly reminiscent of Basil and Sybil Fawlty, and one could almost imagine John Cleese and Connie Booth penning an instalment of Basil's misadventures along these lines on a particularly sour day for both the writers and their character! Towards the end of *Revenge*, there's a shot of James Booth emerging into the bar to be confronted unexpectedly by two plain clothes policemen — the actor's swift pirouette, forced rictus grin and hearty handclap are pure Cleese/Fawlty, to the point where one wonders if the erstwhile Python might have been inspired by viewing it.

This is a film set in a world where Formica, Bakelite, Bri-Nylon and Brillo Pads dominate the environment, and where the introduction of one shabby little man into the enclosed, insular pub setting can turn friends and family against one another. Griffith works hard to keep the figure of Seely relatively clichéd and nondescript, recognising that he's of considerable symbolic value — on the face of it he's your common-or-garden sex pest (as parodied cleverly by Harry H. Corbett's clean-

Revenge: a seedy subgenre.

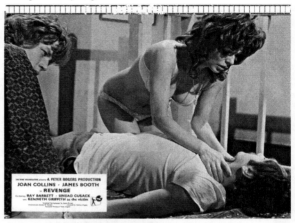

up campaigning psycho in 1959's *Cover Girl Killer*) but in the bigger picture he's nothing less than an emblematic embodiment of the chaos festering beneath this clan's veneer of normality.

Seely's apparent death in the iron grip of Booth's hands early on, followed by his surprise revival, and his subsequent refusal (or simple-minded inability?) to cooperate sends his captors into unanticipated rages both displayed and internal, and as the tight structure they've come to rely on slowly starts to fall apart, it's almost as if they've merely been waiting for this cataclysmic catalyst all along. In the guise of a cheap little exploitation thriller, then, here's something carrying significantly greater weight and import.

Darrell Buxton

SOMETHING TO HIDE (1971)

a.k.a. Shattered | Avton/Avco-Embassy | 99 mins | colour

Director Alastair Reid; **Producer** Michael Klinger; **Screenplay** Alastair Reid, from the novel by Nicholas Monsarrat. **Starring** Peter Finch (Harry Field), Shelley Winters (Gabriella Field), Linda Hayden (Lorelei), Colin Blakely (Blagdon), John Stride (Sgt. Winnington).

Isle of Wight civil servant Harry Field tells neighbours and colleagues that his wife has left him and gone back home to California. Frequently missing work to go and wait for her at the airport (she's never there) and drinking heavily, Harry's mental state becomes increasingly fractious. Things get much worse when he picks up a pregnant hitchhiker, who later ensconces herself in his house.

F ilm academic Martin F. Norden coined the term 'cinema of isolation' to define the representation of physical disability in the movies.[1] But I feel the term could be equally well applied and expanded to include a brace of movies that externalise a character's mental isolation in his or her isolated surroundings. In these pages, we explore two films that very much fit that bill — Robert Altman's IMAGES and Jose Larraz's SYMPTOMS — and there are a host of others that could be cited, not least Polanksi's *Repulsion* (which is set in central London, but who says isolation can't occur in cities?) and Kubrick's *The Shining*, which could be the apotheosis of this alternative 'cinema of isolation.' These films are generally more unhinged than some of the New Hollywood movies that fall under the banner 'cinema of loneliness' (although there is some crossover): their hostile environments are mirrored in their characters' sociopathic tendencies. *Something to Hide* is another addition to this pantheon, and while falling a long way short of *The Shining*, it does at least prefigure that film's exploration of the malevolent power of the 'remote' and how it can exacerbate an already troubled psyche. In this case, we see Peter Finch going doo-lally on the Isle of Wight.

The film starts very much in *Who's Afraid of Virginia Woolf?* territory, on a booze-fuelled Christmas evening where the emasculated Harry Field (Finch), a middle-aged local government executive, is taunted to breaking point by his shrewish American wife (Shelley Winters, parachuted in just for this five minute scene). There's a lot of exposition here, but it's well delivered (Finch and Winters could have played George and Martha as well as Burton and Taylor): Harry is mild mannered, vegetarian and what's more, impotent. His homesick wife feels she was tricked into marrying him all those years ago by his posh accent and fleeting charm. That's long since evaporated, along with his virility; she wonders aloud what it will actually take to get him to perform

in the sack — maybe some alcohol, or a meat dish? This pushes Harry over the edge and he lunges towards his wife. We see a bottle smash to the floor.

Has he killed her? Well, the film doesn't want us to know. Some time after this exchange, Harry is telling his work colleagues that his wife has gone back to the States, and we follow him around as he anxiously awaits her return. At one point, he goes to the airport and watches a lady that looks like his wife disembark. But it's not her and he turns away, dejected. Is this the first glimpse of his deluded mind? Or just a lumpy and ineffective red herring?

Still, *Something to Hide* has its moments. Just after a minor auto collision on the way back from London airport, teenage hitchhiker Lorelei (a pudgy Linda Hayden) plants herself in the dazed Harry's car and instructs him to drive her to wherever he's going. Seeing she's a pregnant runaway, he caves in, so much so he ends up taking her all the way back to the Isle of Wight and to his home, where she demands to stay the night, threatening to tell the police he's been fiddling with her if he turfs her out. Harry looks defeated and bewildered, but he allows her to stay, as long as she stays concealed; he's terrified of what the neighbours will think — on the Isle of Wight, everyone's got their noses in your business.

Harry's attempts to maintain the pretence of an ordinary man awaiting the return of his wife as he goes about his daily business are further strained when Lorelei's baby is born and screams the place down for all to hear. Still, he puts on a brave, but clearly cracking, façade. One evening, however, he comes home to find the baby dead and Lorelei gone (events that the film doesn't bother to explain, despite the source novel making them clear). He sets about trying to dispose of the baby's body, eventually burning it in an incinerator; unfortunately for him, this gets the local Auschwitz survivor's nose twitching.

In a rambling confession to his policeman friend, Sgt. Winnington, Harry comes clean about the whole sorry affair, but also announces that his own wife killed *their* baby, and that *he* then killed *her* and buried her in the bay. So — wait a minute — are the burnt remains the police have found the remains of Harry's own child? Was the hitchhiker a fantasy all along? (After all, we never actually see the baby.) Is this what Harry had to *hide*? Before we have time to try and piece it all together, Harry goes bananas on the beach with his shotgun, blasting a hole through Sgt. Winnington before killing himself.

Throughout this hysteria, Finch is nonetheless very effective. It's interesting to see an imposing and charismatic star take on such a dismal, wet weekend

Slightly misleading poster for *Something to Hide* (but one later appropriated to advertise horror films on the US grindhouse circuit).

of a character, and it's a testament to his skill that you really feel for Harry. He seems genuinely unable to deal with the world around him, from the mundane demands of his job to the innocent concerns of his neighbours. He's a more likeable version of *Falling Down*'s D-Fens but with smaller balls: on the surface a respectable, white collar executive, underneath a bubbling stew of paranoia, fear and impotence. The tragic thing is that you know Harry is actually a sweet guy; he wouldn't want to hurt a fly.

He's just lumbered from mishap to mishap while events have spiralled out of his control, a Basil Fawlty without the comic aggression.

If Finch couldn't save *Something to Hide*, no one could. But director Alastair Reid does lend it some moments of effectiveness and, despite its holes and herrings, his script makes a number of improvements on Nicholas Monsarrat's unrepresentative novel (not least by relocating it to the Isle of Wight from an unconvincing 'generic American' setting). And it's all very handsomely photographed by Wolfgang Suschitzky.

Julian Upton

1   Martin F. Norden, *Cinema of Isolation: A History of Physical Disability in the Movies* (New Brunswick, NJ: Rutgers University Press, 1994).

UNMAN, WITTERING AND ZIGO (1971)

David Hemmings/Mediarts/Paramount Pictures | 102 mins | colour

Director John Mackenzie; **Producer** Gareth Wigan; **Screenplay** Simon Raven, based on the play by Giles Cooper. **Starring** David Hemmings (John Ebony), Douglas Wilmer (Headmaster), Anthony Haygarth (Cary Farthingale), Carolyn Seymour (Silvia Ebony).

Starting a new career as a master in a private boys school, John Ebony soon learns the fate of the man who proceeded him, and also that the class he has taken over may well be murderers. Reluctantly caught in the web of their endeavours, Ebony finds his life — and the lives of others — increasingly in danger as he attempts to break away and uncover the truth.

There is a scene midway through *Unman, Wittering and Zigo* where schoolmaster John Ebony visits colleague Cary Farthingale in his workshop. Farthingale is reading a copy of *The Fifth Pan Book of Horror Stories*. Curiously, the half-ghoulish female face on the cover resembles Ebony's attractive young wife, Silvia. Even more curious, the collection itself contains a story — 'Bonfire' by C.A. Cooper — in which an insane headmaster plots murderous revenge against a younger teacher.

Murder fuels *Unman, Wittering and Zigo*, but it is not between masters; nor is it ever seen. Instead, the film carries with it a fug of threat, mixed in with dead language and male genitals to drift alongside the cold wood panelling of the school's endless corridors. David Hemmings plays Ebony, a young ex-advertising employee looking to radically change his life and give something back to society. The character is one of his earnest-yet-naïve creations, fitting as *Unman*... lies almost dead centre between those two Hemmings landmarks of innocent investigation: *Blowup* (66) and *Profondo Rosso* (75). Accompanied by Silvia, Ebony takes up a residential position at Chantry, a private school housing 300 boys, and is handed Form Lower 5b, stepping tentatively into a dead man's shoes. Pelham, the previous master, was found at the foot of nearby coastal cliffs. "It's just not done for a schoolmaster to die in term time," the headmaster informs Ebony. "What do you think the holidays are for?"

Never an actual character in the film, Pelham haunts Lower 5b, as does Zigo, the last name on the register and ghostly non-occupant of the classroom's only empty chair. On his first morning, Ebony is told by the boys that "His father's taken him to Jamaica," an explanation that becomes more suspect after the class also inform their teacher of what actually happened to Mr Pelham: "We killed him, sir." Ebony at first dismisses the statement as bravado, but soon comes to realise that it might actually be true, especially after some macabre

246

Unman, Wittering and Zigo: teacher David Hemmings has some trouble with the boys in 5b.

tricks are played on him: one of Pelham's shoes is secreted in his desk at home, and the proud boys present him with Pelham's wallet.

"You can see the bloodstains, sir."
"There was two pound ten in it but we spent that."
"On cupcakes."

Faced daily with a class full of polite, dead-eyed maybe-killers, a revelation of no interest to his wife, Ebony confides in Farthingale ("One of the damned," as he describes himself) over booze and dinner. The guilt of 5b does not shock Farthingale however: he knows that concepts such as 'idealism' and 'morality' soon get bored and wander off in a place like Chantry. "I'm a connoisseur of failure," he proclaims. "I can smell it." With little room to navigate, Ebony reluctantly turns victim and co-conspirator, as the class outlines a modus vivendi that promises 'collective security.' The intelligent boys need to pass their exams in order to take their place in the greater society outside Chantry; the less intelligent (who spend their hours reading news-stand novels such as *Surgeon's Oath* by William Johnston) couldn't care less. Thus Ebony is primed, broken and assimilated ("After all, there's no reason why we shouldn't peacefully co-exist"), and yet he still attempts to uncover the truth, eventually refusing to play the game of Lower 5b: a decision that forces the boys to turn against each other, with escalating consequences for Ebony, his wife, and the unfortunate Wittering, second to last on the register.

Director John Mackenzie (*The Long Good Friday*) and screenwriter Simon Raven manage to wrestle *Unman, Wittering and Zigo* away from its radio/TV

play origins to transform it into a major studio picture that has — bizarrely — remained unheard of for many years. Maybe the chill atmosphere and adolescent amorality turned audiences away? The source material must have been one of the attractions for novelist, bon vivant and scallywag Raven, although there's no mention of the film in Michael Barber's biography of him, *The Captain* (it should be noted that *Incense For The Damned* is also ignored, with Raven's source novel *Doctors Wear Scarlet* itself allowed less than a page).

Unman, Wittering and Zigo.
If only they had stopped at murder...

UNMAN, WITTERING and ZIGO.
DAVID HEMMINGS

Notoriously bisexual — although his tastes veered more towards the male form — Raven obviously seized at the chance to adapt such a dark story in an all male, public school setting, and his demonic signature reveals itself in a few brief scenes, as Ebony begins to have harsh visions of the boys attacking him, or caressing each other in the school gym: the white PE shirt and shorts standard uniform for a thousand postwar middle-aged male fantasies. There is also an understanding of how absolutely vicious young men can be, as displayed early on when the boys, on a climbing lesson at the very cliffs where Mr Pelham perished (actually the headland at Llandudno), descend on a perching Ebony and recount to him the confrontation and murder of their former teacher with all the emotionless vigour of a Latin oral test. And later, there's the incredible scene where the boys trap the alienated Silvia Ebony ("There are no beautiful women in this hell, I'll tell you that.") in a squash court, and attempt to execute a terrible act against her person, excited shouts and squeaks of gym shoes the only sounds, the light of a dozen torches the only illumination. "We're going to show you how grown up we can be. In a very special way. In a way you won't want to tell him about. You won't dare tell him. You'll be so ashamed, feel so dirty, so disgusted with what's happened to you."

Recommended for viewers who felt that Lindsay Anderson's *If....* was perhaps too liberal.

Martin Jones

IMAGES (1972)

Hemdale/Lion's Gate | 101 mins | colour

Director Robert Altman; **Producer** Tommy Thompson; **Screenplay** Robert Altman.
Starring Susannah York (Cathryn), Rene Auberjonois (Hugh), Hugh Mallais (Marcel), Marcel Bozzuffi (Rene), Cathryn Harrison (Susannah).

Cathryn, a children's writer ensconced with her photographer husband in the isolation of a country house, is plagued by invasive images of lovers, past and present. Pushed to hysterical limits, she attempts to dispatch her ghosts by killing them, but her inability to separate fantasy from reality puts the people around her in danger.

I*mages*, one of the oddest films on Robert Altman's CV (and that's saying something), is a world apart from those multi-character epics of American satire and tragicomedy that he became most celebrated for in the 1970s: *M*A*S*H* (70) and *Nashville* (75). An intense chamber piece, it is very much an 'interior' work, reflecting Roman Polanski's *Repulsion* (65) and Ingmar Bergman's *Persona* (66) in its intimate, darkly sexualised observation of a woman's mental breakdown.

On a surface level, the film almost succeeds as a tense psychodrama with a splashing of the supernatural. Altman shows a previously unseen aptitude for delivering horror movie thrills as he evokes the encroaching madness of a children's writer (Susannah York), isolated in a country farmhouse with her demons and her distracted husband for company.

But the film is best seen now as a bold showcase for the leading lady's kinky side. (She was a bit of a dark horse, that Susannah York.) Just when people had accepted her, at the height of the sixties, as a corn-fed English ingénue of finishing school refinement, she went and bedded down with Coral Browne for the heated *Killing of Sister George* lesbian scene. And just when they thought she was all set for a glittering Hollywood career after her Oscar nomination for playing a disintegrating blonde bombshell in *They Shoot Horses, Don't They?* (69), she retreated from the mainstream to choose 'challenging' arthouse projects, like the film of Jean Genet's perverse *The Maids* (74), and this. York gave herself to *Images* almost beyond the call of duty, not just by appearing in every scene, showing herself raw and naked (literally), but also in allowing Altman to use lengthy passages from a children's book she was writing at the time (*In Search of Unicorns*). Indeed, Altman's touch of directorial genius is drawing York so far into the movie that it looks like a

vehicle of her own making. Developing the character of the children's writer around her personality and her own writing puts the actress' indelible stamp on the piece. And it paid off — she won the Best Actress award at Cannes.

Despite this, her performance is uneven: she is constantly shifting, not altogether believably, from screeching madness to glacial somnambulism and back again. Often she is simply grating (especially when she screams, which comes out as a rasping, broken wail that goes through you like claws on a blackboard). And there are times, for all her emotional investment, that she looks like she literally doesn't know how to play the scene — which was probably true, given Altman's methods. (It is left to twelve-year-old Cathryn Harrison, as a neighbouring, pubescent girl who idolises York in the way a frumpy child might look up to her delinquent older sister, to deliver the film's only truly convincing performance.)

So, for all York's immersion in the material, *Images* remains very much Altman's work. (He'd even tried setting it up previously with other actresses, such as the much more 'Altmanesque' Sandy Dennis, and got so far as beginning to shoot it in Milan with Sophia Loren in the lead.) Accordingly, he must take most of the blame for it — especially for foregrounding the pretentious symbolism and baffling us with conspicuous displays of 'meaning.' For example, as York's photographer husband, Rene Auberjonois (a then Altman regular, laughably out of place here) spends most of the movie pottering about the house in his driving gloves. A comment on his clinical detachment from his surroundings? Or on his clinical detachment from his wife? When York fires a gun at one of her imagined invaders, she actually shoots out her husband's camera lens. Are her husband's photographs the 'images' the film is really about? Is Cathryn's torment at the hands of her male abusers symbolised by the camera's objectification of Susannah York? What's it all about, Altman?

And the character names puzzlingly reflect the real names of the cast: York is Cathryn, and young Cathryn Harrison is 'Susannah'; Rene Auberjonois is 'Hugh,' Hugh Mallais is 'Marcel' and Marcel Bozzuffi is 'Rene.' A blogger on the Internet Movie Database was urged to speculate: "I wonder if this is a clue to the story, or is it just Altman's wicked sense of humour?"

Or perhaps it's just horse shit. Perhaps it's one of those half-baked ideas that comes out during the rehearsal process — suggested on a whim by an acclaimed director and lapped up by his idolising cast — that might be enlightening for those in on the joke but serves no purpose for the end user (if, indeed, the end user even notices it). Ingmar Bergman might have got away with it, but here it looks like a contrived attempt to inject some arthouse beard-stroking. The problem with *Images* is the deeper you look into it (and the film encourages you to look deeper), the less you see in it. For all its intentions as a complex and deathly serious exploration of schizophrenia, you get the feeling it would have worked better as exploitation (see Larraz's SYMPTOMS).

Even so, it's beautifully shot by Vilmos Zsigmond, who darkly captures the desolate magnificence of the countryside (the

setting is never identified — it's Ireland, but it could be Britain) and it has a satisfyingly haunting, Bernard Herrmann-type score by John Williams (en route from his strident TV themes to the orchestral majesty of *Star Wars*).

Most effective though are the atmospheric 'sound sculptures' of Japanese composer Stomu Yamash'ta. Indeed, it is the sound design that helps to rescue the film from its more risible arthouse pretensions and drag it back into the realm of psychological thriller. Let loose it would doubtless have meandered further into visual psychobabble and pseudo-feminism.

The sounds, then, constitute *Images*' true innovation. Altman would no doubt have been amused by the irony.

Julian Upton

THE LOVERS! (1972)

British Lion | 88 mins | colour

Director Herbert Wise; **Producer** Maurice Foster; **Screenplay** Jack Rosenthal. **Starring** Richard Beckinsale (Geoffrey Scrimshaw), Paula Wilcox (Beryl Battersby), Joan Scott (Mrs Battersby), John Comer (Mr Scrimshaw), Rosalind Ayres (Veronica).

Eager to take advantage of the sexual freedoms that the 'permissive society' purports to allow, Manchester bank clerk Geoffrey finds his efforts constantly rebuffed. He's more optimistic when he starts going steady with the spirited Beryl, but it turns out Beryl is even more sexually uptight than other girls — she refers to sexual intercourse as "Percy Filth." Needless to say, the path of young love does not run smoothly.

othing confirmed the seventies British film industry's desperation and monumental lack of imagination more than its pillaging of the country's most conservative television format — the half hour sitcom — for material. Almost overnight, a few enterprising producers seemed to realise that a theatrical version of a popular sitcom need only pull in a tiny fraction of its TV audience to become a huge money-spinner. And, initially, they were proved right; famously, the movie version of *On the Buses* was one of the top grossing films at the British box office in 1971. Other notable early hits on the big screen were *Up Pompeii* (71), *Please, Sir!* (71) and *Steptoe and Son* (72).

The British 'sitcom spin-off' craze lasted from 1968 to 1980, during which time more than thirty films were adapted from successful comedy shows. In most cases, they were woefully vulgarised and overblown (although the vulgarity of *On the Buses* on TV took some beating), but a handful, like some of the later *Carry On* films, were somehow endearing in their mischief. Still, only three of them can actually be said to have been any good: *The Likely Lads* (76), *Porridge* (79) and *The Lovers!*

The Likely Lads, written by Dick Clement and Ian La Frenais, keeps the essence of its original series — which followed Bob (Rodney Bewes) and Terry (James Bolam) around Newcastle as they grew from adolescence to maturity, from cheerful, laddish optimism to resignation and disillusionment — while further developing, to great tragicomic effect, a sense of loss and reflection. *Porridge*, by the same writers, works nicely because the series' abundance of well-drawn characters could be profitably featured in the leisurely pace of a film. The prison setting looks harsher than in the studio-bound TV series, but the warmth of the characterisations still shines through.

FILM REVIEWS

The Lovers! double-bill. Well, it's got birds in both of them.

The Lovers!, for its part, has more laugh-out-loud moments than either of the above. Yet it has been far less exposed. This is a shame, because it is a good British sex comedy in its own right. By retelling, in condensed form, the whole story of Manchester couple Geoffrey and Beryl's faltering relationship — from its awkward beginnings to the frustrated slanging match it becomes — writer Jack Rosenthal avoids having to pad the material out with the kind of lame devices so prevalent in the other sitcom spin-offs, such as the obligatory holiday to the seaside/holiday camp/Spanish resort, or the introduction of a toothless subplot about nefarious property developers/gangsters/interlopers (delete as appropriate).

Rosenthal's script is also subtle and intelligent enough not to have to ramp up the crassness to sustain our interest for ninety minutes (a trap that even writers as brilliant as Ray Galton and Alan Simpson fell into). There is a lot of nudge-nudge talk about sex, but that was always the series' raison d'etre; the comedy comes from the fact that the characters aren't 'getting any.' Instead, the film is awash with non sequiturs and funny comeback lines, typical of Rosenthal at his best:

Geoffrey: My name's Geoffrey. I don't happen to be attached.
Beryl: Mine's Beryl. I don't happen to be surprised.
Beryl: Tell me about your terrible past, Geoffrey.
Geoffrey: I haven't had one yet!
Mrs Battersby (consoling Beryl after splitting up with Geoffrey): Joan of Arc never married and she led a full and happy life. Or am I thinking of someone else?

True, a lot of the lines are rehashed from Rosenthal's original first series (Geoffrey Lancashire wrote the second and final one), but, in most cases, they deserve another airing, and any patchworking on the writer's part is at least expertly sewn. And there are lots of new things to enjoy. There's a marvellously absurd scene, courtesy of young Bruce Watt as Jeremy, the kid brother of Veronica, one of Geoffrey's rebound conquests. After stumbling in on Geoffrey and Veronica's attempt at lovemaking, Jeremy proceeds to reel off everything he knows about the facts of life in merciless physiological detail. Maybe it's just me, but the sight of a scruffy, pyjama-clad urchin articulating words like 'spermatozoa,' 'uterus' and 'fallopian tubes' in a strangulated northern accent has got to be one of the funniest moments in British comedy cinema. It's a priceless little cameo. What happened to little Bruce Watt?

Whether you were a fan of the original series or have no knowledge of it, *The Lovers!* works as a tartly funny time capsule, revealing the frustrations of a provincial courtship at the beginning of the seventies, when the so-called permissive society was meant to be raging. As Geoffrey and Beryl, Richard Beckinsale and Paula Wilcox are on their best form as the lovebirds who don't really know how to behave, regardless of the opening of the sexual floodgates.

The Lovers! came and went, and the sitcom spin-off era continued apace. It finally ground to a halt in 1980 with *Rising Damp* (whose original series had also featured Beckinsale) and *George and Mildred*. *Rising Damp* took the safe option and simply reworked scenes that had already established the series as a classic. As a result, it's very watchable (save for the conspicuous absence of Beckinsale, who died the year before it was released, aged thirty-one). But that anybody thought *George and Mildred* was fit for theatrical release is almost beyond reason; it is undoubtedly one of the worst films ever made in Britain. To add insult to injury, it was also released just after the death of one of its stars, Yootha Joyce. ('A blessing, of sorts,' notes the website TV Cream.)

This, and the fact that the revenues were drying up, amounted to the final nail in the sitcom spin-off coffin. But the films were soon to prove they had an enduring appeal almost as strong as the *Carry On*s. Since they were first broadcast back in the late seventies, they have lived on, fittingly enough, on television. Not many months go by without the big screen versions of *Dad's Army* or *Bless This House* or *Are You Being Served?* being aired. At Christmas, you can expect to see half a dozen or more crop up in the schedules somewhere. But, frustratingly, there's rarely a showing of *The Lovers!*

Julian Upton

NOTE Parts of this article originally appeared in *Headpress 24* (2002) and in *Bright Lights Film Journal*, http://www.brightlightsfilm.com/35/britishsitcoms1.html.

MADE (1972)

Anglo-EMI/Vic Films/Janet Productions | 101 mins | colour

Director John Mackenzie; **Producer** Joseph Janni; **Screenplay** Howard Barker, from his play, *No One Was Saved*. **Starring** Carol White (Valerie Marshall), Roy Harper (Mike), John Castle (Father Dyson), Sam Dastor (Mahdav), Margery Mason (Mrs Marshall), Doremy Vernon (June).

Valerie lives with her illegitimate son and invalid mother in an East London tower block. Resistant to the men in her life — work colleague Mahdav and local priest Father Dyson — she eventually clicks with up-and-coming folk singer Mike. But happiness with Mike is shortlived. By the time he has moved on to success in California, Valerie has lost her baby and her mother, and looks set to face her humdrum life alone.

"Father McKenzie," sang Paul McCartney in Eleanor Rigby, "wiping the dirt from his hands as he walks from the grave / No one was saved / All the lonely people / Where do they all come from?"

In titling his second play *No One Was Saved*, staged in 1970, it looked like twenty-four-year-old Howard Barker was offering an answer to Lennon and McCartney's catchy question above: some might come from high rise blocks in Woolwich. But Barker was never one for straight answers, and *No One Was Saved* was as much a critique of Eleanor Rigby (and its writers) as it was an exploration of the song's nod to a redundant religion.

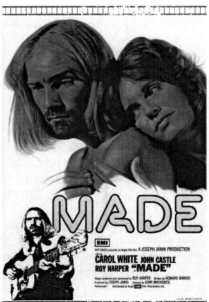

No One Was Saved has been succinctly described as 'Eleanor Rigby meets John Lennon' and the film version — although emerging as *Made* and serving as a vehicle for folk singer Roy Harper — captures this idea quite pertinently. Before the film's Eleanor, the put-upon but attractive Valerie (Carol White), has her first conversation with singer Mike (Harper), she encounters him holding court in

a very Lennon-esque way on Brighton Pier, being publicly interviewed by 'Whispering' Bob Harris, answering questions on love and religion with a cheeky northern chutzpah that ranges from low, ribald humour to a confident grasp of the big themes and concepts.

But, as quite a few have said of John Lennon, Mike could well be a fraud.

Valerie cherishes her short affair with him because he is, in her eyes, 'sincere.' Her work colleague Mahdav (Sam Dastor) has tried to woo her with naff poetry and old Indian charm, but, when that failed, ended up leaping on her after a curry. The self-consciously modern Father Dyson (John Castle) has tried 'saving' her, but in the process only revealed murkier motives underneath his pious sermonising. Only Mike talks to her on the level; he doesn't promise her anything outside the few casual couplings they experience, but she respects him for this. And the sound-bitey morsels of godless, anti-establishment wisdom he offers her touch her more deeply than anything the church could muster up — pop music bettering religion.

Some time after Mike's departure for Los Angeles, however, Valerie hears him singing unmistakably about her life on the radio, and the effect is heartbreaking. Mike/Lennon and his music have offered her only temporary and, ultimately, meaningless respite. Was he just a cold observer all along? After all, he had the means to take Valerie away from all this, but didn't even offer. ("No one you can save that can't be saved," Lennon once sang.)

The Beatles/Lennon commentary is enough to see *Made* re-evaluated, but those looking more deeply at its place in postwar British drama will appreciate it as a 'riposte' to Edward Bond's notorious play about disenchanted underclass life in south London, *Saved*, first staged at the Royal Court Theatre in 1965. At the centre of both *Saved* and *Made* is the shocking killing of a baby; both hold up this atrocity as an example of the impoverished 'state of the nation.' In *Saved*, a baby in its pram is stoned to death by youths in a park. In *Made*, Valerie's baby, in its pram, is caught up in a crowd of football hooligans and sent careering, *Battleship Potemkin*-like, down a flight of concrete steps.

But if Bond concluded *Saved* with a note of communal optimism and redemption, Barker's emphasis is indeed that 'no one was saved.' There is no solace in family or community for Valerie here. She ends the film truly alone.

Despite adapting his own play for the screen, Howard Barker did not — and, as he pointed out to me, still does not — approve of *Made*. Calling the experience 'an extremely brutal introduction to the world of film,' he laments the conversion of his 'bitter, partly satirical, somewhat surreal play' into a 'lump of tedious social realism.' He goes on: 'The producer had no grasp of my intentions, or cared even less. Harper and Carol White were encouraged to write their own text, or improvise it. All this was catastrophic.'[1]

Certainly, from the changing of the play's title to the film's more sympathetic treatment of the Mike/Lennon character, *Made* dampens and obscures Barker's original angry exposé of a fraudulent Lennon exploiting a vulnerable woman's dismal history (we know now, of course, that Eleanor Rigby was very much McCartney's song). Mike seems quite heroic compared with the other men in Valerie's life, and although there is a sense of betrayal when she hears his song about her on the radio, it could be that she is just as devastated by the poignant revelation of her hopeless condition in his lyrics.

As for the accusation of 'tedious social realism,' there is a clear attempt to emulate the dramas of Ken Loach (not least in the presence of Carol White, whose bedraggled beauty had powered Loach's *Cathy Come Home* [BBC TV, 66] and *Poor Cow* [67], which *Made*'s Joe Janni also produced), at the expense of the semi-surrealism of the original. But to call it all catastrophic is arguable. *Made*'s attempts to provide a critical commentary on the state of modern Britain through the sad eyes of a single mother may amount to a middlebrow objective, but, let's face it, most films are made to be seen by as many people as possible — they don't have the theatre's luxury of preaching to the converted.

In his first (and only) significant film role, Roy Harper is awkward, but better than, say, Bowie or Jagger (or indeed Lennon) would have been. (Harper's original songs for *Made* turned up on his *Lifemask* album in 1973, but they're more powerful and illuminating in context, particularly the track that cruelly exposes Valerie's life to her: The Social Casualty.)

Carol White, making a conspicuous return to 'acting' after an abortive Hollywood sojourn, is impressively dowdy; her blonde hair traded for anonymous brown, she trudges through the drab cycle of changing nappies and washing down her disabled mother with a touching resignation. It's a great passive performance, up there with Barbara Loden in *Wanda* (70) and Isabelle Huppert in *The Lacemaker* (77). It's a shame that White herself was already set on a self-destructive path in her own life. In the end, not even she could be saved.

Julian Upton

---

1   Howard Barker, email to the author, 19 January 2010.

THE OFFENCE (1972)

Tantallon Films/United Artists | 112 mins | colour

Director Sidney Lumet; **Producer** Denis O'Dell; **Screenplay** John Hopkins, from his play, *This Story of Yours*. **Starring** Sean Connery (Johnson), Ian Bannen (Baxter), Vivien Merchant (Maureen), Trevor Howard (Cartwright).

Johnson, a veteran detective sergeant investigating a series of attacks on young girls, muscles in on the questioning of Baxter, a suspect picked up one night in the local town centre. But as the interrogation proceeds, the policeman's troubled psyche, bruised by years of exposure to violent crime, begins to flood out in a torrent of brutality.

uitting the role of James Bond after 1967's *You Only Live Twice*, Sean Connery was keen to expand his acting horizons, believing that working for 'actors' directors' like Sidney Lumet was the way forward. He'd worked with Lumet on *The Hill* (65), a tough WWII drama in which he stood out in a gritty role as a demoted sergeant being put through his paces in a North African military prison. But after that he hadn't been so lucky, taking roles in some decidedly patchy non-Bond films: *A Fine Madness* (66), *Shakalo* (68) and *The Molly Maguires* (70).

Meanwhile, the Bond producers replaced Connery with George Lazenby and made *On Her Majesty's Secret Service* (69), one of the best of the series. But Lazenby didn't win the public over and, more damagingly, he believed there was no future for Bond as the 1970s began. So Lazenby also quit the role as *OHMSS* reached the cinemas, leaving a lot of egg on the producers' faces (and, later, when he realised the foolishness of the decision, even more on his own).

In some desperation, United Artists lured Connery back to Bond 'one last time' for $1.2 million plus twelve-and-a-half per cent of the box office gross, an unprecedented fee that the star duly donated to the Scottish Educational Trust. Connery was actually more attracted by the deal's other sweetener: the pledge by UA to fund, to the tune of $2 million, two of his subsequent 'personal' film projects.

As he auto-piloted through *Diamonds Are Forever* (never once disguising his contempt for the franchise), Connery's mind was clearly on these next projects, which now more than ever needed to cement his acting credibility. One was to be a new adaptation of *Macbeth*, with Connery starring and directing. The other, for which he'd re-teamed with Sidney Lumet, was a film version of a more modern but similarly brutal stage play, *This Story of Yours*.

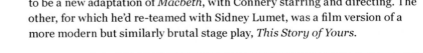

FILM REVIEWS

Written by the celebrated TV scribe John Hopkins (of *Z Cars* fame), *This Story of Yours* is an intense character study of a cop (Johnson) whose long exposure to murder and sex crime has jaded his psyche, and who fails to recognise, until it's too late, that his own warped preoccupations have been masked by his take-no-prisoners approach to law and order. The focus on self denial, on skewered perspectives, informed the working title of the film, *Something Like the Truth*, which (fortunately) was later dropped for the more prosaic, but somewhat more palatable, *The Offence*.

AFTER 20 YEARS, WHAT DETECTIVE-SERGEANT JOHNSON HAS SEEN AND DONE IS DESTROYING HIM.

SEAN CONNERY as Detective-Sergeant Johnson
TREVOR HOWARD in
"THE OFFENCE"
with **VIVIEN MERCHANT · IAN BANNEN**
Written by JOHN HOPKINS · Produced by DENIS O'DELL · Directed by SIDNEY LUMET
United Artists

Hopkins' play divides the story into three scenes: an explosive argument between Johnson and his wife, an unapologetic interview with his superior, and the climactic, tortuous interrogation of Baxter, a suspected child molester, a man by turns odious and audaciously incisive, who Johnson sees as his nemesis but who might actually be his mirror image. The film retains these lengthy passages (to its detriment — the wife and boss scenes could have benefited from cutting), while opening out the material and juggling (to no great effect) the sequential narrative.

Where *The Offence* does succeed is in Connery's unforgiving portrayal of a man whose demons have hijacked his humanity — he's like a provincial British version of Harvey Keitel's *Bad Lieutenant*. And the physicality he brings to the role emphasises its menace and aggression. As a husband, he

is abusive; at work, he is a bully. Any tenderness within him, glimpsed as he scoops up the terrified young girl he finds discarded in the woods, is tinged with brutality. He doesn't look entirely trustworthy as he struggles to calm the hysterical twelve-year-old, and as he sits with her in the ambulance, he tries to delay the administering of painkillers so that he can get her to talk.

The Offence was shot quickly — not unusual for Sidney Lumet — and, of course, cheaply. As an actor's piece, its stagey theatrical origins are much in evidence. But, for all that, there is also a visual sense at work, however unattractive. The opening scene, with police observing worried local parents hastily collecting their children from school, looks almost defiantly pedestrian: a series of shots of a nondescript new town, all featureless concrete buildings, redbrick houses and scraps of urban wasteland (it's actually Bracknell, that paean to prosaic civic planning that was equally exploited for its drabness in I START COUNTING three years earlier; clearly, Bracknell is the town of choice for your discerning sex murderer). It's about as far from the exotic vistas of a James Bond location as you can get. Similarly, the interiors — the colourless, modernist police station, like an adjunct to a multi-storey car park, and Johnson's decidedly un-homely high rise flat — emphasise the clinical bleakness of the proceedings, and the bleakness of Connery's character. Had the film been set in a quaint English village, or even central London, it would be less uncomfortable, and probably less powerful.

Not surprisingly, given the above, *The Offence* bombed at the box office. Indeed, sometimes it feels like anti-entertainment; there's a soporific stillness to it that would test even the hardiest fan of the police procedural. (It would have worked better as a one hour TV play.) For United Artists, its failure proved an opportunity to backtrack on the *Diamonds Are Forever* sweetener: Connery's *Macbeth* project was duly cancelled (which it probably would have been anyway, since Roman Polanski had just released a version).

Connery did manage to score some subsequent offbeat critical successes — *The Man Who Would Be King* (75), *Robin and Marian* (76) — but a series of flops saw him donning the Bond toupee once more for the unofficial *Never Say Never Again* (83). In 1987, a supporting role as an Irish cop in Brian De Palma's *The Untouchables* re-established him, at fifty-seven, as a star. But none of the varied roles that followed were as brave as what he'd attempted in *The Offence*. The film stands as a worthwhile reminder that, between the high-key antics of Bond and the scene-stealing character parts of his late middle-age, Connery was prepared to try something edgy and dangerous, to let us see how ugly he really could be.

Julian Upton

FILM REVIEWS

Porridge it ain't. Ian McShane and Oliver Reed in *Sitting Target.*

SITTING TARGET (1972)

Peerford Ltd./MGM | 93 mins | colour

Director Douglas Hickox; **Producer** Barry Kulick; **Screenplay** Alexander Jacobs, from the novel by Laurence Henderson. **Starring** Oliver Reed (Harry Lomart), Jill St. John (Pat Lomart), Ian McShane (Birdy Williams), Freddie Jones (Macneil), Edward Woodward (Milton), Frank Finlay (Marty Gold).

Hardman convict Harry Lomart's wife informs him during a prison visit that she's pregnant by another man and is leaving him. Harry smashes through the glass and tries to strangle her on the spot. When he gets out of solitary confinement, he stages an escape with his friend Birdy and another inmate. Birdy suggests they lie low, but, consumed with rage, Harry acquires a gun and sets off to kill his wife and her lover.

Sitting *Target* has got to be one of seventies British cinema's best kept secrets. Bankrolled by MGM a year after the studio released *Get Carter*, *Sitting Target* has steadily sunk into complete invisibility, however, while *Carter*, at least from the point of its laddish rediscovery in the 1990s, has gained a reputation as the ne plus ultra of the British crime film. But *Sitting Target* is far better than its obscurity suggests, and *Get Carter*, as I tell anyone who will listen, is considerably less brilliant than the pundits keep telling us it is.

There are, however, lots of similarities between the two films. *Get Carter* set a new benchmark for casual sex and violence in the British crime movie; *Sitting Target*, on *Carter*'s heels, pushes the violence and general nastiness even

further (breaking out of their prison cell, Lomart [Oliver Reed] and Birdy [Ian McShane] beat up one screw by repeatedly smashing his head against the wall and cosh the other with his own truncheon after pouring a bowl of piss over him — *Porridge* it ain't). Both films root their glacial, irredeemable villains in ugly urban frontiers (Jack Carter returns to an ungentrified Newcastle, *Target*'s Harry Lomart to the tower blocks and railway lines of south London). And both are shot through with heavy, brutal cynicism; a far cry from the upbeat villainy of a late sixties crime caper, *Carter* and *Target* reflected the new nihilism of an already darker, more desperate decade.

But where *Get Carter* is photographically flat and episodic, like a boundary-pushing but nonetheless formulaic regional TV crime thriller shot on 16mm, *Sitting Target* is aesthetically bold and vivid. The first thirty minutes — in which the taciturn, poker-faced con Lomart finds out his wife is pregnant by another man and rounds up two fellow inmates to stage an audacious prison break-out — amount to a virtuoso piece of staging and visualisation from director Douglas Hickox, one of the unsung heroes of British cinema. The night-time escape is a gripping piece of reverse *Rififi*, as Lomart and his cohorts daringly scale the barbed-wired walls and slide an aerial tightrope to

freedom. Later, Hickox frames the colourless tower blocks of south London with a uniquely cinematic eye. As Lomart takes aim at his wife in her high rise flat through the telescopic lens of his rifle, we could be watching *Dirty Harry*'s Scorpio pick off San Franciscan citizens, or Frederick Forsyth's Jackal honing in on Charles de Gaulle. At the film's climax, there's a deftly executed car chase, which, in its smaller way, is as tense and exciting as Popeye Doyle's pursuit of his would-be assassin in *The French Connection*, only this time we're racing through the drab streets of 1970s Battersea.

Perhaps unwittingly, Hickox also stages a scene that emulates *Get Carter*'s car chase through the washing lines. But here, as if to further emphasise *Target*'s visual superiority, the action becomes balletic, almost dreamlike, as Lomart is pursued through billowing white sheets by a pair of motorcycle cops. Hickox was confident enough a stylist to know that flourishes like this can have their place even in a gritty piece of thick ear. One wonders what he could have done with a Bond film, or a big Hollywood budget.

Oliver Reed, who looked pretty mean at the best of times, is at his unsmiling, aggressive best in the early scenes. There really was no other English star like him at the time; it's no wonder Hollywood wanted him to decamp Stateside (he never did). Reed projects the inherent violence and charismatic danger of a Steve McQueen or a Lee Marvin, something few other British stars, save the non-English Stanley Baker and Sean Connery, could really do. The effect is lost a little when Lomart starts to talk — Reed's clipped tones belong more to a public school bully than a south London hoodlum — but then Michael Caine's Jack Carter didn't exactly sound like he hailed from Newcastle, and no one complains about that.

Ian McShane (who, *Lovejoy* aside, is surely one of the true crime movie icons of the last forty years) lends solid support as Lomart's associate, Birdy. Jill St. John, however, is almost laughably miscast as Lomart's long suffering wife, Pat. (Surely this role needed Carol White or Billie Whitelaw, someone who could convincingly dish out a fried breakfast, rather than the powdered, diamante Ms St. John, who looks as much at home in a Battersea council flat as Audrey Hepburn in a Robin Reliant.) That aside, the rest of the cast — Edward Woodward, Frank Finlay, Freddie Jones, Robert Beatty — is impressive, if under-used.

Sitting Target has its plot holes and narrative flaws (don't most British crime movies?) but it deserves recognition as a corking, kitchen sink action thriller. At the very least it is *Get Carter*'s equal, not its B-side.

Julian Upton

WHAT BECAME OF JACK AND JILL? (1972)

Amicus/Palomar Pictures | 93 mins | colour

Director Bill Bain; **Producers** Max J. Rosenberg and Milton Subotsky; **Screenplay** Roger Marshall, based on the novel *The Ruthless Ones* by Laurence Moody. **Starring** Vanessa Howard (Jill Standish), Mona Washbourne (Gran), Paul Nicholas (Johnny Tallent), Peter Jeffrey (Dr Graham).

Twenty-one-year-old Johnny Tallent lives with his housebound grandmother in suburban London. Unemployed and shiftless, he dreams of the better life that will come once Gran dies. But Johnny's wicked girlfriend, Jill, is impatient for the inheritance, so between them the pair devise an audacious plan to do away with the old woman as soon as possible.

hilst Hammer Films journeyed into the 1970s unaware that its reign would soon be over, the horror giant's two main rivals continued to carve their own individual marks onto the British landscape. Tigon had established itself through plentiful naked flesh and eerie, almost pagan locations; Amicus, master of the portmanteau feature, developed a — perhaps accidental — fetish for urban corridors and clinical theatres, white plaster and damp basements. Any film from Amicus usually carried the promise of one or more characters perishing between four walls. Messrs Rosenberg and Subotsky cultivated their projects away from sunlight and fresh air, allowing the dark and stuffy atmospheres to breed madness. The most obvious examples can be found in the titles of classic Amicus releases — *Dr Terror's House of Horrors* (65), *The House That Dripped Blood* (70), *Tales from the Crypt* (72), *Asylum* (72), *Vault of Horror* (73) — which suggest horrible fates lurking beyond the doorway, far removed from the fairytale sets and foreboding woods of their competitors' own films.

The main interior of *What Became of Jack and Jill?* offers the sort of gloomy mise en scene even Amicus associate Harold Pinter would have recoiled from: all dust-filmed mirrors and grin-and-bear-it wallpaper, grey walls and silence punctuated by that pensioner's friend, the TV set. The kind of home where electric blankets are a rare treat. Here, fast car obsessed twenty-something Johnny lodges with his elderly grandmother. Preening, work shy, sarcastic Johnny nicks cash and heart pills off his unwitting relative and dreams of a better life for him and his Juicy Fruit-chewing harlot of a girlfriend, Jill, who is first seen in the graveyard where Johnny's grandfather lays, tormenting the dead with her body and selfish free will. She announces her intentions to all by scrawling the word 'GRAN!' on the accompanying, waiting headstone. "Not sleeping," she spits. "Dead." Johnny and Jill have a plan to do away with

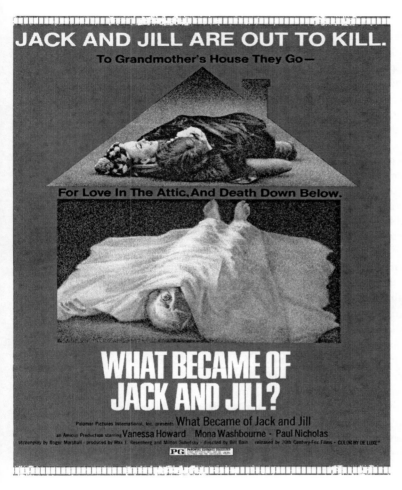

JACK AND JILL ARE OUT TO KILL.

To Grandmother's House They Go—

For Love In The Attic, And Death Down Below.

WHAT BECAME OF JACK AND JILL?

Palomar Pictures International, Inc. presents What Became of Jack and Jill
an Amicus Production starring Vanessa Howard · Mona Washbourne · Paul Nicholas
screenplay by Roger Marshall · produced by Max J. Rosenberg and Milton Subotsky · directed by Bill Bain · released by 20th Century-Fox Films · COLOR BY DE LUXE®

PG

the old woman and inherit her house and money, via swiftly planted geriatric paranoia, courtesy of a deeply contrived invention, 'Youth Power.' Johnny simply tells Gran that one day the young will come and take all the old away. To a background of student riots on the TV, he cuts out newspaper articles under the pretence that he doesn't want her to see them; he pretends that sexy Bible bashers ("I've just been talking to God, does that surprise you?" "Yeah. Yeah, I'd say it did.") are from the 'Y.P.' movement; he gets Jill to make fake census phone calls from her travel agent workplace. All this builds on their fanciful hope of a peaceful art school rag day procession passing through Acacia Avenue (even that imaginary act and road goes on beyond the scope of Amicus' walls), literally coming to get you, Grandma.

Somehow, the plan works. At Gran's funeral, Johnny has a vision of owning a flash black sports car. But his dreams are not founded on hard graft, and can only be fed through the purely materialistic filter of a TV advert. The same applies to Jill: "All I want is a passport full of visas, a twelve-month suntan and some good clothes on me back." Their desires are cut short, however, through an amendment presented by Gran's lawyer: Johnny will only inherit everything as long as he never marries Jill. Despite making a start on alternative marriage plans at a local discothèque, life for Johnny and Jill falls apart soon after. The house is too big, too old for these young people. They become trapped, the shadows like thick bars, casting suspicious glances at each other from dark corners. Taken out of the house, they fall even further apart. There is an altercation where Johnny stabs Jill with a knife. With Jill dying out on the street — sordid lives and plans now in plain sight for all to see — Johnny remains inside, hunted and haunted by the gravity of his actions and the foreboding walls of the house.

A rare curio, *What Became of Jack and Jill?* appears to have suffered from the usual multiple-interest editing process that has hindered many a project that falls short of a specific genre. It somehow fails to gel as a whole, undecided as screenwriter Roger (*...And Now The Screaming Starts*) Marshall is as to whether it should stay true to its thriller fiction origins, stand tall as harsh social commentary, or wallow in the macabre comfort of 'Gran' Guignol. The film is worth it alone, however, for Johnny's insane fantasy — thirty minutes in — of pensioners being pulled from a mini-bus, lined up against a wall and machine-gunned to death by himself, dressed in full Nazi SS uniform. It's a perverse moment that temporarily redeems Paul Nicholas — another actor strangely out of step on the seventies disco floor — from his future crimes in asinine TV sitcoms.

As for Vanessa Howard, after the jaw-dropping nymphette in MUMSY, NANNY, SONNY AND GIRLY (70), this would be her last role in a British film before relocating to America. Her one credit there before following the path of married life with producer Robert Chartoff was — fittingly — a 1973 production of *The Picture of Dorian Gray*. Thus her cinematic achievements remained flawless and intact, whilst her real self got on with the important business of life. British cinema's loss was Beverly Hills' gain, and the miniskirted and turtlenecked Jill became a fine, sleazy closure to a short career. An alternative title for *What Became of Jack and Jill?* was *Romeo and Juliet '71*, although Jill ("I get bored so easily") could actually have come from one of Shakespeare's darker plays: a high street Lady Macbeth who dreams of Las Vegas, Capri and Barbados, but in actuality would only get as far as Torremolinos.

Martin Jones

BLUE BLOOD (1973)

Mallard Productions | 82 mins | colour

Director Andrew Sinclair; **Producers** John Trent, Kent Walwin; **Screenplay** Andrew Sinclair, adapted from the novel *The Carry-Cot* by Alexander Thynne. **Starring** Oliver Reed (Tom), Fiona Lewis (Lily), Anna Gaël (Carlotta), Derek Jacobi (Gregory), Meg Wynn Owen (Beate).

Flamboyant aristocrat Gregory is threatened by his faithful but wayward butler, Tom, whose control over the family home is unnerving. Nanny Beate's arrival in the house coincides with mysterious injuries inflicted upon the children. In the end, not only are Gregory's home and family at stake, but also his sanity.

> **"He's looking up your dress."**
> **"I'm stepping on his face."**

ith dialogue like this, you could be forgiven for thinking that *Blue Blood* is a run of the mill British sexploitation flick with miniskirted mod girls and lashings of hepcat dialogue, but the reality is unfortunately rather less exciting. Oliver Reed is Tom, butler to Gregory (Derek Jacobi) and reminiscent of a straining pit bull in collar and tie, serving a master who spends an inordinate amount of time desecrating the walls of the family home with childish murals and entertaining his extramarital companions with trips to the on-site safari park.

If the vague image of an eccentric, long-haired, waistcoated aristocrat pops into your head at this point, give yourself a gold star; notably one of Britain's more colourful aristocrats, the Marquis of Bath, is nowadays to be found doing the occasional cringeworthy turn on daytime TV's abominable *Animal Park* series. *Blue Blood* was based on his 1972 novel *The Carry-Cot*. Written under the name Alexander Thynne, it is a tedious tale more manifesto for polygamy and drug experimentation than anything with a semblance of plot. "Why do we have to go around pretending that mankind is monogamous," opines Thynne, "when the whole of society is copulating like rabbits?" [1] An arduous read, *The Carry-Cot* is by no stretch an obvious choice to translate to the big screen, and the difficulty of doing so is clear within the first half hour of *Blue Blood*.

Derek Jacobi as the thinly disguised Bath character, replete with embroidered waistcoat, is a thoroughly unlikeable gent from start to finish. Raising his two young children is "a bore" and on one occasion, having accused nanny Beate of hitting his daughter, he suggests he might make a clandestine visit to her room in the small hours. Meg Wynn Owen puts in an interesting performance as Beate, hovering between tearful submissiveness and seething

anger, whilst Fiona Lewis is her usual effortlessly glamorous self as Gregory's unfathomably understanding wife, Lily. She plays a singer whose regular tours lead her husband to employ various replacements in the marriage bed. *Carry-Cot* author Thynne makes a fleeting appearance as a guest at Gregory's party — look out for the gaudy red satin shirt and questionable dancing. There's also some light relief in the form of a Mr Humphreys-style groundskeeper duo. But the film is stolen by Reed's frankly astonishing performance as the slightly camp yet sexually menacing — and somehow inexplicably attractive — Tom.

The Carry-Cot describes Tom as 'a Jack-of-all-trades' with 'a curious blend of cultural influences... half way between hippydom and a caricature of a Dickensian gentlemen's gentleman,' sporting tattoos alongside Edwardian trousers and winkle-pickers.[2] Reed's incarnation as Tom is reasonably true to the book, with slicked down hair and Victorian sideburns, though he succeeds in looking more like an East End heavy than a sixties lovechild. He cuts a massive, hulking presence next to the other cast members, offset by his strange mincing walk and really quite ridiculous voice: think a fey English gentleman with a hint of South African. "You know, with a voice like yours," sniffs Lily, "it's very difficult to take you seriously." In the final scenes of the film, as order in the house unravels, it's almost disappointing to see Reed in his more familiar guise of general dishevelment.

Tom exerts terrific control over the whole household, including Gregory, and throughout the film there is the suggestion that he is involved in something very unpleasant indeed, with occasional crimson-drenched intercuts of Tom in ceremonial robes, surrounded by unclad ladies and a variety of occult paraphernalia. Only very late do we discover that Tom is leading the estate personnel in Satanic rituals, but even this development is rather sketchy and not as jarring as it should be. The sacrifice sequence could easily be construed as one of Gregory's acid-induced hallucinations rather than any definitive conclusion. Thankfully director Andrew Sinclair chose not to remain faithful to the book's description of this climactic scene (although one cannot doubt it would have pleased Reed if he had):

> [Tom] cast the cloak from his body... It was Tom all right: but an intensely phallic Tom, with an erection such as my imagination had never given him credence: painted in vivid colours, and garlanded with a ring of small seashells.[3]

1   Alexander Thynne, *The Carry-Cot* (London: W.H. Allen, 1972), p.10.

2   Ibid., pp.4–5.

3   Ibid., pp.149–50.

Thynne's novel cannot be held wholly responsible for the generally messy progression and ill-managed scenes that crop up in the film time and time again. Filling out the sparse plot are shots of the grounds, while the animals of Longleat safari park are credited with lengthy appearances that ultimately resemble the stock mondo footage of a low budget cannibal flick. In one bizarre shot, Tom has a tense exchange with Lily whilst polishing the silver, the lower half of his face completely obscured by a large tea urn. Whether the composition is intended to be artistic, or simply the result of some lax camera work, is open to debate.

Perhaps under different direction *Blue Blood* would have been a reasonably enjoyable horror romp. (It's easy to imagine Peter Cushing as the leisured aristocrat and Christopher Lee as the sinister, charismatic butler.) The relationship between hippy master and Satanic servant is exploited to no greater end than a scene of the two smoking marijuana together. *The Carry-Cot* offered very little to build upon and the film takes nothing more from it than the interminable aristocratic ramblings on the inadequacies of modern 'straight' society. By the time anything definitive happens, the viewer's attention has fixed inextricably on the quixotic Reed. Without him *Blue Blood* would have disappeared from even the most avid B-film fan's radar. Sensational as the film may think itself, only Reed's looming presence elevates it from being anything beyond a cut-rate version of Losey's *The Servant*.

Jennifer Wallis

DARK PLACES (1973)

Glenbergh/Sedgled | 91 mins | colour

Director Don Sharp; **Producer** James Hannah Jr.; **Screenplay** Ed Brennan, Joseph Van Winkle.
Starring Christopher Lee (Dr Ian Mandeville), Joan Collins (Sarah Mandeville), Robert Hardy (Edward Foster), Herbert Lom (Prescott).

Edward Foster inherits a crumbling mansion from Andrew Marr, a dying patient in a mental institution. He quickly realises he has inherited more than he bargained for, plagued not only by money-hungry neighbours, but the restless spirits of the former inhabitants. Obsessed with a search for the Marr fortune said to be hidden in the house, it transpires Foster may not be all that he seems.

Dark Places is an oddity, hanging somewhere between cheap drama and potential cult status, but shy of both. It wants to be an old-fashioned ghost story but becomes a messy concoction of psychological drama, love story and cut-rate horror. Marketing of the film seemed to reflect this confusion, with the video from Embassy Home Entertainment promising naught but a glamorous Joan Collins, shamelessly capitalising on her *Dynasty* fame. There's certainly no hint of glamour in the film, although Joan up a ladder, dusting down cobwebs, is certainly a sight to behold.

Joan Collins made no secret of her dislike of the genre that helped make her name. Discussing horror, she was to the point. "It makes me sick," she said.[1] Her pairing with Christopher Lee in *Dark Places*, then, is an interesting one, the patron saint of horror having just finished filming *The Wicker Man* and already beloved by the film-going public as Count Dracula. As brother and sister Ian and Sarah Mandeville, Collins and Lee are a perfect team. Sarah is candid about the primitive way in which she extrapolates information about Edward Foster and his newly-acquired home, and Lee has a hint of incestuous possessiveness in his angry response: "Dirty, filthy little slut!" "Can't you keep your hands off anyone?"

Unfortunately, the presence of such a high-profile duo isn't enough to redeem *Dark Places*. It was described by *Variety* as a film 'of no distinction, bound for TV' – which 'from *Variety* in 1974 [was] the greatest curse imaginable.'[2] The film certainly does have a TV movie quality, right from the clunky opening credits that pan across the courtyard of St. Columba's Mental Institution accompanied by a remarkably uninspiring score. Without the presence of Collins, Lee and Herbert Lom (as neighbour Prescott), *Dark Places* may perhaps have fared better. Removing from it the stigma of star material, the film is at heart a perfectly passable psychological thriller.

Edward encounters local superstition as he travels to see his new home, Marr's Grove, warned by his driver that people who go there "get hurt." Right on cue, Edward exits the car only to fall into a hole in the driveway; "I told you, didn't I?" cries the trembling driver. The dilapidated house is the perfect creepy setting. Located not far from Pinewood Studios, it was described by Lee as 'empty and abandoned, water dripping down the walls, no proper plumbing, no heating,' a set which made filming 'thoroughly uncomfortable.'[3] It mirrors the fragile mental condition of Edward, an engaging performance from Robert Hardy that alternates between shy passivity and the actor's typical impassioned outbursts ("Put those bloody lights on!" "Alright you bastards, who are you?" and so on). Edward becomes progressively unstable in his search for the elusive cash secreted by the late Andrew Marr. He may simply be

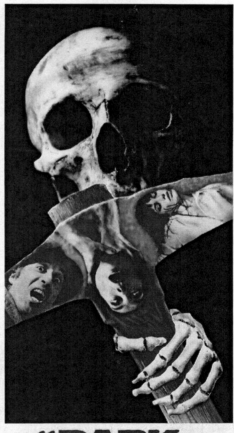

There's more than death
waiting for you
in dark places.

"DARK
PLACES"

"DARK PLACES" A JAMES HENNESSY JR. PRODUCTION STARRING CHRISTOPHER LEE · JOAN COLLINS
HERBERT LOM · JANE BIRKIN · ROBERT HARDY Guest Star JEAN MARSH

Joan Collins gets it in the neck. *Dark Places.*

"DARK PLACES"

FROM CINERAMA RELEASING

272

losing his mind, but Edward's frantic tapping of panelled walls for signs of a hidden recess and his moody pacing of the halls ultimately suggests supernatural forces are afoot. He is intermittently possessed by the spirit of Colonel Marr, a portrait of whom hangs menacingly above the drawing room fireplace, whilst the house relives the brutal events that took place within its walls.

Someone behind the scenes evidently didn't think this in itself was enough. Consequently the ghostly element is accentuated by a set that looks like a fairground ghost train, with theatrical cobwebs strewn impossibly over the kitchen and abandoned nursery, the latter fitted with the requisite shattered porcelain doll and a decrepit rocking horse. Picking things up a pace, a swarm of plastic bats emerge from a chimneybreast to flap about on strings. It is a shocking scene, but only because of its decidedly vintage execution.

Is Edward mad? Possessed? And why does he so closely resemble Colonel Marr? The confusion behind *Dark Places* and its shoddy effects constitute a watered-down version of things far better — the B-movie finesse found in *The House That Dripped Blood* (70), for instance. The television adaptation of Susan Hill's *The Woman in Black* (89) mirrors many elements of *Dark Places* — ghost children and eerie nurseries included — and is tellingly far more effective. *Dark Places* is one for the most serious of Collins and Lee fans and all-star misfires in general.

Jennifer Wallis

1   Jeff Rovin, *Joan Collins: The Unauthorized Biography* (London: Bantam, 1985), p.147.
2   Robert Levine, *Joan Collins, Superstar: A Biography* (Bath: Chivers, Windsor, Paragon & Co., 1986), p.95.
3   Christopher Lee, *Lord of Misrule: The Autobiography of Christopher Lee* (London: Orion, 2003), p.130.

THE HOUSE IN NIGHTMARE PARK (1973)

a.k.a. Crazy House | Associated London Films Limited/Extonation Productions Ltd. | 92 mins | colour

Director Peter Sykes; **Producers/Screenwriters** Clive Exton and Terry Nation. **Starring** Frankie Howerd (Foster Twelvetrees), Ray Milland (Stewart Henderson), Hugh Burden (Reggie Henderson), Kenneth Griffith (Ernest Henderson), Rosalie Crutchley (Jessica Henderson).

Hammy, unpopular thespian Foster Twelvetrees is invited to perform at the large isolated manor of the Henderson family. Unbeknownst to Foster, he is the illegitimate son of their late murdered brother, and has been left his entire estate. The remaining family try to avail from Foster the secret hiding place of their brother's treasure before trying to bump him off.

This film has become harder to see of late but it's not for want of quality. Oh no! Not on your nelly!! But don't expect *Carry On Screaming!* — which in my book is the best of the *Carry On* films and arguably the best movie ever made. For a start there are no monsters here — just a large, creepy house full of strange siblings: the Henderson family. There's Stewart (Ray Milland), haughty, sometimes charming, money grabbing and not averse to a bit of murder; his brother, Reggie, a bad tempered, stuck-up military type, money grabbing, not averse to a bit of murder; their other siblings, Ernest and Jessica, money grabbing, not averse to... you get the picture. Ex-pats of India, they are converts to Hinduism. We see them worship a frightening icon covered in skulls with its tongue stuck out. Nasty bunch.

This is *Cat and the Canary* territory. The Henderson's horrifically aged mother tells our hapless hero, ham actor Foster Twelvetrees (Frankie Howerd), from whom the family are trying steal an inheritance, "Don't trust the others! They are all mad here!," before trying to chop off his head.

But things aren't always this funny; indeed, some of *The House in Nightmare Park* is actually quite unsettling. Director Peter Sykes gives the proceedings the ambience of Hammer Films (he'd directed a few), and screenwriter Terry Nation, who worked on *Doctor Who*, certainly knew how to create tension. One scene in particular makes the whole film worth watching. After Foster 'entertains' the family with one of his awful renditions, they decide to reciprocate and perform an old song and dance routine from their childhood stage act, dressed as dollies and a golliwog. Their wizened faces covered in white makeup, the eeriness of the song and the skewered choreography is so

The House in Nightmare Park: all told, the poster is better than the film.

creepy that you find yourself unsure whether to laugh or recoil. *The League of Gentlemen* eat your heart out! Their song ends suddenly with the golliwog collapsing on the floor with a knife in his back.

In one of his few starring roles, Frankie Howerd is excellent as Twelvetrees, his timing impeccable. Still recognisably Frankie Howerd, his comic asides are however rendered more subtly, as if he's talking to himself. Forties Hollywood legend Ray Milland, defiantly bald, plays it arrow-straight as the villain (and Frankie's foil), but still gives a good, nuanced performance; it's often harder to be the straight man to a clowning buffoon (take Jerry Desmond to Norman Wisdom, or Dean Martin to Jerry Lewis). The other siblings play their parts with relish, especially Rosalie Crutchley as the mainly mute sister.

You may need a treasure map to be able to get hold of a copy of *House in Nightmare Park* nowadays, but if you do manage it, don't blame me if you have nightmares. Or, then again, you might want to. Please yourselves![1]

Andrew Syers

---

1   Frankie Howerd does not actually use any of his usual catchphrases in this film.

TALES THAT WITNESS MADNESS (1973)

World Film Services Ltd./Cinema International Corp | 90 mins | colour

Director Freddie Francis; **Producer** Norman Priggen; **Screenplay** Jay Fairbank (Jennifer Jayne).
Starring Donald Pleasence (Dr Tremayne), Jack Hawkins (Dr Nicholas), Russell Lewis (Paul), Peter McEnery (Timothy), Joan Collins (Bella), Michael Jayston (Brian), Kim Novak (Auriol Pageant).

Keen to hear about his colleague's new breakthrough in treating the insane, Dr Nicholas visits Dr Tremayne at his futuristic institution where he meets four of Tremayne's patients and hears their stories — but could their strange tales possibly be true, as Tremayne believes, or are they all in the mind?

The opening titles come on like a cut-price Bond movie, with X-rayed skulls (instead of silhouetted girls) suggesting that we're going on a journey into the unexplored recesses of the human mind, to some Freudian space of aberrant behaviours and their deep seated, yet ultimately explicable, hidden springs.

Of course, the unexplored recesses of the mind were anything but by this point; all sorts of insanity and murderous delusion — as well as their pat diagnoses — had been grist to horror's mill ever since Hitchcock's *Psycho* (60). For a while it looked as if the psychopathic was set to oust the supernatural, and as if the modern monster — no longer diabolical, but all too human — was a suitable case for treatment, amenable to the screen trick cyclist's armoury of talking cures and taboos. British cinema, for the next decade, was full of murderous kooks and one-word movie titles like *Paranoiac* (63) and *Hysteria* (65).

While *Tales That Witness Madness* presents some fine assorted loons, and suggests that the men in white coats might be equally unhinged, it also emerges from another subgenre of British horror, the portmanteau film, in which disparate weird tales are told by various individuals within a framing story set in a single location — a crypt, a funfair... or a lunatic asylum.

The template might have been laid down in 1945 by Ealing's *Dead of Night*, but it was perfected in the series of films made by Amicus Productions, starting with 1965's *Dr Terror's House of Horrors*, drawing on a distinctly un-English tradition to create a viable alternative to Hammer's established Gothicism. The twisted and darkly humorous EC comics *Tales from the Crypt* and *Vault of Horror* (to which Amicus secured the rights) had outraged American parents and delighted budding juvenile delinquents with their short, sharp and shocking stories of cruelty, murder and supernatural revenge, all

Two of the *Tales That Witness Madness.*

topped off with bloodily satisfying twists. It was a perfect formula for screen adaptation, and Freddie Francis — who also turned in the aforementioned *Psycho* knock-offs — directed *Dr Terror* and others for Amicus before cooking up *Tales That Witness Madness* with actress-turned-screenwriter Jennifer Jayne. The film pinches the established Amicus formula of four linked stories played out by a cast of British stalwarts and some international names, and bears not a little resemblance to Amicus's own, and far better remembered, *Asylum* (72).

Things start reassuringly enough with icon of dependability Jack Hawkins (in his final role) driving up to a country house and ringing the doorbell. When an automatic door ushers him into a futuristically white and eerily empty institution we may be slightly disconcerted, but it's only when another door slides open to reveal a beaming Donald Pleasence that we sense something might be seriously awry. Pleasence's Dr Tremayne explains to his visiting colleague that he has made a breakthrough — a psychiatric theory of everything (he's sketchy on details) that his four current patients will somehow prove — and invites Dr Nicholas to tour their cells and hear their stories.

First up is Paul, the lonely, only child of squabbling parents who's invented an invisible feline friend. His awful ma and pa don't believe in Mr Tiger; bones under Paul's bed and scratches on the door simply confirm their suspicion that the youngster is becoming "uncontrollable." All the more satisfying, then, when, in a neat inversion of Belloc's cautionary tale, the ghastly pair are ripped to pieces by the 'imaginary' beast; and all the more disappointing that the scene relies on intercut shots of a roaring circus cat, an outrageously fake cuddly toy paw and the head of a stuffed specimen chowing down on a pile of offal. Nonetheless, the gouts of blood that splash the bedroom walls as the blank-eyed kid bangs out a nursery tune on his toy piano, and the camera's final impassive survey of the carnage in an otherwise typical child's bedroom, attain a vicious poetry that's worthy of the EC ethos.

Next is antique dealer Timothy, in a tale that initially seems an analogue of the golfing episode in *Dead of Night* but emerges as something nearer the same film's haunted mirror story. "It was hard in this next case to discover the patient's reasoning," says Dr Tremayne; it's hard, too, to take a possessed bicycle, or the hilarious expressions animating the haunted photo of Uncle Albert, very seriously. But the central conceit of a man caught in a time loop and dragged repeatedly into the past is a strong one, and the genuinely surreal image of the deerstalker-sporting protagonist riding a blazing penny-farthing through a genteel Victorian park is like a page of Ernst's *Une semaine de bonté* come to life.

And then there's Joan Collins and the tree — the bit everyone remembers. It's another tale in which an object takes on a life of its own — or articulates the repressed desires bubbling in the brains of the characters. Brian and Bella appear to have a perfectly good relationship — until he comes back from a jog through the woods clutching an ugly tree stump and plops it down in the middle of the living room. Bella believes she has a wooden rival for Brian's affections when 'Mel' — so christened for the graffiti carved into her trunk — starts heavy-breathing and clenching her twigs in a jealous fit. Quite why a hot-blooded 1970s male would fancy a tree instead of Joan Collins is never made clear, but the twiggy temptress triumphs, and in a dreamlike sequence that unites Algernon Blackwood's visions of malevolent nature with Japanese tentacle porn, Bella is pursued and attacked, Mel's branches clawing at the exposed breasts of a body double.

The final segment — in which Kim Novak's wealthy literary agent falls for a dodgy Hawaiian hunk with human sacrifice on his mind — is predictable and overextended, but it does contain the film's most gruesome twist, in which Novak (a last minute replacement for Rita Hayworth) ends up consuming her own daughter's flesh at a wonderfully naff Tiki barbecue.

And Tremayne's great theory? Well, the framing story wraps things up in a double-twist that leaves us none the wiser really, but given the kitschily inventive craziness we've already enjoyed, it's hard to feel too short changed.

David Sutton

A DANGEROUS MADNESS

OPENING THE DOOR TO ASYLUM HORROR

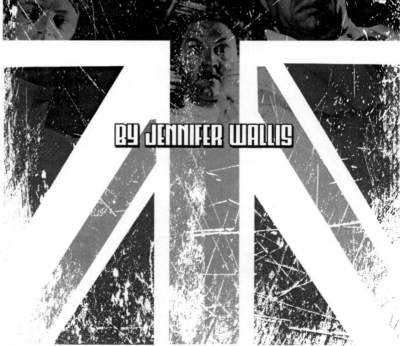

BY JENNIFER WALLIS

Madness and film are a match made in heaven. Unhinged characters allow action to take place that would otherwise be nonsensical, playing on the viewer's fear of the animalistic side of human nature and, ultimately, of becoming mad oneself. In the first half of the twentieth century, *Bedlam* (46) presented a Hogarthian view of madness that capitalised upon the Gothic qualities of the lunatic asylum, whilst Rudolf Maté's *The Dark Past* (US, 48) portrayed the mentally ill as dangerous, sociopathic killers. In the late sixties and early seventies, there was a sudden rush of British films whose sensationalist and sometimes visceral take on mental illness left the viewer in no doubt about the dangers posed by those of unsound mind. Drawing upon widely publicised developments in psychiatric policy, these films held no pretensions of being sympathetic portrayals of the mentally ill patient, or even the asylum doctor. Throats are slit, innocent victims are strangled, and the overarching feeling is one of distrust, as the most unlikely characters are revealed to be homicidal maniacs intent on satisfying their murderous urges.

It didn't take long for the asylum and its patients to become established in the world of film. The silent short *Le Systeme du Docteur Goudron et du Professeur Plume* (a.k.a. *The Lunatics*, c.1912), with a screenplay by grand guignol writer André de Lorde, saw a group of asylum inmates attempting to cure their doctor's 'insanity' using varying degrees of butchery, whilst 1920's *Das Cabinet des Dr Caligari* offered a nightmarish vision of madness in which even the key players were unaware of their own fragile mental state.

Interest in the asylum heightened in the immediate postwar period, particularly in the US. As cinema audiences revelled in the abominable horrors of *The Snake Pit* (48), American journalists and photographers were immersing themselves in the reality of 'the total institution.'[1] During WWII conscientious objectors were often assigned positions in mental hospitals; one such individual, Charles Lord, photographed dishevelled and naked patients housed in filthy wards, in some cases shackled to beds. When *LIFE* magazine ran the pictures in 1946, the response was an angry one. Two years later, Albert Deutsch's book, *The Shame of the States*, presented a shocking picture of American psychiatric hospitals, and magazine editors played on a horror still fresh in the public's mind by comparing such visions of incarceration to German concentration camps.[2]

It was against this background that attempts to integrate asylum patients into the wider community were made, both in the US and the UK, with initiatives such as the 'open door' policy to allow patients greater freedom of movement.[3] In the UK, the 1959 Mental Health Act made it much easier for people to

Madness in Hollywood: 1948's *The Snake Pit.*

receive psychiatric treatment on an informal basis — without a hospital stay or being 'certified' — reorienting mental health care towards the community and away from the remote mental hospital.

Although deinstitutionalisation seemed simple in theory, it proved more difficult in practice. Replacing the asylum wholesale was in actuality an impossible task as a good number of patients still required twenty-four hour care. There was, however, a huge reduction in psychiatric beds: 72,000 in England in 1982, down from 152,000 in 1954. High patient turnover though, suggested a 'revolving door' effect to many observers, who suspected the same patients were repeatedly admitted and discharged.[4]

The public were not overly impressed. Asylums had kept the mentally ill out of sight and out of mind, and moves towards community care and outpatient clinics threatened to place the mentally ill at the heart of 'normal' life. The collective imagination worked overtime to produce a stereotypical image of the ex-asylum patient who was calculatedly evil. Such a mythical character was ideal for the big screen.

In 1972, Amicus released *Asylum*, a portmanteau horror set in a small private asylum in rural England. Dr Martin (Robert Powell), hoping to secure a new job at the institution, is set the task of determining which of the patients is Dr Starr — the asylum director whose recent breakdown has caused the emergence of a new personality. After hearing the horrific tales of the inmates, we discover that the mysterious Dr Starr has taken the place of the hospital orderly, indiscriminately murdering visitors. Apparently motiveless killings like these had begun to be given special interest in psychiatric literature of the seventies. Whilst earlier 'social psychiatry' had emphasised the centrality of environment, a decade later such senseless killings began to be explained as the result of sudden 'explosions' of feeling arising from unresolved trauma. Murder then, was almost a behavioural trait, with no visible signs to warn a potential victim.

In another Amicus offering, *The House that Dripped Blood* (70), horror writer Charles Hillyer (Denholm Elliot) is terrorised by his literary creation, Dominic: a grinning, maniacal escapee from a criminal lunatic asylum. The tale explores the fear of losing one's sanity as Dominic appears to be another side of Charles's personality with murderous designs on his wife, Alice (Joanna Dunham). We discover that these visions of Dominic are being set up by Alice and her lover Richard (Tom Adams), an actor, but the fine line between sanity and madness is crossed as Richard is taken over by the Dominic persona, brutally strangling Alice as he laughs maniacally: the classic picture of the deranged psychopath whose real nature is concealed beneath a 'normal' man.

The British television series *Thriller*, broadcast between 1973–76, a compelling mixture of crime, ghost stories and psychological horror, had rather a penchant for psychiatrists and madmen. An episode from season four, 'Killer with Two Faces,' follows a man who escapes from a criminal asylum and assumes the identity of his twin brother. Bob, the innocent half of the duo, is distinguishable to the police only by a unique scar on his arm, suggesting that the homicidal maniac is so skilled in his subterfuge that detection can only rely on physical markers.

Such flawless deception is also evident in DEADLY STRANGERS (74), which sees Hayley Mills play her usual wide-eyed, vulnerable young miss to perfection as Belle Adams, who hitches a lift with stranger Stephen Slade (Simon Ward). Her real identity is a genuine shocker, as the end of the film sees her dispassionately throttling Stephen to death with a scarf, emotionless and unrepentant. Upon the arrival of the police, she obligingly walks to the car to be taken back to the asylum, carrying a box containing an ostrich egg acquired on her brief travels. "Do you know," she marvels in the back of the police car, "it

takes four hours to boil an ostrich egg. Four hours!"

Belle is clearly incurable, exhibiting no remorse for her actions, and this concept appears repeatedly; in some cases, such as TWISTED NERVE (68), mental illness is explicitly genetic and irreversible. This was a far cry from the picture of drug-induced madness seen in the same year's *Lila* (a.k.a. *Mantis in Lace*), in which a stripper develops a taste for butchering men after experimenting with LSD. TWISTED NERVE's problematic message — that Down's Syndrome was in some way linked to murderous motivations — was sensationalised further with the suggestion that mental instability, if present in one sibling, was likely present in the other, even if no outward symptoms were visible. The possibility of a whole family of unhinged murderers was explored in Pete Walker's *Frightmare* (74), in which it seemed that homicidal and cannibalistic tendencies had been passed from parent to child.

Frightmare, like DEADLY STRANGERS, was unusual in its choice of woman as murderous psychopath. Moral panics of the 1930s had focused on the male psychopath as inhuman beast (exemplified by 1931's *M*), but now the definition widened to include the prospect of the female psychopath, with the Moors murders confirming the horrific possibility of a glamorous woman inexplicably

drawn to sexual sadism and murder. Even if she was thought to have been coerced into the act of murder, the female killer was a more shocking figure than the stock male, and *Frightmare* pushed the envelope even further by placing white-haired grandmother figure Dorothy Yates (Sheila Keith) at the centre of the bloody action. Dorothy and husband Edmund (Rupert Davies) are released from a lengthy spell in an asylum after a series of gruesome killings but quickly revert to old habits, luring unsuspecting strangers into their house before

Care in the community? Sheila Keith in *Frightmare*.

murdering and eating them. It transpires that daughter Debbie (Kim Butcher) seems to have inherited her mother's tastes and the film capitalises on the fear, debated by psychiatrists long before the twentieth century, that our fate is determined by our parents.

The film outraged British film critics who found Walker's simplistic interpretation of mental illness disturbing. Walker was unapologetic, framing *Frightmare* as a criticism of the psychiatric profession:

> ... I really did believe that people were being let out of jails and mental asylums before they were properly cured. The week before the film went to the censor, a man was released from Broadmoor by a load of well-meaning psychiatrists who said he was ready to take his place in society again. A week later he killed two more children... I was just saying we should be more careful.[5]

His comments came against a backdrop of increasing dissatisfaction with the mental health system. The association of mental illness and criminality proved perfect fodder for an excitable tabloid press; indeed, despite the good intentions of community care some patients — having lived in institutions for many years — found it difficult to cope and ended up homeless. Although a few may have been drawn into petty criminality out of necessity rather than any inherent criminal tendency, they were a group easily used to illustrate the apparently 'natural' link between mental illness and criminal behaviour.[6]

That such impoverished groups existed at all, regardless of their numbers, fuelled the criticism of the psychiatric profession that had its roots in the

work of such 'anti-psychiatrists' as Thomas Szasz and R.D. Laing.[7] Filmmakers certainly produced some damning portrayals of mental health professionals: *Psycho* homage *Dressed to Kill* (80) was a direct attack on the psychiatrist, with Michael Caine cast as the transsexual razor-wielding murderer, whilst 1973's *Tales that Witness Madness* portrayed a psychiatrist apparently as mad as his patients (albeit with a last minute reprieve for the disturbed Dr Tremayne, played by Donald Pleasence).

Not to be confused with Ed Wood's *Orgy of the Damned*.

Since the turn of the twenty-first century, despite being a diminished presence in real life where it has been replaced with more modern 'secure units,' the traditional asylum has made a comeback on the big screen with another wave of themed films. The emphasis however, has done an about-turn since the horrors of the early seventies, with the threat no longer embodied in the maniacal man or woman, but the fabric of the asylum itself. *House on Haunted Hill* (99) inaugurated a cycle of (mostly American) films that place the psychiatric establishment centre stage. In updating William Castle's 1959 film, *Haunted Hill* director William Malone situates the exclusive party in an abandoned asylum, where gurneys line the damp corridors and electroshock equipment languishes in basement treatment rooms. The criminal here is asylum director Dr Vannacutt (Jeffrey Combs), whose brutal experiments on his helpless charges have imbued the empty building with an evil presence that constantly seeks new victims. The hospital's central lock-down button — originally an emergency measure — becomes a means of containing the party-goers within the building whilst the ghosts of the former inhabitants stalk the halls. *Death Tunnel* (2005; a shameless rip-off of *House on Haunted*

Hill), *The Sick House* (2007), *Dark Floors* (2008) and *Mirrors* (2008) have continued the trend, situating horror within the walls of derelict asylums and hospitals that are malevolent, predatory entities, whilst *The Devil's Chair* (2006) attempts an ironic swipe at the genre that only succeeds in placing it firmly within the category it seeks to critique.

The atmosphere of the 'urbex horror' film — drawing on the urban exploration tradition to place the building, as much as the actors, centre stage — is a far cry from the vintage sensationalism of *Asylum*, but shows that madness and its institutions hold an enduring fascination. Sociologist René Lourau called this 'schizophilia' — an 'overvaluing' of madness, in which its symptoms are used with a degree of artistic licence in books, films, stage plays etc.[8] Lourau's definition is usually invoked in a positive sense — to refer to the growing popularity of exhibiting patient art for example — yet its darker side can be seen in films such as Twisted Nerve and *Frightmare*. In these screen representations, mental illness is credited with massive power to harm that bears no resemblance to the lives of the majority of psychiatric patients. Yet as institutions across Britain closed or downsized, Dr Starr, Belle Adams and Dorothy Yates were stark symbols of the fear of the mentally ill prevalent in many sections of society at the time. The films, coupled with tabloid sensationalism, represented a popular commentary on government policy that was neither subtle nor compassionate but which neatly articulated the concerns of the general public when it came to opening the doors of the asylum: whilst the ramshackle, archaic asylum itself was frightening, it was nothing compared to what might happen in its absence.

1   See Erving Goffman, *Asylums: Essays on the Social Situation of Mental Patients and Other Inmates* (Harmondsworth: Penguin Books, 1968).

2   Cynthia Erb, '"Have you ever seen the inside of one of those places?": Psycho, Foucault, and the postwar context of madness,' *Cinema Journal* 45:4 (Summer 2006), pp.45–63, 49.

3   See Arthur Bowen, 'Some Mental Health Premises,' *The Millbank Fund Quarterly. Health and Society* 57:4 (Autumn 1979), pp.533–51.

4   Sarah Payne, 'Outside the walls of the asylum? Psychiatric treatment in the 1980s and 1990s,' in Peter Bartlett and David Wright (eds.), *Outside the Walls of the Asylum: The History of Care in the Community 1750–2000* (London: Athlone Press, 1999), pp.244–65, 247.

5   Cited in Steve Chibnall, *Making Mischief: The Cult Films of Pete Walker* (Surrey: FAB Press, 1998), p.146. *Films Illustrated* (March 1976) [page no. unreferenced].

6   See Noam Trieman, 'Patients who are too difficult to manage in the community,' in Julian Leff (ed.), *Care in the Community: Illusion or Reality?* (Chichester: John Wiley & Sons, 1997), pp.175–87.

7   See for example, Thomas Szasz, *The Myth of Psychotherapy: Mental Healing as Religion, Rhetoric, and Repression* (NY: Anchor Press, 1978).

8   Erb, '"Have you ever seen the inside of one of those places?,"' p.45.

NOTE I am very grateful to Chris Millard for his comments and suggestions on an earlier version of this piece, particularly in clarifying some of the historical issues surrounding twentieth-century mental health policy.

THAT'LL BE THE DAY (1973)

Goodtimes Enterprises/Anglo-EMI | 91 mins | colour

Director Claude Whatham; **Producer** David Puttnam; **Screenplay** Ray Connolly.
Starring David Essex (Jim MacLaine), Ringo Starr (Mike), Rosemary Leach (Mrs MacLaine), Robert
Lindsay (Terry), Rosalind Ayres (Jeanette).

*Nineteen fifty-eight. Sixth former Jim MacLaine abandons his studies and
takes to the seaside holiday camps and fairgrounds, where his life becomes a
procession of easy kicks and casual sex, sustained by a background of rock and
roll music. Facing up to 'adulthood,' he marries a local girl and starts a family.
But the call of rock and roll is too strong for him to ignore.*

That'll Be The Day isn't a forgotten film as such; it was a domestic box office hit, generated a sequel — *Stardust* (74) — and will no doubt be kept alive while there are still legions of David Essex and Ringo Starr fans walking the Earth. But it's generally seen as a footnote in British cinema, a minor exercise in rock and roll nostalgia, chiefly memorable for providing screen roles for a roster of British pop stars, past and present, whose faces lend the piece a degree of novelty even if their performances don't (as well as Essex and Starr, there's Billy Fury and Keith Moon in the first film; Adam Faith, Marty Wilde and Dave Edmunds turn up in the sequel).

But this is much better than just a vehicle for a couple of musicians to try their hand at acting. As an evocation of the birth of rock and roll in Britain, and, especially, as an exploration of what that really meant to the first wave of 'teenagers,' *That'll Be The Day* is up there with the contemporaneous *American Graffiti* (73) for encapsulating an era with just the right level of feeling and authenticity.

The story has parallels with John Lennon's early life (although David Essex, in his 'period' haircut and clothes, is actually a dead ringer for the young Paul McCartney). A lower-middle-class grammar school kid, Jim MacLaine (Essex), abandoned as a youngster by his wayward father, drops out and drifts, sows his wild oats, marries and has a baby, and then walks out on his family, just like his old man did, but this time giving it up for a guitar and a rock star dream.

All this happens without Essex — one of the biggest pop stars of the day — singing a note. That's because this is a story about how the music influences a young man, how it begins to course through his veins and provide the score for the events of his life, not how he becomes a great practitioner of it. By the end of the film, MacLaine may be following his dream, guitar in hand, but there's no suggestion he will be able to make it as a singer or a musician (it's doubtful he can even play a chord). Rather, he is like thousands of late fifties teenagers: some might have carried on chasing rock stardom, a few lucky ones might have achieved it, but most would have been back home to their dead end lives within six months.

The Lennon parallel extends to the sequel, which sees MacLaine's band become the biggest in the world while his ex-wife and child are kept under wraps. But *That'll Be The Day* and *Stardust* can work as separate, standalone films. *Stardust* is an epic attempt to condense the destructive journey that was the 1960s and show it through the eyes of a superstar band very like the Beatles; in its way it is a fascinating and prescient film (given that it was made so soon after the sixties ended). But it's less concerned with detail and the minutiae of teenage fantasies; instead, it falls prey at times to its own portrait of overindulgence and pretentiousness.

That'll Be The Day, on the other hand, is surprisingly modest and earthy; it belongs in many ways to the social realist wave of films that preceded it by at

least ten years — *Room at the Top, Saturday Night and Sunday Morning, A Kind of Loving*, films that were nudged out of popular view by the onset of the swinging sixties. But it differs in that it's a 'period' film, even though only fifteen years had elapsed between the year of its release and the time it is depicting. In terms of attitudes, fashion and culture, the gap between 1958/59 and 1973 seemed thirty years wide. Some misguided early seventies movies were still hanging onto the coat-tails of swinging London; *That'll Be The Day*'s very existence was proof positive that the sixties were over, man.

But if you think it was easy to capture 1958/59 accurately in 1973, you only have to look at the hash Franc Roddam made of trying to recreate 1964 in 1979's *Quadrophenia* to realise there was some considerable skill to it. There is real understanding in *That'll Be The Day*'s attention to detail. It's not just in the clothes and the decor; it's evoked in the dated teenage lingo, in the claustrophobia of lower middle-class aspirations, in the sheer visceral power that the early rock music held over a generation eager to break away. Director Claude Whatham may have been consigned to history as serviceable and pedestrian, but he had the good sense to let the details speak for themselves, and to understand that 1958 was already another country. It's a pity Roddam couldn't see there was a similar gulf between 1964 and 1979.

While he's no Laurence Olivier (or Laurence Harvey, for that matter), David Essex holds his own rather well here. He's passively charismatic enough to be able to drift amiably from one sequence of events to the next. But when he makes a decision, it tends to be a major one. And it's interesting that Essex is not yet required to 'play the rock star' as he was to do in *Stardust*. He gives a straight, low-key, naturalistic performance, and does it better than most pop-star-turned-film-actors.

But the real acting revelation of *That'll Be The Day* is Ringo Starr, whose extended cameo gives the movie its comedy and its central drive. As Mike, Jim's more experienced but equally directionless holiday camp room-mate, Starr plays the lecherous Scouse scamp bit to the hilt. Obsessed with getting his end away and bursting with colourful stories of life on the fairgrounds, it looks like a role he was born to play.

Sadly, Ringo didn't come on board for the sequel. There was apparently a role for him in *Stardust*, but that film's depiction of a band that becomes the victim of its own success was all a bit too close to home.

Julian Upton

DEADLY STRANGERS (1974)

Silhouette Film Productions/Rank | 88 mins | colour

Director Sidney Hayers; **Producer** Peter Miller; **Screenplay** Peter Levene, from his original story.
Starring Hayley Mills (Belle Adams), Simon Ward (Steven Slade), Sterling Hayden (Malcolm Robarts), Ken Hutchison (Jim), Peter Jeffrey (Uncle).

After she is molested by a lorry driver, Belle, a young woman, accepts a lift from Steven, a travelling salesman. But a patient has escaped from a nearby mental institute and, as they start to avoid the police roadblocks, the pair's unhappy memories begin to catch up with each of them, and it soon becomes very clear that one of these strangers is in the grip of madness... and murder.

A private room in Greenwood Mental Hospital. A nurse enters and is attacked by an unseen patient. A suburban home is broken into and clothes stolen. A man stops his car to make a call in a telephone box. He is run over and then robbed of his wallet. These are the events that begin *Deadly Strangers*, clues that drag it into a rain-soaked Somerset on a peculiar, and yet very English, road trip...

So, an escaped lunatic is on the loose. In a roadside public house on a dead end Sunday, whiskey-quaffing Steven Slade is among the many men who notice the arrival of Belle Adams, an attractive young woman trying to get to Greenwood Station. After accepting a lift from a lorry driver ("You a model, eh?"), she narrowly avoids being raped (part of the job description for such men in 1970s films) and then is almost run over by Steven in his car. Bottle in hand, he comes out with remarks such as "You know how long it takes to boil an ostrich egg?" and offers to drive Belle to her station.

The ice is broken, but neither Belle nor Slade is revealing the whole truth about where they've been, or where they're going. Traumas from the past follow

TWO ON THE RUN...
one leaving a trail
of sudden death
the other about
to become
a victim!

DEADLY STRANGERS

STARRING
HAYLEY MILLS · SIMON WARD
and STERLING HAYDEN
produced by PETER MILLER directed by SIDNEY HAYERS music by RON GOODWIN
associate producer PATRICK BROMILODGE original screenplay by PHILIP LEVENE

Simon Ward gets an eyeful. *Deadly Strangers.*

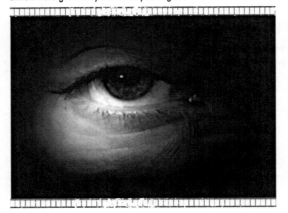

close behind in Vaseline-smudged flashback: Belle's childhood joy of riding a horse along a deserted beach is cut short when her parents' car hits a lorry head on; Steven offers up a brief sexual encounter with a cocktail dolly bird, clues added to his own makeup when he asks her to leave her heels on. Something is not right with either of these strangers, a fact made clear when Steven pulls in to a deserted petrol station to fill up. Wandering around for signs of life, he spies on a shapely, raven-haired female attendant (reliable sitcom stand-in Nina Francis) changing out of her overalls into an impractical yellow mini-dress. Before the film can turn into *Confessions of a Psychopath*, the girl is stabbed to death in her office. But by whom? Neither Steven nor Belle is letting on, as they get back onto the roads, roads, roads and a world of cigarettes, booze, roadblocks, newspaper headlines and egg and chips. After a speeding altercation with two *Psychomania*-style bikers, which ends with an exact reproduction of the fiery climax of *Easy Rider*, both Steven and Belle appear to have genuine reason to evade the police.

But nothing is what it seems in *Deadly Strangers*: the biker doesn't die, and the places Steven and Belle pass through and head for do not appear to exist. Greenwood? Whickham? Southcliffe? Springfield? Apart from the recognisable, strangely grim seafront at Weston-super-Mare, the only actual location mentioned in the film (aside from a briefly-seen road sign for Cheddar) comes from an envelope Belle peaks into whilst in the car: Richmond Hill, Bath. Steven explains that he travels the country selling farm equipment, and the envelope belonged to the man who had the job before him. A lie? The only truths so far seem to be their respective flashbacks: orphaned Belle goes to live with her uncle; Steven can't satisfy his girlfriend in bed.

Avoiding a roadblock by spending the night down a country lane, Steven wakes to find himself alone, unaware that Belle has merely walked to the nearest village to buy food. "Bloody bitch!" he mutters as he speeds off. Walking back to nowhere with her lonesome groceries, Belle becomes entranced by a horse in a field. More schizophrenia: Belle becomes Hayley Mills, the horse a reminder of her own past, on and off screen. A Disney child. Another career

FILM REVIEWS

All grown up: Hayley Mills in *Deadly Strangers*.

in another life. For Belle, it's the alternative Disney vision, childhood of nightmare. Peter Jeffreys as the uncle (Uncle Walt?). She discovers him seducing a servant girl in the hayloft. Later, he interrupts her taking a bath, salaciously commenting: "And to think I used to hold you on my knee. Nature's a wonderful thing." And Steven's trauma? Voyeur, masturbator, reliant on top-shelf filth. "So this is what you like?" his girlfriend shrieks. "Well no wonder you couldn't make it! You want me to whip you then?"

Whether Steven is the killer or not, it soon becomes apparent that perhaps we should not be watching this film. Like the unsettlingly intimate GOODBYE GEMINI (70) before it, there is the uneasy feeling with *Deadly Strangers* that the viewer is in fact privy to events they have no right to see, not even alongside Steven, as he spies through a keyhole in a makeshift hotel room towards the climax. A *Mayfair* fantasy of Belle in black underwear, suspenders and garter belt is replaced by the actual sight of her topless. Steven using the trusted *Psycho* hole-in-wall method. Hayley Mills topless. An extraordinary yet unnerving sight: like the look in Mills' eyes throughout; like the audacious quarter-of-an-hour cameo, forty-four minutes into the film, by American actor Sterling Hayden. As if sent over by misguided agents to audition for the role of the next *Doctor Who* (almost perfect timing, in fact, for the Jon Pertwee/Tom Baker changeover), he appears out of nowhere, sending the film off the rails of its thriller origins for the duration of his presence. In *Chitty Chitty Bang Bang* car, flat cap, tweed cape and extensive chin beard, Hayden appears to be reading from his own interpretation of the script, overbearingly playing the gent to Belle, within minutes suggesting marriage. His reaction when Belle and Steven are reunited, prompted by a lingering newspaper headline, makes perfect sense at the end of *Deadly Strangers*, but in reality for Hayden, this is a long way from working with Stanley Kubrick.

And as for Hayley Mills... Her stocking-clad legs — amongst other things — may captivate men throughout the film, but deep down even she (and Belle) knows that Weston-super-Mare is a long way from Disneyland.

Martin Jones

GHOST STORY (1974)

a.k.a. Madhouse Mansion | Stephen Weeks Company/Nationwide Distributors | 89 mins | colour

Director/Producer Stephen Weeks; **Screenplay** Philip Norman, Rosemary Sutcliff, Stephen Weeks. **Starring** Larry Dann (Talbot), Murray Melvin (McFayden), Vivian Mackerall (Duller), Marianne Faithfull (Sophy), Leigh Lawson (Robert), Anthony Bate (Dr Borden), Barbara Shelley (Matron).

England, late 1920s. Three former college friends, Talbot, Duller and McFayden, meet for a weekend's shooting at the country pile McFayden has just inherited. But the new homeowner is fearful of the building's aura and has really invited his friends for support. Sure enough, Talbot, the most impressionable of the trio, is soon assailed by ghostly visions of events that took place in the house many years before.

Stephen Weeks was twenty-two when he directed his first film (*I, Monster*) and twenty-five when he scripted, financed and directed *Ghost Story*. But this impressive example of artistic and commercial precocity has remained somewhat overshadowed by the story of British horror's more tragic-romantic director, Michael Reeves. Reeves died at the age of twenty-four, after making waves with his third feature, *Witchfinder General* (68). There has since been much speculation on the heights he could have gone on to reach at the forefront of gothic cinema. *Ghost Story*, similarly, was Weeks' third feature, but it made no commercial impact and, far from the outrage that *Witchfinder* caused, was only damned with faint praise. So, while Weeks himself remained very much alive, his feature film career stalled. This is a shame, because in its careful, quiet and rather civilised way, *Ghost Story* has moments that are as effective and unsettling as *Witchfinder General*, and it shows Weeks as a filmmaking talent every bit as assured and inventive as his ill-fated rival.

The central haunted house tale is an oft-told one (it isn't adapted from any particular story but aims to evoke an M.R. James ambience). But the 'devil' here is very much in the detail. Weeks took the remarkably adroit step of shooting almost entirely in Tamil Nadu, India, where he found a wealth of colonial relics still in operational use, not least a baronial-style mansion whose interior was steeped in Victoriana and which serves as the film's haunted house. Further, there were vintage cars, steam trains and country estates and roads that had been imported or fashioned by those homesick, Raj-era Brits, all readily available for use at a much lower price than the cost of designing a period film back home. Thus, Weeks cleverly added tens of thousands of pounds' worth to his production values at relatively little cost, a decision that

FILM REVIEWS

Chic heroine. Marianne Faithfull in *Ghost Story*.

has to rank as one of the most astute a low budget film producer has ever taken (and low budget film producers are not known to be slack on cost saving). What's more, India offered a good chance to capture that perfect English 'Indian summer'; in England, even filming in July or August runs the risk of rain stopping play.

While *Ghost Story* benefits immeasurably from the 'authenticity' of the location shooting, Weeks also showed good taste in the casting decisions. Having a heroin-ravaged Marianne Faithfull as the tortured soul that still haunts the house (she's a young woman condemned to an asylum by her brother [Leigh Lawson], who harbours incestuous feelings for her) may have been a calculated pitch to secure some cut-price star quality (Faithfull's career was at a low ebb), but her pallid appearance and vacant stare turn out to be rather effective. The film has gained further pop culture credibility by featuring Vivian Mackerall as the sneering house guest Duller. The late Mackerall, who shared a flat with Bruce Robinson in the late sixties, has gained posthumous notoriety as the real life inspiration for the eponymous drunken actor in Robinson's *Withnail and I* (87). But here, in his only significant film role, he is perfectly cast as a dastardly 1920s rogue, all chiselled, matinee-idol looks, pencil moustache and clipped delivery, like a young Laurence Olivier. The one concession to conventional horror movie casting is Barbara Shelley as the matron of the asylum. But this also works well: the Hammer stalwart has rarely looked as haunted. (Of course, this may have been down to the food poisoning, which all the cast suffered at one point during their Indian sojourn. Another of Weeks' clever ideas to save on makeup costs?)

Only Larry Dann as the hapless Talbot seems a touch out of place. His befuddled face looks more suited to an episode of *Last of the Summer Wine* than a scary film. The eerie visions start to break him down, but his toothy, jovial features seem to have a hard time registering abject horror (or food poisoning, for that matter). But it's a minor quibble: Dann can certainly do

China girl: Larry Dann gets dolled up. *Ghost Story.*

hapless, and he bounces off Mackerall and Murray Melvin (as the house owner McFayden) nicely.

There are other problems, of course. The china doll that instigates much of the eeriness looks suitably creepy, but having it move around in front of the camera like a hovering muppet isn't likely to strike terror in many people today. At the other extreme, much of the film is just too tepid and forceless, like a waning torch in a freezing night fog. The sense of restraint is admirably arthouse (I'm sure if the same film had Peter Weir's name on it, it would enjoy a far more privileged status), but a horror movie released some months after *The Exorcist* should probably have let rip a little more, thrown something genuinely nasty at us. That said, the asylum scenes are quite disturbing, all the more so for descending into hysteria as gently as they do.

Ultimately, the film reflects the careful (and propitious) design of its creator — from the evocation of a vanished England to the precise ear for period language. An outfit such as Hammer may have thrown (a bit) more money at such a project, but the studio-bound artificiality and po-faced dialogue that would have inevitably resulted would jar now. Nearly forty years on, Weeks' film still looks solid and credible — as credible as such things can look. Like its mansions, vintage cars and antique trinkets, *Ghost Story* appears built to last.

Julian Upton

DVD print under review supplied by Nucleus Films.

FLAME (1974)

a.k.a. Slade in Flame | Goodtimes Enterprises Ltd./Spouberry Productions Ltd. | 91 mins | colour

Director Richard Loncraine; **Producer** Gavrik Losey; **Screenplay** Andrew Birkin, from a story by Dave Humphries. **Starring** Alan Lake (Jack Daniels), Dave Hill (Barry), Jim Lea (Paul), Don Powell (Charlie), Noddy Holder (Stoker).

Members of two rival pop groups get together to form Flame. They are signed by a powerful marketing company and become successful. But their ex-manager uses violence to try to get a cut of their profits, and soon the constant touring causes the band to implode and break down in acrimony.

Flame opens with a wedding party — a dreary wedding party full of conventional people, the men wearing their hair only slightly longer than they would have done in the 1950s. The swinging sixties have yet to touch Wolverhampton, even though it's 1974. The camera follows the groom from the bathroom of a large detached house as he descends the stairs to the marquee in the garden where a band is providing entertainment. As this is a film featuring Slade, we expect to find Noddy Holder at the mic, but he is nowhere to be seen. Only Dave Hill and Jim Lea are present. Instead, on lead vocals is one Jack Daniels (Alan Lake).

Barry (Hill) soon becomes bored with the gig and uses his foot to prop up the back of the bride's dress, providing himself with some extra entertainment. The groom registers his displeasure by diving head-first into the group. A fist fight ensues, and Jack panics that the drum kit will get damaged, which indeed it does.

The next scene sees Charlie (Don Powell) working in a furnace. The credits begin and the great title track (How Does It Feel) accompanies shots of him leaving work, jumping into an ancient motorcycle sidecar and being driven past old terraced houses and tower blocks, one of which he lives in with his parents. When he gets home his parents tell him the debt collectors want his drums back. Instead, he takes them and heads off to audition as the new drummer for Jack Daniels' group. Jack gives Charlie the job — but only because he has a good drum kit.

It's a pity that *Flame* is a semi-forgotten film, but more so that Alan Lake is a forgotten performer. Although his role here is small — Jack is soon ousted from the band in favour of, predictably, Mr Holder — he is so engaging as a pathetic, washed-up rocker, trying unsuccessfully to emulate Elvis, that the film could have easily centred on his anguish at being deprived of the big time

Slade in *Flame*.

yet again. Even the black and white photo of him that briefly appears on the
screen as the end credits roll is impressive. Lake's look of enraged defiance
stays with you long after the film has ended.

But director Richard Loncraine also solicits surprisingly good, deadpan
performances from Holder, Hill et al. It's a credit to them that they were
prepared to play scenes that could have alienated their fans. (For example,
they treat their roadie more and more like a slave as they rise in the pop
charts.) And it's impressive that they were prepared to appear in a pop music
film that does not conform in any way to the madcap, Richard Lester template.
Instead, *Flame* is a slice of life without the crusts cut off: a gritty, realist
depiction of what it was actually like for working class youths trying to make
it in the music business, performing in seedy clubs and dives where nobody
appreciates their music — including their manager.

Over thirty-five years old now, this is very much a period piece. It shows a
different, vanished England — albeit an England almost as depressing as
the one we have today. The group's manager, Ron Harding (played with
fantastically seedy gusto by Johnny Shannon), epitomises the nasty side
of the era: the brutish, criminal element that contaminated the music
business, along with many other enterprises. Tom Conti's marketing man,
Robert Seymour, however, displays a ruthlessness far more effective and
sophisticated, and one that's more sly, as it resides beneath a veneer of polite
respectability. It's also timeless. Seymour arranges for Flame to do a live
interview on a pirate radio ship. They get shot at, almost killed, but he is
pleased that the media coverage is excellent. Some things will never change.

Andrew Syers

SYMPTOMS (1974)

a.k.a. The Blood Virgin | Finition/New Realm Entertainment | 91 mins | colour

Director Joseph (José) Larraz; **Producer** Jean Dupuis; **Screenplay** Joseph Larraz, Stanley Miller. **Starring** Angela Pleasence (Helen), Lorna Heilbron (Anne), Peter Vaughan (Brady).

Returning to her family's isolated country house after a period of convalescence, the neurotic Helen is joined by her friend Anne. Despite evidence all around of Helen's previous housemate (and lover), Cora, Helen is reluctant to talk about her. Helen's hatred of the house's odd job man, Brady, however, seems to implicate him in Cora's disappearance. Disturbed by this and the strange noises at night, Anne decides to investigate further.

W hen a director like José Ramón Larraz tackles the subject of a woman's madness, the result is filed for posterity as exploitation, despite the occasional credible intervention of a critic. When someone like Robert Altman does it (see the earlier IMAGES), it's art.

However, in exploring a young woman's spiralling neurosis from the inside, and fashioning her fragile grasp of reality with the tools of the horror film genre, *Symptoms* more than matches IMAGES as an effective addition to the alternative 'cinema of isolation' (see SOMETHING TO HIDE). Indeed, it outclasses it, achieving its haunting power with rather more subtlety and restraint. As brave as Altman was, he didn't have the audacity to let lonely, quiet scenes unfold with this much eerie languor. (It's doubtful whether Larraz was influenced by the Altman film. He certainly owes a debt to Roman Polanski's *Repulsion*. But even Polanski was far from the first director — hack, artist or otherwise — to be enticed by the potential for erotic horror inherent in a tale of a young woman's mental disintegration.)

Larraz is a director unafraid of silence or stillness (even his more attention-seeking follow-up, *Vampyres* (74), which boosted the sex and gore to grindhouse levels, builds much of its atmosphere from an entrancing wordlessness); in *Symptoms*, he makes long passages of next to nothingness so absorbing that you forget — or no longer care — that you're supposed to be watching a horror film.

This, of course, makes the little moments of shock all the more effective. But don't expect too many shocks. The atmosphere is sustained by an evocation of the unsettling inertia of rural England as much as it is by the central character's murder spree. Like Polanski, Larraz's outsider's view of the mundane trappings of English life seems to infuse them with a dark sense of 'otherness'; like

Altman (who shot IMAGES in Ireland), his foreigner's eye captures the beauty of the countryside while suggesting menace behind its charm.

But *Symptoms'* real trump card is Angela Pleasence as the troubled protagonist Helen. If Donald Pleasence's full moon face, X-ray blue eyes and quiet, psychotic manner lent themselves well to the horror genre, then daughter Angela looks born for it. Not too fortunately for her, she resembles the old man very closely. Yet, for all that, she also has a skewered sexiness about her, and by injecting some gentle lesbianism into the film (Helen harbours fantasies about her female house guest), Larraz draws this out quite successfully. More importantly, Pleasence knows screen acting; like her father, she can convey as much emotion (or emotional dysfunction) in one creepy stare as many an actor can project in a full soliloquy. It's a performance equally as good as Catherine Deneuve's in *Repulsion* and Susannah York's in IMAGES; if anything, Angela Pleasence is even more convincing as someone going completely off her rocker.

José Larraz had been a comic book artist in his native Spain before launching his directorial career with a couple of Danish-financed, sexy horror movies, *Whirlpool* (70) and *Deviation* (71), both of which involved some shooting in England. Stimulated by the environment, he came back to make the fully English-set *Scream... and Die!* (73), another woman-in-peril psychodrama, before signing on for *Symptoms*.

Rather surprisingly, *Symptoms* was chosen, along with Ken Russell's *Mahler,* as a British entry to the 1974 Cannes Film Festival, generating some word-of-mouth interest in the process (Jack Nicholson apparently liked it). Perhaps not so surprisingly, many critics of the time were not keen to endorse a cheap indie horror and the film struggled to get adequate distribution despite the Cannes selection. (It surfaced in the US under the misleadingly salacious title *The Blood Virgin* two years later.)

Nevertheless, Larraz cracked on with what became his cause célèbre, *Vampyres*, which did relatively well in the more relaxed markets, but in Britain (where it was "edited for the Vatican," as Larraz later commented) failed to make much initial impact. So, the director returned to Spain, where, although working occasionally with higher budgets and more diverse subjects, he generally succumbed to less inventive horror and sexploitation fare. The more well known of his later films — *The Coming of Sin* (78) and *Black Candles* (81) — struggle to compare with *Vampyres* and, particularly, *Symptoms*.

Julian Upton

ESKIMO NELL (1975)

Salon Productions/Eagle Films | 85 mins | colour

Director Martin Campbell; **Producer** Stanley Long; **Screenplay** Michael Armstrong.
Starring Michael Armstrong (Dennis), Christopher Timothy (Harris Tweedle), Roy Kinnear (Benny U. Murdoch), Terence Edmond (Clive).

Three novice filmmakers are commissioned by Poverty Row producer Benny U. Murdoch to make a sex film based on the raunchy poem 'The Ballad of Eskimo Nell.' But Murdoch's three backers are each expecting a different film — a gay western, a hardcore porno and a kung fu musical — and all have to be accommodated.

I n the 1970s, Britain was unique in the western world in censoring its legitimate 'adult' films to the point where nothing remotely erotic remained. Despite this, the nation's more thrill-addicted cinemagoers were constantly fooled by heated marketing campaigns into parting with their money for 'X' rated fare that promised far more than it could possibly deliver.

More strangely, thanks to the Eady Levy, the British soft porn film was effectively a government-sanctioned enterprise. If you were a producer, it didn't matter whether your project was about Elgar, rambling in the Yorkshire Dales or spying on ladies in shower rooms; all you had to do was prove to the Eady board that your cast and crew were British and you could be on your way to getting some end-money back, courtesy of the mandatory tax on exhibitors set up to support British film production.

This curious state of affairs was not lost on the young Martin Campbell, a Kiwi who'd come to Britain in the mid sixties and who was working as a video cameraman at ATV by the end of the decade. Increasingly confident that he could direct better than the hacks he was working with, Campbell had struck up a relationship with the enterprising screenwriter-producer Tudor Gates, who had set up a company, Drumbeat, to get on the sex film bandwagon.

Campbell launched his big screen career as 'assistant to the producers' on Drumbeat's *The Love Box* (72), a cut-price romp that focused on the sleazy stories behind the personals section of a fashionable magazine. As dreadful as it was, *The Love Box* didn't lose money. So Gates set up an immediate follow-up, *The Sex Thief* (73), and this time handed the directorial reins to the eager Campbell.

299

The Sex Thief — about a 'gentleman' jewel thief who breaks into the plush London homes of married ladies, seducing them 'to keep them quiet' after he is invariably caught red-handed — is hopelessly dated now (and hardly likely to have appealed to burgeoning women's libbers of the time), but acquits itself somewhat better than expected. The script (by Gates and Michael Armstrong) is quite engaging, and the acting a cut above the usual softcore fare. More importantly, Campbell achieves some visual inventiveness on what is clearly an infinitesimal budget.

One man who noticed this resourcefulness was the irrepressible cameraman-cum-producer-cum-distributor Stanley Long, who roped in Armstrong and Campbell for the sex film he was next preparing, *Eskimo Nell*.

Eskimo Nell is now regarded as the high point — if there is one — of the British soft porn wave of the 1970s. It is, at least, powered by the genre's only half-decent script (again by Michael Armstrong). Wittier and more ambitious than most of its ilk, it attempts to construct a satire on the sex film industry itself, assimilating much *Producers*-style showbusiness talk and in-joking into its narrative. The film's 'adult' credentials rest more on its salty dialogue than on its sex and nudity (of which there is precious little), but most of the 'risqué' dialogue seems lame now, as are a lot of the jokes (Roy Kinnear's tit-obsessed producer is called Benny U. Murdoch, and his production outfit B.U.M. Films). Nevertheless, Nell's extended central sequence — in which the three outrageous versions of the same film are shot on the same set, unbeknownst to the respective actors — is a small triumph, and certainly one of the most frenetic episodes in seventies British cinema (even if the Goodies had already done something similar — and better — on television). The fact that it is actually funny at all sets it head and shoulders above other British sex comedies of the era.

Nell owes a lot more to Armstrong's script than to Campbell's direction, but it does show Campbell progressing as visual stylist. The central interlude gives him an opportunity to fool around with slow-motion, undercranking and cartoon violence, which keeps the pace up when the ideas start to flag. But in the subsequent 'action' sequence — wherein the desperate filmmakers attempt to stop a mix-up of the film cans bound for the premiere by staging a car pileup on the streets of suburban London — Campbell really brings a bit of kinetic muscle to the proceedings, choreographing a low octane car chase that compares to the opening moments of Peter Yates' *Robbery*. The fact he achieves this on a budget that wouldn't have covered Roger Moore's cigar allowance on a Bond movie was an early indication that Campbell was destined in some way for more ambitious action projects.

Inspired by the bawdiest ballad ever written...

STANLEY LONG'S ESKIMO NELL ®

Starring
ROY KINNEAR · ANNA QUAYLE · KATY MANNING
MICHAEL ARMSTRONG · SHEILA BERNETTE · RICHARD CALDICOT · TERENCE EDMOND
JEREMY HAWKE · ROSALIND KNIGHT · DIANE LANGTON · GEORGE MOON
BETH PORTER and CHRISTOPHER TIMOTHY

It is hard to position *Eskimo Nell* as anything like a 'gem' of British cinema. To those who remain enviably unexposed to the British sex film of the seventies, it will doubtless look tawdry and mediocre. But for those who've seen more than, say, five examples of that genre, it has to be regarded as something of a classic.

For all that, *Nell* didn't launch the ambitious Campbell into the major league. He returned (with Michael Armstrong) to Drumbeat to direct the unfathomable THREE FOR ALL (75). Then he gained producing experience on *Black Joy* (77) and the big screen version of *Scum* (79) before returning to television, this time as a director. After notching up credits on shows like *The Professionals* and *Bergerac*, he finally hit the big time with BBCTV's rapturously received *Edge of Darkness* in 1985. By then, the lengthy and unglamorous apprenticeship he'd served stood him in good stead for the Hollywood years to come — *No Escape* (94), *The Mask of Zorro* (98). But it wasn't until he revived the James Bond franchise, *twice*, with *GoldenEye* (95) and *Casino Royale* (2006), that Campbell was finally regarded — well into his sixties — as the A-list director he'd always wanted to be.

Julian Upton

SULLIVAN'S TRAVAILS
THE ROLDVALE SEX FILMS OF DAVID SULLIVAN

BY DAVID KEREKES

David Sullivan and George Harrison Marks: two British pornographers a generation apart, one on his way up and one on his way out. Their meeting in the seventies kickstarted a series of sex films that would become huge money spinners, despite failing on almost every other level. Given the brouhaha that accompanied the release of these films it seemed a British sexual revolution was imminent, much like the one in Denmark. But it was all hot air.

Having discovered money in smut, David Sullivan launched Roldvale Ltd. in 1975, an umbrella company under which he would publish adult magazines, produce adult films and breed racehorses. He courted controversy from the outset, drawing attention to a growing stable of publications that pushed the boundaries of decency and buckled Britain's top shelves with explicitness hitherto unseen. He named the first of his magazines *Whitehouse*, serving to inflame the nation's moral guardian, Mary Whitehouse, and *Ladybirds*, a name belonging to the publisher of children's books. Sullivan was forced to acquiesce on the latter and *Ladybirds*, amidst more publicity, became *Playbirds*. These titles were also the names of the horses he was racing, in a cross-promotional ploy.

George Harrison Marks was a photographer supplying Sullivan with picture layouts. Regarded as a pornography pioneer, Marks had been in the business since the fifties, effectively inventing glamour photography with his partner, model Pamela Green. He established the long-running beauty magazine *Kamera* in 1957 and moved

Come Play with Me ran at London's Moulin for several years.

Mary Millington 'leads' *The Playbirds*.

into feature films with the nudist romp *Naked as Nature Intended* in 1961. The magazine, his models, films and signature 8mm loops made Marks a rich man, but it was all decidedly antiquated by the mid sixties and, refusing to change the formula, sales declined for Marks, leaving him to squander what was left on booze.

The irony of employing Marks, the man who had introduced nudity to Britain, could not have been lost on Sullivan, the man who had foisted upon it the split beaver shot. During one of their meetings, Sullivan asked Marks why he hadn't made a film for some time. It happened that Marks had an idea kicking around for a film called *Come Play with Me*. Sullivan unhesitatingly agreed to finance it for £100,000 (or £130,000; accounts vary).

The story was a simple one: a couple of counterfeiters on the run take refuge in an exclusive health resort. It was a nod from Marks to the gentle comedy style of Ealing Studios as much as it was his own antiquated nudie films. He even brought in some old chums, such as Alfie Bass, Irene Handl, Ronald Fraser and Tommy Godfrey. Sullivan's only stipulation was that *Come Play with Me* should feature his own models and star his girlfriend Mary Millington. Millington was the masthead and greatest asset in the Sullivan publishing empire; he wanted *Come Play with Me* to help turn her into a star,

'Britain's own Linda Lovelace' as he put it.[1]

Marks brought the film in under budget. During the course of a boozy afternoon, he then surrendered his twenty-five per cent of the picture to Sullivan for a one-off payment of £15,000. Sullivan now owned the picture outright, and it would play for five years at Soho's Moulin cinema, grossing over £3 million.

The success of *Come Play with Me* is entirely attributable to Sullivan's shrewd eye for publicity and the fact he blitzed his magazines with advertisements. Knowing the type of picture Marks would make, and the respectable actors with which he was making it, Sullivan announced that a special export version of *Come Play with Me* would contain hardcore material. These additional sex scenes "will make Linda Lovelace look like Noddy," he told a reporter for the *News of the World*. "They show the lot. Nothing is simulated." The octogenarian cast was suitably rattled at the prospect and a very public furore ensued, as Sullivan had intended.

They needn't have worried. In the time-honoured tradition of the British sex comedy, *Come Play with Me* promises sex every two minutes but keeps its thighs locked resolutely together. And while it isn't particularly sexy, it isn't very funny either. Marks himself plays one of the counterfeiters, wearing a ridiculous wig and theatrical goofy teeth, prancing about in a nightshirt as if reliving the days of the music hall. There is a sad inevitability about the arrival of a bevy of buxom nurses, who can provide little more than bad acting. Nevertheless, this, proclaimed producer Sullivan, was Britain's best sex comedy and also its most hardcore.

The runaway success of the film surprised everyone, not least Sullivan, who immediately began cooking up a follow-up. This became *The Playbirds* (78), a wholly different picture for which Sullivan replaced the protesting Marks with Willy Roe; Roe was assistant producer on *Come Play with Me* but had never before directed a picture.[2]

Opening with a woman being strangled to death, the story here concerns a spate of apparent ritual murders. The police suspect Harry Dougan (Alan Lake), a publisher of pornographic magazines. Some of Dougan's recent photo spreads have incorporated a black magic theme, and Dougan himself is interested in the occult. "Sex, witchcraft and horses," he determines, "the unholy trinity." Dougan of course is innocent and in the end a corrupt Cabinet Minister is arrested on suspicion of the murders.

Ads used in this chapter taken from Sullivan's magazines.

The film is a commentary from the point of view of the pornographer, possibly Sullivan himself, who was certainly no stranger to the police. Dougan, like Sullivan, publishes a magazine called *The Playbirds*. As the police are busy raiding Dougan's printer for obscene material, an undercover officer (Mary Millington) is slain by the murderer at large — the 'real criminal.'

Millington enjoys a slightly bigger role than she had on *Come Play with Me*. Her role as a WPC is intended as ironic, given the harassment she suffered from the police because of her fast and loose lifestyle and links to the sex business.

Next from Roldvale was *Confessions from the David Galaxy Affair* (79). Sullivan clearly thought he was on a winning team with *The Playbirds* and he brought Willy Roe back as director, Alan Lake as the leading man, and of course the ubiquitous Mary Millington as the star attraction. The film tries to be adventurous despite a story that goes nowhere, but Lake as the wisecracking, womanising David Galaxy (effectively a pot-bellied vision of Michael Caine's *Alfie*) is so unlikeable that it's very much a losing battle. During a sex scene, Lake suddenly farts loudly. Given this unpleasantly impromptu moment, viewers will be relieved that much of the sex in the *David Galaxy Affair* is the static kind, comprising material seen on display in the windows of Soho sex shops, as evidenced when Lake takes one of his walks. Alas, Soho in 1979 looks a lot more exciting than the movie that is unspooling before us.

Confessions from the David Galaxy Affair turned a profit, but it was nowhere near as successful as *The Playbirds*, or *Come Play with Me* before that. Consequently, Sullivan's interest in film was waning. He devoted less of his time (and less of his money) to the Roldvale filmmaking arm, the result being that each picture faced a tighter schedule and an increasingly thin artifice of a storyline.

Queen of the Blues (79) followed *Confessions from the David Galaxy Affair* by

THE ONLY BLUE FILM MADE IN BRITAIN – THE FUNNIEST SEX FILM OF ALL TIME!

MARY MILLINGTON 'meets' SUPER STUD with ROSEMARY ENGLAND in a sensationally funny film for both sexes

ALAN LAKE
GLYNN EDWARDS
MARY MILLINGTON
ANTHONY BOOTH
KENNY LYNCH
ROSEMARY ENGLAND

BERNIE WINTERS

DIANA DORS

DAVID SULLIVAN
JOE IRELAND
WILLY ROE

Confessions from THE DAVID GALAXY AFFAIR

SEE NEARLY TWO HOURS OF SEXSATIONALLY FUNNY, NON-STOP PORNO! BE ONE OF THE FIRST PEOPLE IN BRITAIN TO SEE CONFESSIONS FROM **THE DAVID GALAXY AFFAIR** SHOWING FOR A SEASON AT THESE CINEMAS!

LONDON
Eros, Piccadilly Circus, Thursday June 28th – continuous performances from 11.00am daily, late show nightly, showing 7 days a week, continuous performances.

BLACKPOOL
Studio Cinema, from July 5th.

GT. YARMOUTH
Empire Cinema (late night shows only) from July 5th.

only a few months. Clocking in at sixty-two minutes, most of it is striptease and comedy routines playing out under the spotlight of a Soho club (with some scenes repeated two or three times). In between the stage acts a couple of heavies lean on the management. That's it for story. Directed once again by Willy Roe, *Queen of the Blues* introduces John M. East, a fresh and soon to be a regular face on the declining Roldvale film arc, familiar to some for his bit parts in television since the fifties. East had interviewed Sullivan for a BBC radio series on entrepreneurs and struck up a friendship. He was Old School, like George Harrison Marks. In *Queen of the Blues* East plays a compère, subjecting the audience to appalling banter that draws on East's obsession with Max Miller, Britain's top comic of fifty years ago. Mary Millington is the star, playing one of the strippers, the titular Queen of the title. It would be the last film she would make before her suicide in August 1979.

Queen of the Blues managed a solid thirty-eight week run at the Eros in Piccadilly, overlapping another new Roldvale production, *Boys and Girls Together* (79), which opened next door at Cinecenta in October. Directed by Ralph Lawrence Marsden, *Boys and Girls Together* was almost a proper

Emmanuelle in Soho: the British sex film's last, desperate gasp.

film, making a narrative effort and depicting the sex life of a multicultural household in north London. One of the more adventurous films to emerge from Roldvale, it even went so far as to show male genitalia and an instance of homosexual sex (both absent from Sullivan's other efforts). But this sort of progressiveness, together with the death of Mary Millington, may account for the comparatively muted promotion Sullivan gave to *Boys and Girls Together*; certainly *Queen of the Blues*, released only three months earlier, got the lion's share of advertising. Success lay not with critics (they never thought anything good of his pictures), but rather Sullivan's fervent campaigns, such as the promise that *Queen of the Blues* showed 'every form' of sexual behaviour. This sort of ridiculous hyperbole however, was soon to catch up and land Sullivan in hot water.

Unsurprisingly the next film to emerge from Roldvale was a 'tribute' to Mary Millington. Loved by all, except authority figures, Millington had actually attained the kind of star status that Sullivan had projected for her. The quasi documentary, *Mary Millington's True Blue Confessions* (80), was not instigated by Millington's former boyfriend and manager, however, but the ingratiating and irritating John M. East, who had become the model's acting coach, close friend and confidante during *Queen of the Blues*. The film is presented more as a sensationalist exposé, and of course acts as a marketing tool for Roldvale. In it East reads from his own cockeyed script over footage of Millington, mixed in with reconstructions of questionable taste (such as a Millington lookalike in a coffin).

Sullivan made no pretence that he was even trying anymore. His next production, *Mary Millington's World Striptease Extravaganza* (81), intercuts scenes from some of Sullivan's other movies with shots of strippers in a Soho nightclub, supposedly performing in a competition for a cash prize. Our hosts for the evening are the now ubiquitous East and family entertainer Bernie Winters, an unlikely and quite frankly scary pairing. Mary Millington is represented by a solitary clip from *Queen of the Blues*, which is rather apt as *World of Striptease* (all forty-six minutes of it) essentially repeats that formula, being another tribute of sorts.

Emmanuelle in Soho (81) was a last hoorah for Sullivan, a vehicle he hoped would launch a star career for Julie Lee in the manner of Mary Millington. But Lee was an even worse actress, and as a consequence was dropped to a supporting role in her own movie. Directed by one David Hughes and an uncredited Ray Selfe (responsible for the comedy *White Cargo* [73] starring

a young David Jason), *Emmanuelle in Soho* is an unofficial cash-in of the *Emmanuelle* franchise owned by ASP films. It tells the story of a young porn photographer who discovers that his publisher is ripping him off and seeks revenge. Needless to say events unfold at a plodding rate, and it is the incidental detail — the genuine sex film posters on the wall of the publisher's office, for instance — that proves a more entertaining diversion.

Trading Standards Officers brought Sullivan to task on *Emmanuelle in Soho*, challenging him over ads that claimed the film to be more hardcore than

ATTENTION NORTHERN READERS – BLACKPOOL!

An Erotic Experience!

Emanuelle meets the Wife Swoppers

X

MONIKA MARK · CARMEN JECKYL · INGRISD STEEGER · MICHAEL MAIEN
BRITT CORWIN · HENRIA WINSTON · CLAUDIA FIELDERS · DEBBY DELIGHT
Produced by ALOIS BRUMMER   Directed by NORBERT FRARS

SPECIAL PRESENTATION FOR A SEASON FROM JULY 5th AT THE STUDIO CINEMA
BLACKPOOL

it actually was. The ads also featured images not in the actual movie, but Sullivan said these were taken from an export version. Ironically, while Trading Standards accused *Emmanuelle in Soho* of not being strong enough, the BBFC were putting pressure on to dilute the picture even further.

Emmanuelle in Soho was Sullivan's most successful film for some time, but it was still grief. All that remained for Roldvale films was another quickie by the name of *Hellcats: Mud Wrestling* (83), which was simply mud wrestling and foxy boxing filmed in a club in Croydon over the course of a sweaty afternoon. It was barely a film at all, and in fact went straight to video when Sullivan refused to acquiesce to the demands of the BBFC. It was re-edited and reappeared in the guise of *Queen Kong: The Amazonian Woman* (84). By this point no one was counting. Roldvale films still made money, and as far as British films go are a success story, but Sullivan's sights were set on much bigger fry. (In 1986 he launched a national newspaper, the *Sunday Sport*, and in 2010 became joint chairman of West Ham United football club.)

For almost a decade Sullivan tried to emulate on screen what he had managed in print, the magazines having made him rich and something of a working class hero. His celluloid aspirations were ultimately dashed with *Hellcats*, an insult of a film that served only to underscore the end of the Eady Levy. Had Sullivan not surrounded himself with eccentric characters, jettisoning George Harrison Marks only to adopt John M. East, it might not have become such a folly. East adopted a key position in originating and scripting the films, and sought to give himself key parts. (The *Monthly Film Bulletin*'s review of *Emmanuelle in Soho* describes his character — though it may well have been describing him — as 'a sinister individual of abiding charmlessness.'[3]) Of course, Roldvale was highly unlikely ever to have produced any great films, but with East on board their degeneration was all the more swift and absolute.

---

1   Mary Millington wasn't the only British contender for the Lovelace mantle: Fiona Richmond, over at rival publishers Paul Raymond, was another. Her film, *Hardcore*, was released the same year as *Come Play with Me*.

2   Roe's name on the print is Willy Pope, while ads credited him as Wilhelm Roestein, 'Denmark's leading "blue film" director.'

3   John Pym, *Monthly Film Bulletin*, 48:564/575 (1981), p.152.

A version of this article appeared in *Headpress* 15 (2000).
NOTE Sullivan was executive producer on a couple of non British films: *Die Nichten der Frau Oberst* and *Julchen und Jettchen, die verliebten Apothekerstöchter*. Produced, written and directed in 1980 by exploitation Übermensch Erwin C. Dietrich, these were released in Britain under the titles *Come Play with Me 2* and *3* in 1980 and 1982, respectively.
SOURCES Mark Killick, *The Sultan of Sleaze: The Story of David Sullivan's Sex and Media Empire* (London: Penguin 1994). Simon Sheridan, *Keeping the British End Up: Four decades of saucy cinema* (London: Reynolds & Hearn, 2007).

THE LIFETAKER (1975)

Onyx Film Productions | 98 mins | colour

Director/Producer/Screenwriter Michael Papas. **Starring** Terence Morgan (James), Lea Dregorn (Lisa), Peter Duncan (Richard).

When her husband leaves her to go on a business trip, a bored, beautiful woman takes a lover for a day of passionate sex. Returning to apologise, the husband finds the couple in bed, but leaves without revealing his presence. Next morning he returns to find his wife and her lover relaxing in the garden, but greets his rival as a guest, insisting that he stay. By evening, the three are drunkenly engaged in a series of deadly games.

M ade in the wake of a period of excess and, some might say, over indulgence in the British film industry, *The Lifetaker* is one of a number of audacious and challenging films produced during the 1970s that ardently clung to the belief that it was still possible to simultaneously push the boundaries of generic convention and survive the perils and pitfalls of audience attendance and critical reaction, even without major studio backing. Like many of its contemporaries, *The Lifetaker* has remained all but absent from theatrical and home cinema distribution since it was made,[1] and has never been granted a proper place within any serious history of British cinema. More's the pity, because Michael Papas' stylish and erotically charged tale of obsession is not only the quintessence of the kind of film they don't make anymore, but is also radically unlike the kind of film they made even then.

An intense three-hander, the film feels at times like Pinter; its carefully constructed and hermetically sealed universe working towards an inevitable

Onyx Films presents

The Lifetaker

A Film by Michael Papas

EURO LONDON FILMS LTD.

and devastating eruption. At others, it exudes the flavour of international art cinema. Ultimately, though, Papas' lush widescreen frame is his own, and his consistent use of inch-perfect composition, bold camera moves, sumptuous colour schemes and daring set pieces ensures that this unjustly obscure work is as unique as anything you're ever likely to see from these shores.

Essential to the film's success, though, is its perfectly selected cast. As the bored wife, Lisa, the virtually unknown Lea Dregorn is immediately and consistently striking. And yet, her character is deliberately one-dimensional — her delivery measured and almost monotonous, her gaze almost expressionless. She is an unwitting player in a game that she feels she has a hand in, when in fact she is nothing more than the prize (and only that as long as she observes the rules).

Youthful energy and naïve idealism exude from the slender and athletic frame of Peter Duncan (later to present TV's *Blue Peter*) as Richard. First seen literally 'diving in head first' to the lake where Lisa secretly watches him, and then swimming underwater for so long we think he may have drowned, Richard spends the entire film well and truly out of his depth. Not yet jaded by life, he is an innocent. But his seduction by the trophy wife brings him into direct conflict with a world way beyond his youthful experience or comprehension. In this world, what appears to be happiness or freedom is actually the product of a highly controlled existence, with a well kept secret at its brutal core.

And it is this brutality that is the province of Terence Morgan who, as James, is the film's trump card. A veteran of 1950s and sixties B-movies and studio pictures (including TREAD SOFTLY STRANGER [58], *The Curse of the Mummy's Tomb* [64] and *The Penthouse* [67]) Morgan's many meaty character roles saw him take on a number of tough guy and fall guy personas, but in *The Lifetaker* he is the locus of total experience, cultured wisdom and calculated survival. What's more, he is a professionally trained military assassin. Throughout the film, Morgan is required to give a performance that is more nuanced and emotionally complex than either Dregorn or Duncan, and the film's bloody finale is made almost unbearably intense by his actions alone.

That it should be Richard's curiosity that undermines James' deadly plan for the lovers at the film's climax is supremely ironic; it raises essential questions about the possibility of total control and containment, and about the effectiveness of discipline and order when faced with the unpredictability of youth. With its dizzying abandonment of the measured art of formal combat, the final sequence clearly echoes the ape sequence in Kubrick's *2001: A Space Odyssey* (68) and even perhaps pre-empts the visceral nightclub scene in Gaspar Noé's *Irreversible* (2002), both of which explore the relationship between intelligence and violent rage. In Kubrick's sci-fi epic, the beating of a rival ape with a bone-turned-weapon marks the transition from unthinking animal to intelligent being capable of horrific acts, while in Noé's dark vision, the intellectual Pierre goes from complete passivity and verbose criticism of his best friend's base urges to committing an uncontrollably violent revenge murder, the like of which his friend would never contemplate.

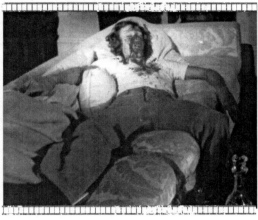

Brutality at the core. *The Lifetaker.*

In *The Lifetaker*, too, the relationship between knowledge and violence is key. By spending much of the second half of the film patronising Richard with martial arts demonstrations that are, first and foremost, intended to affirm his own physical and intellectual superiority, James also begins to introduce the young man to the philosophy of violence, and taints him with newfound knowledge. And yet it is not necessarily due to any newly acquired physical or intellectual experience that Richard manages to triumph. Rather, it is that his innermost urges and natural instinct for violence as a force for self preservation are — despite James' narcissistic 'lessons' — not kept in check by a full understanding of the art of self control.

But it is inevitable that the old should give way to the new, and at the film's close the youthful Richard finally strips James of the title of 'lifetaker.' Rather than a feeling of optimism at the death of the old dictator, though, one is left with the uncomfortable sense that this young man has inherited a world he neither understands nor knows how to take charge of.

And here lies the question at the heart of the film: How did we manage to let the vibrant self confidence of Terence Morgan's 1960s give way to the bleak uncertainty of Peter Duncan's seventies?

Sam Dunn

---

1   *The Lifetaker* was never released in the UK. Says director Michael Papas: "It was scheduled to be released nationwide on the ABC cinema circuit. But on completion the then managing director of EMI distribution (formerly ABPC) 'chickened-out' after viewing the completed film and the release was cancelled." Email to the author, dated March 7, 2012.

HENNESSY (1975)

American International Pictures/Hennessy Film Productions/CIC | 104 mins | colour

Director Don Sharp; **Producer** Peter Snell; **Screenplay** John Gay, based on an original story by Richard Johnson. **Starring** Rod Steiger (Hennessy), Lee Remick (Kate), Richard Johnson (Insp. Hollis), Trevor Howard (Comdr. Rice).

Niall Hennessy is a law-abiding citizen with distant ties to the IRA. When his wife and daughter are accidentally gunned down by a British soldier on the streets of Belfast, Hennessy snaps and plots to blow up the Houses of Parliament in retaliation. A manhunt ensues across London, with both Scotland Yard and the IRA on his tail to stop him before it's too late.

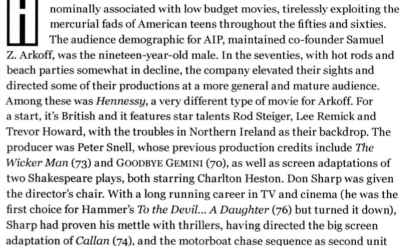

merican International Pictures was an independent film company nominally associated with low budget movies, tirelessly exploiting the mercurial fads of American teens throughout the fifties and sixties. The audience demographic for AIP, maintained co-founder Samuel Z. Arkoff, was the nineteen-year-old male. In the seventies, with hot rods and beach parties somewhat in decline, the company elevated their sights and directed some of their productions at a more general and mature audience. Among these was *Hennessy*, a very different type of movie for Arkoff. For a start, it's British and it features star talents Rod Steiger, Lee Remick and Trevor Howard, with the troubles in Northern Ireland as their backdrop. The producer was Peter Snell, whose previous production credits include *The Wicker Man* (73) and GOODBYE GEMINI (70), as well as screen adaptations of two Shakespeare plays, both starring Charlton Heston. Don Sharp was given the director's chair. With a long running career in TV and cinema (he was the first choice for Hammer's *To the Devil... A Daughter* (76) but turned it down), Sharp had proven his mettle with thrillers, having directed the big screen adaptation of *Callan* (74), and the motorboat chase sequence as second unit director on *Puppet on a Chain* (71).

Critical reaction towards *Hennessy* was generally favourable, with the film being described as real edge-of-the-seat stuff, fast, tense, suspenseful. It failed to make much of an impact at the box office, however. A brief dissection of it suggests why: Hennessy is the focus of the film and, having lost his family, is clearly a victim. But he's gone raving mad! What's more, despite the political upheaval against which the film is set, the crusading Hennessy doesn't have a political inclination one way or another: If he succeeds in blowing up Parliament, the Queen and half the Ministers of State with it, the IRA fear it will turn the whole world against them and so have instruction to kill him on sight, as do the police.

The IRA is portrayed as a merciless and untrustworthy bunch, while Scotland Yard fare only slightly better, with Inspector Hollis doing what he pleases, beating up anyone he wants in his own pursuit of the wanted man. Hollis is played by Richard Johnson, seemingly minutes away from boarding the boat that will take him to Lucio Fulci's *Zombie Flesh Eaters* (79), where a similarly arrogant role as Dr Menard awaits. Johnson, who also wrote the original story for *Hennessy*, plays well off an electric Trevor Howard as the no-nonsense Commander Rice, and indeed spirited performances all round make for compulsive viewing.

Rod Steiger adds to his repertoire of provincial accents. Having tackled Irish brogue in THE MARK (61) and a peculiar sort of Yorkshire for *Three Into Two Won't Go* (69), the appeal of *Hennessy* undoubtedly lay in the fact it required not one but two accents: a very passable Irish and, later, an Irishman mimicking an Englishman, so that Hennessy may pass himself off as a government official and get into the House of Lords.

Steiger isn't afforded much opportunity to chew the scenery. Early on, when Hennessy discovers his wife and daughter (an infant Patsy Kensit[1]) are dead and breaks down in the street, we seem to be tipping towards a legendary Steiger moment. But Hennessy's sombre retinue, encircled by British soldiers, is a nicely composed sequence that director Sharp curtails in good time. Likewise, Hennessy's death scene, having been shot down by Hollis outside the House of Lords, is wisely played just short of the usual Steiger histrionics. Sharp's concession is that Hennessy manages to trigger the explosives strapped to his body and becomes a mushroom cloud rising above the London skyline. (Compare this death to the one in *No Way to Treat a Lady* [68], where Steiger is shot down by police on a theatre stage no less and falls about the place forever.)

Hennessy ran into some problems. Archive footage of the Queen opening Parliament (which dates from 1970) is intercut throughout the final act in a

American playing an Irishman playing an Englishman. *Hennessy.*

manner that suggests Her Majesty is a part of the action, and deft editing makes it look as if she is reacting to the sound of the explosion. It is very unusual to see footage of royalty used like this, and *Hennessy* remains possibly the only instance. I don't know whether there is an arcane British law that frowns upon disingenuous use of the Queen, but the filmmakers thought it prudent to preface *Hennessy* with a statement outlining the fact the royal family took no part in the making of it. Furthermore, BBFC records show that the original release of the film may have been delayed for a few months, whilst satisfactory assurances were received from the makers about the non-viability of an explosive device demonstrated in the film and for local authorities in Northern Ireland to be informed about the content of the film, specifically the presence of a Republican song at a funeral wake and what their then current attitude to this was.

Director Don Sharp's written assurances concerning the lack of imitability due to the absence of sufficient information to make the device viable satisfactorily allayed concerns in the first instance. With regard to the second matter, that of local authorities in Northern Ireland and their opinion, it seems assurances here were also satisfactory, although, regrettably, there is no record in the BBFC files as to what form these assurances took. (This is not uncommon for the time, because such assurances may well have been made by telephone. Or the documentation could be lost, which is also not uncommon.) In any case, AIP chose to omit any overt reference to the IRA when it came to promoting *Hennessy* in the USA, calling them simply a 'radical underground organisation.'[2]

One promotional tie-in that appears in the AIP pressbook encourages local theatre owners to partake in a best disguise contest; another idea is a manhunt in a busy shopping centre, awarding cinema tickets for the capture of a designated 'felon' who would be identified by his or her false moustache and hairpiece.

David Kerekes

---

1   Other bit parts in *Hennessy* include Patrick Stewart as a shortlived IRA henchman, and an uncredited David McGillivray, screenwriter and critic, as an extra in the riot scenes that open the picture.
2   Thanks to David Hyman for the BBFC references cited in this review.

NEVER TOO YOUNG TO ROCK (1975)

GTO Films | 99 mins | colour

Director Dennis Abey; **Producers** Greg Smith, Ron Inkpen; **Screenplay** Ron Inkpen, Dennis Abey.
Starring Peter Denyer (Hero), Freddie Jones (Mr Rockbottom), Sheila Steafel (café proprietress), Joe
Lynch (Russian soldier), Peter Noone (army captain), Mud, The Rubettes, The Glitter Band, Slik.

*The near future (i.e., late seventies Britain). Pop music is under threat as a TV
station proposes to end its coverage of the scene, unless groups agree to appear
at an imminent 'Pick of the Hits' concert. A young television employee has less
than a week to scour the country for willing bands and artists.*

Along with *Confessions of a Pop Performer* (75), FLAME (74) and
Stardust (74), here's another neglected example of 1970s glam rock
cinema (assuming such a sub-subgenre exists). I first saw *Never Too
Young to Rock* on its original release, at the Lucky 7 twin-screen in
Chaddesden (nowadays an insalubrious suburb of Derby) in 1975, and later
caught a mid afternoon television screening in the eighties, finally managing
to acquire a VHS bootleg via a fellow aficionado after years of tracking down
this elusive sparkling gem. I'm not ashamed to reveal that a spectacular
three-colour poster for the movie takes up wall space in my bedroom, either,
screaming as it does '14 Smash Hits!' and 'The All Family Musical Of Today!'
above weird-looking tinted photos of the various star groups whose agents
providentially enrolled them for this big screen escapade.

The film could be said to possess a vaguely sci-fi premise, being set in a
possibly totalitarian future England where it is hinted that pop music may be
banned. Our hero, coincidentally named 'Hero' (played by Peter Denyer from
TV sitcom *Please Sir!*) travels the country in his 'Group Detector Van,' driven
by the great Freddie Jones, seeking out pop acts to feature at a huge protest
rally in favour of keeping young people's music on our TV screens. The duo
encounter Mud performing The Cat Crept In at a transport café filled with
rival scarfed and bobbled-hatted footie fans, pick up the Glitter Band filming
at the River Thames en route, and espy the Rubettes riding on the back of a
lorry while blasting out their top twenty smash, Tonight. Jones' character, Mr
Rockbottom, an admirer of old-time 'Silver Bands,' has no love for such long-
haired layabouts, however, and does his curmudgeonly best to scupper the
entire scheme. But he is eventually won over to the charms of Supersonic-era
bubblegum during the film's delirious climactic party.

At one point, the van detects a musical presence at an old Tudor house —
Denyer and Jones venture inside to find the place haunted! Denyer opens a

door to reveal a body within, blood oozing from the mouth. Various ghostly noises and rattlings are heard; a spook appears carrying his head underneath his arm, and announces "I was alright until I had the hysterectomy!" (a gag that went over my twelve-year-old head in 1975, and I'm not entirely sure I understand it now). Another portal is opened to reveal Radio Luxembourg DJ Peter Powell broadcasting from inside a cupboard (the sheer number of disc jockeys who appeared in British horror films is remarkable — try counting 'em sometime — and I suppose Powell's cameo here just about qualifies as an addition to the expanding list). Eventually our heroes meet Bob Kerr's Whoopee Band, who storm through an enormously entertaining number before revealing that they are all ghosts too! (I was lucky enough to meet Bob after a Bonzo Dog Band gig in late 2006, and asked if he remembered his participation in this movie — he said he'd had a lot of fun guesting in it, and reminded me that his fellow Bonzo, Vernon Dudley Bohay-Nowell, had taken part too as a member of the Whoopees.)

Never Too Young to Rock, as indicated by the hysterectomy gag, smacks of Eady-funded filmmakers having a great time and trying to throw in material way beyond their target teeny-bop audience's comprehension. The crazy edits, frequent and inexplicable appearance of chickens and other tomfoolery would probably win this the Turner Prize nowadays, if it were offered up by some Nathan Barley-esque member of the glitterati. The jaw-dropping concert for the massed bands at the end is what Bob Geldof's charity fundraisers would have looked like in a perfect world — it's the closest that white musicians have ever come to resembling one of George Clinton's Parliament/Funkadelic extravaganzas, with four drummers pounding away, three bassists, balloons and kaleidoscopic colour everywhere, and a whole crowd of dancing girls and football hooligans (not to mention a wizard) rushing on at the end!

This was the middle film in a trio of semi-related productions from Laurence Myers' GTO company — preceded by *Remember Me This Way*, a now understandably notorious and rarely screened 1974 featurette cashing in on the Gary Glitter phenomenon, and followed by *Side By Side* (75), directed by future Oscar nominee Bruce Beresford and top-lining Terry-Thomas and Barry Humphries as nightclub owners futilely attempting to prevent the rival discothèque next door from hiring newfangled pop acts such as Mac and Katie Kissoon, Desmond Dekker, Hello and Kenny for live performances. Mud turned up at the end of this one too, delivering a perfunctory knees-up rendition of Side By Side. But it was all a far cry from the heights of Tiger Feet and Rocket and the giddy glam fun of this, their major motion picture debut.

Darrell Buxton

FILM REVIEWS

THREE FOR ALL (1975)

Dejamus/Drumbeat/Fox-Rank | 90 mins | colour

Director Martin Campbell; **Producers** Tudor Gates, Harold Shampan; **Screenplay** Tudor Gates, Michael Armstrong (uncredited), Harold Shampan (story). **Starring** Adrienne Posta (Diane), Graham Bonnet (Kook), Lesley North, Cheryl Hall, Robert Lindsay, Christopher Neil, Richard Beckinsale, George Baker, Simon Williams, Diana Dors.

Up-and-coming pop band Billy Beethoven, led by singer Kook, are booked on a tour of Spain by their seedy promoter. Angry at not being invited, their spirited girlfriends, led by Kook's other half Diane, decide to follow the band abroad surreptitiously — but cause mayhem along the way.

P oor Adrienne Posta — she's the star that never was. One of the busiest young character actresses of the sixties and seventies, she was unfortunately blessed with the kind of face that you faintly recognise but can never put a name to. And more unfortunately, it's not one of those faces that makes you think of the silver screen. Rather, you wonder if you've seen her scanning your groceries at the local Tesco checkout, or sitting across from you on the bus, lost in thought.

But Adrienne wasn't short of talent; indeed she was brimming with it (and no doubt still is). She could do sexy, she could do funny; she could be serious and downbeat. She might have been as at home gambolling around in hot pants in a late *Carry On* film as playing a beleaguered prostitute in a gritty *Play for Today*. And she could sing too, providing vocals for music producers like Jonathan King and Andrew Loog Oldham on a handful of now forgotten 45s.

In 1974, still to make a name for herself, Posta was in a relationship with singer-songwriter Graham Bonnet, formerly of the Marbles, who was just establishing himself as a solo performer. Their potential for exploitation in the 'youth market' was not lost on one Harold Shampan, a music publishing executive who'd dabbled in film. Shampan assembled a 'package' consisting of Posta, Bonnet and a storyline for a family-

What a drag. Robert Lindsay pops up in *Three for All*.

oriented musical comedy film set in sunny Spain, and took it to his friend Tudor Gates, whose Drumbeat production outfit was in the low budget film market, even if it had so far only made soft porn comedies.

Gates wrote a script around the storyline, and then gave it to Michael Armstrong, who re-wrote it, injecting it with much *Blazing Saddles*-type irreverence (or so he told me), only to see it rejected by Shampan, who ordered the whole thing rewritten. But Shampan's vision for the film was hopelessly out of touch, Armstrong says, as he'd "not been to the cinema probably since the advent of sound." Neither could Shampan attract any talent to the project. So Armstrong was tasked with assembling a cast: 'I phoned my mates and mates of my mates and said, "Come in and do a couple of days' work and I'll write you a scene." So I wrote almost all the cameos. And the result was this kind of strange, hybrid script.'[1]

With the strange, hybrid script in hand, the production team set off for Torremolinos, where, says Armstrong, "almost every day I had to go to the airport to bring back some star who was walking off in a temper." The hotel in which the cast were ensconced was right out of *Carry On Abroad*: all pneumatic drills and falling masonry. In the face of total disaster, Armstrong and director Martin Campbell made a pact: 'He said, "I'll hold the crew together if you can hold the cast together." And we staggered through it like that.'

Staggered through it is right. To say *Three for All* is a mess is a mountainous understatement. The film can't decide if it's a musical comedy or a comedy with music, and fails to get going as either. It's also a bit like a sex comedy with no references to sex: it's pitched at a juvenile level, yet looks as if it might become 'X' rated at any moment (it doesn't, which is probably for the best).

Posta struggles perkily with the material, trying to breathe some life into the lame knockabout routines, but she and her girlfriends just end up looking silly. She even has to get through a straight-faced musical number, singing a sickly lullaby over the crib of a hastily introduced infant, a scene that Shampan apparently demanded and that seems to prove Armstrong's point about him being hopelessly out of touch (it's the sort of cloying aside Norman Wisdom would have put us through, circa 1959).

More strangely, the up-and-coming band that comprises Bonnet, Paul Nicholas, Robert Lindsay and Christopher Neil languish pointlessly at the bookends of the film. Bonnet's music is kept to a minimum, and he only has two lines of dialogue.

The only thing that makes *Three for All* curiously interesting today is the incredible cast of cameos that Armstrong conjured up from his address book. Roles were scarce for screen actors in seventies British cinema, and many were prepared to take one or two day's work in anything that was going, scoring a nice bit of money for very little effort, and giving the producers a 'star' name to put on the marquee. Hence Diana Dors in *Swedish Wildcats* (74), Roy Kinnear in *The Amorous Milkman* (74), John Le Mesurier in *Rosie Dixon, Night Nurse* (78), and all three's involvement — along with Hattie Jacques, Richard Beckinsale, Arthur Mullard, George Baker, Liz Fraser, Ian Lavender, Dandy Nichols and even Edward Woodward — in this fiasco. That *Three for All* manages to waste a cast like this, albeit a fleetingly glimpsed one, makes the whole thing seem even more tragic.

Armstrong concludes: 'They premiered it at Brighton. But it died an absolute death at the box office. Showaddywaddy were in it, but that didn't seem to draw the crowds in.' (Funny, that.)

As for Adrienne Posta, she picked herself up and followed the rest of the would-be stars of the then-depressed British film industry — into television. There she worked just as hard for the next twenty years, turning up in everything from episodes of *Minder* to Maureen Lipman's British Telecom commercials. Later she worked less onscreen and went into drama teaching in London. I'm sure her talent was even more infectious there.

So perhaps you did see her on the bus, lost in thought.

Julian Upton

1   Author's interview with Michael Armstrong, December 2008.

THE BLACK PANTHER (1977)

Impics Productions/Alpha Films | 102 mins | colour

Director/Producer Ian Merrick; **Screenplay** Michael Armstrong. **Starring** Donald Sumpter
(Donald Neilson), Debbie Farrington (Lesley Whittle), Marjorie Yates (Neilson's wife), Sylvia O'Donnell
(Neilson's daughter), Andrew Burt (Lesley's brother).

*Donald Neilson is the identity of the masked man the press calls 'the Black
Panther,' responsible for a series of armed raids on post offices that leave three
people dead. He is caught following the kidnap and murder of a teenage girl,
Lesley Whittle. Based on actual events, this is the story of the Black Panther, the
most wanted man in England.*

The Black Panther is a rare example of a British movie based upon a
real life killer case, in this instance Donald Neilson, who terrorised
north and middle England as 'the Black Panther' in the early to mid
seventies.

Neilson is played by Donald Sumpter, whose utter contempt for the world
is drawn into a marvellous acidotic sneer. Not that it is much of a world for
Neilson. The only people with whom he has any contact are his wife and
daughter, usually with a dinner plate perched on his lap while watching the
telly. Interaction is a regimental admonishment that the tea is too hot or the
cutlery not clean enough.

Obsessed with his National Service days, Neilson plans a series of robberies
on sub post offices with military precision, training in the woods and then
drawing up plans in a room in his house that resembles a bunker. He robs
at gunpoint, concealing his identity beneath a black hood, which gives rise
to the name 'the Black Panther.' The film shows Neilson to be a vacant entity
outside of the crimes he commits, and for the most part it concentrates on
the botched raids in which someone is killed before it turns to the kidnapping
of seventeen-year-old heiress Lesley Whittle (an idea Neilson extrapolates
from an article he reads in *Reader's Digest*). She too is left dead following a
succession of unsuccessful ransom drops.

Whittle's body is found hanging in a drainage shaft in Bathpool Park, a dismal
recreational area near Kidsgrove in Staffordshire. Neilson later maintained
the girl's death was an accident, that the wire around her neck was to prevent
her escape and that she slipped. Contrarily, the film would appear to show
Neilson pushing Whittle from the platform when his cover is blown.

FILM REVIEWS

The Black Panther opens with Heywood Post Office, 16 February 1972, the scene of a bungled robbery that sends Neilson into the first of many violent rages, and ends with a fracas and arrest outside a fish and chip shop in Nottinghamshire. It makes no attempt to follow police procedural, but concentrates solely on Neilson; his military tactics, his callous determination, his emotional incapacity when confronted with a sad film on the box. Only when he is in his bunker, plotting jobs and flicking through a scrapbook of 'Black Panther' newspaper clippings, do we see a momentarily content Neilson.

Behind the mask: Donald Sumpter as Donald Neilson.

There are no theories posited on his psychological makeup. Financial gain doesn't improve Neilson's quality of life and we feel ultimately that money is only one factor driving him to crime, and possibly not the most important one either. It is the dull, disorganised suburban funk in lieu of army discipline that would appear the greater incentive. He has a dislike of black people, which is manifest in a ridiculously affected Jamaican accent when communicating from behind his Black Panther hood (barking syncopated phrases like "You are good girl!"). In court the real Nielson argued there was no sexual impetus in his kidnapping of Lesley Whittle. The film doesn't contest this outright, but it shows Neilson to have no sexual interest in his wife, while a fleeting moment with an unexpectedly nude Whittle carries some licentious suggestion. In one curious scene he pulls a schoolgirl's pleated skirt from a desk drawer, which hints at a wholly different path the film may easily have taken.

The Black Panther is level headed throughout, presenting a cruel story in a measured and realistic fashion without tipping over into sensationalism. It is not perhaps the type of film one might expect of Stanley Long's distribution outfit, Alpha Films, nor the creative team of Ian Merrick and Michael Armstrong, none of whom are strangers to exploitation. Director Merrick travelled from London in the late sixties to end up in the New York office

of Barry Mahon, a prolific producer of 'Adults Only' features. He returned to Britain to work with Harry Bromley Davenport, later to direct *Xtro* (83), the only British entry on the DPP's list of 'video nasties.' *Black Panther* screenwriter was Armstrong, who had courted much controversy with his own film, a bloody period piece *Mark of the Devil* (70).

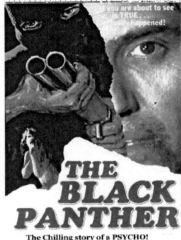

THE
BLACK
PANTHER

The Chilling story of a PSYCHO!

Armstrong says he was drawn to *The Black Panther* because it presented him a challenge, and also because director Merrick had an "obvious commitment to making a serious film." The focus was on Neilson, he said, because there was no way to show another side "without turning the film into an exposé of police ineptitude and media interference, the combination of which could be claimed was partly responsible for the events which directly led to Lesley Whittle's death."

There aren't many films based on real life British killers. Removing Jack the Ripper from the equation, a genre unto himself, there haven't been many British killers of note and filmmakers tend not to want to tell their tale. Two exceptions are *10 Rillington Place* (71) and *Cold Light of Day* (89), equally level headed in their approach to sensationalist subject matter, but different to *The Black Panther* in that they allowed the public some breathing space.

This is one reason the film bombed at the box office. *The Black Panther* came barely a year after Donald Neilson was sentenced to life imprisonment. The mass psyche was repulsed by the film, following as close as it did to its heinous source material. But what's more, its release in 1977 met head on a new climate of fear in the form of the Yorkshire Ripper murders. Posters utilising the menacing police photofit of Neilson were most unwelcome.

David Kerekes

---

1   Read all about the case, as I did, in 'The Black Panther and the (Tragic) Kidnapping of Lesley Whittle,' *True Crime* (December 1993/January 1994). Here, I discovered that one of the Black Panther's targets was the post office in Chapelfield, Lancashire, next door to where I grew up.

2   Michael Armstrong, *The Black Panther*, Michael Armstrong Online, http://www.michaelarmstrong.co.uk/film/blackpanther/history.htm [Last accessed 26 July 2010].

THE GLITTERBALL (1977)

a.k.a. Glitterball | Mark Forstater Productions/Children's Film Foundation | 56 mins | colour

Director Harley Cokeliss (credited here as Harley Cokliss); **Producer** Mark Forstater; **Screenplay** Howard Thompson, from a story by Harley Cokeliss and Howard Thompson. Additional dialogue by Michael Abrams. **Starring** Ben Buckton (Max Fielding), Keith Jayne (Pete), Ron Pember (Filthy), Barry Jackson (Mr Fielding), Marjorie Yates (Mrs Fielding).

A tiny silver ball — actually an alien life form — crash lands into the Fielding family's garden shed and enlists the help of young Max Fielding and his friend Pete to return to its home planet. But the local petty thief, Filthy, has other plans for the alien's powers, which include the ability to unlock padlocks without a key.

T**he Glitterball** is perhaps what *E.T.* would have looked like if it was wholly funded with the takings from a modest car boot sale. But *Glitterball* was actually five years ahead of Spielberg's sci-fi blockbuster, and is no less charming despite its vastly humbler origins. It's probably not the best of the relentlessly chirpy Children's Film Foundation (CFF) entries, but it represents CFF at its late period perkiest, and is a useful reminder that, once upon a time, family films could be engaging without 3D CGI, $150 million budgets and a bevy of cheerfully patronising superstars lending their 'voice talents' just to get into their own children's good books.

The 'glitterball' itself is nothing more than a ping pong ball sprayed silver; even so, this is something of a pyrotechnical bonanza for a CFF film. Director Harley Cokeliss pulls off some very passable special effects scenes, from the alien's radar-eluding crash landing to its greedy, stop motion animated rampage through the Fielding family's kitchen cupboards, where it indiscriminately relieves them of every brand of produce known to the 1970s British grocery shopper: Heinz soup, Winalot, Kellogg's Bran Flakes. (You could be forgiven for thinking this was the first CFF film financed by product placement.)

Naturally, it's the kids, Max and his friend Pete, that 'get' the glitterball's mission (it needs

Distinctly lo-tech climax of *The Glitterball*.

to harness all available energy to contact its home planet), while Max's parents (Barry Jackson and Glenda-Jackson-a-like Marjorie Yates) remain very much in the dark. This being the world of CFF, the boys are well meaning, polite and unassuming — they make *E.T.*'s California brats look like volatile delinquents. And, as usual, the adults are on hand just to mess things up. If they're not trying to impose some debilitating or misunderstanding authority onto the situation, then their objectives are altogether more villainous.

The film's visual novelty doesn't extend much beyond the spherical alien's stop-motion feasting. Generally, everything looks like a wet afternoon in a nondescript new town (which, largely, it is). The suburban, outer, outer London setting — shopping precincts, B-roads, pylons — might be depressing if it wasn't for the lively zip of the action. Cokeliss keeps the plates spinning nicely and draws spirited performances from the boys and most of the adults, particularly Ron Pember as the rather provocatively named Filthy.

The key thing here is the good-natured inventiveness of the enterprise. It's wholesome and resourceful, the filmic equivalent of a *Blue Peter* empty-toilet-roll-and-sticky-back-plastic model. Where the stirring final scenes of *E.T.* are set in a misty, flashlight-illuminated Californian forest, *The Glitterball*'s climax takes place in the biscuit aisle of a Hertfordshire supermarket. For this alone, it deserves a pat on the back.

CFF films were always rather like upmarket home movies with trained actors and professional focus pulling — you sometimes wondered if children had actually written the scripts or directed them (they hadn't). But for all their infinitesimal budgets (this one cost somewhere between £30,000 and £50,000, the director strained to recall for me[1] [it's probably nearer the former]), the best ones are industrious and agile, winsome and uplifting. *The Glitterball* is all these things and more.

Julian Upton

---

1   Director's email to author, 5 July 2010.

SEEN BUT NOT HEARD OF
THE CHILDREN'S FILM FOUNDATION

327

BY JAMES OLIVER

I n an age where pop culture nostalgia is big business, it's strange that polite society still treats the work of the Children's Film Foundation as some sort of national embarrassment. After all, the CFF — as the Children's Film Foundation shall henceforth be called — played a unique role in the cultural life of the UK. Chances are that every boy and girl born in these isles between — ooh — the Coronation and the Silver Jubilee will have strong memories of at least some of their wares.

Such ubiquity should ensure a degree of at least grudging affection; instead, the CFF is treated with snarking contempt. The stale plots! The gurning actors! The woeful effects! Oh, what were they thinking? This is not a judgement of hindsight: such verdicts were common currency even when your present correspondent was part of the target audience for CFF films.

There was a feeling that these were a slightly out-of-touch grown-up's idea of what a film for children should be: worthy, well mannered and wholesome. These were movies that even an unsophisticated audience found unsophisticated. In other words, they treated their audience like — well, like children.

Fair? Kids are harsh critics, ready to jump on and exploit even the slightest sign of weakness. But here's the thing: such authoritative criticism suggests considerable familiarity with the material. Plainly, the nitpickers consumed more CFF product than they might care to admit; they would hardly have put themselves through such agonies if these films were as bad as popularly remembered.

Could it be that the CFF has been unfairly maligned? That their merits have been forgotten in the rush to recollect their (undeniable) failings? The first point to make is that the modern viewer doesn't — or cannot — experience them in the same way as their original audience. To watch them on DVD is to watch them in captivity, away from their natural habitat. These films were tailored to a very specific environment: the Saturday Morning Matinee.

Outdoor adventures. *Five on a Treasure Island.*

The plot thickens. *Five on a Treasure Island.*

The Saturday Morning Matinee began in 1927; harassed mothers keen to gain a morning's respite from the ankle biters would drop their little angels at the local Adelphi or Odeon, to be entertained by the latest Ken Maynard or *Hopalong Cassidy* romp. The films shown were almost exclusively American — cowboy serials, jungle adventures, slapstick comedy and short cartoons.

It was a source of longstanding chagrin that there were no British films for Her Majesty's younger subjects to enjoy. The CFF evolved as a way of remedying this deficiency, crafting films where the heroes demonstrated good posture and pronounced 'tomato' properly. Funding would be provided by the Eady Levy, a small tax placed on cinema tickets in the UK, the proceeds of which were ploughed back to fund production and distribution.

The CFF was established in 1951 and, initially at least, saw its mission statement as providing "Clean, healthy, intelligent adventure" untainted by "sensationalism or unhealthy excitement or vulgarity." "Films and good fellowship" were to be the order of the day at the matinees; the first films — *John of the Fair* and *The Stolen Plans* — arrived in 1953.

Matinees were rowdy affairs, as one would expect when 500 hellions gathered in one place. Terry Staples' invaluable book *All Pals Together*

No, not a knitting pattern — a shot from *Go Kart Go.*

quotes one cinema patron who gives a flavour of the 'extremely unruly'
Saturday mornings:

> The name of the game was being there with friends and having a good
> time running around, throwing things, climbing over seats, being ticked
> off or chased by the usherettes [...] The front row was a good place to be
> for a while, because then you could try to trip up the ice cream ladies.

> Among the things being thrown around, blown out or dropped inside
> shirts were half-eaten Zoom lollies, Kia-Ora juice cartons, cornets,
> beakers of Coke, bits of bubble gum — girls with long hair were in
> particular danger from that — spit balls, peanuts, rice, dried pies,
> water balloons and stink bombs. If you could not afford to go in the
> circle, then at the very least it was imperative not to sit in its line of fire,
> otherwise you'd end up with an ice-cream or a sticky boiled sweet or the
> remains of a packet of crisps on your head. The atmosphere was great.[1]

One of the best of the early CFF flicks is *Go Kart Go* (64), an entertaining
tale of rival go-kart teams. Lacking the resources of the leather-clad go-kart
champions, a gang of kids build a kart from parts liberated from a junkyard
and an engine borrowed from a lawnmower. It's a story straight out of the
Beano, a world of gang huts, home made inventions and ineffectual authority
figures. Will the good guys triumph? Will their unsporting rivals get their
comeuppance? The stakes are low but there's a great deal of satisfaction in

Powell and Pressburger's last hurrah: *The Boy Who Turned Yellow*.

seeing the underdogs hoist the trophy at the end.

Technically, it's a mixed bag. There's a poorly executed extended slapstick chase sequence that's an obvious manifestation of the film's tiny budget. The set piece racing scenes, however, are first rate. Often filmed from the cockpit of the vehicles, they're effective even on a small screen — one can easily imagine a temporary cessation of airborne confectionery bombardments as the yahoos in the cheap seats paused to watch the action.

Watched today, *Go Kart Go* is a startling film — and not just because the star driver is played by a youthful Dennis Waterman. There's an innocence that can sting the eyes of the ironic modern viewer. The word 'gang' has acquired an altogether more threatening meaning since 1964 — the worst mischief these 'gangs' get up to is some light sabotage; no one gets shot. Most heartbreakingly of all, there is a casual assumption that all the children live with both parents.

Perhaps the most famous of the CFF films is *The Boy Who Turned Yellow* (72), the final collaboration of Michael Powell and Emeric Pressburger, the (by then faded) lions of British film. It is the story of John, a young lad with a penchant for extreme fashions — he dresses as though newly returned from a blissed out weekend at Glastonbury Fayre. Things become more peculiar when he turns, as the title promises, yellow.

This is the work of 'Nick' (it's short for 'electronic'), a friendly alien who feeds off electricity. (Those who bewail modern Britain's restrictive health and safety practices will surely approve of Nick's method of consuming his favourite tangy voltage: he sticks his fingers in the wall socket, with no ill effects. In a children's film.)

Nick travels via television rays and invites John to join him on an adventure. They travel to the Tower of London, to retrieve the pet mouse John mislaid during a school trip. The lad is nearly beheaded by the Beefeaters until Nick saves the day. It might just have been all a dream (shades of *A Matter of Life and Death*) but it must have been a very special dream, for John is now

Battle of Billy's Pond: late-era CFF classic.

conversant with the whys and wherefores of electricity.

It is far from Powell and Pressburger's finest work but it's never condescending. Indeed, contemporary viewers liked it well enough to award it 'best CFF film' for two years running.

As the costume designer of *The Boy Who Turned Yellow* had realised, times had changed. Matinee audiences were shrinking and those who did turn up were increasingly sophisticated. And yet the CFF could still come up with worthwhile films, as THE GLITTERBALL (77) proved. Made the same year as *Star Wars*, on a budget less than *Star Wars*' catering bill, Harley Cokeliss' engaging film shows the CFF at (close to) its best. Two boys discover a miniature space ship and seek to help it leave Earth. Since the craft is technically a UFO, the RAF is on the case; more worryingly, Filthy, a local ne'er-do-well, thinks the ship will help him in his criminal endeavours and steals it from the boys.

Cokeliss, who directed another CFF classic, *The Battle of Billy's Pond* (76), knew that unless a director took the film seriously, no one else would. His two lads (Max and Pete) are credible and likeable. Perhaps more importantly, the great Ron Pember makes the noxious 'Filthy' one of the most effective CFF villains, striking a perfect balance between buffoonery and genuine menace.

THE GLITTERBALL makes one wonder why CFF films are held in such low regard. Sure, it looks cheap and the effects are worthy of an episode of BBC's *Blake's 7* but it's a lot of fun, even for a jaded adult.

As cinema audiences receded in the 1970s, there was a commensurate decline in the funds raked in by the Eady Levy, which paid for the CFF. More pertinently, the very concept of children's matinees was under threat. Saturday morning television was now more popular than a morning at the pictures. Kids would rather tuck into the delights of *Tiswas* or *Multi-Coloured Swap Shop*, with their Phantom Flan Flingers and Posh Paws, than films from the CFF.

Although television was the CFF's biggest threat, it also offered a lifeline. Film quiz show *Screen Test* regularly screened clips from CFF films (invariably *Tightrope To Terror* [83], if memory serves) and, in later years, the BBC took to playing the films on Friday afternoon.

With a guaranteed slot, perhaps the unit might have been able to shift their focus from the declining matinees to the more fertile pastures of television. Certainly, later CFF productions were more thoughtful and better suited to television. *Terry on the Fence* (85), for instance, dealt with delinquency in a measured way, pointing towards a more contemporary sort of film.

As it was, this new dawn did not last. In 1985, the Thatcher government abolished the Eady Levy and the CFF was collateral damage. The name survived and its staff consulted on other projects but it is foolishness to pretend this was the same organisation as before.

The Foundation was arguably the last vestige of the British tradition of seeing the public information film as art. From the earliest days, when John Grierson began using his 'documentaries' to educate the workers, there was a belief that films could be more than just transitory entertainment but an actual public good. Whatever the faults of the CFF, it was possessed of a quality that has — regrettably — fallen into obsolescence: it meant well.

No, children did not appreciate its efforts, but do they ever appreciate those who mean well? It's only with the hindsight that comes with maturity that

The Five have a mystery to solve in *Five Have A Mystery to Solve.*

Things get choppy. *Five Have A Mystery to Solve.*

they realise just how much the teacher who they thought was an overbearing tool helped them at school, or how lucky they were to have a youth club leader who cared more about helping the kids than he cared about his own dignity. It says too much about the bastardised values of our own times that such laudable values are 'innocent.'

As we look back and snigger knowingly at the clothes, the wholesome values and the all-round lack of sophistication, we should keep our ears open for the sound of future generations laughing at us. What will they make of the fact that today's children's entertainment is basically an exhortation to buy product? (You want an e.g.? How about that omnipresent fuschia money-vampire Hannah Montana, et al?) Even the otherwise estimable Pixar willingly whore their creations into Happy Meals.

Banish both adult cynicism and rose-tinted spectacles. In the final analysis, the CFF comes up rather well. If we cannot ignore their deficiencies, then we shouldn't overlook their tremendous merits. For over thirty years, they saw entertaining children as a public service. More than this, the popular perception of these films as worthy-but-crap is simply wrong: the best are fast, well-paced fun. Let's be honest now; whatever you might have told your friends, you enjoyed them really, didn't you.

---

1   Terry Staples, *All Pals Together: The Story of Children's Cinema* (Edinburgh: Edinburgh University Press, 1997).

THE SQUEEZE (1977)

Martinat Productions/Warner Bros | 104 mins | colour

Director Michael Apted; **Producer** Stanley O'Toole; **Screenplay** Leon Griffiths, from the novel *Whose Little Girl Are You?* by David Craig (a.k.a. James Tucker). **Starring** Stacy Keach (Jim Naboth), David Hemmings (Keith), Edward Fox (Foreman), Carol White (Jill), Freddie Starr (Teddy), Stephen Boyd (Vic), Alan Ford (Taff), Hilary Gasson (Barbara).

Alcoholic ex-Scotland Yard detective Jim Naboth is drawn back into the violent London underworld when his ex-wife Jill and her daughter Christine are kidnapped by a gang of thieves working for Irish crime boss Vic Smith. But Naboth's efforts to help Jill's rich new husband foil the kidnap plan are continually hampered by his helpless addiction to drink.

At the time of writing, after languishing in obscurity for a good twenty-five years (it had a primetime TV showing and a video release in the mid eighties), *The Squeeze* looks as if it is making some tentative steps into the 'official' chronicles of British cinema history: 2010 saw it featured in the Edinburgh Film Festival's 'After the Wave' programme of unjustly neglected films. But it has yet to be made available on DVD, and subsequent TV screenings have been scant, so it's still a long way from being talked about in the same breath as, say, *Get Carter*, *Villain*, *The Long Good Friday*, or even *The Sweeney* movies. This is a shame, because *The Squeeze* is in many ways better than all of them.

On its 1977 release, the film was so keen to trample over similar TV fare and live up to its 'X' rating that it seemed almost pornographic in the way it revelled in newly-broken mainstream cinema taboos. Films had already been featuring excessive violence, nudity, swearing and the grim reality of urban life for some years, of course, but none seemed to relish them quite as much as *The Squeeze*. Its milieu is one of heavy duty viciousness, stinking drunks, smoke-browned wallpaper, soiled Y-fronts and cheap suits. It is ugly, brutal and messy. The characters we care about are debased and humiliated; the characters we don't like are as egregious as any the cinema has produced.

Such unpleasantness might be harder to take if *The Squeeze* wasn't a film of alarming scenes and revelatory performances. Most prominent is Stacy Keach as washed-up ex-cop Jim Naboth, a man so entrenched in the gutter you can almost smell his B.O. Few stars, certainly American ones, have let themselves look quite this wretched on screen. Keach stumbles through most of the movie inebriated and dishevelled, thinning hair hanging limply over his face, shabby clothes falling off him (when he's not completely unclothed,

having been stripped and dumped in the road by his enemies). But he's far from an amusing drunk; his desperate alcoholism is more like an unshowy counterpoint to Ray Milland in *The Lost Weekend* or Albert Finney in *Under the Volcano* — all consuming, but tragic and pathetic. For a Hollywood lead, he comes very close to pulling off a very English performance: not so much with his accent, but with his sad, weary eyes and his beleaguered countenance. But then there was always something in Keach that seemed to identify with the downtrodden, troubled but essentially decent Englishman, albeit one who can handle himself in a fight. Witness the footage of his release from Reading jail in 1985 (he'd served six months after being picked up at Heathrow in possession of cocaine). The news cameras catch him emerging to speak to the assembled press, sans toupee (as in *The Squeeze*), contrite, ashamed, but unwaveringly courteous. He emanates such sincere humility that you're rooting for him, just as you are Naboth when he finally gets himself in order at the end of the film.

Then there are the irredeemably loathsome bad guys — villains for a grown-up audience, not the grotesque parodies of gangsters that underworld thrillers are usually so keen on presenting. David Hemmings as Keith — pudgy, greying, looking older than his years — gives an expert performance of sly, callous menace beneath a wafer-thin veneer of civility and politeness; he is by far the most dangerous presence in the film. But Stephen Boyd, as Keith's Irish boss Vic Smith, steals all the scenes. Vic is the sort of character who would wipe the floor with *Sexy Beast*'s Don Logan and then piss on him for a laugh while enjoying a cigar. The memory of Boyd's award-winning turn as *Ben-Hur*'s friend Messala in 1959 may long since have given way to obscure westerns and Europudding actioners, but in *The Squeeze* he comes into his own, delivering what is surely one of the nastiest bastards in crime film history. It's more like a terrifying debut than a comeback from a faded matinee idol. His towering physique, weather-beaten face and Northern Irish accent (his own) make the character even more intimidating: he looks so hard you'd cross the country to avoid him. The actor could very well have revived his career with this performance; sadly, the following year, he died of a heart attack on a California golf course, aged forty-five.

There's Carol White as Jill. This isn't one of her best roles — she has little to do most of the time except be pushed around and shouted at by the kidnappers — but the film does give her its most disconcerting moment. A couple of days into her captivity, Keith instructs her to strip for the gang; he puts on the Stylistics' You Make Me Feel Brand New to ease her into it. It's one of the most uncomfortable scenes in British cinema, as unnerving in its degradation of the actress as it is of her character. White brings a raw power to the strip,

performing it with
tangible anguish;
the camera itself
initially seems
complicit in her
exploitation. But
the scene soon goes
beyond anything
resembling
titillation. By
the end, the
audience is left
feeling grubby
and ashamed. *The
Squeeze* is not a
film to throw a veil
over the naked
humiliation of
one of its nicer
characters.

Finally, there's
a surprising
presence in
the midst of all
this barbarity
in comedian
Freddie Starr. He is chirpy cab driver Teddy, Naboth's heart-of-gold Scouse
sidekick. On paper it shouldn't work, but it does. There's more than a touch
of 'bromance' to Teddy and Naboth — Teddy goes far beyond the call of duty
to help the ex-cop, making sure he's eating and dressing properly, driving
him around, looking after him more like a doting wife than a buddy — but the
warmth and camaraderie Starr brings provides some much-needed relief.

I could go on: Michael Apted's edgy direction, the original electro-rock score
by Genesis producer David Hentschel, Edward Fox and Alan Ford and a close-
mouthed Roy Marsden. Perhaps when *The Squeeze* earns just a fraction of
the praise that's hurled at *Get Carter* and *The Long Good Friday*, there'll be
plenty of room to discuss its qualities further.

Julian Upton

JUBILEE (1978)

Megalovision/Whaley-Malin Productions Ltd. | 109 mins | colour

Director Derek Jarman; **Producers** Howard Malin, James Whaley; **Screenplay** Derek Jarman. **Starring** Jenny Runacre (Queen Elizabeth I/Bod), Adam Ant (Kid), Little Nell (Crabs), Toyah Willcox (Mad), Jordan (Amyl Nitrate), Ian Charleson (Angel), Jack Birkett (Borgia Ginz).

Queen Elizabeth I is transported by her alchemist John Dee to a lawless and broken-down Britain of the late twentieth century. As she surveys the death and destruction left behind by a group of violent misfits on the fringes of the punk music scene, she is forced to consider a distant future of godlessness and anarchy.

Jubilee is one of the key British films of the seventies, but it is still looked upon as something of a novelty, a fringe item, both in terms of British cinema and the later career of its director, Derek Jarman. Ostensibly a 'punk' film set in the near future, it was really the only commercial British film of its time to advance a social critique: its ugly vision of Britain was closer to the reality of a country crippled by strikes, social unrest and the real prospect of civil breakdown than anything else seen in 'worthy' pictures of the era.

Striking parallels with the earlier *A Clockwork Orange*, *Jubilee*, however, gives itself to anarchy where Kubrick's film is a cool-headed experiment. It is impulsive where *Clockwork Orange* is measured, and raw where the earlier film is stylised. But it seems less like Jarman's vision than one of a punk cinema collective: it could have feasibly been made by Paul Morrissey on a

Jubilee: late seventies dystopia through a punk lens.

sabbatical from Andy Warhol's Factory, or perhaps even John Waters, Russ Meyer, and, fittingly for Jarman (who designed *The Devils* [71]), Ken Russell.

Not a punk music film per se, *Jubilee* is an encapsulation of the punk aesthetic and the ethics of punk cinema. Like Morrissey's *Trash* (70) and Waters' 1970s films, it has a permissive abandon that serves to unnerve the conventional viewer. The characters could have emerged from a contemporary Carrollesque nightmare: they are unrestrained, unpredictable, volatile. They have names like Crabs, Chaos and Amyl Nitrate, and fill their time with straight and bisexual gang bangs and casual murder. They suffocate a post-coital lad with a polythene sheet

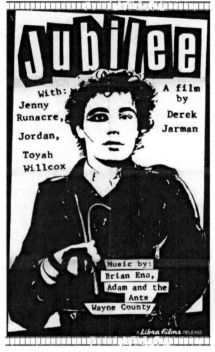

for a laugh. They attack a waitress in her own café and smother her in ketchup. They walk around naked and tattoo each other with carving knives, sealing the wounds with salt. It is all decidedly un-British.

A reaction to the pomp and ceremony of the 1977 Silver Jubilee celebrations (it's a pity it wasn't released concurrently), *Jubilee* takes punk's customary anti-Royalism and anti-establishmentarianism to their limits. It observes a broken-down Britain through the eyes of Queen Elizabeth I (Jenny Runacre), who is transported from the sixteenth century by the magician John Dee (Richard O'Brien) to witness violence and anarchy reigning in the streets. The current Queen lies dead, murdered on some waste ground; Buckingham Palace is under the control of a blind megalomaniac (the unhinged Jack Birkett), who has turned it into a recording studio.

The cast is remarkable: Jenny Runacre (doubling up as Bod, the leader of the misfit gang) had appeared in Pasolini's *The Canterbury Tales* (71), the Michael Moorcock adaptation *The Final Programme* (73) and Antonioni's *The Passenger* (75); Richard O'Brien and Little Nell (a.k.a. Nell Campbell) were already midnight icons from *The Rocky Horror Picture Show* (75);

a young Adam Ant wanders through the film, two years before his run of British pop success; and Toyah Willcox, also ahead of her shortlived, post-punk chart reign, scowls and swears as ginger suedehead Mad. The late Ian Charleson, three years away from 'respectability' in *Chariots of Fire*, is also here, shamelessly naked. (He later tried to deny he'd ever been in *Jubilee*, a touch ambitiously, since by the mid eighties it was available for all to see on video.) No one gives a 'conventional' performance; like John Waters' repertory company — Divine, Mink Stole, et al — they generally prefer shouting to acting. But this is what gives *Jubilee* its absurdity and edge.

Where it differs from earlier US 'punk' films by Waters, Meyer and Morrissey is in Jarman's apparent aversion to out-and-out comedy: *Jubilee* is more concerned with evoking the immoral and amoral, and with shocking the serious-minded. Although time has tamed it, on its release it seemed more deliberately disturbing than funny; perhaps Jarman thought jokes would diminish the shocks. (Even before its UK TV premier in 1986, eight years after its appearance in cinemas, there were questions in the House of Commons about *Jubilee*'s suitability for transmission.)

But what was perceived as an arthouse approach also saw the film attacked by key members of the punk community, who criticised what they saw as a conservative selling-out of the movement (the Clash apparently pulled out of appearing for this reason). More damagingly, there was a vehement backlash from one of the heads of punk's own 'establishment.' Designer Vivienne Westwood, whose King's Road boutique was the fashion Mecca of the British punk wave, printed up a T-shirt calling *Jubilee* 'the most boring and disgusting film' she'd ever seen, adding, in a particularly personal dig at Jarman, that she couldn't get off 'watching a gay boy jerk off through the titillation of his masochistic trembling.'

Attacks on the film's 'street cred' continue to this day: TV Cream calls *Jubilee* 'spit-drainingly pretentious.' But it endures where other British punk films have failed to leave a mark — *The Punk Rock Movie* (78), *Rude Boy* (80), *Breaking Glass* (80) and, not least, the Sex Pistols' *The Great Rock 'n' Roll Swindle* (80). And what is a punk film if it doesn't upset people, even punks? *Jubilee* may share some of its sensibilities with the self-consciously progressive, occasionally didactic (and, dare we say, liberal, middle class) plays of the BBC's *Play for Today* strand, but at least in this it is in more powerful company than any of its contemporaries on the UK cinema screen. It remains a crucial window on the desperate Britain of the late seventies.

Julian Upton

This chapter is adapted from an article that first ran in *Bright Lights Film Journal* (October 2000).

Horror upstages sex comedy. *Killer's Moon.*

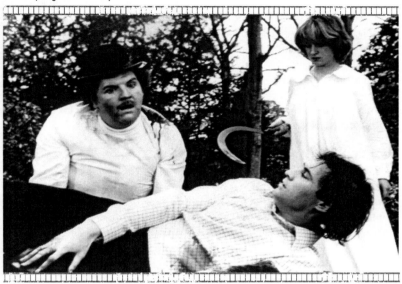

KILLER'S MOON (1978)

Rothernorth | 90 mins | colour

Director Alan Birkinshaw; **Producers** Alan Birkinshaw, Gordon Keymer; **Script** Alan Birkinshaw.
Starring Anthony Forrest (Pete), Tom Marshall (Mike), Georgina Kean (Agatha), Alison Elliott
(Sandy), Jane Hayden (Julia), Nigel Gregory (Mr Smith), David Jackson (Mr Trubshaw), Paul Rattee
(Mr Muldoon), Peter Spraggon (Mr Jones).

Four psychopaths with a shared history of child assault, mass murder,
homosexuality and religious delusion escape an institution where progressive
treatment with psychotropic drugs has eradicated their ability to distinguish
dreams from reality. They encounter a party of stranded schoolgirls. Believing
they are still in the institute and merely dreaming, they perceive their acts of
sex and violence to be just what the doctor ordered.

I n the echelon of British exploitation filmmaking, director Alan
Birkinshaw is not unique in that he cut his teeth working in
commercials and TV before a directorial debut in that most
charmless of institutions, the British sex comedy. In this case it was
the 1974 feature *Confessions of a Sex Maniac*. A purely commercial venture,
Birkinshaw and his investors decided they wanted to make and distribute a
movie, and the sex comedy was seen as the easiest, more risk-averse way to go
about it. Birkinshaw followed *Confessions of a Sex Maniac* with *Killer's Moon,*

some four years later. "We decided that the horror film was more upmarket than sex comedy," the director told this author,[1] "and it would sort of lead us onto bigger and better things. That was the idea. We decided that horror film was a sort of natural progression."

This 'natural progression' proved timely in that *Killer's Moon* was released the same year as *Carry On Emmannuelle*, a rather flaccid poke at the new permissiveness that succeeded only in sounding the death knell for *Carry On* and the British sex comedy in general.

Killer's Moon is a downbeat, relatively gory horror film so basic in concept and execution that it borders on the surreal: a group of vulnerable people become isolated and are left to thrash out the next twenty-four hours with a group of vulnerable psychopaths. Shot for the most part on location in Birkinshaw's childhood stomping ground the Lake District, the traditional green and pleasant associations of English pastures has never before appeared so muted and drab. The film opens with a coach containing the Maidenhill school choir (one of our vulnerable parties) trundling through the countryside, whose flat rendition of Greensleeves sizes up the well. The coach is destined for a concert in Edinburgh but when it breaks down the girls find themselves trapped in a brown landscape threatened by rain and are forced to spend the night at an out of season hotel. Their neighbours are few and far between, not unlike the twists and turns of the story. Nevertheless, compounded with the schoolgirl cast, psychopaths on LSD and an appearance by a dog with a missing leg, *Killer's Moon* is primed to be satisfyingly unwholesome. The stilted dialogue is entertaining, too, and eminently quotable. The four psychopaths are unsure of where, what or why, and converse in a series of psychedelic catechisms.

"Have you ever been hungry in a dream before?" queries one of the killers in one typical scene. Another of the men is busy reciting a bowdlerised nursery rhyme. He thinks a fainted woman is his mother.
"Never wake a sleeping lady, for we are gentlemen. Even in our dreams."
"Are you sure you said mother? I often dream of mother — she doesn't look like that."

Birkinshaw wrote some of the dialogue with his sister, the author Fay Weldon, who didn't want a credit on the movie and contributed for fun. "Some of the fun lines actually came from Fay," Birkinshaw says.

Asked whether *A Clockwork Orange* had been an influence, Birkinshaw says not. All the same, *Killer's Moon* makes an interesting addendum to Kubrick in that the government's radical treatment is a failure and the 'Droogs,' still

NINE ATTRACTIVE GIRLS...FOUR DANGEROUS MEN... ONE ENDLESS NIGHT OF TERROR!

ANTHONY FORREST

Killer's Moon x

with TOM MARSHALL JANE HAYDEN NIGEL GREGORY

ALISON ELLIOTT and GEORGINA KEAN

an ALAN BIRKINSHAW film

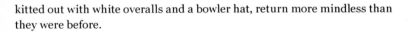

kitted out with white overalls and a bowler hat, return more mindless than they were before.

The first we see of the lunatics they are jumping single file over a small stream as darkness falls, their white overalls failing to register stains or marks.

"Well the idea was that, in a strange sort of way, they were innocent too," says the director. "And the girls racing round in their nighties were also innocent and that was just a sort of a thing in the background really. I mean one tries to put a bit of depth in these things although sometimes it doesn't really come through." [2]

Nothing upsets the film's unhealthy drive or its distorted, childhood fable quality. Despite a brief discussion in Whitehall about the escape no one actually comes looking for the lunatics and none of the schoolgirls try too hard to leave the danger zone. Indeed, cornered in the "wilds of nowhere," any suggestion of outside help is instantly dismissed when one person remarks, "I don't think there are any cops around here."

Much of the filming took place in Armathwaite Hall, a secluded luxury hotel framed by Bassenthwaite Lake and the Skiddaw mountain. The crew was under strict instruction not to disturb any of the guests. One scene involved the maniacs carrying a girl into the main hall, depositing her on a

School choir trip takes a turn for the worse. *Killer's Moon.*

sofa and tearing
off her clothes.
But crashing
the impromptu
set was an old
American couple
in no great hurry
to leave, having
decided to take
tea. The crew's
relationship with
management was
already frayed
enough and so,
not daring to
ask the guests
to move, they
erected instead a

polystyrene wall on the sofa and proceeded to shoot the rape in silence.

One of the first victims in the film is a dog, whose leg is hacked off by the
killers. Birkinshaw recalls having a massive casting session for a three-legged
dog at his Greek Street office in London. A Doberman called Hannah got the
part and she brought *Killer's Moon* its big break. The exhibitors had hitherto
not been enthusiastic about the film and offered three trial dates, one of
which was Gravesend. "The other two were not better," Birkinshaw recalls.
"Gravesend really is the pits as far as cinema." But Hannah was a publican's
dog and had lost her leg in gunfire thwarting a pub robbery, a deed for which
she received the doggy VC for bravery. When it came to promoting *Killer's
Moon* Hannah attended a press call at a cocktail lounge (Peppermint Park,
next door to Stringfellows). It must have been a slow news day because all the
daily newspapers turned out, including the *Times* and *Telegraph*, and they
ran photographs of Hannah seated at the bar, a straw in her mouth and a girl
from the film on each side. Consequently, the film did incredibly well when
it opened in Gravesend and the other two awful cinemas, and a full national
release followed, playing second bill to *The Last Hard Men*, a western starring
Charlton Heston and James Coburn.

David Kerekes

1   David Kerekes, 'An Interview with Alan Birkinshaw,' in David Kerekes (ed.). *Creeping Flesh* (Manchester:
    Headpress, 2003), p.88.
2   Ibid., p.89.

FILM REVIEWS

PREY (1978)

a.k.a. Alien Prey | Tymar Film Productions/Premier releasing | 85 mins | colour

Director Norman J. Warren; **Producer** Terry Marcel; **Screenplay** Max Cuff. **Starring** Barry Stokes ('Anders'/ Kator), Sally Faulkner (Jo), Glory Annen (Jessica).

A shape-shifting alien lands on Earth to investigate potential food sources; taking human form, he is injured in a skirmish and is offered refuge by a lesbian couple, Jo and Jessica. His arrival exacerbates tensions in their relationship: fascinated by this strange man, Jessica is happy for him to stay, to the consternation of her lover. But the alien has not forgotten his mission and humans are on his menu...

During the late 1970s, British film basically curled up and died. Once the American studios who'd bankrolled the industry withdrew their largesse, film production in the UK became, essentially, the preserve of low budget exploitation producers.

Prey might be the most interesting film produced in that interregnum. By turns a sexploitation flick, a sci-fi/horror movie and a sub-Polanski, sub-Losey psychodrama, it's a ragged film but one so wonderfully odd, so filled with ideas that it is in quite a different class to the dispiriting tits'n'bums epics that were the staple fare of UK Poverty Row outfits.

It's worth dwelling on the circumstances of its creation, for they go some way to informing the film's unique qualities. With little work available for industry professionals, experienced assistant director Terry Marcel decided to promote himself to producer and put a film together. To direct, Marcel picked Norman J. Warren. A one-time amateur filmmaker, Warren turned pro to make a couple of undistinguished sex comedies before gravitating to horror. Used to straightened circumstances, he was just the man for Marcel, who was on a very strict timetable: Warren had just three weeks to prepare the film and

Penis envy? Sally Faulkner in Prey.

Prey. Special makeup effects *not* by Rick Baker.

a further ten days in which to shoot. This truncated schedule resulted in a film guided more by instinct than intellect. The script, by Max Cuff, was essentially written as they went along, guided by an outline prepared in advance. That synopsis was enough to make any exploitation hack salivate — Gore! Aliens! Lezzers! — but as it developed into a screenplay, a slightly different story emerged.

True, no one will ever hail the film as a progressive depiction of a same-sex union. There's an extended bout of girl-on-girl action (or rather a heterosexual's vision thereof) for the dirty mac brigade and the relationship of the two women echoes earlier lesbian-themed films, such as *The Killing of Sister George* (68), by emphasising the unhappiness of these characters.

Their partnership is not what it was and the arrival of the newcomer moves it towards breaking point. Jessica — the younger, more carefree woman — is keen to establish a degree of independence. For her, the stranger represents a break in the monotony (claustrophobia?) of their relationship and perhaps more; she is happy to flirt with her guest.

This troubles her more dominant partner, Jo. While not quite a classic bull dyke, she despises men ("Do you take sugar?" she asks her new guest. "I suppose so. Most men do.") Jessica wonders why their friend Simon no longer comes to see them; she finds out when she discovers his bloodied clothes and a vicious bayonet locked in a trunk. Jo is terrified of losing Jessica and behaves accordingly. Although Jo wants rid of the interloper, she has a certain sympathy for him too. Both women believe him to be a refugee from a psychiatric hospital and we later discover that Jo has her own experiences of such places. Evidently they caused more problems than they cured.

While the film's sexual politics are very much of its time, it deserves praise for developing the women into characters rather than just using them as an excuse for titillation. It should also be pointed out that despite the discord between Jo and Jessica, lesbian sex is presented as enjoyable and mutually satisfying. By contrast, when Jessica finally seduces her guest, he is so overcome by his passions that he kills and eats her.

The alien, of course, has no idea of the friction he's causing. Calling himself 'Anders Anderson' (Anderson being the name of his first terrestrial victim), he displays a childlike bewilderment at his predicament. Indeed, he's barely aware of his surroundings: there's a wonderful scene where the two women rescue him from the river — he hadn't realised the difficulty of walking on water.

Barry Stokes — otherwise best known as the star of *The Ups and Downs of a Handyman* (76) — distinguishes himself as this otherworldly intruder, suggesting both curiosity and uncertainty as he absorbs his new world. This is perfectly displayed in the film's highlight, as his hosts throw 'Anders' a party. Naturally, everyone dresses up... even 'Anders.' In an intriguingly perverse touch, the women doll him up in a glamorous frock and slap on some makeup. Yet for the alien this is no more bizarre than the other human clothing he is obliged to wear.

But 'Anders' — or Kator as he's known back home — hasn't come to Earth to put on his glad rags. He's here to find alternative food sources for his people. Humans — "rich in protein" — seem like the perfect resource.

Like *The Texas Chain Saw Massacre*, *Prey* is a film much interested in the food chain. Jo and Jessica are proud vegetarians, while Kator is the ultimate carnivore: he finds the vegetarian meals he's served literally indigestible. Yet despite her herbivorous ways, Jo has no compunction about going after the fox who disembowelled her chickens. The strong will always prey on those weaker than themselves. So it is at the film's conclusion when Kator consumes his hosts.

It's rare to find an exploitation flick with a single idea, let alone so many. It's a shame, then, that the film never ties these two strands — the psycho-sexual stew and its musings on meat — together more convincingly. The closest it gets is with the sub-plot of Jessica's parrot, an awkward metaphor for her own caged existence: 'Anders' is fascinated by the bird and eventually devours it, just as he does its owner.

It would be easy to overstate the film's qualities. The low budget is frequently evident and Cuff's script could only have benefited from a polish (where lines like "Ours is a pure love, without the foul animal functions of breeding" could have been painlessly extracted). And yet, the white heat of production resulted in something remarkable. Mad, feverish and often inspired, *Prey* is a much better film than it has any right to be.

James Oliver

TOMORROW NEVER COMES (1978)

Classic Klinger/Montreal Trust/Neffbourne/Rank | 109 mins [1] | colour

Director Peter Collinson; **Producer** Michael Klinger, Julian Melzack; **Screenplay** David Pursall, Jack Seddon, Sydney Banks, based on an original story by David Pursall. **Starring** Oliver Reed (Wilson), Susan George (Janie), Stephen McHattie (Frank), John Ireland (Captain), Donald Pleasence (Dr Todd), John Osborne (Lyne), Raymond Burr (Burke).

On the day of his retirement from the police force, detective Jim Wilson is landed a hostage situation. A man named Frank is deranged with jealousy, threatening to kill his former girlfriend, Janie, who has shacked up with Lyne, the owner of a luxurious beach hotel. Wilson refuses to resort to violence to end the situation, but the pressure is mounting.

Peter Collinson's big screen directorial debut was the 1967 psychological drama, *The Penthouse*. He followed this with the respected cabbage soup opera, *Up the Junction* (68), adapted from a celebrated social realist BBC TV play that wallowed in underclass English life. Then came *The Italian Job* (69), a crime caper, and one of the most enduring British pictures that in itself has become an evocation of Britishness. But from the mid seventies to his death in 1980, Collinson bounced around the world, making whatever was presented to him, wherever: *Ten Little Indians* (74) in Iran, *Open Season* (74) in Spain, *Tigers Don't Cry* (76) in Africa, *The Sell Out* (77) in Israel, *The Earthling* (80) in Australia.

A report published by the BFI in 1983 attempted to determine what exactly constituted a British film.[2] The paper duly notes that some films qualify as British despite evidence to the contrary, such as overseas funding or an international cast and crew adrift in exotic locations. Collinson's *Tomorrow Never Comes*, a Canadian/UK coproduction, is one of these anomalies. It is set amidst an expansive landscape familiar to everybody as America (in actuality Canada), opening with a shot of the sort of truck that exists to ferry hitchhikers from one limitless US highway to the next, or at least to a used car lot, where our grateful stranger (in this instance, Frank) leaves his ride to converse with a toothy kid washing big cars. It then jumps through some familiar American hoops — a hardnosed detective, an amusement park, a dead junkie, a barroom brawl — before arriving at a beach resort where a standoff between a crazed gunman (Frank again) and armed police officers ensues under the blistering sun.

Furthermore, there is a *Dirty Harry* anti-cop element to the proceedings, along with a crowd that gathers to observe the police engage the gunman in negotiations. Indeed, the crowd becomes omnipresent, a tanned and fractious fixture. But this is no *Dog Day Afternoon* (75) and the crowd here has no Attica to get fired up about; they simply ponder whether the situation is real or merely a TV show in production, while looking for Telly Savalas from *Kojak* in the wings.[3]

According to the 1983 BFI report, there is a criterion that determines a film as British, but this is befuddled and most or

Stephen McHattie and Susan George in *Tomorrow Never Comes,* a violent picture according to cinema mags of the day.

all of it can be disregarded anyway. The empirical idea of a British film is a lot more satisfying. Or rather it is if we turn to Rosamund John, a much loved actress of the forties and fifties, who once claimed that British films are 'films which present the British.'[4] In applying this rule, *Tomorrow Never Comes* is as British as they come. The very British John Osborne, embittered playwright, pops up in another of his very few movie appearances. He reprises, or attempts to reprise, his effete big shot persona, used to great effect in *Get Carter* (with which this film also shares composer Roy Budd), playing Lyne, the owner of the resort where the main action takes place. As brief as it is, the performance is a car wreck that creates an ugly tailback. A notoriously heavy drinker in life, Osborne is clearly pissed behind his sunglasses to the point he must remain seated to deliver the few lines expected of him. He literally falls over for his final scene, which I'm inclined to believe isn't acting or scripted.

Another heavy drinking Brit, of course, is Oliver Reed as Jim Wilson, the 'anti-cop' who is determined to resolve the hostage situation without resorting to violence. Everyone around him thinks otherwise, even the Chief, and Wilson has to fight them all the way. One of Wilson's ideas is to use beer to lure the gunman out. More beer proposals follow (it's a blistering day, remember), such as lacing the beer with a knockout drug. Reed hides it better than Osborne, driving his hands into his barrel chest suit pockets and striding about with a wistful determination. He collides with another actor only once.

"I want you to use smoke and teargas and move in fast!" demands the Chief. "I won't do it!" snaps back a resolute Wilson. And so on.

Displaced person. Oliver Reed considers another beer ruse in *Tomorrow Never Comes*.

Donald Pleasence as Dr Todd has very little to do but cough and wheeze. It's one of Pleasence's wonderfully crisp character observations, if in this instance undermined by a ridiculous accent; possibly it's German but at times it might be French, or perhaps a deliberate act of treason to nullify his performance next to that of his sot compatriots? Finally among the British stars is Susan George, who, as Janie, is the love interest that completes the triangle between Frank and Lyne, which triggers the whole hostage business. Susan George's film career is in trouble and the desperation shows. At one point she becomes a bawling, flailing paroxysm of emotion that is more like primal scream therapy than any notion of acting. Stephen McHattie's reaction to it, as Frank, is to try and stifle a laugh.

To further align it with Rosamund John's definition, *Tomorrow Never Comes* is British in that it presents the British film industry in crisis. Oliver Reed, John Osborne and Donald Pleasence are like displaced persons here, although they are having a ball with Johnny Foreigner and not bothering to wait for the pub to open. Poor old Susan George, however, is just stuck indoors. The film was made in a climate of economic recession in the UK, and when notions of national identity were becoming more complex and boundaries more blurred.

Tomorrow Never Comes followed Collinson's *The Italian Job* by only a few years, but the gap is wide enough for one to have created an institution of the other.

David Kerekes

---

1   This is the US running time, the print under review. The film was cut to 106 minutes in the UK.

2   Linda Wood, *British Films 1971–1981*, BFI National Library. Republished 2005 and made available online at http://www.bfi.org.uk/filmtvinfo/publications/pub-rep-brief/pdf/britfilms.pdf [Last accessed 28 December 2010].

3   The onlookers are right to be confused: One of the American stars of *Tomorrow Never Comes* is Raymond Burr, playing the Chief of Police. The burly actor had only just finished *Ironside*, the long running TV show in which he starred as the Chief of Police.

4   New Theatre cited in Linda Wood, *British Films 1971–1981*, BFI National Library. The original date of the source material is unclear.

BLOODY KIDS (1979)

a.k.a. One Joke Too Many | Black Lion Films/ITC | 91 mins | colour

Director Stephen Frears; **Producer** Barry Hanson; **Screenwriter** Stephen Poliakoff.
Starring Derrick O'Connor (Ritchie), Gary Holton (Ken), Richard Thomas (Leo), Peter Clark (Mike),
Gwyneth Strong, Jack Douglas.

*Southend-on-Sea. Eleven-year-old Leo enlists his school friend Mike in a
prank to fool the police. They stage a fight outside a football ground in which
Mike brandishes a knife. But when Mike accidentally stabs his friend for real,
he goes into hiding with a gang of local delinquents, while Leo is rushed to
hospital to cause more trouble.*

Bloody Kids is more proof, if we needed it, that the most provocative
and stimulating British films of the late seventies and early eighties
were made for television. (It did receive subsequent theatrical
screenings in London and New York.) Filmed in 1979 and broadcast
in early 1980 — just months into Margaret Thatcher's premiership — it has
all the ingredients of the typical (of the time) gritty, social realist TV play:
shot-on-16mm film, left-wing agenda, themes of social decline and alienation.
But where, say, the contemporary TV work of Ken Loach or Alan Clarke was
largely channeled through an ultra-naturalistic, drama-documentary style,
Bloody Kids conjures up something else entirely.

From the outset, Chris Menges' dream-like night photography and George
Fenton's wayward, genre-hopping score smack more of telefantasy than social
realism. An eleven-year-old boy, Leo (the poker-faced Richard Thomas),
wanders morbidly through the aftermath of a car crash, where a weary copper
is struggling to restore order from the chaos. Leo is hypnotised by the scene,
while at the same time deeply unimpressed by the bumbling police. He nabs a
bobby's hat from a nearby squad car in a show of contempt.

The next day Leo formulates a plan to exasperate the stupid coppers further
by staging a mock knife fight with his hapless friend Mike (Peter Clark). Mike
is reluctant to get involved, but his vacant temperament is no match for the
icily manipulative Leo. When the knife fight goes wrong (Mike stabs Leo for
real), Leo is whisked to hospital while Mike goes on the run, falling in with
a gang of 'post punks.' Meanwhile, interviewed by the beleaguered Detective
Ritchie (Derrick O'Connor), Leo coolly shakes things up even more by
describing his pal Mike as a psychotic, would-be killer who'd been threatening
to stab him all along.

Bloody Kids. Derrick O'Connor (left) stands in for the late Richard Beckinsale.

By now we're in more recognisably urban territory — the prosaic civic buildings, concrete schoolyards and high rise developments of a bleak Southend-on-Sea. But that doesn't see *Bloody Kids* surrender to realism. If anything, it becomes even more heightened and eerie.

For all their involvement at the centre of the drama, Leo and Mike are as inexpressive as zombies. (This isn't a criticism; Thomas and Clark are both excellent — whatever happened to them?) Leo's dead eyes are like CCTV cameras made flesh: the 'footage' he stores fuels his hatred of the incompetent authority figures around him. He seems motivated by a rage against the system, but this isn't expressed with anger or emotion; instead, he glides blankly through streets and corridors, causing maximum damage with minimum effort. Mike is similarly catatonic; his pallid, passive face looks almost drained of life.

The unruly adolescents Mike hooks up with maraud through Southend's teenage wasteland like a pack of ghouls. Sporting dyed blond hair and New Wave threads, they channel *Grange Hill* through *Dawn of the Dead*, or *The Warriors* through the Children's Film Foundation. But where *The Warriors'* gangs were vibrant and foul-mouthed, these nocturnal souls are stifled and numbed by living in a ghost town.

The exception is their 'leader' Ken, played with chirpy virtuosity by Gary Holton. Ken is the only person who seems alive: a cheeky tearaway in his early twenties who has street cred to spare. He takes the fugitive Mike under his wing and attempts to show him the criminal ropes. In the process, he becomes an oddly paternal presence, providing the nearest thing to warmth in the film. Perhaps inevitably, he gets a sticky comeuppance. It's doubly affecting to see Holton as Ken now, knowing that the actor died just a few years later.

Similarly, *Bloody Kids* is haunted by sitcom star Richard Beckinsale, who was originally cast as Detective Ritchie but died soon after filming began. As

Britain in meltdown. *Bloody Kids.*

director Stephen Frears has testified, the actor remains in some of the long shots. The nation grieved when Beckinsale died at thirty-one, and *Bloody Kids*, inevitably, gained even more dark poignancy from the tragedy. But as well loved as he was as a comedy actor, *Kids* wouldn't have been an easier film had Beckinsale lived to finish it: unused footage shows him as a darker, heavier, more serious character, with close-cropped hair and an aggressive physicality. It's a further step in the murkier direction he had taken a couple of years before in Frears' similarly unheralded TV film, *Last Summer*.

Leo and Mike are reunited at the hospital, which by the end of the film is in meltdown: the police, fire and medical services have all given up under the strain of a collapsing Britain. Nobody notices the boys as they wander through the chaos and carnage of civic breakdown. They light up a cigarette and brazenly smoke it. It's like Leo says: they're young, they're just kids, they can get away with anything. Not even the ubiquitous CCTV surveillance cameras can faze them. Author and critic Ali Catterall has drawn a chilling parallel here: "… [I]n Leo and Mike we might also see future echoes of two other emotionally damaged boys who, like our juvenile screen pair, were also once picked up on a CCTV camera, leading a trusting toddler through a shopping centre."[1]

As with Nigel Kneale's gloomy, updated *Quatermass* miniseries for Thames TV (broadcast just a few months earlier), the fantasy elements of *Bloody Kids* reflect the real societal concerns of late seventies Britain, as well as presenting a remarkably prescient harbinger of the violence of the Thatcher years and beyond. Prophetic and darkly portentous, it is a film of ghosts — of the past, the present and those yet to come.

Julian Upton

---

1 Ali Catterall, *Bloody Kids* review, Film 4, http://www.film4.com/reviews/1979/bloody-kids [Last accessed 1 August 2010].

This article first appeared in *Bedabbled!* (Issue 1, 2011).

HOME BEFORE MIDNIGHT (1979)

Peter Walker (Heritage) Ltd./Columbia-Warner | 111 mins | colour

Director Pete Walker; **Producer** Pete Walker; **Screenplay** Murray Smith. **Starring** Alison Elliott (Virginia Wilshire, 'Ginny'), James Aubrey (Mike Beresford), Debbie Linden (Carol).

Fourteen-year-old Ginny, leaving her friend Carol chatting to a lorry driver in a roadside café, is offered a lift by songwriter Mike Beresford. This chance meeting quickly leads to an intense and blissful relationship. But matters take a turn for the worst when Ginny's father, discovering the full extent of their familiarity, calls in the police.

Never a man for subdued social commentary, Walker's *Home Before Midnight* is an in-your-face portrayal of the relationship between twenty-eight-year-old Mike Beresford (James Aubrey) and fourteen-year-old Ginny (Alison Elliott), released just as debates over the British age of consent were reaching a crescendo. Ginny initially introduces herself to Mike as a design student, but quite early in the film we realise that Ginny is not all she seems. After a brief sex scene, Ginny asks Mike about his 'sexual preferences'; we cut to a fresh-faced Ginny in school uniform, late to detention: "Sorry I'm late, Sir. Art class went on a bit." The audience is immediately implicated in what has just happened, and this is a clever touch on Walker's part: whoever was titillated by the sight of the two lovers in bed together is now guilty of an altogether worse transgression. Ginny's true identity is only revealed to Mike later, when he finds a bracelet engraved with her birth date; confronting her with the evidence, he is stern in telling her there will be "no more sex" (predictably, this pledge lasts about a week).

Throughout, Ginny is revealed to be a manipulative and untrustworthy character. She and her schoolfriend Carol (Debbie Linden) joke about the sexual prowess of schoolmate Malcolm (Ian Sharrock) — an unusually pathetic and insipid boy — and from the outset it is clear that Carol makes a habit of sleeping with strange men. Leaving a café with the lorry driver who has picked them up hitchhiking, she has no concerns about having sex in his porno-strewn cab, even mocking his eagerness: "Bit basic, aren't you?" Ginny's subterfuge extends to her parents, as she assures them that she and Mike are just good friends (though

Illicit lovers Ginny and Mike.
Home Before Midnight.

her mother [Juliet Harmer] does seem remarkably liberal in allowing her teenage daughter to go out in a car with a "good looking boy," even lending her a dress to wear to a party thrown for the band he works with, Bad Accident). Faced with explaining the whole messy situation after her father (Mark Burns) has called in the

Mike gets a shock. *Home Before Midnight.*

police, we begin to feel slightly sorry for Ginny, as she encounters the short-sighted bureaucracy of the law. "Did sexual intercourse take place?" asks a female police officer. "Did he first attack you in the car?" Ginny's distress is construed as being a response to Mike's 'attacks,' when in fact the trauma is the unravelling of a loving relationship: "It's so bloody sordid!" she cries. The ridiculousness of the situation is conveyed in this excruciating conversation between Ginny, parents and police, as her mother expresses caution: if Ginny "went back again and again" it could hardly be unwilling, she argues, and of course Ginny "could pass for nineteen or twenty." The police keenly inform her that, due to Ginny's age, it is a straightforward case of rape; her father states, in a sickeningly satisfied tone, "Rape, dear. It's rape now."

This confusion about what constituted rape, and the issues of consent that Ginny finds herself entangled in, mirrored the key concerns of many bodies arguing for reform of the law in the seventies. The Young Persons Act of 1969 had redefined young people to refer to under eighteens — a lowering of the previous threshold of twenty-one — and by the mid seventies a whole host of groups were putting forward their recommendations to lower the age of consent.[1] In 1974, the Sexual Law Reform Society suggested replacing the age of consent with an 'age of protection,' challenging the legal assumption that consent was only possible above a certain age. In 1976, the National Council for Civil Liberties (NCCL) produced what *The Sun* sensationally dubbed a 'Lolita's Charter,' arguing for the abolition of the crime of incest, more liberal sentencing for paedophiles, and the lowering of the age of consent to fourteen.[2] The National Council for One-Parent Families further argued that the law was not a deterrent to young people pursuing sexual relationships, and only led to reluctance on the part of girls to seek contraception or abortion advice.[3]

Unsurprisingly, these arguments were echoed by less savoury groups: the Paedophile Information Exchange, set up in 1974, put forward hysterically eager claims that children were sexual beings, couching these in the language of liberty introduced by the NCCL.[4] *Home Before Midnight* though, makes a clear distinction between the relationship of Ginny and Mike and paedophilia. As the charges against Mike are made public, he is visibly disturbed by telephone calls he receives from a heavily-breathing pervert who suggests they team up to kidnap two children. "Did you get her to suck you off?... What was it like inside her?... I'm a big fan of yours, Mike," he gasps.

It is elements such as this that lead the film over the line from intelligent social commentary to sleazy exploitation, and no doubt one of the main reasons it remained beneath the general public's film radar. Gratuitous reference to incest ("I always used to think if I had an older brother — good looking — I don't think I could keep from doing it with him") and allusions to the allure of young girls ("You're even hornier since you found out I'm only fourteen," "There's something about her... a bit of a turn-on") are unnecessary but completely expected from Walker. The boundaries of acceptable and unacceptable behaviour are further questioned by the character of Ginny's father, who has a habit of merrily slapping his daughter's and her friend's backsides, accompanied by a greeting of "Hi, sexy!" The best line of the film though, has to be that uttered by Bad Accident manager, Johnny (Jeff Rawle): "You were humping a minor. That's death to a band like Bad Accident."

It's easy to see why *Home Before Midnight* would offend fragile sensibilities, with the contradictory responses Ginny prompts in the viewer confused further by a sensationalistic script, but at its core the film is a tragic love story. The victim of the piece is not a terrorised schoolgirl, but a heartbroken man who remains, to the last, utterly confused by the accusations made against him. Just as he did with *Frightmare* (74), Walker takes a contemporary debate and runs with it — much further than is necessary and well past the finishing line — to produce a remarkably intelligent if completely unsubtle take on British legal apparatus.

Jennifer Wallis

1   Matthew Waites, *The Age of Consent: Young People, Sexuality and Citizenship* (Basingstoke: Palgrave Macmillan, 2005), p.132.
2   Ibid., pp.134–36.
3   Ibid., p.136.
4   See David Cox and Glenn Wilson, *The Child-Lovers: A Study of Paedophiles in Society* (London: Peter Owen, 1983).

THAT SUMMER! (1979)

Film and General Productions/Columbia | 93 mins | colour

Director Harley Cokeliss; **Producers** Davina Belling, Clive Parsons; **Screenplay** Janey Preger, from a story by Tony Attard. **Starring** Ray Winstone (Steve), Julie Shipley (Angie), Tony London (Jimmy), Emily Moore (Carole), Jan Morrison (Tam).

Recently released from Borstal, Steve Brody quickly leaves his dead end life in London behind and travels down to the Devon coast for the summer. There he meets others who are also looking for escape, romance, adventure and low paid jobs. However, when he decides to enter an annual swimming contest, Brody soon finds himself up against a gang of Scottish lads willing to do anything to stop him from winning.

Michael Winner's 1964 film *The System* casts a brooding, über-confident Oliver Reed as Tinker, the leader of a group of males in the fictional Devon resort of Roxham (actually the three towns — Brixham, Paignton, Torquay — that make up Torbay), whose 'system' ensures a healthy turnover of female tourists every summer. For these men, there are three choices in life: freedom, abortion or the family way. They exist as threadbare creatures deprived of fresh meat for eight months of the year, and there lies the melancholy undercurrent of Winner's film. Beneath the B-movie surface are glimpses of the reality of life in a seaside town. The summers may be a feast, but the winters bring on famine, especially in a place like Torbay in the early 1960s. The lack of girls, shops and good weather do nothing to make the bedsitting rooms of a thousand single men any warmer.

No such introspection in *That Summer!* The protagonists here descend on Torquay full of the kind of hope that only the searing heat of 1978 could ignite. After serving eight months for GBH, Steve Brody leaves Borstal with no future and no skills, save his strength as a swimmer. He is unceremoniously dumped on the seafront by a National Express coach and swiftly finds a job — and lodgings — in a local pub. Angie and Carole, factory girls from Leeds, have summer chambermaid jobs lined up at one of the resort's posher hotels ("They're ever so grand down south, aren't they?"). Another Londoner, Jimmy, drives there because he has nothing better to do. To all four, the town is a Xanadu, offering fresh starts and new opportunities; and, of course, beer and sex. The fly in the ointment here is a group of aggressive Scotsmen, led by Tam, who rub Brody up the wrong way right from the start. Tam has also signed up to compete in the across-the-bay swimming contest, but whereas he and his cronies are drunken, pill-popping, leery thugs, Brody (a nod to that other fish-out-of-water protagonist in *Jaws*?) is determined to get something

Misleading 'rock music' poster graphics for *That Summer!*

right in his life for once, and even the amorous, confident attentions of Angie can't distract him.

Set against backgrounds of Technicolour harbour lights, exotic palm trees and red and green illuminated night gardens, Harley Cokeliss' film captures perfectly the fecund four months a year that drive the characters in *The System*, but without the Beat-ish gloom. This is a world of aftershave, Durex and cut-off denim shorts, where you're either a local or a 'grockle' (tourist). Viewers resident in Torquay may well be amused by the geographical liberties taken by Californian Cokeliss (one of whose productions of note to that date was *Crash!*, a 1971 BBC film written by and featuring J.G. Ballard), who reduces the town to a beach (Babbacombe), a nightclub (the 400 on Victoria Parade), a hotel (The Imperial) and a pub (The Pickwick Inn). The view from Brody's lodgings down the side street of Pimlico takes in the harbour, when in reality he'd be looking at somewhere near the rear of Marks and Spencers. He also effortlessly jogs from there to Babbacombe beach, a good half hour hilly walk at the best of times. Other local landmarks include the omnipresent Thatcher Rock, the Odeon cinema up Abbey Road, EF foreign language students and the Coral Island nightclub/swimming pool, which in later years became — for a while — a haunted landscape worthy of a Ballard story. There is also a bizarre punch-up between Brody and the Scots at the Babbacombe Model Village, a long-standing attraction that here becomes a surreal arena: feet and fists flailing and crushing the very places that the characters live in.

FILM REVIEWS

For years there has been an unchallenged understanding that *That Summer!* is an unofficial 'sequel' to Winstone's breakthrough role in *Scum* (79), with Steve Brody being a continuation of that film's Roy Carlin. There are some casting crossovers between the two, aside from Winstone. John Judd — Mr Sands in *Scum* — is Brody's swimming coach at the start of *That Summer!* John

A fresh-faced Ray Winstone. *That Summer!*

Fowler (the hapless Woods) is seen briefly as Brody's brother. Tony London originally played Woods in Roy Minton's original — and banned — *Play for Today* version for the BBC in 1977. *That Summer!*, however, was released a few months before the film version of *Scum*, suggesting that the connection was made only in the minds of younger, more enthusiastic viewers.

What with these two roles and *Quadrophenia*, in the space of one year Ray Winstone made his presence known in a trilogy of films that became required viewing by every subsequent post-punk generation. *That Summer!* is not hardcore cult material, but something that fits the more leisurely pace of its surroundings, a traditional and straightforward story, with only the excellent new wave soundtrack (seen by some at the time as a cynical cash-in) connecting it to any notion of 'hip.' In truth, though, *That Summer!* reveals more about punk rock than the likes of JUBILEE (78) ever could. [Steady on! *Ed.*] Outside the main cities of London and Manchester, life in the late 1970s carried on more or less as normal, enlivened perhaps only by a free Sex Pistols badge in *Smash Hits* magazine. The soundtrack to teenage lives may have changed, but the rituals remained the same. This is why Jimmy can fix up his car whilst Richard Hell's Blank Generation blares out of the stereo, or couples can slow dance to Patti Smith's Because The Night in the 400 Club.

Interestingly, almost thirty years later, one of Winstone's daughters, Jamie (b.1985), would star in the dire British 'thriller' *Donkey Punch* (2008), where a group of Leeds girls meet a group of London lads on holiday, but this time with an altogether more unsavoury conclusion than either *The System* or *That Summer!*

Martin Jones

SIR HENRY AT RAWLINSON END (1980)

Charisma Films/Virgin Vision | 71 mins | b&w/sepia

Director Steve Roberts; **Producer** Tony Stratton-Smith; **Screenplay** Vivian Stanshall and Steve Roberts. **Starring** Trevor Howard (Sir Henry), Patrick Magee (Slodden), Sheila Reid (Florrie), Vivian Stanshall (Hubert), J.G. Devlin (Old Scrotum), Denise Coffey (Mrs E) Harry Fowler (Buller Bullethead), Gary Waldhorn (Max), Simon Jones (Joachim).

Following the adventures of the titular aristocrat as he drinks, quaffs, swills, chugs, bends his elbow, wets the baby's head, carouses, gets rat-arsed, tipples, knocks 'em back, imbibes, swigs, hits the bottle, fortifies himself, indulges, enjoys a brisk 'sharpener,' wassails, re-fills the old tank and otherwise consumes alcohol. Some other stuff happens, too.

Deep in the heart of olde England, down Southampton way, lies Rawlinson End, imposing ancestral seat of one of Britain's most celebrated clans. Set on the river Riddle, near the picturesque hamlet Wankers Grunge, its copious rooms play home to Sir Henry Rawlinson, miscellaneous family members and a devoted staff (headed by Old Scrotum, the wrinkled retainer). There's a ghost in the corridors, a POW camp in the garden and a brace of ne'er-do-wells trying to break in. And given the way Sir Henry treats the local peasantry, it's probably best that the house is not open to the public.

It says something about the blissfully haphazard state of the British film industry in the late seventies that anyone even contemplated setting a film in such a place, let alone actually making the damn thing. True, the British film industry has a long and ignoble history of painting pretty pictures of the landed gentry but *Sir Henry at Rawlinson End* is a world away from the forelock tugging of Merchant Ivory. It is a dashed queer affair, but that's hardly unexpected, given its parentage.

Apparently, Vivian Stanshall (Sir Henry's creator, co-writer and narrator) disliked the term 'eccentric' but there's no better way to describe him short of invoking mental illness. Stanshall first claimed a place in the nation's affections as ringleader of the Bonzo Dog Doo-Dah Band, the bonkers multicoloured musical comedy troupe that provided the missing link between Captain Beefheart and 'Big Hearted' Arthur Askey. Unlike his contemporaries, Stanshall's creativity owed little to LSD-25; his world view was naturally psychedelic. *Sir Henry* was born when Stanshall deputised for John Peel and interpolated spoken word stories about life at Rawlinson End amidst the records. These tales gained a cult following and a film was proposed.

FILM REVIEWS

CHARISMA FILMS LTD PRESENTS
TREVOR HOWARD in VIVIAN STANSHALL'S
Sir Henry
AT RAWLINSON END

SHOWING WITH
PETER SELLERS AND SPIKE MILLIGAN IN
THE RUNNING? JUMPING STANDING STILL FILM

Producer Tony Stratton Smith
Executive producer Martin Wesson Director Steve Roberts
Screenplay Vivian Stanshall and Steve Roberts
Soundtrack and narration Vivian Stanshall

Original soundtrack recordings Charisma Records Ltd
Get the book from your local bookshop £3.95 Fat Pie Publishing Ltd
Special thanks Richard International Film Festival 1980

Steve Roberts, an experienced TV director, came on board and somehow, Stanshall's ramblings were turned into something a bit like a story.

It should be emphasised that Stanshall was an alcoholic by this point and the film follows a drinker's logic, shifting and free-associating. Much of the dialogue is made up of non-sequiturs ("I never met a man I didn't mutilate," or "Incidentally, before I get drunk — have you killed?"). The plot, such as it is, drifts in and out of focus — the most substantial part of the film follows the attempts to exorcise the ghost of Henry's late brother Humbert, doomed to wander the Earth because he wasn't wearing trousers when he died.

Like his creator, Sir Henry is a bibulous sort. "If I had all the money I'd spent on drink," he muses, "I'd spend it on drink." He only finally decides to banish the troublesome spectre when it oversteps the mark and dilutes his brandy. As his wife says, "Henry detests water. He even cleans his teeth with rum."

Although Sir Henry is painted in the worst possible light —he's an unreconstructed (and thoroughly racist) imperialist — he's treated with a certain affection. Indeed, the film can be seen as a bizarro world version of Visconti's *The Leopard* (in which Burt Lancaster plays a Sicilian prince gradually accepting his era has passed). Here, Trevor Howard is too drunk to realise he's an anachronism and no one else has got around to pointing it out yet. The film even concludes with him reasserting his feudal privileges, hacking away at the assembled yeomanry with a bloody great sword.

361

As the above suggests, this is hardly a typical example of British cinema, which has always preferred the polite and the worthy. And yet, ironically, *Sir Henry* is one of the most profoundly British films, drawing on explicitly British traditions. It's one of the few films to walk in the frazzled footsteps of Lewis Carroll or even Laurence Sterne, indulging a taste for the absurd and the ribald; celebrating peculiarity rather than banishing it to the attic. (For example, the war is long over but Sir Henry keeps German prisoners in the garden for the sport of foiling their escapes.)

Sir Henry has been described (lazily) as 'surrealism.' Nope. This is Nonsense — which is to say the 'Nonsense' of Edward Lear, whose imagination inspired so many of Stanshall's generation, not least John Lennon and Syd Barrett. Stanshall's mellifluous opening narration gives a flavour of this influence: "English as tuppence, changing yet changeless as canal water, nestling in green nowhere, armoured and effete, bold flag-bearer, lotus-fed Miss Havishambling opsimath and eremite..."

Despite *Sir Henry*'s multiple transgressions, the film is never less than amused and even indulgent. Like his influences, Stanshall is more interested in being silly than doing anything so dull as make a point, a very English attitude to life.

Tempting though it is to ascribe the credit to Stanshall alone, Steve Roberts deserves more than just a nod. He worked miracles with the pacing and finding exactly the right tone for what could have been the most god-awful mess. It's a surprisingly graceful film, looking beautiful in sepia tinged black and white and crammed with subtle visual jokes to reward attentive viewers.

At the heart is Trevor Howard as Sir Henry. It's not the sort of role normally associated with the film actor who was arguably Britain's greatest — especially not the part where he rides a unicycle dolled up in stockings, a tutu and blackface — but by all accounts he was thrilled to be involved, as was Patrick Magee: as might be expected from Samuel Beckett's favourite actor, he was an ardent admirer of Stanshall.

Situated somewhere between Toad Hall and the mouldering turrets of Gormenghast castle (the gothic pile of Mervyn Peake's best work) Rawlinson End stands empty now, a monument to its builder. Stanshall died in 1995; his bed caught fire when he passed out smoking a cigarette. We can regret that he did not accomplish more but should be grateful he gave us what he did, most especially this film; it's one of the great masterpieces of English eccentricity.

James Oliver

WINGS OF DEATH

THE DEMISE OF THE SHORT FILM AS SUPPORTING FEATURE

BY DAVID KEREKES

The theatrical short film approaches its demise. *Wings of Death.*

I didn't know it at the time, but one of the people who joined us that night had a nerve condition and was under doctor's orders to avoid any excitement because of it. He reacted badly to *A Nightmare on Elm Street* (84), the new shocker from Wes Craven, and suffered a breakdown that was a distraction for everyone in the cinema.

Another thing I could not have known was that the film supporting *A Nightmare on Elm Street*, a short fictional drama involving drug abuse called *Wings of Death* (85) was destined to be the last short I would see as supporting feature on a British cinema screen.

The era of the short had come to its end. There was no obituary and few people would have cared had they even noticed. The short had been a puzzling and largely unwelcome appendage to the main feature; it had been clinging for years in all the wrong places like a debilitated grandparent, popping up when one least expected it and then sticking around, clueless.

Wings of Death proved to be an apt title for the departing of the short. These half pint oddities may have dragged on a little longer in other places, but *Wings of Death* was the last I would see of them.[1] The year was 1985 and the cinema some forsaken place in the north of England. *Wings of Death* and *A Nightmare on Elm Street* are a well matched pair, but the same cannot be said of many other programmes absent of aforethought. Short films were commonplace in British cinemas, appearing in the mid to late sixties as a cheap substitute for the B-picture, gradually replacing it, and then disappearing in the mid eighties when cinemas ceased to exhibit a full supporting programme and the cash incentive for short filmmakers was pulled by the BFI. Today the short is all but forgotten with even some ardent cinemagoers of the seventies and eighties having scant recollection of them, as I was to discover courtesy of my fellow OFFBEAT authors.

GARY RAMSAY: *To be honest I have a very sketchy memory of supporting features. I can remember very few, especially Brit offerings. I remember going to see either* Grizzly *(76) or* Conan the Barbarian *(82) with a supporting pic that involved someone being chased into a house by a giant claymore that embedded itself in the surround of a big roaring fireplace in a stately home somewhere. It is a scene that has stuck in my head for years. God knows what that was. It's all I can remember...*

The Film Act 1960 defines the British theatrically released short film as anything less than thirty-three-and-a-third minutes duration. But this basic criterion was eventually proven redundant, and a short became in essence anything less than 'feature length.' Kenneth F. Rowles' *Take an Easy Ride* (77), which we'll discuss later, is a short that runs over forty minutes. Content and form was of no matter, whether documentary or travelogue, live action drama or music promo. Sometimes the short bore a thematic relation to the feature it supported, but quite often there was no logical connection. When Steven Spielberg's *Jaws* (75) reached the Mayfair cinema in Whitefield, Manchester, it was packaged with *The Line to Skye* (74). This fifteen minute film by Edward McConnell took the viewer from Inverness to Kyle of Lochalsh via the scenic West Highland railway, a journey I endured twice for the sake of Spielberg's blockbusting shark. There was no bar at the Mayfair in those days either, so the auditorium was packed in agonising anticipation on both occasions, making

Take an Easy Ride began as a public information film.

Eddie McConnell a most fortunate man and his film hugely unpopular.

MARTIN JONES: *I couldn't help with the 'cinema fillers' question you sent out. My <u>only</u> memory now is of watching a* Pink Panther *film and the short before it being about skiing!*

DAVID HYMAN: *The grandmaster of tedious travelogue documentaries was auteur writer-producer-director Harold Baim, whose Harold Baim Productions inflicted more tedious travelogues and shorts on the population than they deserved to endure. Among them was the 1981 unholy trinity of* Telly Savalas Looks at Aberdeen, …Portsmouth, *and* …Birmingham. *I think these shorts may have recycled bits of the same scripts with the different local landmarks dropped in. I saw* Telly Savalas Looks at Aberdeen *when it supported* Tenebrae *in 1983 at the Classic Tottenham Court Road. I can still remember Telly segueing seamlessly from talking about Aberdeen Castle to introducing Aberdeen University, describing the latter as "a castle of learning."*

Baim also used Pete Murray to narrate a similar trilogy: Pete Murray Takes You To Coventry, …Hastings, *and* …Nottingham. *I think I saw the Coventry short as I can remember seeing a documentary with a male narrator prattling inanely about wartime bombings and the new Coventry cathedral.*

By contrast, a rather inventive choice of short accompanied Stanley Kubrick's *2001: A Space Odyssey* (68), again at the Mayfair cinema. This was a documentary on deep sea exploration called, as best I can remember, *A Sea Odyssey*.[2] The unknown terrain in this instance was far from Kubrick's own particular frontiers of space and mind, but its aquatic craft did closely resemble his EVA pods, nonetheless. Or so I thought at age twelve. *A Sea Odyssey* didn't grace the original run of *2001*, but played on a repeat screening sometime in the early seventies, and possibly only regionally. Material that had local flavour was a clear incentive for booking agents. One example is *Croydon Airport*, a short that was popular with the patrons of the Fairfield cinema in Croydon, where it played more than once.[3]

'Good shorts make good programmes,' stated distributor Connoisseur Films in one trade ad.[4] Among a catalogue of foreign language and repertory type features, Connoisseur boasted a 'magnificent collection of 100 short films hand-picked for quality and interest.' These included an early Bob Godfrey animation, *The Plain Man's Guide to Advertising* (63), and a three minute vampire film, *Darling, Do You Love Me?* (68), starring Germaine Greer.

Kim Newman: *I saw most of these things [short films] in Somerset, Brighton and Kingston, though I remember a few in the West End. I had the impression that shorts tended to be yoked to specific features. People tend to remember the silly nude ballet effort, which came round* with The Exorcist *(73),* or Black Angel *(79) (a mediaeval-set imitation*

Germaine Greer in the three-minute *Darling, Do You Love Me?*

of An Occurence at Owl Creek Bridge, *directed by Roger Christian), which was billed with* The Empire Strikes Back *(80), because they were billed with widely-seen films. Those Stanley Long featurettes (did you see that one of them,* Dream Home, *was recently remade as a feature called* Psychosis?*) were shoved out several times, as was David McGillivray's* The Errand *(80) — presumably to fill a hole. There was also that dire comedy about the flea-infested mattress, which was put out with* Friday the 13th *(80).*

Before the days of MTV, music promos would occasionally play in theatres as record companies found new avenues for the promotion of bands and their albums. Unfairly, some truly tiresome music suddenly had a captive audience. A film of Dire Straits performing songs from *Making Movies*, which played prior to Michael Apted's *Coal Miner's Daughter* (80), is an exercise hardly removed from that of the Nazi propagandists, whose rubbish was also screened to locked houses. (I liked that album. *Ed.*) At fourteen minutes *The Pretty Things* (67), by Caterina Arvat and Anthony West, is an early example of a theatrical short for a pop group, in this instance the Pretty Things.

DARRELL BUXTON: *Hmmmm, November 1982, Derby ABC, John Carpenter's* The Thing *(82) supported by a film about the making of The Who's* Face Dances *album...*

DAVID HYMAN: *To Russia... With Elton (79) was double-billed with* Porridge *(79) and was directed by Dick Clement and Ian La Frenais. According to the BFI database library, it features 'highlights of Elton John's concert performances in Moscow and Leningrad in spring 1979.'*

Trippy imagery from *The Oriental Nightfish.*

I remember seeing the trippy Oriental Nightfish *(78), directed by Ian Emes (who later made one of the Duran Duran music videos deemed too sexy for TV) with Walter Hill's* The Driver *(78) at the ABC Shaftesbury Avenue in 1978. As one IMDb correspondent notes, it's a 'short film based on an unused song that Linda McCartney recorded with Paul McCartney and Denny Laine (Wings) during the sessions for* Band on the Run *in 1973.'*

The short film is not best remembered as an entity in and of itself. It conjures the memory of a greater experience, such as the programme on which it played and the cinema that played it. Understandably, it is the fantasy tinged dramatic short, more than the music promo, documentary or travelogue, that has had anything of an impact on those old enough to remember. Christian Marnham's *The Orchard End Murder* (82), which opened for Gary Sherman's horror film *Dead and Buried* (82), has generated a cult reputation despite being unseen for almost three decades. It was a bill I saw at the Classic in Bury, Lancashire, but from all accounts it played across the UK, too. The tale is a very English one (and at forty-nine minutes one of the longer shorts), which involves a cricket match, a train station, a murder and its attempted cover up. The curious atmosphere and imagery (a breast poking through the dirt where the body is buried) has made a lasting impression of this particular double bill, which is greater than the individual parts: because of *The Orchard End Murder* I better remember *Dead and Buried*.

WINGS OF DEATH
THE DEMISE OF THE SHORT AS SUPPORTING FEATURE

KIM NEWMAN: *I remember quite a few of these things, mostly the odd little psycho thrillers: I saw* Jaws *with* Panic *(78), the Avis Bunnage hatchet-carrying hitchhiker film, but more typical were* Deep End *and* The Dumb Waiter *(79), proto-slasher movie chase scenes with a homicidal maniac persecuting the lead character. And ghost stories, the shorts that became* Screamtime *(83), for instance, and some period literary adaptations like* The Man and the Snake *(72) and* The Return. *Also, the parade of* Land of the Grape-*type travelogues which were killed by the murderous parody John Cleese put out with* Life of Brian *(79). I also remember an Elizabethan sexy horror story called* Red *(76), with Ferdy Mayne and Gabrielle Drake, which came round with* The Final Conflict *(81).*

DAVID HYMAN: *Supporting* Creepshow *when I saw it at the ABC Harrow was a film called* That's The Way To Do It *(82), directed by Stanley Long. It starred Robin Bailey (Uncle Mort from TV's* I Didn't Know You Cared*) and Ann Lynn. Bailey plays a Punch and Judy man, who discovers that his wife has been cheating on him and kills her with Mr Punch's club, whilst repeatedly shrieking "That's the way to do it!" This short can also be found on the compilation* Screamtime.

When I think of *Wings of Death* I cannot help but think also of *A Nightmare on Elm Street*, and the guy with bad nerves, owner of the car in which we travelled to see it. The experience has overtaken the film, as time is slowly overtaking the experience, relegating it to hazy memory for people like me who have only just realised it has gone. I decided I should at least try and speak with someone who had inside knowledge of short films, about how they were made and distributed. *Wings of Death*, as noted, was the last short I saw in British cinemas and in this instance the end seemed the logical place to start.

Michael Coulson is one half of the filmmaking team behind *Wings of Death*. He wrote and directed it with Nichola Bruce, having worked together since meeting as students at Hornsey College of Art in the seventies, and establishing Muscle Films for the production of

Screamtime was a horror shorts compilation. Was it screened with a short supporting feature, too?

'Easier for young kids to get heroin than a job.' Thatcher's
Britain in *Wings of Death*.

experimental art films.
One of their earlier films,
the five minute *Clip*
(83), was screened at the
ICA as support to Slava
Tsukerman's *Liquid Sky*
(82). These early films
were visual abstracts
geared for television
and festivals. *Wings
of Death* on the other
hand was envisaged as
a mini feature, because,
as Coulson puts it, "we
wanted to get it seen."

MICHAEL COULSON: Wings of Death *was produced by the BFI. Our
producer Paul Webster was instrumental in getting it seen once it had been
made. He was working with Palace Pictures at the time and knew they
were going to be distributing this picture called* A Nightmare on Elm Street.
Palace became interested in Wings of Death *and encouraged the BFI to let
them distribute the film in the UK. Palace made thirty prints of the film at
least, so that it went out with the feature* Nightmare on Elm Street *all over
the UK. This was unusual. Normally, they wouldn't put up the money to
make that many prints.*

*The BFI was interested in us making a feature film, but they wanted to see
what we would do with a short film first of all. As we had a reputation for
being visual rather than narrative filmmakers, something like a horror
movie seemed to be a good avenue for us to go down. We call* Wings of
Death *a tragedy. The tragedy at the time was that it was easier for young
kids to get heroin than get a job in the UK. So, the film was based loosely
around the whole heroin thing that was going on, but we didn't really want
it to be a commercial against taking heroin. In the end, the BFI persuaded
us to put in this opening sequence that made it more specific to heroin than
we actually wanted it.*

*We were told to go off and write a script. So we did. It was originally going
to have more of a William Burroughs influence to it. I don't know if we were
told what length it had to be. We had made a twenty minute short before, so
maybe that's where we were guided.*

Wings of Death.

I've just discovered we've got about six to ten 35mm prints in our archive, which we didn't know we had. Channel 4 had a remit to broadcast it, probably a certain number of times. I don't know whether they will broadcast it again because it'll probably mean they are going to have to pay for it. It was a big calling card for us showing it to people. In America they were very interested in it. Europe liked it a lot; the Italian festival audience really liked it. It won the first prize at the Cinema of the Fantastic in Sitges, Spain. So it got a lot of exposure at the time, and now unfortunately there's no venue to see it so it's disappeared.

Another filmmaker I spoke with was Ken Rowles, who had directed *Take an Easy Ride*, a rather untypical exponent of the short film but a fascinating example all the same. *Take an Easy Ride* was initially envisioned as a documentary for television, warning young people of the perils of hitchhiking, but it found its way as sexploitation following the advice of porn producer David Hamilton Grant. Grant encouraged Rowles to pad the running time with sex scenes and play it theatrically, notably at one of Grant's own cinemas, the Pigalle in Soho. Here, the film enjoyed a solid forty-eight week run. Rowles eventually pulled the plug on Grant due to lack of payment, and *Take an Easy Ride* found a new life playing nationally with *Erotic Young Lovers*, a retitled episode from the German *Schulmädchen-Report* film series.

Rowles has production credits on a number of exploitation films, including *Venom* (71) and *The Ups and Downs of a Handyman* (76). But *Take an Easy Ride* is wholly different. Part public information film, part grindhouse, it remains a wonderfully outrageous piece of sleaze quite unlike any other short — or indeed any other film — produced in Britain during the seventies. Ken

Take an Easy Ride ended up as one half of a sexploitation double bill.

A CHILDS ASSOCIATES RELEASE

Rowles had this to say about *Take an Easy Ride*, its genesis as a production intended for television which then became a modest hit nationwide.

KEN ROWLES: *Southern TV knew that we had an interest in making a film about the danger of young people hitching a ride. They said make the film and show them the finished film. After David Grant offered me a deal I did not think the sex content would be suitable for television. We did the deal with Oppidan distributors, the company owned by David Grant. The film was then distributed by Child Associates after I took it away from David Grant. It was second feature with another film of Child Associates [*Erotic Young Lovers*] and played in most Classic, Essoldo, Granada and Star group cinemas in towns up and down the country. There were so many cinemas in towns that would screen such films.*

The film was played uncut when David Grant screened it at the Pigalle, a cinema club in Piccadilly. (Grant promoted it as, simply, An Easy Ride.) On its national release it had an 'X' rating. I cut the rape scene in the woods, the close-up shots with black gloves between the legs and the close-up shots between the legs, as well as the Tara Lynn and Alan Bone close-up intercourse shot.

WINGS OF DEATH
THE DEMISE OF THE SHORT AS SUPPORTING FEATURE

The music in *Take an Easy Ride* is interesting. The rock song that plays in the opening nightclub scene and recurs throughout is from the De Wolfe production music library — in actuality a track called *Alexander*, recorded by the Pretty Things under an assumed name. It is familiar from other Brit movies, including Menahem Golan's *What's Good for the Goose* (69) and Michael Armstrong's *The Haunted House of Horror* (69), where it is again used as a backdrop to a party scene. Also on the *Take an Easy Ride* soundtrack, but not credited, is Get It On by T. Rex.

Nudity upstaged by wallpaper. *Take an Easy Ride.*

KEN ROWLES: *I was working with record producers who came in with various recording artists who wanted to promote their early work. I had been working with Polydor on the pilot of the [unaired] television series Go Girl (70). They introduced me to groups like Slade and the Iguana. Yes, Get It On was a coup!*

I then asked Ken Rowles about *The Perils of Mandy* (80), a sex comedy he made after *Take an Easy Ride*, which has the distinction of being an early shot-on-video short but one lacking any success. Ken qualified his answer with an introduction to his own career and life now as director, writer and producer of an altogether more formal type of short film, the kind that carry titles like *Tribute to Her Majesty* (86), *U.S.S. Richard Montgomery* (2003) and *Remembering Merton Park Studios* (2008). It is an insight to another side to film production, but concurrent with many themes, ideas, and personalities noted elsewhere in this book.

KEN ROWLES: *I came into films at fifteen wanting to be a cameraman. At sixteen I was given the opportunity to go into the editing department at Merton Park Studios, where I worked on the* **Edgar Wallace** *and* **Scotland Yard** *series — they were B-movies that played in the cinema with full length features films. I then went on to edit documentaries, programmes for ATV and Anglia and television commercials. I worked with director Phil Wrestler who directed second unit on* The Italian Job. *Phil said I would make a better*

producer than I was as editor. I was given various feature scripts that we wanted to make. Another editor friend of mine had Venom *and so, in 1970, I produced* Venom, *my first feature film at Twickenham film studios. I always wanted to produce or direct big movies and Phil and I had many projects that we wanted to make. Having made* Ups and Downs of a Handyman *I had ideas to follow it with other sex comedies, such as* Ups and Downs of a Soccer Star. *This was never made due to being let down by our investors and distributors. KFR Productions Ltd. went out of business. David Grant gave me a job in his cinema clubs. After a few months a director friend, Ted Frances, asked if I would join him to run a company, Film Archive Services, advising the Nigerian Government on setting up their own film marketing in West Africa. I spent the next two years buying and selling films in Africa. In 1979, the contract ended and I joined Phil Wrestler and set up a company to make an action drama based on the book,* Truck, *by Peter Cave, with George Kennedy and Oliver Reed. Phil wanted to direct but the investors would not agree and the American distributors said it was too British. At the same time I was asked to find films for the new video companies as I had contacts, having been buying films for Africa from most of the British distributors, such as Rank and EMI. I also set up my own video sales company, The Best of British.*

Phil and I made a short film On The Bridge, *which we hoped to sell to television. One of the companies I was selling features to was Vision On owned by Tony Maldoon. He asked if I would make a film of approximately sixty minutes and he would put up the money. We agreed to make a series, the first being* Perils of Mandy. *I don't think Tony had any idea of the commitment needed to produce such a series. There was also a disagreement on the sex content. I don't think it had as much heavy sex as he wanted. We made no more films together and I went on to run my new production company in the Medway Towns. I had a lot of bad publicity about* Perils of Mandy *in the local press. I had just lost my marriage, my three children and my home. So I started making documentary films for industry and television commercials.*

[For more on the short film, see the Appendix.]

---

1   Says OFFBEAT contributor, James Oliver: "I think the short was dying out by the time I started to go to the pictures, although it seemed to survive longer in the West Country (where we holidayed) than elsewhere."

2   Although *A Sea Odyssey* was referred to as such in the cinema listing of the local press, I have been unable to turn up any information on a film by this name. However, it was certainly not the same documentary that played with *2001* on its original screenings, which, from all accounts, was an investigation into the possibility of extraterrestrial life.

3   As advertised in *Films and Filming*, June 1970.

4   *Films and Filming*, July 1970.

NOTE The author would like to hear from anyone on the subject of short films that were screened theatrically in Britain, be it anecdotal information or otherwise. Contact David Kerekes via the publisher.

THE APPOINTMENT (1981)

First Principle Film Productions Ltd. | 90 mins | colour

Director Lindsey C. Vickers; **Producer** Tom Sachs; **Screenplay** Lindsey C. Vickers.
Starring Edward Woodward (Ian, the father), Jane Merrow (Diana, the mother), Samantha Weysom (Joanne, the daughter).

When an unavoidable work commitment forces a businessman to miss his teenage daughter's school orchestra performance, supernatural forces are unleashed to punish him for his neglectfulness.

As a young girl walks home from school through a woodland shortcut, eerie noises and a feeling that someone is watching throw her into a state of unease. Her name is whispered menacingly by an unseen presence, and something hidden moves in the bushes. Then, when the tension has become almost unbearable, we are delivered one of modern cinema's most effective, yet little-seen, shock moments: out of nowhere, an invisible presence snatches the innocent victim and drags her through the air and into the bushes with such ferocity that her body literally folds in two as she disappears. Having dispensed with the girl, the presence then retrieves any evidence that she ever existed, slowly dragging her violin and sheet music into the undergrowth. With every trace removed, all that survives are the words of a missing person's report, spoken in monotone over the soundtrack. And so begins *The Appointment*.

After the titles, the film settles down to become something seemingly more humdrum and uneventful than this visceral introduction promises. We meet middle-aged father Ian (Woodward), his wife Diana (Merrow), and their teenage daughter Joanne (Weysom), an only child. Within this domestic setup, played out in a nondescript suburban home according to the rules of unremarkable middle-class engagement, we learn that, due to a last minute change of plans, Ian is forced to attend a work-related tribunal in place of a colleague, and that he must therefore disappoint his daughter by missing her end of term concert. This bad news gives rise to an incredible sulk from

A Sgt. Howie for the eighties: Edward Woodward as Ian in *The Appointment*.

Joanne, leaving her parents to argue over the best way to handle her emotions. But just as we experience the distinct and uncomfortable feeling that the film's powerful opening may have given way to a potentially tedious story about a moody teenager who would be better seen and not heard, Vickers' low-key tale of the extraordinary-within-the-ordinary starts to offer some subtle hints that something sinister is afoot. And, sure enough, as a succession of finely crafted set-pieces begins to unfold, we discover that Joanne's disappointment in, and anger towards, her father runs so deep that a force has been triggered within her which, unconsciously or otherwise, is intent on exacting revenge on him through powerful supernatural means.

With the clock counting down to the moment when Ian turns the key in the ignition to start out on his long journey, Joanne turns her mind to her dark project. While she and her family sleep in the comfort of their home, we witness a pack of mysterious dogs roaming through the house, see a mechanic slaughtered by the tools he uses to fix Ian's car, and experience a sinister shared dream that offers a portent to both husband and wife. Then, as the sun comes up and Ian prepares to leave, it is clear that the scene has been set for the film's gripping and daring final act — the punishment of the father.

In his role as Ian, Joanne's father, Edward Woodward comes the closest he ever would to reprising one of his most celebrated and enduring characters — Sgt. Howie in *The Wicker Man* [73]. Here, just as in Hardy's wonderful folkloric tale, his uncompromising sense of duty, and his distinct lack of intuitive understanding of the things he cannot rationalise, both defines him and brings about his downfall. And just as the road to Sgt. Howie's demise is

Woodward comes to another sticky end. *The Appointment.*

mapped out right before his eyes, with only the righteous investigator himself unable to see it coming, so too is Ian's downfall designed for him to walk — or rather drive — right into.

At the end of *The Appointment*, when the brutal punishment is over, we return to the site of the film's shocking opening sequence to find Joanne sitting at the mouth of the woodland shortcut, now barricaded by a wrought iron fence, calmly stroking the pack of mysterious dogs. The satisfaction at the way things have turned out — as well as the film in general — belongs to her.

An audacious exploration of the dawning of womanhood, and of the danger that unassimilated 'otherness' — as embodied by the maturing female figure of Joanne — poses to the order of things (the rules of the house, the importance of a man's work), *The Appointment* could reasonably be thought of as a very British *Carrie*. But with its palette of muted colours and its understated 'horror' sensibility, Lindsey C. Vickers' restrained, radically pared-down style is about as far from the uber-flashy cine-referentiality of De Palma as it's possible to get. Menstrual shower scenes and "dirty pillows" are here replaced with far more subtle suggestions of maturation and fertility, such as the blooming flower garden which Diana tends, and the lush countryside through which Ian must navigate. And though the film certainly has its moments of intensity — not least during the pre-title sequence — chills are generally to be found in the quietest of places, such as when a bedside photo of Ian and Joanne becomes animated in the dead of night, and she moves her previously fixed gaze away from her hero/father in an attitude of hatred.

Despite the potential for comparisons with popular and successful titles like *Carrie* and *The Wicker Man*, *The Appointment* was met with little enthusiasm upon its original release. Its desire to challenge rather than conform to generic expectations — evidenced by the minimal, even perfunctory, plot, as well as the film's deconstruction of mainstream horror film tropes — did not find favour with audiences. And although it was made available on VHS briefly in 1983, courtesy of the 3M label, all traces of the film have since vanished. However, its unique take on horror, as well as the notable performance from Woodward, is more than deserving of a wider audience and of an acknowledged place within the history of British cinema.

As for Lindsey C. Vickers, he went on to produce a lavish four-part television drama for Channel 4, entitled *Zaztrossi: A Romance*, in 1986. And, aside from an effective short film, *The Lake* [78] — which shares many stylistic and thematic concerns with *The Appointment* — he never directed another film.

Sam Dunn

HOW SLEEP THE BRAVE (1981)

a.k.a. Combat Zone | Lindsay Shonteff Film Productions/Palm Springs Enterprises | 88 mins | colour

Director Lyndon James Swift (Lindsay Shonteff); **Producer** Elizabeth Laurie (Elizabeth Gray, a.k.a. Mrs Shonteff); **Screenplay** Robert Bauer (Lindsay Shonteff). **Starring** Lawrence Day (Lieutenant Young), Luis Manuel (Stress), Thomas M. Pollard (Flak), Christopher Muncke (Captain Hansen).

Vietnam, late 1960s. Having completed one hazardous mission, a platoon of rookie US soldiers are sent back into the jungle by their body count-hungry captain to destroy a village harbouring Viet Cong weapons and supplies. But this time no one makes it back alive.

The late Lindsay Shonteff once told a story of a valuable lesson he took away from working with director William Davidson on a long forgotten Canadian film called *Ivy League Killers* (59), right at the beginning of his career. The crew were watching a couple of incompetent actors thoroughly mangle a scene, and were aghast when Davidson said "Cut! Print it!" Accompanying Davidson in the cutting room a couple of weeks later, Shonteff observed how the director "zapped straight through the take without even looking at it. What he was looking for was a certain reaction from one particular actor. He kept about three feet from a take that ran about three hundred feet... I guess that no one else saw this reaction at the time except him." Shonteff added: "I've had the same kind of experience on just about every film I've made."[1]

It seems to me that this was a particularly bad thing for the impressionable young Shonteff to see. For, with only one or two exceptions, his films serve as evidence that he regularly used *entire takes of crap*, regardless of the final three feet. Perhaps if he was convinced there was some magic in them, you could almost sympathise with him. But Shonteff knew his films, certainly the later ones, were garbage, and yet he continued to make them, each one nearly bankrupting him in the process. For forty years he carried on like this, wading through critical invisibility and public apathy with complete indifference.

What is it that drove Shonteff? There's no question he loved film, and he loved the idea of being a filmmaker. But after what could have been an auspicious start — coming to Britain to direct DEVIL DOLL (64) and *Curse of Simba* (64) while still only in his late twenties, and having a modest hit with *Licensed To Kill* (65), a cheap but cheerful James Bond cash-in — he quickly revealed signs of what became his unwavering inability to distinguish between the vaguely promising and the utterly worthless.

Although he was being courted by Columbia Pictures, Shonteff set off for Hong Kong to make the ludicrous, Frankie Avalon-starring spy romp *The Million Eyes of Su-Muru* (67) for fugitive producer Harry Alan Towers. When he came back, he was surprised to find the Columbia deal had fallen through. So, after a couple more films of varying merit (PERMISSIVE, *The Yes Girls*) he became a one-man production outfit, ploughing his own money into project after project, each of which turned out to be a lame variation on *Licensed To Kill* with added sex and violence: *The Fast Kill* (72), *Big Zapper* (73), *Zapper's Blade of Vengeance* (74), *No. 1 of the Secret Service* (77), *Licensed to Love and Kill* (79). As they went on, they got worse: they play like cheap, jokey coffee commercials, and feature cheap, jokey coffee commercial actors, trussed up in wide-lapelled dinner jackets, delivering third-rate bon mots to semi-naked ladies.

Undeterred by the dismissal of his oeuvre on his own turf, Shonteff took solace from making his films' minimal budgets back from sales to far off territories such as Korea and Japan. He was, at least, in complete control of his projects; being his own man meant he was still working when some of his more talented peers couldn't get arrested. He just wasn't always getting paid.

Perhaps the declarations on the website lindsayshonteff.com (now defunct, last accessed January 2010) held the key to what really fuelled Shonteff:

A director who offered three of his films to the BBC Film Acquisition Dept. — *without even viewing the films they were rejected out of hand...*

A director who turned down a deal related to the purchase of three of his films by ITV because they wanted to make changes to it after a done deal — *they never purchased another film from Shonteff...*

A director who sued the Rank Organisation over a distribution contract concerning one of his films Rank were releasing — *they never distributed another film from Shonteff.*

These quotes were positioned boastfully on Shonteff's home page, but surely to most reasonable eyes they constitute a catalogue of utter failure. The claims went on: 'This maverick of mavericks is a talent that has made twenty-two English feature films, in spite of no support whatever from the British Film Industry and being forced into the film wilderness for twenty-five years.' It seems then that Shonteff looked upon himself as a Skid Row Stanley Kubrick: a maverick, independent North American, controlling his own pictures in Britain, whatever the critical or public reaction.

And this self image is surely best attested to by his attempt to recreate battle-torn Vietnam in England — as Kubrick was to do six years later — in *How Sleep the Brave* (81), one of the true staggering oddities of British Poverty Row cinema.

It's fair to say that the entire budget of *How Sleep the Brave* wouldn't have covered the toilet roll bill on Kubrick's *Full Metal Jacket*. But that's the least thing wrong with the film. If anything, necessity is the mother of invention: restricted to filming just a bus ride away from his home, Shonteff uses the woods and fields of Gerrards Cross, Berkshire, reasonably well to stand in for the lush green badlands of South Vietnam, and at least he appears to have made the film in summertime. (For all *Full Metal Jacket*'s power, Kubrick failed to make south London and Essex look convincingly like Vietnam even with millions of dollars and set designer Anton Furst at his disposal.) Similarly, Shonteff's (rather overzealous) use of stock 'jungle sounds' on the soundtrack serves as another minor distraction when other attempts at verisimilitude break hopelessly down.

But whether you're filming in a forest near the M25 or in a southeast Asian jungle, raiding the local army surplus store for costumes and having your actors run around with toy guns shouting "fuck" a lot is not enough to tell a moving story about the horror of combat. That, at least, takes a degree of storytelling skill. The scenes in *How Sleep the Brave* could almost be viewed in random order, but no amount of shuffling them would relieve the tedium or unveil the point. It is utterly devoid of pacing, narrative flow or emotional engagement. The dialogue comprises a litany of obscene, US army grunt clichés, delivered by actors struggling to sound American. ("We're all animals in this jungle, and it's the meanest motherfucker that's going to survive," growls Captain Hansen in an accent that lies somewhere east of Vancouver and north of Cornwall.) Not one exchange comes anywhere near to being convincing. It's all about as stimulating as a milky drink at bedtime. But don't be fooled into thinking *How Sleep the Brave* is so bad it's funny — it is as close to unwatchable as anything Shonteff ever did.

FILM REVIEWS

To Shonteff's chagrin, the film didn't make his fortune or establish him as an artistic presence. Whatever miniscule reputation *How Sleep the Brave* has in Britain, it gained from adolescent boys who rented it during the early days of home video and were shocked by its copious bad language (which can still raise an eyebrow today — did Shonteff even submit this to the

A rare instance of 'authenticity' in *How Sleep the Brave*.

BBFC?) and bursts of gory violence. By 1990, the director was back yet again to his *Licensed To Kill* shenanigans with *Number One Gun*. He completed a western in 1992 (*The Running Gun*) but couldn't sell it anywhere, and then suffered a decade of inactivity.

Shonteff was never shy to apportion blame for his films' failings; it was often the fault of the ubiquitous, party-pooping 'they' — "They just didn't get behind it" (on the Rank Organisation and *Zapper's Blade of Vengeance*); "They cut every one of these funny scenes out of the picture... they thought I was a madman" (on the distributors of *The Million Eyes of Su-Muru*);[2] "They printed the wrong screening room, the wrong theatre, the wrong day. So nobody saw the film" (on the organisers of the Cannes Film Festival, where Shonteff had arranged a screening of *The Running Gun*) — or on his perennial lack of funds. But, for the most part, Shonteff was answerable only to himself, so the 'them and me' excuse could wear a bit thin. And, as far as the sunken budgets were concerned, well, as we've charted throughout this book, cheap movies just don't have to be this bad.

Shonteff died in 2006, 'on the last day of filming' a US movie, *Angels, Devils and Men*, his website ominously (and perhaps a little fictitiously) pointed out. (This straight-to-video, tongue-in-cheek opus emerged on DVD in 2009; I haven't had the resolve to seek it out.) He was seventy-years-old — the same age as Stanley Kubrick was when he died, as the official announcement had it, just days after 'finishing' *Eyes Wide Shut*.

Julian Upton

---

1   Interview with Lindsay Shonteff, '*Last Of The Independents*,' *The Dark Side*, July 1993.
2   Ibid.

Parts of this article first appeared in *Bright Light Film Journal* (July 2001).

THE PLAGUE DOGS (1982)

Nepenthe Productions/Rowf Films/United Artists | 103 mins/86 mins | colour

Director/Producer/Screenplay Martin Rosen, from the novel by Richard Adams. **Voices of** John Hurt (Snitter), Christopher Benjamin (Rowf), James Bolam (The tod), Nigel Hawthorne, Dandy Nichols, Patrick Stewart, Bernard Hepton, Bill Maynard, Judy Geeson, Rosemary Leach.

After a chance escape from an animal testing laboratory in the Lake District, two dogs, Rowf, a labrador, and Snitter, a terrier, take refuge in the Cumbrian fells. Befriending a canny fox, the dogs begin to fend for themselves. But their trail of ravaged sheep alarms the local farming community, and speculation mounts that they are carrying a plague bred at the research centre. Soon, the dogs are being hunted at every turn.

Watership Down (78), the animated film based on Richard Adams' 1972 bestseller, was a labour of love for its Canadian producer Martin Rosen, but so beset by problems that few people expected it to be the runaway success it became. Rosen struggled for years to raise the cash to make it, eventually accepting investment outside the film industry from a consortium of UK financiers. Then, his chosen director, the American animator John Hubley, died only a few months into production. Rosen considered scrapping the project before being convinced to assume the directorial duties himself, albeit very anxiously (he had never directed a short film before, let alone an animated feature).

When the time came to record the *Watership* score he'd commissioned from Malcolm Williamson, Rosen found that the eminent composer had left only five minutes of music before disappearing on another assignment. Angela Morley was hastily recruited, and wrote the rest of the score in a matter of weeks. Mike Batt was also brought in to supply some songs, one of which, Bright Eyes, was chosen to feature.

When the film was finished, Rosen couldn't get a distribution deal. Eventually securing a limited run in five top London cinemas, he and his investors had to stump up for their own prints and advertising.

But *Watership Down* the movie caught on. Word of mouth was strong — perhaps because adults who'd loved the book wanted their children to experience the tale — and business was amplified when Bright Eyes, sung by one Art Garfunkel, went on to become the biggest selling UK single of 1979. By the end of that year, the film was cleaning up, not just in Britain but around the world.

ESCAPE TO A DIFFERENT WORLD...
AND SHARE THE ADVENTURE OF A LIFETIME.

NEPENTHE PRODUCTIONS PRESENTS
MARTIN ROSEN'S FILM OF

The Plague Dogs

A SPECIAL KIND OF MOVIE MAGIC FROM THE
CREATORS OF 'WATERSHIP DOWN'

From the novel by RICHARD ADAMS
Music composed by PATRICK GLEESON "Time and Tide" composed and sung by ALAN PRICE
Production Design GORDON HARRISON Directors of Animation TONY GUY and COLIN WHITE
Written for the screen, Produced and Directed by MARTIN ROSEN Color by CFI Soundtrack released by Columbia Records.

Snitter approaches the dead bounty hunter. *The Plague Dogs.*

It was inevitable that Rosen (and his investors) would want to recapture that success, especially as there had emerged, during *Watership Down*'s lengthy production, a new Richard Adams novel, *The Plague Dogs*. A searing indictment of vivisection wrapped in a gripping adventure of two laboratory dogs who escape to the fells of the Lake District, the new novel was just as powerful and poignant as the first book.

Accordingly, Rosen's *Plague Dogs* amplifies *Watership Down*'s savagery, retaining — even enhancing — all the harshness of the original novel, and then some. Rosen even sacrifices a happy, if ambiguous, ending for a distinctly downbeat one. Any negative reaction, such as there was, to *Watership Down* tended to focus on how it could disturb its young audience, but *The Plague Dogs* takes things a step further: few mainstream cartoon features have made so few concessions to the genre of the 'family movie' or to the cathartic comforts of Disney-style anthropomorphism.

The vision of the research animals' plight is uncomfortable and cheerless, but it's also brave and uncompromising. These dogs may be able to talk to each other (rather incongruously, like the rabbits in *Watership Down*, with somewhat cultivated accents), but they very much remain animals: they tear hungrily at bloody sheep carcasses, they gnaw and scratch themselves, they dig pitifully at the ground when their situation seems hopeless. Like Halas and Batchelor's ANIMAL FARM, there is a strong resistance to 'cute' here, and the effects can be vivid, such as when Snitter unintentionally kills a welcoming man by standing on the trigger of his shotgun, or when the starving dogs are seen to have fed on the body of a bounty hunter who has fallen to his death from a crag (a shot cut from later prints, along with seventeen minutes of other footage). And it wouldn't be a stretch to call the climax, when the weakened dogs swim towards 'their island,' emotionally devastating.

So, if anything, it's all a little too much. The atmosphere of *The Plague Dogs* is one of overwhelming pessimism. After watching it for the first time, young children aren't about to go buzzing out into the garden following a few moments of naïve contemplation; they're more likely to stare silently into space, nursing the angry seeds of an ambition to crusade violently for animal rights. Or considering putting a plastic bag over their heads.

Ultimately, *Watership Down* and *The Plague Dogs* can only offer faithful but crude distillations of Adams' tales. The novels aspire to the literary epic, as opposed to the simple 'children's book'; ninety-minute cartoons can never really do them justice (just as Ralph Bakshi's noble but doomed cartoon adaptation of *Lord of the Rings* — released at the same time as *Watership Down* — failed to do much justice to Tolkien's tale). What we get instead is a potent concentration of the powerful scenes, but without any of their texture and playfulness. Adams' *Plague Dogs* has touches of comic relief, even crude satire (the Animal Research, Scientific and Experimental facility's acronym, for example), but there is no time for this in the film. The only whiffs of humour come from James Bolam's lovingly voiced fox, 'the tod,' whose chipper sagacity and devious appeal capture the lighter tones of the book. But even he ends up throttled by hunting dogs.

Still, there's no arguing that the novel's message about the cold cruelty of nature and man's brutality to his fellow mammals is trenchantly delivered. Indeed, Rosen's *The Plague Dogs* is as powerful an anti-vivisection statement as burning down a drug company boss's holiday home.

Julian Upton

WHO DARES WINS (1982)

a.k.a. The Final Option | Richmond Light Horse Productions/Various Entertainment Trading/Rank | 125 mins | colour

Director Ian Sharp; **Producer** Euan Lloyd; **Screenplay** Reginald Rose, based on an original story by George Markstein. **Starring** Lewis Collins (Peter Skellen), Judy Davis (Frankie Leith), Richard Widmark (Arthur Currie), Edward Woodward (Commander Powell).

Apparently dismissed from the SAS after allegations of brutality against visiting soldiers, Captain Peter Skellen has in fact been assigned to infiltrate a peace organisation that may have terrorist connections. Gaining the trust — and bedroom favours — of Frankie, its nominal leader, Skellen soon discovers that the People's Lobby may pose a greater threat than originally thought.

> **"Hood 'em up!"**

I f it had been made in a previous decade, *Who Dares Wins* might now be considered an exploitation classic. The wily producers earned their percentage in the standard fashion by first identifying an occurrence of great public interest, and then thoroughly exploiting it. The six-day Iranian Embassy siege instigated by terrorists in April/May 1980 was brought to a sudden, unexpected end by the appearance — seemingly from nowhere — of silent, black-clad soldiers: the Special Air Service, or SAS as they became more popularly known. Leaving seven dead in their wake, the anonymous force suddenly found themselves in the public spotlight, thanks mainly to riveting television coverage of the assault. Camera crews had descended on South Kensington quicker than it took then-Prime Minister Margaret Thatcher to crack a smile behind her empirical desk...

These were grim times for fair Albion. 1982 saw the Falklands War begin and end, *Boys from the Blackstuff* made its groundbreaking, yet depressing, debut on BBC2, and the Protect and Survive leaflet became available to the general public, coldly informing parents and children what to do with deceased family members after a nuclear conflict. The country needed heroes, men who kicked the door in, shot first, and then asked questions to whoever could string a few lines of English together later.

Enter Lewis Collins and Ian Sharp, both fresh — as star and director — from LWT's *The Professionals*, leaping from one covert organisation to another. An ideal vehicle for the woefully underused Collins, *Who Dares Wins* cast him as Captain Peter Skellen (definitely not to be confused with the similarly monikered easy listening singer/pianist), an ice-cool SAS killing machine

recruited by the government to infiltrate a sub-CND organisation called the People's Lobby after one of their number is murdered by a crossbow through the mouth on a protest march.

For Skellen, the view of the world is beautifully simple: you are either a decent citizen or a hippy bastard. Impeccably suited, with a little-seen wife and daughter posted in Westminster's exclusive Bathurst Mews, he's a two-sugars-in-coffee man who considers the American and German armed forces inferior to his own maverick brand of combat. We first see him at training camp, a place run on the choreography of death — near-ballet poses over roofs, dancing through windows — berating the failure of yet another bunch of trainees. How his superiors expect him to get in with the People's Lobby is never explained, especially as it is run by nervy Judy Davis and everyman socialist foil John Duttine. But Skellen charms his way there with lines such as "I know more about nuclear devastation than you ever will," and goes above and beyond the call of duty by attending appalling performance art shows that attempt to be a cross between *A Clockwork Orange* and *Breaking Glass*. Later on, he even accompanies the conquered Frankie to a gig at the Union Chapel, Islington, where a proggish new wave band are playing (its members a mash-up of actual Fairport Convention/Jethro Tull musicians); easy work to a man who thinks nothing of evading pursuers by jumping onto moving pleasure boats or off speeding double-decker buses.

Armed and dangerous. Lewis Collins, *Who Dares Wins*.

But all this is merely foreplay to what the audience really wants: *an exact replication of the Iranian Embassy siege*. In *Who Dares Wins*, the US Embassy takes the flak, with members of the People's Lobby getting through the door on the stolen uniforms and instruments of a busload of service musicians, with a vague plan in action to fire a nuclear missile at a submarine base. Enter the crowd-pleasing black-clad abseilers, and the chance for Captain Skellen to show his true colours to Frankie and terminate their relationship, with extreme prejudice.

The climax also ushers in Richard Widmark as the US Secretary of State. Here Widmark becomes another recipient of the Sterling Hayden Award for Confused American Actor Cameos in British Films, there to lend gravitas and credibility in exchange for a day's work and a week's pay. But in the end he's just one of a short line of distinguished actors overshadowed by Lewis Collins' brute force. Despite being fourth billed, Edward Woodward appears to have little to do, stuck in an office away from the action. Future TV wine expert Oz Clarke emerges briefly as a Special Branch officer. As for Ingrid Pitt, her role as a hydrogen cyanide gas-injecting assassin seems out of place even in this film, and she wears the same facial expression throughout, the one that in subsequent years will guide her through the Faustian torment of countless film conventions, framed by those glossy Hammer stills of an eternally younger self...

If the end of the film is ambiguous, and suggestive that the 'good guys' are merely pawns in a greater game, then the actual message of *Who Dares Wins* is extremely clear cut: the SAS are an invisible killing machine, and nuclear war is a very real threat that will destroy all humanity. Appropriately, a minor role is played by Patrick Allen, death-bell voice of the Protect and Survive adverts. *Who Dares Wins* captures the zeitgeist like a marine's hands around the throat of a jelly-spined foreigner, and probably says more about the state of Thatcher's Britain in 1982 than anything written by Alan Bleasdale.

"Live bastards! Dead soldiers!"

Martin Jones

FILM REVIEWS

THE BOYS IN BLUE (1982)

Elstree Production Company/Apollo Leisure Group/MAM Ltd./Rank Organisation | 87 mins | colour

Director Val Guest; **Producer** Gregory Smith; **Screenplay** Sid Colin and Val Guest, based on the original story *Ask a Policeman* by Sidney Gilliat. **Starring** Tommy Cannon (Sgt. Cannon), Bobby Ball (PC Ball), Suzanne Danielle (Kim), Jon Pertwee, Eric Sykes.

Sgt. Cannon and Constable Ball of Little Botham police station find their jobs under threat due to a lack of local crime. Salvation comes in the shape of a gang of art thieves led by local working class-boy-done-good Lloyd, but their capture is of course far from simple.

The 1970s and early eighties saw a slew of largely unfortunate forays into film territory by established British sitcoms: *Dad's Army* (71), THE LOVERS! (72), *Love Thy Neighbour* (73), *Are You Being Served?* (77), and so on. All transferred an already flagging concept to the big screen in the mistaken belief that feature films were the perfect showcase for the talents of their small-screen stars. Such a project was less than straightforward for a comedy act like Cannon and Ball, whose television efforts lacked the stock characters or established jokes that *Dad's Army* or *Porridge* had to their advantage.

Cannon and Ball met whilst working in an Oldham factory, quickly establishing themselves as popular club entertainers as well as the clowns of the shop floor, frequently reprimanded for their spontaneous tomfoolery. Changing their original name — The Harper Brothers — to the catchier Cannon and Ball, their success began to seep beyond the environs of Manchester as they moved into television and appeared on *Opportunity Knocks* and *The Wheeltappers and Shunters Social Club*. Their self-titled television show first aired in

A master of comic timing. And Cannon and Ball. *The Boys In Blue.*

1979 and attracted very respectable viewing figures. Even so, the duo leapt at the chance to expand offered to them by *Boys in Blue* producer Gregory Smith. "I saw them on television some two and a half years ago and thought them unique," he said at the time.[1] Having previously worked with the distinguished director Val Guest, Smith chose him to steer the Cannon and Ball project.

By this time, Guest's career had slowed down somewhat, though in his heyday he had worked with comedy greats such as Ronnie Corbett, Peter Sellers and Frankie Howerd (as well as delivering some assured films in many other genres). He had also co-written the script for Will Hay's *Oh, Mr Porter!* (37) and *Ask a Policeman* (39), the latter being exploited for *The Boys in Blue*, which serves effectively as a remake.

The link to the great Will Hay, however, fails to help *The Boys in Blue*. *Ask a Policeman* told the story of three inept country policeman (Hay and his regular stooges Graham Moffatt and Moore Marriott), whose half-hearted policing efforts are interrupted by the activities of a local smuggling ring. Not quite a scene for scene remake — Marriott's quaint shop has been replaced with a rather decrepit mini-market and the smuggler's ruse of a headless horseman has been replaced with rumours of alien spacecraft (inexplicably, a car with a red flashing light attached to the roof which surely, even in deepest rural Cornwall, would have fooled nobody) — *Boys in Blue* nonetheless closely follows the template of the earlier film. And by invoking comparison, it comes up severely short. It's cheap looking and flatly made, but these flaws pale into insignificance next to the standard of acting. Cannon and Ball's amateur dramatics may have been enough to breathe life into a ten-minute sketch, but assuming that Tommy Cannon could play Will Hay's part with the same panache is nothing short of slanderous. *Ask a Policeman*'s Marriott and Moffatt characters are rolled into one in the diminutive figure of Bobby Ball — 'the dumb one' next to Cannon's authoritative and self important Sergeant — and he is reasonably convincing in this role. But even Ball can't make Cannon any less excruciating to watch: he has all the flair of a rigid child in a school pantomime. He's not helped by his broad Lancashire accent, which imbues the role with none of the gravitas Hay's clipped schoolmaster tones invariably did.

Elsewhere, there is the promise of some improvement, with Jon Pertwee as the lighthouse keeper and Eric Sykes as the local Chief Constable. Both put in perfectly respectable turns, though Sykes seems distinctly uncomfortable — no doubt mindful of the embarrassing debacle he is participating in. There's also an appearance by Suzanne Danielle, darling of British studios at the time, with appearances on *The Morecambe and Wise Show* and the lead in *Carry*

On Emmannuelle (78) to her credit; she stands out as one of the most competent players in the film.

The Boys in Blue is a warning to future generations of the inherent danger in remaking films whose central charm lies in their often coincidental pairing of actor and era, inseparable from their contemporary context. Cannon and Ball didn't seem to learn from their mistake: a few years later, they gave us six episodes of a dire sitcom, *Plaza Patrol*, which drew strongly on the *Boys in Blue* formula. (Here they were shopping precinct security guards whose watches are filled with all manner of unbelievable dramas, although much of each twenty-five minute episode saw them engaging in domestic squabbles about which tin the tea should be kept in.) Since then the duo has famously found God (releasing books with titles like *The Gospel According to Cannon and Ball*).[2] So perhaps now all is forgiven.

Jennifer Wallis

---

1   From the Cannon and Ball 1983 Spring Tour Programme. Reproduced at *Comedy Kings*, an unofficial Cannon and Ball website, http://www.comedykings.co.uk/index.php/film/articles-and-reviews [Last accessed January 2010].

2   Bobby Ball, Tommy Cannon and Chris Gidney, *The Gospel According to Cannon and Ball* (Norwich: Canterbury Press, 2007).

G.B.H. GRIEVOUS BODILY HARM (1983)

I.R. Productions | 73 mins | colour (video)

Director David Kent-Watson; **Producers** Cliff Twemlow, David Kent-Watson; **Screenplay** Cliff Twemlow. **Starring** Cliff Twemlow (Steve Donovan), Anthony Shaeffer (Murray), Jerry Harris (Keller), Brett Sinclair (Chris), Jane Cunliffe (Tracy), Lenny Howarth (Connor), Steve Powell (Gregg).

Legendary hard man Steve Donovan is hired by the Zoo discothèque as protection when gang boss Keller tries to muscle in on the Manchester club scene. Donovan, a.k.a. 'the Mancunian,' is handy with his fists and with the ladies, and he betters Keller's goons every time. The violence accelerates until a final bloody shootout leaves Keller's empire in disarray. But Donovan's fate is also sealed at the end of a policeman's gun barrel.

"He can have the house in Bury," offers Murray, the owner of the Zoo discothèque — if Steve Donovan will agree to work the door he can have it. Fresh out of Strangeways prison, Donovan takes the job and soon enough the fists are flying. The movie is barely five minutes old by the time the second punch up is over. These fight scenes are a counterbalance to the soppy sequins of the disco dancefloor, which sparkle every ten minutes in a lamentable love scene; they are brutal and edgy, and give the film the character sorely lacking in the flat, if spirited, acting. That said, Jerry Harris, who plays the evil gang boss encroaching on Manchester club life, does a reasonable turn at mimicking Bob Hoskins, which encouraged the distributor to draw a comparison with *The Long Good Friday* when marketing the movie.

G.B.H. Grievous Bodily Harm is one of the first British productions shot on video. Unlike the other films discussed in this book it was never intended for theatrical release, but rather the home video market, where it had moderate success. Due to the reluctance of major studios to commit to the fledging technology, the formative days of home video were dominated by entrepreneurs quick to feed a public eager for product of any stripe. Exploitation films that hadn't a hope in hell of gracing a British cinema screen were catapulted into the nation's living rooms. Step forward *G.B.H.* According to director David Kent-Watson, *G.B.H.* sold 9,000 copies within six months of its release (on the World of Video 2000 label) and reached number nine on the video rental charts. Part of the appeal lay in the blood and action it offered, which was in excess of anything being broadcast by the television networks. Another part lay in the kitsch value and the tart, eminently quotable dialogue ("I'll smash the bastard!" being a typical example). Ironically for a home entertainment medium, a thriving social network evolved around

FILM REVIEWS

BOUNCER WITH PLENTY OF BOTTLE

JULIE DAVIES
visits a
film set in
Patricroft

Cliff Twemlow, right, attacks actor Charles Cassar in a scene from "The Mancunian". Filmgoers will see blood spurt up from the direction of Charles's mouth. But in fact the "blood" is made from an insect and is squirted from a washing-up liquid bottle by a woman crouching below.

THE Rainbow Rooms, like any other nightclub, is the scene of the occasional scuffle if an awkward customer has perhaps had too much to drink.

But the club has never experienced anything like the scenes there for three days the other week.

A man stood at the bar with blood pouring from his head while another pushed a glass into his skull.

Bullets splattered into the back wall of the club and numerous brawls took place.

But it must be explained that these incidents were scenes being shot for a film — a film which is to have its world premier at the Rainbow Rooms.

It is to be called "The Mancunian" and the script and music were written by its star, former night-club bouncer Cliff Twemlow who grew up in Peel Green Road, Peel Green.

Cliff, a former pupil at Godfrey Truman C of E School, admits that the film is "slightly autobiographical" in that the hero Steve Donavan is also a bouncer.

Donavan's life is at times by necessity violent. And indeed Cliff has had his fair share of the life which he terms in his autobiography as that of "the Tuxedo Warrior".

But Cliff vehemently denies that the film is unnecessarily violent.

"The violence is an integral part of the film" he told the Journal.

"It is realistic. These things happen in life — a lot of these things have happened to me".

Indeed, in the book, "The Tuxedo Warrior" Cliff describes having a broken bottle driven into his groin in a club in Glasgow a fate which befalls Archie Waterhouse, of Rake Lane, Clifton in the film.

When asked whether he hopes the film will be a success Cliff replies: "I don't hope it will be a success, I know it will be".

This will be Cliff's third film. His first was a screen version of "The Tuxedo Warrior" which is currently on show in America.

This was followed by "The Pike", a freshwater version of Jaws which involves the tale of a killer pike. This is due to be released in this country next year.

Cliff said that "The Mancunian" cost £¼ million to make and has been financed by Swedish multi-millionaire Ingemar Rydstrom — hence the name of the company is IR Films.

He emphasises that Mr Rydstrom is a man of considerable business skill.

He is involved in areas as diverse as road haulage and cosmetics and Cliff points out that Mr Rydstrom owns six Rolls Royces, a yacht valued at £1 million at Cannes in the south of France, 100 acres of land in Sweden, and homes in Spain, America and at Hale, Manchester.

"I met him when I was on the door at a club he used to frequent.

"I talked to him and he said that he thought I was out of place there and that I was destined for better things.

"He knows that this is going to be the start of something big".

The film concerns Donavan's attempts to rid a night-club, which will keep the name of the Rainbow Rooms, of a gangland London mafia — a subject which is close to Cliff's heart.

When someone commented that it made a change to have a film set away from London, Cliff replied: "London where's that?"

"Our aim is to set up a film industry in the Manchester area. Why shouldn't films be set in the Eccles area?" he asked.

"I can remember when Barton Bridge was the eighth wonder of the world —people used to flock here from miles around to see it.

"This is an area of great historical interest — so why shouldn't we make films here?

"This is my town and people like Eric Hale here at the Rainbow Rooms are my kind of people.

"This film is not an ego trip — it is for the people of this area".

Cliff describes "The Mancunian" as being a combination of the Humphrey Bogart film "Casablanca", "Every Which You Can", which star-

red Clint Eastwood and "Streetfighter" which starred Charles Bronson.

He says that Donavan is a loser like each of these characters. He is also a great fighter and a great lover.

He has three affairs in the film before he meets a sophisticated girl who according to Cliff fall sfor his "animal-like instincts".

She tires to tame him and for a while it works — but he reverts to his former self.

And what of the future? Already Cliff has plans for a book of "The Mancunian" to be published.

In addition, he has four more films to be made. They will be called "Dogs of Kane", about a pack of wild dogs; a martial arts film called "Return Me A Man"; a love story called "Twilight of the Gods", and his next film, "Samson was a Jew", a story of a man with great strength.

Cliff now plans to devote his career entirely to films.

He has come a long way since his first job as an apprentice projectionist at the Princes Cinema, Monton.

He recalled in "The Tuxedo Warrior" that this career reached a premature end when he took it upon himself to re-organise the show when the chief projectionist retired for a pint.

"In omitting the news and adverts and only presenting the beginning and end reel of the main feature, a bewildered audience found themselves vacating the premises by 9.15 p.m. — they weren't admitted before 8.15 p.m. not even time for their choc ices."

Film industry in Eccles?

video, thanks to video parties, video rental stores and fan publications, through which *G.B.H.* and films like it managed to acquire cult status.

G.B.H. is a prime example of a cheaply shot, independent film that avoids the traditional means of production and distribution to find its place in a new market. But it is not possible to talk about *G.B.H.* without talking foremost about renaissance man Cliff Twemlow, the film's star, writer, co-producer, stunt coordinator and (under a pseudonym) composer. Born in Hulme, Manchester, in 1937, Cliff Twemlow's career encompassed everything from lifeguard, fairground boxer, labourer in an asbestos factory, through to later years as a nightclub doorman who occasionally doubled as a crooner. He maintained a strict keep fit regime that served him well as a jobbing extra and later in his film roles. He was the creative brains on nine films (which include some that

remain unfinished), working with micro budgets, supported by a repertory cast and crew. He was also a published author (one of his horror novels, *The Beast of Kane*, was rejected by Hammer) and a composer of some 2,000 tunes, among them popular TV themes.

In 1973, Twemlow and his record company Indigo were served an injunction by Paul McCartney. Live And Let Die, a song composed by Twemlow and performed by jazz singer Selena Jones, was a James Bond cash-in but otherwise not related to the film or McCartney's theme of that name. Despite reaching Terry Wogan's coveted 'record of the week' slot on BBC Radio 2, Live And Let Die had to be withdrawn at a huge loss to Twemlow and Indigo. But it was not an incident to faze him. Twemlow would convince the owner of Indigo, David Kent-Watson, to collaborate with him on *G.B.H.* some years later.

G.B.H. has its origins in Twemlow's autobiography, *Tuxedo Warrior*, published in 1981. The book was the subject of an earlier film adaptation, *Tuxedo Warrior* (82), which boasted professional production values. It was directed by Andrew Sinclair, perhaps better acquainted with the work of Richard Burton and Oliver Reed. Twemlow was unhappy: he had a bit part in his own movie and no creative control. Furthermore, the grim Manchester backdrop was relocated to Zimbabwe. Twemlow may not have liked it, but he took from the film invaluable experience and on his return to England quickly set in motion *G.B.H.*, a film closer to the original spirit of *Tuxedo Warrior*.

Cliff Twemlow died in 1993. He made no secret of his admiration for Hollywood actor Charles Bronson, with whom he shares a cinematic camaraderie in *G.B.H.* (and name-checks him twice). But in terms of homage, Bronson is second billing to the city of Manchester, whose presence throughout resonates like one of Donovan's punch-ups. A house in Bury may not be the most glamorous offer in the world, but it says a lot about the cheaply shot, down-at-heel approach of Twemlow.

G.B.H. Grievous Bodily Harm gave rise to a new age of truly independent filmmaking. Unfortunately the very medium that helped to establish these films also sank them. The Video Recordings Act of 1984 was introduced to curb the sex and violence hitherto unchecked on video, making it unlawful for any film to be released without a BBFC certificate. *G.B.H.*, never having been submitted for classification, remains unavailable in any legitimate home entertainment format in Britain, or anywhere else for that matter.

David Kerekes

SOURCE C P Lee and Andy Willis, *The Lost World of Cliff Twemlow: The King of Manchester Exploitation Movies* (Manchester: Hotun Press, 2009).

Terence Stamp and John Hurt in *The Hit*.

THE HIT (1984)

Central Productions, Zenith Productions, Recorded Picture Co. | 98 mins | colour

Director Stephen Frears; **Producers** Jeremy Thomas, Joyce Herlihy; **Screenplay** Peter Prince. **Starring** John Hurt (Braddock), Terence Stamp (Willie Parker), Tim Roth (Myron), Laura del Sol (Maggie), Bill Hunter (Harry), Fernando Rey (senior policeman), Lennie Peters (Corrigan).

Gangster Willie Parker turns supergrass on his former partners in crime and puts them in prison. Ten years later, living in Spain, he is kidnapped by Mr Braddock and Myron, two bungling hit men hired by the men he put away. Along with a beautiful girl that gets embroiled in their plans, they all embark on a violent, semi-philosophical and blackly comical road trip back to England.

Sixteen years before Jonathan Glazer's *Sexy Beast* (2000) used the 'Costa del Crime' as the backdrop to the best British crime flick of the noughties, Stephen Frears took the dusty heat and drenched blue skies of Spain as the setting for a film that somehow seems to have got lost amidst his later, more celebrated mainstream movie career.

After a modicum of early success with the likeable *Gumshoe* (71), Frears eschewed the big screen and spent the majority of the 1970s and early 1980s directing chunks of television drama for BBC and ITV. He only switched back to the big screen when, by his own admission, he felt "mature enough to understand how to make films and connect with that audience." His absence was no doubt also due to the paucity of opportunities available for British filmmakers wanting to make serious films in the 1970s.

The hitman and her: John Hurt and Laura del Sol. *The Hit.*

Either way, with *The Hit*, he returned with a smart piece of storytelling set among the lazy Spanish hills and backed by a soundtrack of soft flamenco guitar by Paco de Lucia. It starts in London, with Willie Parker (Terence Stamp) looking dapper in court and sending his former friends, led by Corrigan (Lennie Peters), down for a taste of porridge. Parker is taken out of court to start his life of immunity in Spain, to the cheery strains of the villains singing: "We'll meet again, don't know where, don't know when..."

Flash forward ten years, and Parker is shocked out of his quiet life when he is kidnapped by a gang of locals that 'sell' him on to Mr Braddock (John Hurt) and Myron (Tim Roth), two hit men sent by the newly released Corrigan to bring Parker to Paris to be killed off. The swap over of Parker to Braddock and Myron comes at a price for the Spanish accomplices, and an innocent abandoned shoe, shown in stark close-up, becomes the first of a series of telling mistakes that sets up the premise for the road trip and subsequent police chase.

As the mercurial Braddock, Hurt stays just the right side of caricature as the sunglasses-wearing, laconic old professional. In his feature film debut, Roth gives Myron a bright-eyed and bushy-tailed air of mild psychosis. He is the novice shooter learning the ropes, packing a cosh alongside plenty of hardman trash talk. Although on his way to his almost certain death, Parker is serene and curiously Zen-like. He has resigned himself to his fate."I have

been waiting ten years for this moment," he tells a cheerless Braddock at one point. "Death is just a stage in the journey — as natural as breathing." He is also the experienced old criminal, who tries to let the increasingly inept Myron know that he might not be the only one that will meet his maker at the end of the journey.

The road trip soon becomes a tortuous affair. After making a detour to Madrid before heading to France, they drop in on what they think is an empty safe house. Inside they find Harry (Bill Hunter), a twitchy old Australian lag and his Spanish girlfriend Maggie, who are in the wrong place at the wrong time. This is an unwanted complication that Braddock has to unpick. After some deliberation, he decides that he has to 'take care' of Harry and take Maggie along for the ride.

The addition of Maggie leads to Braddock and Myron (who is now developing an unhelpful conscience), squabbling about what to do with her. Although Maggie is drawn into the mix, the main focus of the film is the spiky relationship between Braddock, Myron and Parker. Both hit men are dumbfounded by Parker, who is taking his imminent demise with an angelic grace. He has little regard for his fate. Braddock is quietly seething at why Parker is not terrified. Myron is too dumb to bother understanding. After he kills a petrol attendant, it's clear that Braddock's violence is leading quickly to everybody's downfall. At every mistake, the group is closely followed by the Spanish police, led by veteran Fernando Rey, who gain ground on them in a strangely silent, almost mime-like manner. Their role seems to be a creeping full stop, waiting to inevitably end the journey for good.

Still, there is a downbeat ending that you don't really see coming. Instead of a redemptive conclusion or some reflective universal truth, this 'road' movie actually leads nowhere — which is uncommonly refreshing. There is no salvation, only pointlessness to everyone's actions.

Despite some obtuse musings on life and death and a subtle touch of black comedy, there is nothing overly complicated about *The Hit*. Enjoyable throughout, it is elevated by the energetic Roth (who picked up a BAFTA for Most Outstanding Newcomer to Film), Hurt's sneering Braddock and the forever charismatic Terence Stamp. Despite these performances, some gorgeous Spanish scenery and a twangy title track written and performed by Eric Clapton, *The Hit*, sadly, didn't live up to its name at the box office. Shameful.

Gary Ramsay

WILD GEESE II (1985)

Frontier Films/Thorn EMI | 125 mins | colour

Director Peter Hunt; **Producer** Euan Lloyd; **Screenplay** Reginald Rose, based on the novel *The Square Circle* by Daniel Carney. **Starring** Scott Glenn (John Haddad), Barbara Carrera (Kathy Lukas), Edward Fox (Alex Faulkner), Laurence Olivier (Rudolf Hess).

Mercenary John Haddad is hired to spring the ageing Nazi war criminal Rudolf Hess from Spandau prison for the purpose of a TV interview. Haddad assembles a crack team, but is hindered by various government and political factions, each with a vested interest in the most closely guarded prisoner in the world. Ultimately the operation is a success but Haddad reneges on the deal, allowing Hess to return to prison where he might live out his life in peace.

At the core of both *The Wild Geese* (78) and its follow up *Wild Geese II* are soldiers for hire engaged in an increasingly desperate mission. But where *The Wild Geese* is set against the panoramic expanse of Africa, with a top cast that includes Richard Burton, Roger Moore and Richard Harris, by comparison *Wild Geese II* is a misfire, with none of the budget, a fraction of the star appeal and a rather drab Berlin on the verge of rain replacing the tropical skies.

To understand how it came to fall so heavily from grace, we must appreciate that the original *Wild Geese* is a film beloved by many Brits,[1] in the vein of, say, *Zulu* — another 'last stand' picture that begat an idiot sibling.

Directed by Andrew V. McLaglen, *The Wild Geese* was itself a reworking of an earlier British picture, *The Mercenaries* (a.k.a. *Dark of the Sun* [68]) starring Rod Taylor. It tells the story of a band of mercenaries brought out of retirement to free a humanist leader in Rhodesia, but when confronted with a double cross they must face greater odds than anticipated. If *The Wild Geese* didn't exactly return its lauded veteran cast to their halcyon days it was at least a move in the right direction for Burton and Harris, whose careers had taken a very public pounding from booze and a succession of lacklustre performances in forgettable roles. As a result the film opened to a critical sigh of relief. Box office was good, despite a campaign protesting the fact it had been made in apartheid South Africa. (The protests began with the London premiere and filtered down the provinces, through to Bury near Manchester, where this author saw *The Wild Geese*. A small group had gathered outside the Odeon in the town centre to hand out flyers advising people to boycott the film: 'DO NOT FEED THESE WILD GEESE.' I recall that in this instance the

glorification of mercenary activity was also a cause for concern.)

Substituting the African president of *The Wild Geese* with Nazi war criminal Rudolf Hess, incarcerated in Spandau Prison, Berlin, *Wild Geese II* delivers a wholly different set of characters. This hadn't been the plan: Richard Burton was intending to reprise his role as a hard-nosed, hard-drinking Colonel, when his untimely demise necessitated some on-the-fly changes for fear the project would lose its financial backing.

THEY FLY AGAIN!

WILD GEESE II

Originally published as THE SQUARE CIRCLE

DANIEL CARNEY

It's difficult to know what Burton may have done for the movie (the sly poster art makes it look as if he's still in it). Top billing goes to American actor Scott Glenn, who plays Haddad, the mercenary in charge of springing Hess for the purpose of a television interview. It's a deadpan performance but one that selflessly accommodates the gregarious Edward Fox as Faulkner, in the role planned for Burton, a crack British soldier who is Haddad's minder and by contrast devours each scene with relish.

Fox's stiff upper lip is a joy, but Barbara Carrera is shoehorned in with nothing to do. Her appearance with Fox in the Bond movie *Never Say Never Again* was evidently enough of a draw to relegate poor Sir Laurence Olivier to

the bottom of the bill. Olivier is the Nazi war criminal Hess, and he portrays him as a man of quiet nobility, convinced that the TV interview is pointless and that his words are unlikely to change anything in the world for better or worse. Olivier gives the expected measured performance, but it's curiously off pitch in this otherwise unassuming adventure yarn, arriving too late to serve any purpose anyway.

Hess is an old man, whose abominable crimes are already sinking in the snowdrifts of time. And here is part of the problem: the closest the movie gets to a 'real' enemy is a late addition to Haddad's own team by the name of Hourigan (Derek Thompson). The mean-spirited Hourigan is a member of the IRA, whose skills don't extend much beyond a knack for being unlikeable. In one scene he deliberately feeds the wrong drugs to a feverish Faulkner, before goading him on to a bad acid trip. The incident exasperates already frayed relations between the Irishman and the rest of the team, and by extension the viewer; the presence of this "dirty, filthy IRA scum" — one of the epithets levelled at Hourigan — would fan memories and fears of the mainland bombing campaign carried out by the Irish Republican Army since the late sixties. Hourigan is a cynical addition to *Wild Geese II*, arriving only to stir up some casual racism before his premature departure at the end of a British gun barrel, having hurled one too many insults about the Queen.

Wild Geese II suffers by its association with the fondly remembered original movie and the esteem with which that veteran star cast is held. As a sequel, *Wild Geese II* arrived almost a decade too late anyway, being pipped to the post by an Italian cash-in, Antonio Margheriti's *Codename: Wild Geese* (84).

But back we must go to Rudolf Hess. Where *The Wild Geese* was driven by the ignoble institutions of greed and shady government, the sequel has a conceit so preposterous it almost becomes an entertainment in itself: springing Hess for an interview on TV. Towards the end of the movie, the most feared of the Nazi war criminals, played by the most distinguished British theatrical knight, is smuggled away from Spandau and out of Berlin in the guise of a drunken football supporter, bedecked in bobble hat and team colours on a coach load of pissed up revellers. Now that's not an image to forget in a hurry.

David Kerekes

---

1   Take a look at the comments on IMDb if you don't believe me, with viewers describing it as 'an awesome mercenrary adventure film,' 'a man's picture,' and no less 'the greatest war movie ever made.' IMDb, http://www.imdb.com/title/tt0078492/reviews [Last accessed 8 September, 2011].

A rare shot of Tobe Hooper directing *Lifeforce.*

LIFEFORCE (1985)

Cannon/Golan Globus/Easedram | 116 mins | colour

Director Tobe Hooper; **Producers** Menahem Golan, Yorum Globus; **Screenplay** Dan O'Bannon, Don Jakoby, from the novel *The Space Vampires* by Colin Wilson. **Starring** Steve Railsback (Carlsen), Peter Firth (Caine), Frank Finlay (Fallada), Patrick Stewart (Dr Armstrong), Mathilda May (Girl).

A British-American space crew exploring Halley's Comet encounters three naked, humanoid figures in suspended animation. The astronauts attempt to take the life forms home for study, but when their shuttle reaches Earth only the aliens have survived. Later, ensconced in a research centre in London, the aliens are roused and break out in a murderous rampage, unleashing a vampiric plague that infects anyone who crosses their path.

OK, we're at the bottom of the barrel here. The late seventies are desolate enough when it comes to choosing British genre movies to revisit; the eighties are almost completely arid. So perhaps we should raise our hats to Israeli producers Menahem Golan and Yoram Globus — those tireless purveyors of non-stop action and violence — whose Cannon Film Group became the staple exploitation outfit of the era.

But it's hard to muster up much admiration for Golan and Globus, because although it took a certain chutzpah to sustain this kind of lowbrow filmmaking, especially during the eighties and especially in Britain (where they had a production unit), absolutely nothing they put their names to — *House of the Long Shadows* (83), *The Wicked Lady* (83), *Sahara* (84), *Masters of the Universe* (87) and dozens more produced across the pond — has gathered even the faintest layer of charm.

Except, perhaps, for *Lifeforce*, which looks a lot like a sixties sci-fi B-movie would have done if a half-crazed producer of nudie cuties had stumbled upon a hangar full of cash and decided to spend it all on one film. But if it has any charm (and I'm using the word loosely), it's certainly not a result of the Golan-Globus imprint, and it's debatable whether credited director Tobe Hooper, of *Texas Chain Saw Massacre* (74) fame, had anything to do with it. The jury is still out on whether *Lifeforce* is just abominably bad and unintentionally funny, or whether it's a camp pastiche of the dated films it so clearly resembles.[1]

The most perplexing and fascinating thing about *Lifeforce* is the fact that the producers spent $25 million on it. (This was when $25 million was a lot of money. For a British movie, it was obscene.) The failure of Michael Cimino's *Heaven's Gate*, at a cost of $35 million plus, had destroyed a major studio, United Artists, only five years earlier. In 1985, most mainstream Hollywood films were still coming in at around $15 million.

Where the hell did the money go? Admittedly, the credits soak up some of it: Henry Mancini did the (forgettable) score and *Star Wars'* John Dykstra the (forgettable) visual effects. But $25 million's worth? There are no stars here, apart from the ones burning in space. Unless actors like Steve Railsback, Frank Finlay and Peter Firth had suddenly upped their asking price to $3 million apiece, I find it hard to reconcile that final bill with what's up there on the screen.

There is a workaday epic quality to the movie: explosive set pieces abound, and the special makeup effects, which see life drained from various bodies, are satisfyingly gross and visceral in that latex, pre-CGI way. But the outer space scenes aren't that much better than those found in, say, Norman J. Warren's *Inseminoid* (81), which was made for about eight grand, and the costumes and production design wouldn't look out of place in an early live action Gerry Anderson show. (The fictional European Space Research Centre — surely a laughable concept in itself — looks about as architecturally advanced as a provincial 1970s secondary school.)

It took a spectacular level of mediocrity to spend $25 million on a movie in 1985 and come up with something as bad as *Lifeforce*. Only Golan and Globus were capable of it. (Certainly, the money didn't go on costumes for Mathilda May, who, as the alien vampire, spends most of her screen time completely naked. Out there on the internet, one wag comments that there are only two reasons to see *Lifeforce*: Mathilda May's breasts. As a succinct assessment of the film, this isn't too far off the mark.)

Nevertheless, the film ticks a few cozy B-movie boxes that make it hard to completely dislike: it's agreeably populated with sincere, middle-aged British thespians; it fails to execute its action scenes in that quaint way that most British films (James Bond notwithstanding) fail to execute action scenes; and it appears to take itself so seriously it just has to be smiled at. (Peter Firth's sullen, lip-curling performance, for example, reaches giddy heights of ubercorn.)

To no one's surprise, *Lifeforce* was an unmitigated box office disaster on its original release; it failed to make even half its production cost back in the key US market, even though it played there in a more palatable 100 minute version. It did just as badly everywhere else. And while it wasn't solely responsible for the final sinking of the Cannon Film Group (that was down to a larger programme of insane ambition and wretched judgement), it surely played its part.

Julian Upton

---

1   This sort of ambiguity is not new to the world of Tobe Hooper: there's still a division of opinion on how much of the blockbuster *Poltergeist* (82) he actually directed, and how much its producer, Steven Spielberg, did.

AFTERWORD
1985 AND BEYOND

BY JULIAN UPTON

Nineteen eighty-five seems an appropriate place to stop. Named 'British Film Year' in a somewhat desperate attempt to rally support for the domestic industry, 1985 actually saw British film commerce and culture at its lowest ebb for some time. The previous year's admissions tally (fifty-four million) was an all time low for British cinema.[1]

It's tempting to blame a lot of it on Margaret Thatcher's Conservative government. After all, the Tories did finally abolish the Eady Levy and throw the National Film Finance Corporation (NFFC) to the mercy of the private sector (thus destroying it) in 1985. These moves may have simply been in keeping with the radical programme of privatisation they were pursuing elsewhere, but there was a detectable hostility in the Tories' casual abandonment of British cinema. There was also a hint of their favoured Victorian values, certainly in the abolition of the levy, which until then had meant — as mentioned in the review of ESKIMO NELL — that the British soft porn film was effectively a part-government-funded exercise. With the Conservatives embarking on a zealous clean-up of Soho's porn filled streets, there was little chance they'd approve of more films like *Come Play with Me* potentially benefiting from state subsidy. The death of the British exploitation film may not have been widely lamented, but the demise of the Children's Film Foundation (CFF) was a sadder affair. True, the ubiquity of television had been a thorn in the CFF's side for many years. In the mid eighties the Foundation tried in vain to adapt, rebranding itself as the Children's Film and Television Foundation. But the withdrawal of funding severed a lifeline that it badly needed, and its activities ground to a halt soon after.

Nevertheless, as the previous decade's decline suggested, popular British cinema was in the doldrums with or without government hostilities. One widely cited statistic says it all: 1981 saw only thirty-six films registered as British, compared with ninety-eight in 1971.[2]

It was left to the new television channel, Channel 4 (which began broadcasting in November 1982), to support low budget British film. But Channel 4 took the NFFC's 'worthy' approach of the seventies even further. It's unlikely that, in the eighties at least, a film like *Bugsy Malone* would have seen any Channel 4 money. Among the productions supported by the station were dreary, socially conscious, issue-based features (*Giro City* [82], *Remembrance* [83], *Reflections* [84]) and exercises in experimental or avant-garde cinema (*The Draughtsman's Contract* [82], *The Angelic Conversation* [86]). When it did back something 'quirky' (*Shadey* [85], *She'll Be Wearing Pink Pajamas* [85], *Diamond Skulls* [89]), the results were usually smug or half-baked, or both. And the channel's better ventures (*Dance With a Stranger* [85], *Rita, Sue*

British cinema revival, eighties style. *The Draughtsman's Contract.*

and Bob Too! [86], *Wish You Were Here* [87]) seemed too much like TV plays, with a meagre (generally London-centric) theatrical release followed by rapid exposure on television.

As noted earlier in this book, home video dealt perhaps the severest blow to British cinema. (Again, we can't blame the Tories for this.) By the mid eighties, the country was in the grip of videomania. From a tiny percentage of UK households in 1981, some twenty-five per cent owned or rented a videocassette recorder by 1983, rising to fifty per cent by the end of the decade.[3]

Exploitation, and certainly sexploitation, films quickly found a home on video; accordingly, their big screen viability vanished in a matter of months. Even family oriented fare bypassed the theatres to be enjoyed on the small screen. Exhibitors had not helped themselves by letting cinemas fall into shocking states of disrepair — they weren't called fleapits for nothing. Many theatres weren't fit to take young children into. A film in the early eighties had to be a sure-fire blockbuster to make a trip to the cinema worthwhile. *E.T.* (82) might have warranted an outing to the nearest Odeon; sadly, the Children's Film Foundation's *High Rise Donkey* (80) did not.

So, by 1985 — British Film Year — British cinema looked in danger of collapsing completely. Avoiding that, it could only improve.

British cinema revival, nineties style. *Trainspotting.*

RECOVERY AND RECESSION

B y the late eighties, US-style multiplex cinemas were opening in the big towns and cities. They couldn't be said to deliver a culturally British experience, but at least they were clean and comfortable. The state of British filmmaking was still ravaged, but cinema attendance was improving. Or, at least, takings were, since the price of an evening at the multiplex was far more expensive than a night at the fleapit.

There was still no popular British cinema to speak of. It took a few more years before Channel 4 started to back or help develop films that actually appealed to a mass audience (*Four Weddings and a Funeral* [94], *Brassed Off* [96], *Trainspotting* [96]). Even these refused to shake off the shackles of social realism and political correctness. Still, their success (*Four Weddings* made over $250 million worldwide) did help to contribute to a new mood of optimism surrounding filmmaking in Britain.

The launch of the National Lottery in 1995 was another, albeit wildly uneven, boost (the film industry was one of the many benefactors of the Lottery's charitable payouts), and bold producers again began to kickstart projects with more unashamedly commercial ambitions. One genre that took hold was the crime/gangster film. *Lock, Stock and Two Smoking Barrels* was a surprise success in 1998, and was quickly followed by *Gangster No. 1* (2000), *Sexy Beast* (2000), *Love, Honour and Obey* (2000), *Rancid Aluminium* (2000), *My Kingdom* (2001), *Snatch* (2001) and more. Few of these were money-makers,

Toff-directed gangster shenanigans: *Lock, Stock and Two Smoking Barrels.*

and others came and went in an eye-blink, but, refreshingly, they showed there was activity again.

By 2000, things were looking up. The promise of Lottery cash saw the return of the Americans. Sixties 'Bondmania' had something of a reincarnation in the *Harry Potter* series, which was British in talent and execution, yet heavily bankrolled by Hollywood; it rapidly became the most successful film franchise of all time. (UK cinema admissions in 2002 reached 175.9 million, the highest since 1971,[4] a figure boosted considerably by the *Harry Potter* and *Lord of the Rings* franchises). James Bond himself had another commercial revival with the casting of Daniel Craig in *Casino Royale* (2006). US-backed, British-fronted rom-coms such as *Notting Hill* (99) and *Bridget Jones's Diary* (2001) also cleaned up at the box office. None of these offered any poignant insights into British life, but their success trickled downwards; it seemed to be OK to be making films in Britain again.

For more cash-strapped filmmakers, the growing availability of cheaper digital equipment democratised the filmmaking process and also contributed to production rising significantly. The result was an upswing in the production of low and middle brow, commercially minded, British genre and exploitation films. Like the Lottery money though, what it couldn't guarantee was exhibition. An independent film was lucky to get a flash of theatrical exposure and a network TV showing in a graveyard slot two or three years later. Many others wound up on one of the plethora of new digital TV channels. A lot more were not seen at all. But those that did at least get one unheralded network TV showing were, potentially, still seen by a million

Ben Kingsley in *Sexy Beast*: the true successor to the British crime cinema throne.

or so people. It was not unlike the situation in the seventies, when a barely released film eventually found a decent audience on television. Which was where OFFBEAT came in.

But as we go to press, these new 'offbeat' British movies are already becoming an endangered species. One of the early decisions of the incoming 2010 coalition government was to close down the UK Film Council, which had been providing a lifeline for lower budget UK stabs at commercial and genre cinema since 2000. The decision was full of dark echoes of the Tories' abolition of the Eady Levy in 1985. For example, the Children's Film Foundation, which was rendered inactive by the Eady decision, had, after two subsequent decades existing only in an 'advisory capacity,' begun to receive input from the Film Council for a script development fund for 'family friendly' features. But, at the time of writing, although the Foundation's website confirmed that 'five projects have been developed through this fund, and are now at various stages in their development process,' it ominously added that 'the fund is now closed and currently the Foundation is unable to take on any new projects.' Full circle?[5] The subsequent news that the Film Council's role is to be assumed by the BFI might not be a comfort to filmmakers with more mainstream intentions.

This second wave, then, of offbeat British films seems to have occupied an even shorter timeframe than the first. But it was one that, in its own way, was equally frenetic, and it does warrant further exploration. Maybe in twenty years' time we'll be able to look back on it quite fondly. But that is for another book.

1   The Cinema Exhibitors' Association Ltd., http://www.cinemauk.org.uk/ukcinemasector/admissions/annualukcinemaadmissions1935-2009/ [Last accessed 6 June 2010].
2   Linda Wood, *British Films 1971–81* (London: BFI, 1983).
3   Figures cited in Lynn Hamill, 'The Introduction of New Technology into the Household' (University of Surrey, 2000), http://www.hamill.co.uk/pdfs/tiontith.pdf [Last accessed 27 May 2010].
4   The Cinema Exhibitors' Association Ltd., op.cit.
5   The Children's Film & Television Foundation, http://www.cftf.org.uk/ [Last accessed 20 November 2010].

APPENDIX
ADDITIONAL JOTTINGS ON THE SHORT FILM

BY DARRELL BUXTON AND DAVID HYMAN

DARRELL **B**UXTON: Anyone who has appreciated the Proustian elements of David Kerekes' reminiscences in the chapter Wings Of Death: The Demise Of The Short Film As Supporting Feature will surely agree that every main feature demands a supporting short. With that in mind, here's a smattering of additional fevered jottings on the theme, as a sort of personal adjunct to the key attraction. Let's call it 'Fragments of an Endless Dream,' and bestow an 'AA' certificate on it, emblazoned on that once-so-familiar eggshell blue BBFC title background.

A truck backs into a telephone booth on a Greek island, squashing the occupant in a mess of shattering Perspex and bloody bones. This event may never have taken place, before camera or elsewhere, but despite the uncertain hesitancy I'm displaying in verifying my nostalgia, the aforementioned 'scene' is all that I 'recall' from what may or may not have been a dramatized Forces recruitment bill-filler, circa late seventies. The film: *The Angelos Incident*. The place: Derby's Odeon triplex, or was it the nearby ABC? The time? The big budget item it accompanied? The brands of popcorn and orange squash on sale in the lobby? Broken, fractured memories, scattered beyond recollection. (The BBFC website declares that the film, which it mis-spells as '*The Angeles Incident*,' was submitted in 1977, but as late as 1982 it appears to have been playing with *Quest for Fire*.)

Another. A whitewashed pub exterior, at nightfall. Against the blank wall is silhouetted an unwitting victim (male? female?), about to have their skull cleaved. Shock cut to a melon — marrow? cabbage? — being chopped via a single sharp descending, bisecting blow upon a rustic kitchen tabletop. *Retribution* (playing with *Friday the 13th Part II* in 1983), my fading braincells conspire to convince me, starred Geoffrey Palmer and was directed by Gregory Dark. Can all this be real?

I know, I know. If you're anything like me, you crave hard facts regarding cinema's cult past, and this unreliable memoir must be a sketchy, frustrating read. But where the support short is concerned, such muddled confusion seems to go with the territory.

And on we lurch. A BBFC header appears. *Vampyr*, supposedly. It's the early eighties (*Vampyr* supported 1983's *The Hunger*) and at this point I'm yet to experience Carl Dreyer's hypnotic masterpiece. But, no, this one's an impostor! A cheery British comedy on a macabre footing. Again, sadly, the only scenes you'll dredge from me are fleeting and half-remembered. A gag whereby some ancient bound volume leaps from the grasp of its reader, flapping through the air beating its cracked leather like bat's wings; a moment

in which (don't ask) our protagonist scuttles on all fours across the living room floor and the camera angle tilts to give him the aspect of Dracula crawling down a castle wall.

Keith Allen as a panto Satan in rockabilly hootenanny *Meteor Madness* (which I saw supporting *Richard Pryor Live in Concert* at Derby's Metro Cinema, January 1982). The once-in-a-lifetime teaming of Eric Morecambe, Tom Baker and the delectable Maddy Smith in *The Passionate Pilgrim* (which I swear I saw under a different title, *Late Flowering Love*, as part of a poorly attended opening weekend performance of *Raiders of the Lost Ark* [81]). Did this stellar trio work together twice in a lifetime after all?). A grim murder-in-a-rural-setting snippet, *The Cottage* (circa 82) — was this really directed by a filmmaker going by the unfortunate name 'Mark Chapman'? For that matter, did it feature a murder? Nicola Paget might have been involved. Am I imagining Terence Stamp's pre-*Company of Wolves* participation in an earlier Angela Carter adaptation, *The Bloody Chamber*, a miniature retread of the Bluebeard legend, that my 1983 notebooks insist I saw playing prior to *48 Hrs*?

Those of us who have spent too many hours in dark, dank cinema halls, captivated by flickering patterns of light, may have a tendency during self reflective moods to consider that our behaviour may be wasteful, or at best vicarious.

Yet these did-they-actually-occur glimpses of a recent yet impossibly distant past prove that the power of a screen image might be indelible — and, more to the point, that there's something at once comforting and rather chilling about pictures and sequences and moments and happenings from largely forgotten fare haunting one's thoughts with a relentless regularity, vitally and vividly popping into the mind's eye in a way that their contemporaries like *Jaws, Rollerball, Tootsie* or *Kentucky Fried Movie* can never quite achieve, try as they might. Proof, perhaps, of the filmgoing obsessive's ability to grasp at shadows beyond the reach of most. And that's your shock/surprise/twist ending, right there, de rigueur.

DAVID HYMAN: I saw the short film called *Red* that Kim Newman remembers seeing with *The Final Conflict*, but it was supporting *Porky's* at the Granada Cinema, Harrow, when I saw it. The IMDb correspondent stephen-lambe gets most of the details correct.[1] It's a period piece wherein Ferdy Mayne plays a painter who appears to live in a large mansion which, incongruously, from what I remember, has a clearly visible TV aerial on the roof in some exterior shots. Three troubadours played by Gabrielle Drake, Mark Wynter (the

sixties pop star who sang Venus In Blue Jeans and later starred in Michael Armstrong's *The Haunted House of Horror*) and Roy North ('Mr Roy' from *The Basil Brush Show*, appearing under the pseudonym Steve Brownelow) arrive and entertain him with what I (and stephen-lambe) remember as a pretty awful song.

Footsteps: an early short from Alan Parker.

Later that night, the painter witnesses both men apparently holding down and raping Drake — in a scene featuring extensive nudity on her part — before they cut her throat. The painter, seemingly inspired by this scene, begins painting a picture. The following morning, the troubadours — including a very much alive Ms Drake — appear and the painter notices a livid red scar around Drake's throat. He mutters something along the lines of red not being his favourite colour any more.

I guess you could interpret the film as a metaphor for artist's block.

This was the only film written and directed by Astrid Frank, star of *Swinging Wives, Swedish Love Games* and *Au Pair Girls* (another film starring Gabrielle Drake) who also appears as a serving girl. It was shot by Robert Krasker (who won the Academy Award for Best Cinematography: Black and White for *The Third Man*!) and the editor Pat Foster also edited a number of UK sex films of the time, including *Diversions*.

I've always thought this was a wholly inappropriate support film for *Porky's*, but can to this day remember far more about it than *Porky's*!

A support film that I have never seen but which appears to have done the rounds at the time was *The Pledge* (81), which I think also played as a support to *Porky's* in some cinemas. One of its editors was Peter Greenaway who, along with Alan Mackay, adopted the pseudonym Tex Leadcote.

Another popular support film, and one that I believe has been on TV, is *Footsteps* (74), directed by Alan Parker.

The film that Kim describes as 'that dire comedy about the flea-infested mattress which was put out with *Friday the 13th*' is called *Resting Rough* (79). The BFI database library synopsis describes it thus: 'Comedy concerning the adventures of a mattress thrown out of a window by an irate householder,

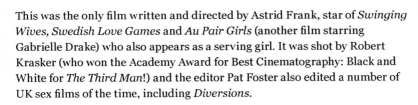

and picked up by a succession of people who use it for different purposes.' [2]
The film was Pierce Brosnan's debut. I remember it because all the onscreen
characters scratching themselves after coming into contact with the flea-
ridden mattress made me feel really itchy! It also has a dire song, some lyrics
of which I can still remember ("Resting rough, resting rough, we are always
resting rough. Scratching all the little fleas in our life"). I seem to recall seeing
this with a Woody Allen film, possibly *Manhattan* (79), at the Golders Green
Ionic circa 1980, but wouldn't stake my life on it.

Another is *Rating Notman* (80). This played like a case history about a
British POW who collaborates with the Nazis and is ultimately brought to
book. I remember this because it starred Maurice Colbourne, who I had
been impressed by in BBC's *Gangsters*. It also stars Jeff Rawle (appearing
in Martin Sherman's play *Bent* at the time alongside Ian McKellen and Tom
Bell at the Royal Court Theatre; he has become a popular character actor,
recently playing Amos Diggory in *Harry Potter and the Goblet of Fire*). It
was classified AA but I can't remember what I saw it with or where, although
Lewis Teague's *Death Vengeance* (a.k.a. *Striking Back*) at the ABC Harrow
comes to mind.

An earlier short I saw as a child was *Crime Casebook — The Big City* (70). The
BFI database library synopsis describes it as the 'story of a WWII air-raid
warden who kills his wife during an air-raid and buries her body in the rubble.
Years later, when a skeleton is found, the search begins for the murderer.' [3]
I remember this as it was very grim and starred John Laurie (Fraser from
Dad's Army). I think I saw it with *The House in Nightmare Park* at the
Edgware ABC circa 1974–75.

There is another film in this series called *Crime Casebook — The Hand of
Fate* (75) which also stars John Laurie and which the BFI database library
synopsis says is 'about a newspaper seller who murders his wife.' [4] However, I
have never seen this one.

The Leonard Rossiter short *Le Petomane* (79) about the 'anal impressionist'
Joseph Pujol, which was directed by Ian MacNaughton (who also directed
many *Monty Python* episodes) and scripted by Galton and Simpson (of
Hancock and *Steptoe and Son* fame) was released with *The Warriors*. I've not
seen it but it seems fondly remembered by some.

Another Leonard Rossiter short that is also fondly remembered by some is
The Waterloo Bridge Handicap (78), wherein a commuter's race to catch a
rush-hour train is narrated in the style of a horse race by TV horseracing

APPENDIX

commentator
Brough Scott.
It also stars
Gorden Kaye
(René from
BBCTV's *'Allo
'Allo!*), Lynda
(OXO mum)
Bellingham
and Patricia
Hodge and was
directed by Ross
Cramer who
subsequently
directed the
Eddie Kidd film
Riding High (81).

There are
also the Bob
Godfrey 'X'
rated animated
short films, like
Dream Doll
(79), which was
co-directed by
Zlatko Grgic,
and *Henry 9 Til
5* (70), which
featured the
voice of Monika

Ringwald (billed as Marylyn Rickard). I can't remember what films they
supported, although I think *Dream Doll* may have supported in some
cinemas.

This film is too long to be classed as a 'short,' but Doug Smith's *The Great
British Striptease* (80), which ran a few minutes short of an hour and
supported George A. Romero's *Dawn of the Dead* (as it was then called)
on its original UK release was 'A recording of a striptease competition in
Blackpool, compèred by Bernard Manning, in which sixteen women compete
for a prize of £500. Manning delivers a spate of racist jokes throughout
the film.' It also featured Su Pollard (presumably presenting, rather than

Comedy sex, please, we're British. Bob Godfrey's *Dream Doll.*

stripping) and a host of comely British talent, including Lisa Taylor from John Lindsay's hardcore sex films, *Jolly Hockey Sticks* and *Juvenile Sex*).

BFI Video has been releasing some old short films. Tony Scott's 1968 short *One Of The Missing* (68),

which is based on an Ambrose Bierce story and stars his brother Ridley, has recently been released as part of a Tony Scott DVD package called *Loving Memory* (70). It was originally classified 'X,' but I don't know what it was originally released with. Gerry O'Hara's *The Spy's Wife* (71), originally classified AA in 1972 and apparently originally released with Stephen Frears' *Gumshoe*, is now on the BFI's *All The Right Noises* (69) and *Kim Newman's Guide to the Flipside of British Cinema* DVD packages.

A short film that won't have been seen on UK screens at the time is John Irvin's 1965 documentary *Carousella*, about the lives of a group of West End strippers, as it was rejected. It has subsequently been classified 15 in 2009 and included on the BFI's *Primitive London* and *Guide to the Flipside of British Cinema* DVDs.

David McGillivray's book *Doing Rude Things* mentions that Arnold Louis Miller (a producer of *West End Jungle*, *The Sorcerers*, *Witchfinder General*, *Sex Farm* and more) and Leslie Berens (brother of the comedian Harold Berens) formed Global-Queensway Films in order to produce documentary films. I can't recall any titles, though.

1   IMDb, http://www.imdb.com/title/tt0218546/ [Last accessed 7 September 2011].
2   BFI Film & TV Database, http://ftvdb.bfi.org.uk/sift/title/123030 [Last accessed 7 September 2011].
3   BFI Film & TV Database, http://ftvdb.bfi.org.uk/sift/title/178041 [Last accessed 7 September 2011].
4   BFI Film & TV Database, http://ftvdb.bfi.org.uk/sift/title/178042 [Last accessed 7 September 2011].
5   BFI Film & TV Database, http://ftvdb.bfi.org.uk/sift/title/223742 [Last accessed 7 September 2011].

FURTHER READING

Justine Ashby and Andrew Higson (eds.), *British Cinema, Past and Present* (London: Routledge, 2000).

Steve Chibnall and Brian McFarlane, *The British 'B' Film* (London: BFI, 2010).

Steve Chibnall and Robert Murphy, *British Crime Cinema* (London: Routledge, 1999).

Chris Diamond and Phil Norman, *TV Cream's Anatomy of Cinema* (London: Friday Books, 2007).

Sue Harper and Vincent Porter, *British Cinema of the 1950s: The Decline of Deference* (Oxford: Oxford University Press, 2003).

Leslie Halliwell, *Halliwell's Film Guide, Seventh Edition* (London: Grafton, 1989).

Pauline Kael, *I Lost It At the Movies* (New York, USA: Little, Brown, 1965).

Wayne Kinsey, *Hammer: The Bray Studio Years* (London: Reynolds & Hearn, 2002).

Stanley Long and Simon Sheridan, *X-Rated: Adventures of an Exploitation Filmmaker* (London: Reynolds & Hearn, 2008).

Brian McFarlane (ed.), *An Autobiography of British Cinema* (London: Methuen, 1997).

David McGillivray, *Doing Rude Things* (London: Sun Tavern Fields, 1992).

Robert Murphy, *Sixties British Cinema* (London: BFI, 1992).

Paul Newland (ed.), *Don't Look Now: British Cinema in the Seventies* (Bristol: Intellect, 2010).

Martin F. Norden, *Cinema of Isolation: A History of Physical Disability in the Movies* (New Brunswick, NJ, USA: Rutgers University Press, 1994).

Danny Peary, *Cult Movies* (New York, USA: Dell, 1981).

David Pirie, *A New Heritage of Horror* (London: I.B. Tauris, 2007).

Jonathan Rigby, *English Gothic* (London: Reynolds & Hearn, 2000).

Jimmy Sangster, *Inside Hammer* (London: Reynolds & Hearn, 2001).

Robert Shail (ed.), *Seventies British Cinema* (London: Palgrave MacMillan, 2008).

Simon Sheridan, *Keeping the British End Up: Four decades of saucy cinema* (London: Reynolds & Hearn, 2007).

Terry Staples, *All Pals Together: The Story of Children's Cinema* (Edinburgh: Edinburgh University Press, 1997).

David Thomson, *A Biographical Dictionary of Film* (London: Andre Deutsch, 1994 edition).

—, *Have You Seen?* (London: Allen Lane, 2008).

Alwyn W. Turner, *Crisis? What Crisis? Britain in the 1970s* (London: Aurum Press, 2009).

Alexander Walker, *Hollywood, England: The British Film Industry in the Sixties* (London: Michael Joseph, 1974).

—, *National Heroes: The British Film Industry in the Seventies and Eighties* (London: Harrap, 1975).

John Walker, *The Once and Future Film* (London: Methuen, 1984).

Linda Wood, *British Films 1971–81* (BFI, 1983).

DARRELL BUXTON is the editor of *The Shrieking Sixties: British Horror Films 1960–1969* (2010). He is also a freelance lecturer, resident 'cult movie historian' at Derby's Quad arts centre, and was a frequent contributor to the UK fanzines *Samhain*, *Giallo Pages* and *We Belong Dead*.

SAM DUNN is head of video publishing at the British Film Institute (BFI), and was previously general manager at Tartan Video. A champion of little-seen and under-appreciated British films, he has contributed writings to *Sight & Sound* and is responsible for shaping the cultural direction of the BFI's internationally acclaimed DVD and Blu-ray label.

MARK GOODALL is a lecturer in media communications at the University of Bradford. He is the author of *Sweet and Savage: the World through the Shockumentary Film Lens* (2006) and editor of *The Firminist*, a journal about the British author Malcolm Lowry. He is lead singer and guitarist with beat combo Rudolf Rocker.

GRAEME HOBBS lives in the Welsh borders, where he writes and podcasts on film for *MovieMail* and makes eclectic chapbooks in his Colva Books series. A regular correspondent for *Vertigo* and *Artesian*, a collection of his writing entitled *Let Yourself Be Broken*, and which is far happier than it sounds, is currently in preparation.

DAVID HYMAN was born in London. He has enjoyed watching films from an early age and often thinks some short films are more memorable than the main features they supported. He is currently employed as an Examiner at the BBFC (British Board of Film Classification).

MARTIN JONES is the editor of *Bedabbled! British Horror and Cult Cinema*. He is also the author of *Psychedelic Decadence: Sex Drugs Low-art in Sixties and Seventies Britain* (2001) and editor of *Lovers Buggers & Thieves* (2005).

DAVID KEREKES co-founded Headpress and is editor of the *Headpress* journal. He is co-author of the books *Killing for Culture: An Illustrated History of Death Film from Mondo to Snuff* (1994 & 2012) and *See No Evil: Banned Films and Video Controversy* (2000) and has written extensively on popular culture.

SARAH MORGAN is the TV Features and Imaging Editor at the Press Association's Northern HQ in Howden, East Yorkshire. She has a degree in Fine Art and has completed a postgraduate course in Film Journalism at the BFI. When not watching obscure movies she can usually be found supporting Sheffield Wednesday.

NOTES ON CONTRIBUTORS

KIM NEWMAN is contributing editor to *Sight & Sound* and *Empire*. His latest books are a new edition of his study of horror cinema, *Nightmare Movies* (2011), and a novel, *The Hound of the d'Urbervilles* (2011). His website is at johnnyalucard.com.

JAMES OLIVER has written for *Sight & Sound*, *Total Film*, *The Idler* and many other less acclaimed (and, indeed, less salubrious) publications.

GARY RAMSAY is a freelance journalist and editor. He has contributed to numerous film and music publications including *Creeping Flesh* (2003), interviewed cult figures such as Tura Satana and Mike Mignola and is currently writing the book *Sonic Celluloid*, on film and music soundtracks.

DAVID SLATER co-founded Headpress. He has worked as a technician in the electronics and engineering industries, co-authored *Killing for Culture: An Illustrated History of Death Film from Mondo to Snuff* (1994 & 2012) and *See No Evil: Banned Films and Video Controversy* (2000) and has written several articles. His interests include movies, books, open country and forteana.

DAVID SUTTON is editor of *Fortean Times* magazine, and has written on film for numerous publications. He has a PhD in Film Studies, has lectured on British cinema history and is the author of *A Chorus of Raspberries: British Comedy Films 1929–39* (2000). He divides his time between London and the Kent coast.

ANDREW SYERS is author of the novel *Long Distance Sleepwalker* (2010) and the play *You've Been a Wonderful Audience* (2008). longdistancesleepwalker. blogspot.com

PHIL TONGE is a cartoonist, writer and painter born and raised in the Forest of Dean, Gloucestershire. His work has meandered through a multitude of so-called 'outsider' publications from the 1980s to the present day. He currently lives in Nottingham and has 'plans' but no money or internet presence.

JULIAN UPTON has written on film for *Headpress*, *Bright Lights Journal*, *Filmfax* and *MovieMail* and is author of the book *Fallen Stars: Tragic Lives and Lost Careers* (2004).

JENNIFER WALLIS is a historian of science and medicine, currently completing her PhD on the pathology of insanity in late nineteenth-century psychiatry. She lives in London.

Titles in CAPS refer to films that are reviewed in full; names in **bold** refer to contributors

8½ (63) 2
10 Rillington Place (71) 152, 324
12 Angry Men (57) 57
24 Hour Party People (2002) 223
48 Hrs (83) 412
80,000 Suspects (63) 91
200 Motels (71) 204
2001: A Space Odyssey (68) 70, 312, 366
ABC (production) 152
Abey, Dennis 317
Abominable Dr Phibes, The (71) 187
ABOMINABLE SNOWMAN, THE (57) 3, 20–22, 28
À bout de souffle (60) 129
Abrams, Michael 325
A Challenge for Robin Hood (67) 83
A Clockwork Orange (71) 99, 160, 221, 338, 342, 387
A.C.T. Films 87
Adam and the Ants (band) 30
Adamski, George 23, 24
Adams, Richard 382, 384, 385
Adams, Ritchie 216
Adams, Tom 281
Addams Family, The (tv series) 11
Adventures of Robin Hood, The (tv series) 83
Afton, Richard 196, 197
Agutter, Jenny 70, 179, 180
Alderdale Films 30
Aldrich, Robert 96
Alfie (66) 9, 306
Alfie Darling (76) 111
ALIAS JOHN PRESTON (55) 15–16
Alien Prey (78) (see: Prey)
All About Eve (50) 35
Allams, Keith 138
Allen, Keith 412
Allen, Patrick 30, 32, 41, 77, 78, 86, 388
Allen, Woody 414
Alliance Film Distributors 51
Allied Artists 117
'Allo 'Allo! (tv series) 108, 415
All Pals Together (book) 329
All The Right Noises (69) 416
Alpert, Hollis 61
Alpha Films 322, 323

Altman, Robert 243, 249–251, 297, 298
American Graffiti (73) 286
American International Pictures (AIP) 10, 36, 92, 314, 316
American Oakshire Films 160
Amicus 152, 205, 264, 275, 276, 280, 281
Amorous Milkman, The (74) 321
Anderson, Ester 167
Anderson, Gene 51
Anderson, Gerry 402
Anderson, Jean 230
Anderson, Lindsay 134, 151, 222, 248
Andre, Gaby 23
Andrews, Harry 139
AND SOON THE DARKNESS (70) 3, 108, 187–188
Angelic Conversation,The (86) 405
Angelos Incident, The (77) 411
Angels, Devils and Men (2009) 381
Anglia television 373
Anglo-Amalgamated 33, 36, 71, 74, 92, 112
Anglo-EMI 235, 255, 286
ANIMAL FARM (54) 11–14, 384
Animal Park (tv series) 267
Animals, The (band) 222
Animated Motion Pictures 115
Anka, Paul 145
Annakin, Ken 100
Annen, Glory 345
ANNIVERSARY, THE (68) 148–151
An Occurence at Owl Creek Bridge (short story) 367
Ant, Adam (see also: Adam and the Ants) 338, 340
Anthony, David 167, 168
Antonioni, Michelangelo 158, 339
Apollo Leisure Group 389
Apple Corps 201, 204
APPOINTMENT, THE (81) 375–377
Apted, Michael 335, 337, 367
Arbeid, Ben 139
Are You Being Served? (77) 231, 254, 389
Arkoff, Samuel Z. 8, 36, 92,

314
Armstrong, Hugh 207
Armstrong, Michael 299–301, 319–324, 373, 413
Arne, Peter 103, 105
Artistes Alliance 23
Arvat, Caterina 367
Asher, Jane 103, 104, 192–194
Ashfield, Kate 237
Ask Agamemnon (novel) 198
Ask a Policeman (39) 389, 390
Askey, Arthur 360
Askwith, Robin 236
ASP Films 309
Aspinall, Neil 201
Assault (71) 240
Assignment K (68) 91
Associated British Picture Corporation (ABPC) 83, 100, 187
Associated London Films Ltd. 273
Asylum (72) 264, 276, 280, 285
A Tale of Two Cities (57) 235
Attard, Tony 357
ATV 373
Auberjonois, Rene 249, 250
Aubrey, James 354
Au Pair Girls (73) 91
Automania 2000 (63) 11
Avco Embassy Pictures 10, 232, 243
Avengers, The (tv series) 114, 187
Average White Band, The (band) 186
Avton (production) 243
Aylmer, Felix 41, 42
Ayres, Rosalind 252, 286
Babylon (80) 222, 223
Baby Love (68) 46, 47, 50
Backbeat (94) 223
Bacon, Francis 135, 137
Bailey, Robin 369
Baim, Harold 366
Bain, Bill 264
Baird, Harry 167, 168
Baker, George 30, 32, 84, 319, 321
Baker, Jane 87, 88
Baker, Pip 87, 88
Baker, Robert S. 26
Baker, Roy Ward 4, 54, 55, 148, 149
Baker, Stanley 59, 95, 140, 262

INDEX

421

INDEX

INDEX

453

ACKNOWLEDGEMENTS

I would like to express my warmest thanks to James Oliver, Jennifer Wallis, Martin Jones, Graeme Hobbs, Gary Ramsay, David Sutton, Darrell Buxton, Sarah Morgan, Sam Dunn, Andrew Syers, David Slater, Phil Tonge, David Hyman, Mark Goodall and Kim Newman, without whose generous input and expertise OFFBEAT would be considerably less insightful (and much thinner). I'd also like to extend special thanks to David Kerekes, for his valued contributions and for making it all possible; to John Krish, for his kind words; and to Jenny, for her help with the sub-editing.

Julian Upton
April 2012

A HEADPRESS BOOK
First published by Headpress in 2012

Headpress, Unit 365, 10 Great Russell Street, London, WC1B 3BQ, United Kingdom
Tel 0845 330 1844   *Email* headoffice@headpress.com

OFFBEAT
British Cinema's Curiosities, Obscurities and Forgotten Gems

Text copyright © Julian Upton and respective contributors
This volume copyright © Headpress 2012
Design & layout: Mark Critchell <mark.critchell@googlemail.com>
Cover: Howard Forbes (based on the poster for the film *Take an Easy Ride*) <takora@gmail.com>
Headpress Diaspora: Thomas Campbell, Caleb Selah, Giuseppe, Dave T.

A CIP catalogue record for this book is available from the British Library

ISBN 978-1-900486-83-5 (pbk)
ISBN 978-1-909394-04-9 (ebk)
NO ISBN (hbk)

Headpress. The gospel according to unpopular culture.

Headpress NO ISBN special editions are available exclusive to World Headpress

WWW.WORLDHEADPRESS.COM

Lightning Source UK Ltd.
Milton Keynes UK
UKOW032208030513

210146UK00004B/40/P